PUBLIC ETHNOMUSICOLOGY, EDUCATION, ARCHIVES, AND COMMERCE

PUBLIC ETHNOMUSICOLOGY, EDUCATION, ARCHIVES, AND COMMERCE

AN OXFORD HANDBOOK OF APPLIED ETHNOMUSICOLOGY

VOLUME 3

Edited by
SVANIBOR PETTAN
and
JEFF TODD TITON

Oxford University Press is a department of the University of Oxford. It furthers
the University's objective of excellence in research, scholarship, and education
by publishing worldwide. Oxford is a registered trade mark of Oxford University
Press in the UK and certain other countries.

Published in the United States of America by Oxford University Press
198 Madison Avenue, New York, NY 10016, United States of America.

© Oxford University Press 2019

All rights reserved. No part of this publication may be reproduced, stored in
a retrieval system, or transmitted, in any form or by any means, without the
prior permission in writing of Oxford University Press, or as expressly permitted
by law, by license, or under terms agreed with the appropriate reproduction
rights organization. Inquiries concerning reproduction outside the scope of the
above should be sent to the Rights Department, Oxford University Press, at the
address above.

You must not circulate this work in any other form
and you must impose this same condition on any acquirer.

Library of Congress Cataloging-in-Publication Data
Names: Pettan, Svanibor, 1960– | Titon, Jeff Todd, 1943–
Title: Public ethnomusicology, education, archives, & commerce :
an Oxford handbook of applied ethnomusicology, volume 3 /
edited by Svanibor Pettan and Jeff Todd Titon.
Description: New York, NY : Oxford University Press, [2019] |
Series: Oxford handbooks | Includes bibliographical references and index.
Identifiers: LCCN 2018031183 | ISBN 9780190885779 (pbk. : alk. paper) |
ISBN 9780190885793 (epub) Subjects: LCSH: Applied ethnomusicology.
Classification: LCC ML3799.2 .P83 2019 | DDC 780.89—dc23
LC record available at https://lccn.loc.gov/2018031183

1 3 5 7 9 8 6 4 2

Printed by Sheridan Books, Inc., United States of America

Contents

List of Figures and Tables … vii
List of Contributors … ix
About the Companion Website … xi

PART I AN INTRODUCTION TO APPLIED ETHNOMUSICOLOGY

Sections

1. Applied Ethnomusicology: A Descriptive and Historical Account … 3
   JEFF TODD TITON

2. Applied Ethnomusicology in the Global Arena … 30
   SVANIBOR PETTAN

3. An Introduction to the Chapters … 57
   JEFF TODD TITON AND SVANIBOR PETTAN

PART II EDUCATION

Chapters

1. Strategies and Opportunities in the Education Sector for Applied Ethnomusicology … 69
   SUSAN E. OEHLER HERRICK

2. Sounds Humane: Music and Humanism in the Aga Khan Humanities Project … 119
   JOHN MORGAN O'CONNELL

3. Intersections Between Ethnomusicology, Music Education, and Community Music … 156
   PATRICIA SHEHAN CAMPBELL AND LEE HIGGINS

PART III AGENCIES

4. Archives and Applied Ethnomusicology 189
   Dan Lundberg

5. The Applied Ethnomusicologist as Public Folklorist: Ethnomusicological Practice in the Context of a Government Agency in the United States 228
   Clifford R. Murphy

6. Applied Ethnomusicology in China: An Analytical Review of Practice 254
   Zhang Boyu

7. The Problem and Potential of Commerce 291
   Alan Williams

Index 323

Figures and Tables

Figures

2.1	A professional dancer at a wedding in Bartang	122
2.2	A professional musician at home in Khorog	126
2.3	A praise singer or *madahkhan* in Khorog	131
2.4	A Mevlevî *Sema* in Turkey ca. 1890	132
2.5	Janbaz Dushanbiyev performing a mortuary dance in Khorog	133
2.6	Abdulvali Abdurashidov playing the Sato in Dushanbe	136
2.7	Musicians from the Academy of Maqâm in a workshop	140
2.8	A musician playing a Maqamboland in Wahan	143
2.9	A skylight or *chahar khaneh*	142
2.10	Rafique Keshavjee in Dushanbe	145
4.1	Other nations in cabinets. Variant register of FMK	196
4.2	Wax cylinders from Karl Tirén's yoik collection 1913–15	198
4.3	Polska from Ore, Dalarna in the FMK collection. Transcribed by Nils Andersson 1906	206
4.4	The music collector Nils Andersson in the home of the fiddler Ante Sundin	213
4.5	The ladder is an illustration of the value scale of FMK. At the bottom we find the music that represents modernity and international influences. At the top we find pastoral music that stands for the good old peasant society	218
6.1	Finnish Jazz musicians playing at the Financial Street in Beijing	260
6.2	Folk instrumental ensembles competition held in Jincheng city Shanxi province in 2013. This is one of the village folk bands that joined the competition. Such activities can be found everywhere across the country	264
6.3	Villages in Wuan county Hebei province are joining a local opera performance during a Taoist temple affair. This is still an important way of spiritual life for current Chinese in rural areas	265
6.4	A Choir has its regular rehearsal at Temple of Heaven Park in Beijing on Saturday morning	271

6.5 A Choir has its regular rehearsal at Zizhuyuan Park in Beijing on Sunday morning — 272

6.6 Musicology Department students at the Central Conservatory of Music giving their first public performance ever at the Recital Hall of the Conservatory during the World Music Days 2010 — 275

6.7 Foreign professors and musicians visited Quantou village at the *Baiyangdian* lake region Hebei province and played the folk music with the folk musicians during the World Music Days in 2007. This was the first time for the villages to see foreigners in their village — 276

6.8 The Chinese music instruments exhibition room at the Central Conservatory of Music — 280

6.9 A set of copied bells exhibited at the Chinese music instruments exhibition room at the Central Conservatory of Music — 281

Table

I.1 Comparative Musicology, Folk Music Research, and Ethnomusicology — 38

Contributors

Patricia Shehan Campbell is Donald E. Peterson Professor of Music at the University of Washington. She is chair of the Advisory Board of Smithsonian Folkways Recordings, and recipient of the 2017 Koizumi Prize, and the 2012 Taiji Award. Her published works include *Lessons from the World* (1991), *Songs in Their Heads* (1998, 2010), *Teaching Music Globally* (2004), *Redefining Music Studies in an Age of Change* (2017), and editorship of *The Global Music Series* and the six-volume series on *World Music Pedagogy*.

Susan E. Oehler Herrick is a middle school social studies teacher in Phoenix, Arizona, who holds degrees in ethnomusicology (Ph.D. Indiana University) and education (M.Ed. Vanderbilt University). In addition to K–16 level teaching, past professional experience includes educational consulting and educational program management for nonprofits, such as the Rock and Roll Hall of Fame and Museum in Cleveland, Ohio (2004–2008). Publications center on the blues, pedagogy, and applied ethnomusicology.

Lee Higgins is the Director of the International Centre of Community Music at York St John University, UK. He has worked on four continents in university, school, and NGO settings and was the President of International Society of Music Education (2016–2018). He is the senior editor for the *International Journal of Community Music* and author of *Community Music: In Theory and in Practice* (2012, OUP), co-author of *Engagement in Community Music* (2017, Routledge), and co-editor of *The Oxford Handbook of Community Music* (2017).

Dan Lundberg is Chief Librarian and Archive Director at the Swedish *Statens musikverk* (Music Development and Heritage Sweden). He is also Associate Professor in Musicology at Stockholm University in Sweden and Åbo Academy in Finland. Between 2004 and 2007 he held a position as Professor of Music and Cultural Diversity at Gävle University in Sweden. His main research areas today are music and identity and music collecting and ideology.

Clifford R. Murphy is the Director of the Folk & Traditional Arts division of the National Endowment for the Arts, and a past Director of the folklife program at the Maryland State Arts Council. He is the author of *Yankee Twang: Country and Western Music in New England* (University of Illinois Press) and co-author of *Ola Belle Reed and Southern Mountain Music on the Mason-Dixon Line* (Dust-to-Digital) with Henry Glassie and Douglas Dowling Peach. He holds a Ph.D. in Ethnomusicology from Brown University.

John Morgan O'Connell is Professor of Ethnomusicology at Cardiff University, United Kingdom. A graduate of Oxford University, he completed his doctoral research on Turkish music at UCLA. He has published extensively on the musical traditions of the Muslim world, acting as a music consultant for the Aga Khan Humanities Project in Central Asia. He also has a specialist interest in applied ethnomusicology, having completed relevant research on music and conflict in Ireland, Turkey, and Tajikistan, among others.

Svanibor Pettan is Professor of Ethnomusicology at the University of Ljubljana, Slovenia. Initiator and first chair of the ICTM Study Group on Applied Ethnomusicology and a founding member of the SEM Section on Applied Ethnomusicology, he contributes to the advancement of the field in the global arena with studies in various formats, addressing war-peace continuum, minorities, conflicts, and education. He currently serves as Vice-President of the International Council for Traditional Music and as Chair of its Study Group Music and Minorities.

Jeff Todd Titon is Professor of Music, Emeritus, at Brown University, Providence, Rhode Island, USA, where for 27 years he directed the Ph.D. program in ethnomusicology. The author or editor of eight books and numerous essays, he is known for developing phenomenological and ecological approaches to ethnographic fieldwork, for theorizing and practicing an applied ethnomusicology based in reciprocity and friendship, and for introducing the concepts of cultural and musical sustainability to the fields of folklore and ethnomusicology. His current research on a sound ecology may be tracked at https://sustainablemusic.blogspot.com.

Alan Williams holds a Ph.D. in Ethnomusicology from Brown University. In the 1990s, his band Knots and Crosses signed to Island Records, and he established himself as a recording engineer and producer in the New England singer-songwriter scene. He has published in the *Journal of Popular Music Studies*, and in *The Art of Record Production* (Ashgate Press, 2012). He currently leads the ensemble Birdsong At Morning, and is a Professor and Chair at the Department of Music, the University of Massachusetts Lowell.

Zhang Boyu is Professor of Ethnomusicology at Department of Musicology, Central Conservatory of Music in Beijing; Vice-Chairman of Chinese Traditional Music Association and China's World Music Association; member of Academic Advisory Board of Humanities Faculty of Helsinki University (2011–2014). He is the author of five research books and over one hundred articles in both Chinese and English. His research is cross-cultural and interdisciplinary, focusing mainly on the meanings of traditional musics in their societies.

About the Companion Website

www.oup.com/us/ohaev3

Oxford has created a website to accompany *The Oxford Handbook of Applied Ethnomusicology*. Audio recordings and color photographs, which cannot be made available in a book, are provided here. The reader is encouraged to consult this resource in conjunction with the chapters. Examples available online are indicated in the text with Oxford's symbol ▶.

PUBLIC ETHNOMUSICOLOGY, EDUCATION, ARCHIVES, AND COMMERCE

PART I

AN INTRODUCTION TO APPLIED ETHNOMUSICOLOGY

Our Introduction to this volume consists of three sections. Although applied ethnomusicology is practiced now in many regions of the world, it has developed differently in various times and places, just as ethnomusicology itself has. We begin in Section 1 (by Titon) with a focused statement on applied ethnomusicology as it has developed from a single representative area (the United States), and then broaden out in Section 2 (by Pettan) to a global perspective, where a greater plurality of voices and viewpoints may be observed, so that we may end with the understanding that applied ethnomusicology is no single field but is instead an ever emergent movement, responding differently at various times and places, by means of music-centered interventions, to different cultures, histories, needs, and conditions. Indeed, this volume as a whole offers just such a plurality of voices and viewpoints. In addition to discussing histories and developments in national and global perspectives, particularly in the contexts of the US-based Society for Ethnomusicology (SEM) as well as the UNESCO-affiliated International Council for Traditional Music (ICTM), the co-editors also each offer personal perspectives, based in many years of involvement. Section 3, jointly written by Titon and Pettan, offers an introduction to the chapters that follow.

We wish to thank many people who have made this work possible. Suzanne Ryan, music editor at Oxford University Press, supported this project from the outset and helped us to understand how to shape the volume in conformity with *Handbook* expectations. The anonymous external reviewers read perceptively and made many useful comments and suggestions. For guidance, vision, and support along the path to applied ethnomusicology, Titon would like to thank colleagues and teachers Alan Kagan, Mulford Sibley, Charlotte Heth, David McAllester, Dennis Tedlock, Burt Feintuch, Erma Franklin, Loyal Jones, Elwood Cornett, Kenneth Irby, Maryanne Wolf, Sandy Ives, Archie Green, Bess Lomax Hawes, Daniel Sheehy, and Robert Baron.

Pettan would like to single out Samuel Araújo, Anthony Seeger, and Kjell Skyllstad, three important visionaries in applied ethnomusicology (among many more), who continue to inspire his own thinking and doing. Both editors thank the contributors to this volume, with whom it was a true honor and pleasure to join forces in creating this essentially important *Handbook*.

SECTION 1

APPLIED ETHNOMUSICOLOGY
A Descriptive and Historical Account

JEFF TODD TITON

Ethnomusicology and Applied Ethnomusicology

I like to think of *ethnomusicology* as the study of people making music (Titon, 1989, 1992b: xxi–xxii). People make sounds they call music, and they also make ideas about music. Those ideas form the cultural domain called music. They include what music is and is not; what it does and cannot do; how it is acquired and how it should be transmitted; what value it has; what it should (and should not) be used for; what it has been in the past and what it will be in the future; whether it should be encouraged and supported, or discouraged and repressed; and so forth. Just as music differs among individuals and social groups throughout the world, so do people's ideas about it differ, and this has been so throughout history.

Applied ethnomusicology puts ethnomusicological scholarship, knowledge, and understanding to practical use. That is a very broad definition. More specifically, as it has developed in North America and elsewhere, applied ethnomusicology is best regarded a music-centered intervention in a particular community, whose purpose is to benefit that community—for example, a social improvement, a musical benefit, a cultural good, an economic advantage, or a combination of these and other benefits. It is music-centered, but above all the intervention is people-centered, for the understanding that drives it toward reciprocity is based in the collaborative partnerships that arise from ethnomusicological fieldwork. Applied ethnomusicology is guided by ethical principles of social responsibility, human rights, and cultural and musical equity. Although some ethnomusicologists regard applied ethnomusicology as a career alternative to academic work—and indeed, it can be—it's not always helpful to make that distinction, because ethnomusicologists who do applied work are employed both inside academic institutions, such as universities and museums, and outside them in government agencies, nongovernmental organizations (NGOs), and client organizations directly. In other words, the place of employment does not determine whether the ethnomusicology has any application outside the world of scholarship. What matters is the work itself: how, where, and why the intervention occurs, and the communities to whom we feel responsible (Titon, 2003; Dirksen, 2012).

Putting ethnomusicological scholarship, knowledge, and understanding to practical use and terming it *applied* implies the usual distinction made in the sciences between pure research, or the pursuit of knowledge for its own sake (as it is often called), and applied research, or knowledge put to practical use. It is possible to minimize this distinction, claiming that the moment a researcher circulates knowledge within a scholarly community it is being put to beneficial use. Classroom teaching is of course another kind of use. Besides, the phrase knowledge for its own sake appears oxymoronic, for in what sense can knowledge possibly be for its own sake if knowledge cannot logically be an agent or a self? If all ethnomusicological knowledge is put to use in one way or another, then the term applied ethnomusicology is redundant. All of this may be so, but for strategic reasons the editors of this volume find the term useful, in order to highlight a certain kind of activity and distinguish an ethnomusicology based in social responsibility where knowledge is intended for beneficial use in communities outside the academic world from an ethnomusicology which is meant to increase and improve the storehouse of knowledge about music and circulate it among scholars. In the absence of this distinction, as I will argue later (see below, "Applied Ethnomusicology in the United States: A Brief History"), applied ethnomusicology has been marginalized or ignored in the definitions and histories of our field that circulate among ethnomusicologists. Indeed, examination of ethnomusicology curricula reveals very few, if any, courses devoted to applied work at the doctoral level. The Ph.D. is a research degree, after all, and the chief criterion for career advancement in the university remains research that enjoys a high intellectual reputation among scholars. Fortunately, however, a sense of social responsibility motivates an increasing number of ethnomusicologists, employed inside and outside the academic world, who find ways to integrate it into their scholarly research, and to apply it in the public sphere. Readers who wish to know more about my personal involvement with, and views on, applied ethnomusicology are invited to consult Titon 2003 and various entries on applied ethnomusicology on my blog at http://sustainablemusic.blogspot.com.

This volume is not meant as a "how-to" handbook, like the *Girl Scout Handbook*. Rather, in keeping with the other Oxford Handbooks in this series, it offers a sampling of current scholarship related to its subject, with contributions from some leading exponents. Applied ethnomusicology is a field of practice and theory, rather than a discipline with a bounded subject and an established, universally agreed-upon methodology. A branch of the academic discipline of ethnomusicology, its scope is still expanding. While its practitioners are in broad agreement over putting ethnomusicological knowledge to use rather than simply pursuing it as an end in itself, we differ in emphasis, whether in definition, method, or purpose (Harrison, 2012). Readers may look here for a variety of subjects, approaches and models.

Applied Ethnomusicology in Contemporary North America: A Brief Overview

What kinds of activities are applied ethnomusicologists involved in? Where, typically, do we intervene in the public sphere? The co-editors of this volume, one active in North America, the other in Europe, have determined to write about these activities in the areas they know best. As I am most familiar with activities in the United States, and the professional organization based there (the *Society for Ethnomusicology*, or SEM), what follows in my part of this Introduction highlights US-based applied ethnomusicology. I will discuss the history (and prehistory) of applied ethnomusicology, and its reception, in the United States since the late 1800s. But before sketching that history, I describe applied ethnomusicology as it is practiced today. What are applied ethnomusicologists doing now? What are our goals, and how are we positioned within the larger world both within and outside the academy?

First, we are involved in promoting traditional music, dance, and other cultural expressions in order to benefit artists, traditions, and communities. Whether undertaken by ethnomusicologists acting primarily on their own behalf, or whether supported by cultural organizations, these *cultural policy interventions* are among the oldest types of applied ethnomusicology and remain one of the most common, particularly as directed toward minority, immigrant, and otherwise underserved populations within developed nations, and among indigenous peoples throughout the world. Sometimes, but not always, these musics are considered threatened or even endangered. Lately, sustainability has become the generally accepted policy goal, whether the musics are endangered or not (see Schippers, Chapter 4, and Titon, Chapter 5, in Volume 1). Cultural trauma has often been an important motivating factor, particularly when cultural renewal appears important in the face of political and economic stress (see Haskell, Chapter 6 in Volume 1). Examples of these interventions include the settlement schools in the southern Appalachian mountains, begun more than a century ago to promote the arts and crafts of mountain folk culture; the immigrant folk music and dance programs for children and adults in large cities such as New York and Chicago, which involved settlement schools and included festivals as well as adult recreation groups and additions to the public school curriculum; national radio broadcasts undertaken by Alan Lomax shortly before World War II to bring the songs and stories of ordinary citizens into media circulation; regional and national festivals such as the Smithsonian Folklife Festival, begun in the 1960s; policymaking and granting agencies that promote community arts, such as historical societies, arts councils, and the National Endowments; and NGOs devoted to expanding the creative economy through musical heritage and cultural tourism, sometimes with a view to recovering from ecological disasters such as hurricanes, urban blight, and mountaintop removal. In the twenty-first century, UNESCO has become the major international force in cultural policy, with its treaties encouraging the preservation of what it calls intangible cultural heritage. The United States has not signed these treaties, but outside the United States many ethnomusicologists are involved with UNESCO activities and indeed, some North American ethnomusicologists participated in the planning and ongoing review stages. Ethnomusicologists have worked as consultants, arts administrators, ethnographic fieldworkers, festival presenters, radio and television producers, podcasters and Internet site developers, educators, facilitators, mediators, writers, expert witnesses, and in various other capacities formulating and administering cultural policies whose purpose is sociocultural, economic, and musical benefit. Ethnomusicologists also have been among those theorizing cultural policy interventions, and have contributed to a growing critical literature evaluating these practices. Many of the chapters in this volume comprise a part of this ongoing scholarship concerning applied ethnomusicology.

Another area of practice is *advocacy*, either on behalf of particular music-makers or a music community as a whole. Rather than adopting the role of the neutral, objective, scientific observer gathering information, the applied ethnomusicologist assumes the role of a partisan, working in partnership toward goals that are mutually understood and agreed upon. Indeed, the most successful advocacy usually arises after ethnomusicologists have visited and listened to the musicians articulate their concerns and what they would like to achieve. Seldom has partnership worked when the ethnomusicologist plays the role of expert and imposes solutions to problems perceived from a distance, or fails to understand the musical community's perspective. Advocacy includes grant-writing on behalf of individuals and communities; writing promotional and press materials; acting as an agent to arrange performances; facilitating community self-documentation initiatives; repatriation of recordings and musical artifacts from museums and archives; political lobbying for arts spaces; facilitating community arts education projects; researching the history of musical traditions for the community; acting as an intermediary between cultural insiders and outsiders; long-term planning for the sustainability of community music cultures; and in general working in partnership and on behalf of musicians and their communities. Advocacy usually arises from relationships developed over time, when an ethnomusicologist is attracted to particular musicians or music cultures, visits them for research purposes and returns, and determines to make a commitment that goes beyond mere study. Academic ethnomusicologists undertaking long-term fieldwork in a community are well-positioned for this, but while an increasing number do become advocates, some prefer to remain neutral observers.

A third area of practice involves *education*. Often educators themselves, applied ethnomusicologists work with other educators designing curricula, and to bring musicians into the schools to demonstrate, teach, and perform; they also facilitate visits to performance spaces where youngsters may observe and participate in music-making activities. Music education once prepared youth to participate mainly in the culture of classical music, or as US academics call it these days, Western art music. As cultural pluralism and multicultural initiatives in North American schools gained traction in the last third of the twentieth century, musical pluralism increased, introducing popular music, jazz, and the music and dance of ethnic communities to the school curricula. Ethnomusicologists have been active in making musical activities more inclusive, fostering interest in local musical artists and traditions, particularly from newly arrived cultural and ethnic groups. In this way, music is viewed as a way to increase intercultural understanding.

Other areas of contemporary practice include *peace and conflict resolution; medicine; law and the music industry; libraries, museums, and sound archives; journalism;* and *environmental sound activism and ecojustice*. Peace-related applications are more frequent outside North America, but work of this sort has been done in Canada in disputes between First Nations communities and the Canadian government, while music has been an important part of labor and civil rights movements in the United States since the nineteenth century. Among the projects of medical ethnomusicology are HIV-AIDS work in Africa, therapeutic work with post-traumatic stress survivors, and music within the autism community. Legal applications have involved ethnomusicologists testifying as expert witnesses, particularly in music copyright infringement cases, and work on copyright and intellectual property issues as the question "who owns culture" becomes increasingly important when money is to be made and cases of exploitation have been documented. Ethnomusicologists have served as advisors to the World Intellectual Property Organization (WIPO), a UNESCO-sponsored group attempting to arrive at laws for protecting intellectual property rights in the international arena. Ethnomusicologists are contributing to ecological studies of the soundscape, and of the effects of environmental noise on physiological and psychological health. We are involved in political action opposing sound pollution, such as noise from ocean vessels and military activities that affect whales, dolphins, and other sea mammals. Applied ethnomusicologists are contributing to the new discipline of ecomusicology, which involves music and sound in a time of environmental crisis. Journalists educated in ethnomusicology bring to world music a broadly informed historical and geographical perspective. Some are writing for newspapers, magazines, and online publications; many are active in promoting music, and some are performing musicians ourselves. Ethnomusicologists working in the music industry serve as consultants, ethnographers, technical assistants, and producers. Many libraries, museums, universities, and other institutions maintain sound archives where archivists with ethnomusicological training offer expertise in acquisition, cataloging, grant-writing, preservation, and outreach.

Since the 1990s, when applied ethnomusicology became a recognizable force within ethnomusicology, other names have been advanced to describe some of the work that applied ethnomusicologists do; but they ought not to be confused with applied ethnomusicology, which is the covering term.[1] *Public-sector ethnomusicology* describes applied ethnomusicology that is practiced by people employed by public-sector, taxpayer-funded (i.e., government) institutions such as (in the United States) the Library of Congress, the Smithsonian Institution, the National Endowment for the Arts, and state arts councils; and whose efforts are directed to the public at large while often targeted at particular communities within it. By definition, "public-sector ethnomusicology" is unable to include applied ethnomusicology as practiced by those who work in the private sector, in NGOs such as museums, historical societies, foundations, and various non-profit organizations, even when part of their funding comes from government grants; nor does it describe the work of applied ethnomusicologists in corporations and client organizations. *Public ethnomusicology* is a better name for this activity, insofar as it focuses on applications in the public arena. But both terms, public sector and public, neglect the private sphere and perpetuate an unhelpful distinction between academia and the world outside of colleges and universities. As I have pointed out, applied ethnomusicology is practiced by those employed inside the academic world as well as outside of it. Ethnomusicology appears to be in danger of replicating the same terminological virus that has infected American folklore studies since the 1980s, one which American Folklore Society President Barbara Kirshenblatt-Gimblett labeled a "mistaken dichotomy" (Kirshenblatt-Gimblett 1988).

APPLIED ETHNOMUSICOLOGY: BEING, KNOWING, AND DOING

Some ethnomusicologists are attracted to applied work, and others not so much. Most ethnomusicologists, I've observed, do share certain characteristics, however. Sound and music are immensely important to the way we orient ourselves. As humans, we are beings "in the world" through all of our senses, but we are particularly aware of vibrations that come to us as sound. Epistemologically, we feel that knowing sound—and knowing by means of sound—is essential to being human in the world and is one of the most important avenues through which to understand the human condition. Certainly it is our special avenue. Where we diverge, somewhat, is in what we *do* as a result of this ontological and epistemological orientation. Some of us are most interested in pursuing and increasing knowledge about sound and music in the world, the music of the world's peoples. This is the usual end of scholarship. Scholars feel a special responsibility to present, discuss, debate, and circulate this knowledge among colleagues and students in the institutional world of universities and professional associations of ethnomusicologists. Others, those of us who practice applied ethnomusicology, also feel a responsibility to help put this knowledge to practical use in the public arena; and so either in addition to our research, scholarship, and teaching within the university world, or instead of it, we also involve ourselves in interventions into musical communities, for public benefit.

Some 45 years ago Mantle Hood wrote a textbook about the nature of ethnomusicology, but instead of titling it *Ethnomusicology* he named it *The Ethnomusicologist* (Hood, 1971). In the Introduction he described an ideal ethnomusicologist's background, education, skills and aptitudes, and personality. It was an unusual emphasis for a graduate textbook in ethnomusicology, but then this was an unusual book, often written in the first person, and to some extent reflecting, I think, the California social and intellectual atmosphere of the 1960s that had also produced public figures like Stewart Brand and Jerry Brown. Although the influence of personality on an ethnomusicologist's accomplishments is not often written about, it is sometimes discussed among ethnomusicologists, especially when we reflect on ethnographic fieldwork, that rite of passage in which ethnomusicologists (like their counterparts in cultural anthropology) traditionally travel to a different, and sometimes strange, culture and while there, try to learn something of the musical universe among that group of people. It is difficult, sometimes alienating, even psychologically traumatic, work (Wengle, 1988); and ethnomusicologists tend to think that certain personality types are better able to accomplish it than others. Applied ethnomusicologists like to interact with our field subjects, not just observe them. We feel a desire to give something back in exchange for what we are learning, and this impulse leads us not only to research but to work directly for the benefit of those we visit. And so although most ethnomusicologists are in the world ontologically and epistemologically in similar ways, we differ somewhat over what we should be doing with those ways of being and knowing. It should go without saying that applied ethnomusicologists engage in research and contribute to the growth of knowledge. Our Ph.D.s are research degrees, after all, and many of us have made substantial scholarly contributions to the flow of knowledge inside academia. But we also feel a social responsibility to put that knowledge to use in the public arena.

Applied Ethnomusicology in the United States: A Brief History

As the co-editors worked on this volume and saw it through an eight-year period of invitations, proposals, abstracts, essays, reviews, revisions, and yet more reviews and more revisions, it became increasingly and unsettlingly clear that many US contributors thought of their work within a local and national context but knew relatively little about the history, ideas, and accomplishments of applied ethnomusicologists living outside the United States. Non-US contributors were similarly knowledgeable about applied work in their spheres of activity outside North America, but generally unaware of the history, projects, scholarship, and cultural policies generated by applied ethnomusicology in North America. Ideas that had been theorized, practiced, and thoroughly critiqued in some localities were being introduced in others as if they were newly discovered. More than once, contributors seemed to be reinventing wheels. Many whose work would benefit from an exchange of ideas with others involved in similar projects elsewhere were not taking advantage of that possibility. Although we believe that the reasons for this insularity have more to do with institutional histories and geography than with any serious divergence over assumptions, approach, and goals, one of the happy consequences of this volume, we hope, will be to increase the dialogue among practitioners of applied ethnomusicology no matter where they work, so that each becomes aware of the ways in which similar problems have been faced, and solutions attempted, elsewhere, while problems and issues that had not even occurred to some will become apparent after reading about the work of others. Another consequence of this insularity, however, was that it became impossible to sketch a unified history and description of applied ethnomusicology apart from those considerations. For that reason, in this section I construct a history of applied ethnomusicology in the United States, related to the growth of ethnomusicology and its professional organization, SEM, founded in 1955. (Svanibor Pettan writes in Section 2 of this Introduction about the communities of applied ethnomusicologists associated with the International Council on Traditional Music [ICTM], and its earlier incarnation, the International Folk Music Council [IFMC, founded in 1947].) In doing so, I draw on a graduate seminar in the history of ethnomusicological thought which I led at Brown University from 1988 until 2013. Reflexivity, postcolonial ethnomusicology, efforts to sustain musical genres and cultures, collaborative ethnography and advocacy, tourism and the creative economy, archival stewardship and repatriation of field recordings, applications to medicine and to peace and conflict resolution, proper roles for government in the arts, the place of world music in education—these are not new themes in our field, but the timing of their entrances, their reception, and their use in applied work has not been uniform among the North American, European, Asian, African, Australian, and Latin American communities of applied ethnomusicologists.

Strictly speaking, the history of ethnomusicology began in 1950, when Jaap Kunst invented the term and it entered scholarly discourse (Kunst, 1950). I prefer to think of the pre-1950 period as ethnomusicology's prehistory, paying particular attention to the two disciplines, comparative musicology and cultural anthropology, that combined in the 1950s as ethnomusicology.[2] I find prototypes of US applied ethnomusicology among nineteenth-century ethnologists and folklorists whose field research in music exhibited both social responsibility and collaborative involvement with musical communities for their benefit. Music was an integral part of early folklore and anthropology, not an afterthought. From the very beginning, scholars writing for the *American Anthropologist* and the *Journal of American Folklore* showed much interest in people making music. The second issue of the former contained an essay by Washington Matthews (1843–1905) on a Navajo sung prayer (Matthews, 1888), for example, while the inaugural issue of the latter featured an article on Kwakiutl music and dance by Franz Boas (1858–1942), the most influential North American anthropologist of his generation (Boas, 1888). Boas's article described some of the group's music, stories, and their ideas and behavior in relation to them; it contained musical transcriptions, and mentioned his 1886 music collecting trip with the German comparative musicologist and music psychologist Carl Stumpf among the Bella Coola. Nothing in Boas's article might be considered applied ethnomusicology per se, but Boas undertook a public anthropology project of enormous import in the early twentieth century when he opposed so-called scientific racism and helped establish the idea that differences in human behavior result from learned cultural, rather than fixed biological, traits.

Matthews's work was aided by a deeply collaborative relationship in which he underwent Native rituals and may have married a Hidatsa woman. Collaborative relationships in which the parties work toward mutually agreed-upon goals became a hallmark of applied ethnomusicology, but their roots may be found in people like Matthews, as well as Alice Cunningham Fletcher (1838–1923), whose collaborative work moved more clearly in the direction of social and economic benefits that would be recognized today as applied ethnomusicology. Fletcher, who became President of both the American Anthropological Association and the American Folklore Society, as well as Vice President of the American Association for the Advancement of Science, lived with the Sioux in 1881, and collaborated with an Omaha, Frances La Flesche, whom she took into her household from 1890 on. Falling ill with a severe case of rheumatoid arthritis in 1883, she was nursed back to health by her Native American friends, who sang to her while she lay recovering. Then, she wrote, "the sweetness, the beauty and meaning of these songs were revealed to me" (Fletcher, 1994: 8). Like the others, Fletcher undertook ethnographic studies of Native music; but she also worked tirelessly on behalf of Native American education, integration, and advancement into mainstream culture.

"Giving back" is the usual term North American ethnomusicologists employ to identify this reciprocity, which has taken various forms over the decades. However, Fletcher's efforts at aiding Native Americans are characterized today as attempts to Americanize them, a "grievous error in the administration of Native American lands and peoples" according to a Smithsonian Institution author (Smithsonian: Fletcher). Ethnomusicologists consider it unfortunate that the Omaha songs she collected were published with Western harmonization, added to them by the musician John Comfort Fillmore, who convinced Fletcher that these harmonies were implicit in the Omaha melodies (Fletcher, 1994). Nonetheless, Fletcher may be understood in her time as a progressive. The principal alternative to Americanization (or Christianization), after all, had for nearly three centuries been genocide. And prominent American composers such as Edward MacDowell were quoting, transforming, and harmonizing Native American melodies in their musical compositions.

Daniel Sheehy and Anthony Seeger trace the history of twentieth-century pioneers in applied ethnomusicology, such as Robert Winslow Gordon, Alan Lomax, and Charles Seeger (Sheehy, 1992; Seeger, 2006). In terming them applied ethnomusicologists, Seeger, Sheehy, and others combine ethnomusicology's historical and pre-historical periods. Certainly, these ancestors would have been called applied ethnomusicologists if ethnomusicology proper had come into being prior to 1950. To some extent their work was related to that of early anthropologists such as A. L. Kroeber and others on endangered Native American languages. The Lomaxes' folk music collections were meant for the general public, to supply a kind of people's alternative to the art music that was being taught in the public schools. Alan Lomax insisted that the treasure trove of folk music should be made accessible through media production, which in the 1940s and 1950s meant radio programs—he produced dozens of them for national broadcast. He issued an appeal for "cultural equity" that articulated many of the principles under which he had been operating for decades (Lomax, 1972). Lomax's "Appeal" may be the single most often-cited document in the literature of US applied ethnomusicology. Charles Seeger, Anthony Seeger's grandfather, had issued a call in 1939 for an applied musicology that would follow from government involvement in the arts, a vision in some ways similar to the situation in China today (Seeger, 2006: 227–228; also see Zhang, Chapter 6 of this volume). Seeger and his wife Ruth Crawford Seeger, John and Alan Lomax, Herbert Halpert, Zora Neale Hurston, and others were involved in efforts to encourage folk music (as the authentic popular music of a democratic society) during the Roosevelt administration. These activities, of course, diminished greatly as the United States concentrated during the 1940s on mobilization for World War II. But Sheehy concludes that "there is a tradition of applied thought and purpose that should be included in the history of ethnomusicology," as well as "an evolving sense of strategy and techniques for action that has flowed through this thought and that demands our attention as ethnomusicologists" (Sheehy, 1992: 329). Anthony Seeger entitled his 2006 essay "Lost Lineages" in the history of ethnomusicology and, like Sheehy, called for a more inclusive history of the field.

The usual historical accounts of ethnomusicology in the United States are not so inclusive: applied ethnomusicology is treated either as a peripheral activity or, more often, ignored entirely. These mainstream accounts trace ethnomusicology's roots to comparative musicology, a scientific project of the European Enlightenment. They do not pay much attention to its roots in folklore and cultural anthropology. In 1885 Guido Adler defined comparative musicology as "the comparison of the musical works . . . of the various peoples of the earth for ethnographical purposes, and the classification of them according to their various forms" (Haydon, 1941: 117). Comparative musicology began in the latter part of the nineteenth century with the systematization of music knowledge, which proceeded with the measurable, classificatory, and comparative procedures borrowed from philology, embryology, and other sciences, generating various hypotheses concerning origins, growth, diffusion, and function. Aided by the recording phonograph and efforts of various music collectors, it included the comparative work on the musical scales of various nations accomplished by the Englishman Alexander Ellis, and the research of the German Carl Stumpf and others in music psychology (or psychophysical science, as it was then called). Comparative musicology was further developed as a research discipline in early twentieth-century Berlin by Stumpf's younger colleague Erich von Hornbostel, Curt Sachs, and others, with related scholarship accomplished by Béla Bartók in Hungary, Constantin Brăiloiu in Rumania, and others in the fields of comparative musical folklore and the sociology of music.

Comparative musicology arrived in the United States in 1925 in the person of George Herzog, who had been von Hornbostel's assistant in Berlin. He went on to study anthropology with Franz Boas at Columbia University, specializing in "primitive music," as it was then called. Herzog received his doctorate in 1931 under Boas's supervision and pursued an academic career at Yale, Columbia, and Indiana University that lasted until the mid-1950s. He was recognized during this period as the leading authority on "primitive music." Among his students were two of the founders of SEM, David McAllester and Willard Rhodes. Bruno Nettl, who has written knowledgeably about Herzog's contributions to comparative musicology, was another of his students (Nettl and Bohlman, 1991: 270–272; Nettl, 2002: 90–92; Nettl, 2010: 168). Herzog's writings exhibited an empirical, scientific method that required large amounts of reliable data, a high standard to which he held himself and others. "All evidence," he wrote, "points to the wisdom of dispensing with sweeping theoretical schemes and of inquiring in each case into the specific historical processes that have molded the culture and musical style of a nation or tribe. . . . So little is actually known . . . that the main attention of this field [of comparative musicology] is devoted to increasing that little, and collecting more material before it all disappears under the impact of Western civilization" (Herzog, 1936: 3). He had learned the importance of fieldwork and data-gathering from his teacher Boas, and he insisted on that, as well as musical transcription and analysis, from his students. His methods added Boas-styled ethnographic research to the comparative analysis that characterized the work of Horbostel and the Berlin school.

A useful summary of comparative musicology, with due attention to Herzog's prominence in the United States, appeared in Glen Haydon's graduate-level textbook, *Introduction to Musicology* (Haydon, 1941). As outlined there, its purpose was to increase knowledge of the music of the world's peoples. Academic research was the means to that end. The work of numerous comparative musicologists, chiefly European, was described, and their most important publications referenced. But comparative musicology soon underwent a facelift. Historical accounts date this to Jaap Kunst's book *Ethno-Musicology* (Kunst, 1950, and two subsequent editions), which defined *ethnomusicology* as the study of "all tribal and folk music and every kind of non-Western art music. Besides, it studies as well the sociological aspects of music . . . " (ibid., 1950: 1). Although he is usually credited with inventing the term *ethnomusicology*, Kunst's argument for the name change rested chiefly on redundancy of the word "comparative." All good science, he argued, is comparative in nature; disciplines like linguistics and embryology had, after all, dropped the adjective for the time being. His argument was persuasive, and some comparative musicologists began to adopt the new name, while others who wished to place more emphasis on the cultural study of music and less on musical analysis welcomed the name change and saw opportunity in it. However, comparative musicology remained the ancestral predecessor for Kunst and in later US historical accounts of the discipline, chiefly by Bruno Nettl (1956, 1964, 1983, 2002, 2005, 2010) as well as others. For nearly 60 years these historical accounts have informed generations of ethnomusicology professors and graduate students, in the United States and elsewhere. Despite increased theoretical sophistication and a growing recognition of historical relativism (e.g., Nettl and Bohlman, eds., 1991; Nettl, 2010; Rice, 2014), different subject emphases by other authors (e.g., Hood, 1971; Merriam, 1964), and an enlarged cast of characters (McLean, 2006), these mainstream histories continue to construct ethnomusicology as a research discipline almost exclusively centered in the academic world. Applied ethnomusicology seldom appears; when it does, it usually is treated with some reservations. As long as comparative musicology remained ethnomusicology's central occupation, applied work would be marginal at best.

The founding of the Society for Ethnomusicology (SEM) in 1955 not only provided an opportunity for a new emphasis on the cultural study of music, but might also have moved applied ethnomusicology to a more central position. Why it did not do so, at a time when applied anthropology was becoming important within US cultural anthropology, is an interesting question. In large part, as this brief history will show, the answer has to do with the founding generation's desire to establish and expand ethnomusicology as an academic discipline, on a firm institutional footing, throughout the university world. In so doing, they missed an opportunity to integrate applied work into the agenda of the new Society. It was left for the next generation to do so.

The early period of SEM was, predictably, taken up with debate over the direction of the discipline. In its first 15 years or so, the SEM journal, *Ethnomusicology*, was filled with essays by many leading practitioners who attempted to define the discipline and influence its course. Research in ethnomusicology's first two decades (ca. 1950–1975) has been characterized as falling broadly into two approaches, one musicological and the other anthropological (Kerman, 1986: 155–181). This is an oversimplification, but it is useful in highlighting the legacies of Hornbostel and Herzog, which in SEM could be seen in the work of Herzog's former colleague Kolinski, William Malm, George List, Mantle Hood, and Nettl, among others. Their focus was on collecting, recording, transcribing, describing, classifying, analyzing, and comparing music in order to increase the music knowledge-base and to test theories concerning musical distribution, diffusion, and acculturation. Like Herzog, most were interested also in the ethnographic study of cultural contexts for music ("music in culture") and in comparing and contrasting music's functions within cultures. Unless one thinks of the polymath Seeger as a comparativist, these comparative musicologists were not represented among the four SEM founders; but their work was prominent in monographs and in *Ethnomusicology*, where they advanced their scholarship and their view of what ethnomusicology ought to be. They also played a major role in establishing ethnomusicology as an academic discipline at the graduate level in US universities during the first 20 years of SEM.

On the other side of the debate over the future of ethnomusicology were the anthropologists, dance ethnologists, folklorists, and various other scholars who shared an interest in music and had been attracted to the new field. Most prominent among these were the anthropologists Alan Merriam and David McAllester, both among the four founders of SEM. Herzog was noticeably absent from SEM's origins, and it is worth asking why. Nettl, who writes movingly and generously about Herzog, observed that Herzog already was behaving erratically in 1952 (he would be hospitalized from the mid-1950s onward, with occasional time off, until his death in 1983, for what we would now call a bipolar disorder) and attributes his absence to this (Nettl, 2002: 90–92; Nettl, 2010: 168; Nettl and Bohlman, 1991: 271–272). No doubt this is correct; but it appears that the founders also wished to escape Herzog's dominance over the field. McAllester reported that as far as he knew, he was the only student ever to complete the doctorate under Herzog's supervision. "The campus was littered with the bodies of failed Herzog students," McAllester said. Herzog's habit was to demonstrate to them time after time that they could not meet his standards. "He never failed them in so many words," McAllester continued, "but they had a very hard time ever getting an appointment with him, and when they finally did, it was all at such a high level that they felt sort of defeated. If they brought in a transcription, it was so bad that he went over it note by note to show them and said, now see if you can't, now that you've had this practice, do better next time. Then a month or so later, when they caught up with him again, then the same thing would happen again." Rhodes was one of the dropouts, but he was already a full professor at Columbia and did not need the degree; yet it remained a sore point with him and his friend McAllester both. Even before Herzog moved from Columbia to Indiana University in 1948, he had been showing signs of the mental instability that would institutionalize him (Memorial Resolution, 1983). Herzog was Nettl's dissertation supervisor at Indiana, but before Nettl could complete his doctorate, Herzog's erratic behavior forced him to move to a different supervisor. "Bruno studied with him [Herzog] when he went out to Indiana, and he [Nettl] had a professor for a father, and so he had a strong position," McAllester said. (Paul Nettl, Bruno's father, was a professor of musicology at Indiana University.) "And he [Nettl] demanded another teacher, and he finished his Ph.D. with Carl Voegelin, the linguist. He left Herzog, but most of us couldn't do that. We were with Herzog and it was do or die, and many died" (McAllester, 1989).

No wonder then, given McAllester's and Rhodes's opinion of him, that Herzog was not invited into the inner circle of SEM founders. At that time they may have been less aware of Herzog's illness and decline than Nettl and the others who worked with Herzog at Indiana. But that must be only part of the answer. The other part is that McAllester, Merriam, Rhodes, and Seeger wanted to take a new direction, to move away from comparative musicology and Boasian ethnography, and toward an ethnomusicology that would make room not only for a greater variety of authoritative voices but also for more emphasis on the cultural study of music. Reaching out to scholars throughout the world, in 1953 the four founders initiated an ethnomusicology *Newsletter*, and two years later they founded the Society for Ethnomusicology (SEM), designed to foster communication and research in the field. SEM immediately began publishing a journal, *Ethnomusicology*, which since its inception has served as the flagship research periodical for the discipline. It is worth pausing for a moment to examine what the founders themselves thought they were up to. Nettl, reminiscing about this early period, the name change from "comparative musicology" to "ethnomusicology," and the founding of SEM, recalls that he (and others, he thinks) regarded these events more as a "revival" of a great scholarly tradition (comparative musicology, which had been all but eliminated in Europe during the Nazi era) than as a revolution (Nettl, 2010: 160–162). Inclined toward his teacher Herzog's understanding of that tradition, Nettl's subject position is understandable. Still a graduate student at the time and not directly involved as a founder, he had nevertheless set his course and was already a major stakeholder in the new field. His memoirs (Nettl, 2002, 2010, 2013) of this transitional period are both charming and invaluable, filled with information unavailable elsewhere and required reading for anyone interested in the history of ethnomusicology. In these memoirs, he tries to deconstruct the "myth" of SEM's "grand entrance," as he puts it, arguing that its historical significance and the importance of the four founders has been overrated (Nettl, 2010: 160–165). In retrospect, it is apparent that comparative musicology continued to exert a strong influence upon ethnomusicology during its first few decades (ca. 1950–1980). But the new Society, the new name, and its founders' orientation toward anthropology is a historical fact that signaled a significant and enduring new direction for the field.

Let me try to reconstruct something of that significance as I believe it to have appeared to the founders at the time. (In so doing, I rely in part on my conversations with Rhodes, Merriam, Seeger, and especially McAllester about that period.) McAllester recalled that after Herzog was finally confined to a mental hospital, he could no longer exercise his former control over degrees, grants, and publications in the field. "He became so ill that he had to be in an institution, and then the lid was off and the Society [SEM] could be established" (McAllester, 1989). For the four founders, SEM represented a move away from comparative musicology, not simply as an escape from Herzog's iron grip, but in establishing a new interdisciplinary field: ethnomusicology. The founders resisted efforts from other Societies who tried to dissuade them from starting a new Society. The American Musicological Society sent representatives to their early meetings and "announced that we should not be a splinter group, but that we should be part of the American Musicological Society . . . . And we said, if we joined them, the AMS, there were a whole bunch of people that would not be any longer members. We had folklorists, anthropologists, ethnologists, acousticians, physicists. . . and they would have dropped out if we had become a part of the American Musicological Society." These same scholars likewise would have left SEM had they allied themselves with the IFMC, McAllester reported. "Maud Karpeles came and pleaded with us to become a wing of the International Folk Music Council. . . . Alan Merriam particularly, well, Charlie Seeger too, they were both very insistent that it not get into the hands of. . . the International Folk Music [Council]. So when we started the society, they [the IFMC] soon got wind of it, and they were very upset because they had their American branch and they were afraid we would simply split their society and draw membership away from them. . . . There were scholars among them, great scholars among them, but they were not anthropologically oriented. And it just happened by the way we operated, that the Society for Ethnomusicology began with an anthropological orientation" (McAllester, 1989). Nettl agreed: "The beginning of the SEM was deeply rooted in the anthropological background of its most influential leaders" (Nettl, 2010: 143).

McAllester recalled the excitement that accompanied the founding of SEM, along with the possibilities of new directions for the Society. For Merriam even more than for McAllester, that direction was to be cultural anthropology. Eventually he termed this direction "the anthropology of music" rather than "comparative musicology," and he lobbied hard for the study of music, not in culture, but *as* culture, a phrase ("music as culture") that Merriam referenced to his earlier "unpublished thoughts" (Merriam,

1977: 204). According to Merriam, music was not something that existed within a cultural context; it *was* culture in the anthropological sense itself, with its own domain of ideas, behavior, and sonic dimension. Obtaining a full professorship in anthropology at Indiana University in 1962, Merriam was not only a founder but a forceful presence in SEM from the very beginning until his untimely death in an airplane crash in 1980. His area interests were in indigenous musics primarily, Native American and African. A former jazz musician, he had little use for the study of folk music, and even less for bi-musicality, about which more shortly. When I taught a summer session in Indiana's Folklore Institute in 1977, he invited me to his home a number of times. He had just remarried, and was in an expansive mood. Relevant for this historical sketch is the attitude he expressed toward the IFMC. He affirmed that the founders had refused Maud Karpeles's invitation to join the International Folk Music Council rather than form their own Society. Nettl attributed Merriam's reasons for objecting to the IFMC to "his perception of the IFMC as specifically interested in music alone, the notion that folk-music scholars were interested in only a small segment of the music of any society; and the idea that the IFMC included a substantial practical component, that is, was in large measure a society of folksingers and dancers" (Nettl, 2010: 143). Merriam's views had evolved since then, for in 1977 he told me the IFMC as a group was insufficiently objective and scientific about music as a human phenomenon. If they had been, they would have been concerned with all music, not mainly the oldest layers of music in what were then regarded as folk societies (Redfield, 1947). And if they had been, they would not have been so concerned with authenticity and so worried about salvaging this music for archival preservation; or worse yet, reviving it for a sophisticated urban audience. Merriam took some pleasure in noting that Indiana University's Folklore Institute did not share this attitude toward musical revivalism; indeed, Richard Dorson, the head of the Institute, had coined the term "fakelore" to describe it, and on the advice of George List, the senior ethnomusicologist in the Folklore Institute, Dorson would not permit amateur folk musicians in their doctoral program to undertake music research unless they had had sufficient formal training in Western music theory and history to be admitted to ethnomusicology courses. As Indiana was one of only a very few universities in the US granting doctoral degrees in folklore, the amount of academic research in US folk music during the Dorson-List-Merriam era was severely diminished as a consequence. For Merriam, ethnomusicology was revolutionary insofar as it elevated anthropology to a position of equality with musicology in birthing the new offspring, ethnomusicology. The *ethno-* prefix (derived from the Greek *ethnos* [= people with a common culture]) firmly established it as a new discipline that was properly part of "the scientific study of man," as anthropology had long been defined. Merriam assiduously pursued this goal, which he called "sciencing about music" (Merriam, 1964: 25 et passim).

With SEM established on the promise of interdisciplinarity and new directions, particularly from anthropology, one might have expected that the new organization would have been hospitable to applied ethnomusicology. Anthropologists had by then started putting their knowledge to use in solving social problems. John Van Willigen dates the rise of a socially committed applied or "action" anthropology to 1945, although he notes that anthropologists had for decades previously taken on community consultantship roles (van Willigen, 2002). But this exciting, albeit controversial, development in anthropology did not cross over into SEM with any success until decades later. The reasons, in retrospect, are not entirely surprising. To establish ethnomusicology within the most secure of institutional bases, that is, within universities, it was necessary to position it as a research science, aiming to increase knowledge of the music of the world's peoples. Musicological and anthropological ethnomusicologists might disagree over the discipline's emphasis, but they agreed that scholarship and the production of knowledge were its goals. Applications of that research in the public arena might be well and good, but the pursuit of knowledge for its own sake had always been valued most highly in university settings, where it could be protected from outside forces. In 1950 ethnomusicology itself was a fringe discipline in the United States, with only a few courses being offered (sometimes in anthropology departments, sometimes music) and only a few professors available to advise doctoral dissertations. For ethnomusicology to expand inside the university world, professors must succeed in establishing courses, programs (especially graduate programs), tenure tracks, and recognition of the discipline as a legitimate academic pursuit. The proven strategy to advance the discipline in the university world would be through research, emphasizing that study of the music of the world's peoples would add to the store of knowledge about human behavior and achievement. Research "for its own sake" was then, and remains, regarded in the academy as more elegant, of higher and "purer" disinterested purpose than research driven by applications. In the arts and humanities, where contemplation of the pure aesthetic object was required for philosophy, literary criticism, and art history, disinterested acts of scholarship were experienced as pleasurable in themselves. Eventually, one could hope, every music department, every music school or conservatory, and every anthropology department would have at least one ethnomusicologist doing research and offering music courses with a worldwide scope; and some would have more than one and would establish graduate programs training future generations of ethnomusicologists as the discipline would expand. Professionalization of ethnomusicology as a research discipline, and with that a need to distance it from well-meaning amateurs who also engaged in music research, was a second reason. Applied work might be done by those who lacked the proper scientific attitude and scholarly training to conduct credible research: missionaries, for example, who had historically put music to use in attempting to convert indigenous peoples, or amateur collectors who became partisans on behalf of those whose music they recorded. I believe that a third reason was the distrust, among this generation of scholars who came of age during or soon after World War II, of social engineering, whether for political, cultural, or musical ends. Applied research put to practical use in musical or cultural interventions, despite intended benefits, was something Americans might well oppose, particularly given the uses to which music was put during the Nazi regime, and was being put in the Soviet sphere during the Cold War. Many in the previous generation of US music scholars had been born in Europe and had fled to North America to escape Nazi persecution and establish a musical scholarship inside the university world where they would be free from political interference. I do not mean to suggest that a cabal of ethnomusicology professors drew up such a plan, but rather that they were inclined by personality and training to move in that direction. Partly as a result, in its first two decades, ethnomusicology became more firmly established as a scholarly discipline; but applied ethnomusicology languished inside the US academic world.

Merriam was perhaps the first US ethnomusicologist to recognize an applied ethnomusicology by that name, although he did not favor it. The phase "applied ethnomusicology" did not appear in the SEM *Newsletter* or journal until Merriam's 1963 review of Henry Weman's *African Music and the Church in Africa*. Merriam wrote that this book is "perhaps most accurately described as a study in applied ethnomusicology, for his principal concern is how African music can be used . . . " in missionary work (Merriam, 1963b: 135). Merriam expanded on his comments a year later in *The Anthropology of Music*, and it is worth looking at them in detail:

> . . . the ultimate aim of the study of man. . . involves the question of whether one is searching for knowledge for its own sake, or is attempting to provide solutions for practical applied problems. Ethnomusicology has seldom been used in the same manner as applied or action anthropology, and ethnomusicologists have only rarely felt called upon to help solve problems in manipulating the destinies of people, but some such studies have been made [here he references Weman's book] and it is quite conceivable that this may in the future be of increased concern. The difficulty of an applied study is that it focuses the attention of the investigator upon a single problem which may cause or force him to ignore others of equal interest, and it is also difficult to avoid outside control over the research project. Although this problem is not yet of primary concern, it will surely shape the kinds of studies carried out if it does draw the increased attention of ethnomusicologists.
>
> (Merriam, 1964: 42–43)

Here, as elsewhere, Merriam privileges "knowledge for its own sake." In criticizing applied work for its narrow focus, Merriam is appealing to the idea that ethnomusicology should study music as a whole; but "outside control" may be viewed as a threat to academic freedom, while the phrase "manipulating the destinies of people" expresses that distrust of and distaste for the political and cultural interventions of applied anthropology and, by extension, of applied ethnomusicology.

Several books and articles critique recent interventions, especially those resulting from UNESCO initiatives to preserve intangible cultural heritage (e.g., Weintraub and Yung, 2005). But this tradition of critique may be traced to Merriam's "white knight" label for those ethnomusicologists who feel called to "function as knights in shining armor riding to the defense of non-Western music" (Merriam, 1963a: 207). Skepticism toward applied ethnomusicology is also evident in Bruno Nettl's histories and descriptions of the field. Nettl, more than anyone else among the founding generation of SEM, shouldered the responsibility to construct a history of ethnomusicology, something which he has come to call his "elephant" (Nettl, 2010). The sole active survivor of his generation of ethnomusicologists, Nettl early on assumed the mantle of spokesperson for the discipline, and today he is recognized in the United States and elsewhere as its elder statesman. As intellectual history is his central concern, he devotes relatively little attention to applied ethnomusicology. His most influential book, *The Study of Ethnomusicology*, treats applied ethnomusicology within the context of applied anthropology: "In the course of the 1950s there developed a concept and a subdiscipline, 'applied anthropology', whose task it was to use anthropological insight to help solve social problems, particularly those occasioned by rapid culture change in the wake of modernization and Westernization." Applied anthropologists also were consulted in attempts to solve economic problems such as third-world poverty. They advised government organizations such as the United States Agency for International Development (USAID), on interventions involving democratization, agricultural modernization, and economic development. Rapid social change and cultural upheaval was the result of the intervention, not the original problem to be solved. No wonder then, as Nettl continues, that although "Anthropologists wanted to help [they] frequently ended up offending the local population and doing what was perceived as harmful. As a result, in the late 1960s and early 1970s they were widely attacked for doing work of no relevance to social problems, of mixing in local politics, of spying. Ethnomusicologists shared in this criticism.. . ." Here, applied ethnomusicologists' efforts to conserve traditional music and culture are conflated with applied anthropologists' efforts meant to aid in the modernization of traditional culture. The implication is that, like applied anthropologists, applied ethnomusicologists were criticized as offensive, harmful, and irrelevant; and that they barged into local politics and were accused of being spies. But if this critique of anthro-colonialism is accurate about interventions meant to bring about modernization and development, it does not follow that it applies to interventions by applied ethnomusicologists meant to conserve traditional music. Nettl then balances the critique with a somewhat more positive view:

> the picture [of applied anthropology and ethnomusicology] is not entirely negative. Some societies are happy to have outsiders come, appreciate their efforts, their respect for the traditions, and their help in restoring vigor to rapidly disappearing musics. Persian and Indian music masters are proud to have Western scholars as students, for it raises their prestige locally and legitimizes their traditional art in the face of modernizing doubters. Even so, there is often the feeling that members of the society itself, given the right training, equipment, and time, could do it better.
>
> (Nettl, 1983: 297; repeated in the 2nd edition, 2005: 206)

Nettl points out that some ethnomusicologists "espouse fieldwork in which informants become collaborators, the members of a community being studied in effect becoming co-collaborators" (ibid.). Yet Nettl's deep unease with applied work as social engineering is embedded in the tone and weight of his discussion and in the examples he offers; and it is apparent where he thinks the majority of ethnomusicologists stand. For the first edition of this book (1983) this was a correct assessment, but by the second edition (2005) it was not. Indeed, in a recent interview he acknowledged applied ethnomusicology's considerable appeal to a new generation (Fouce, 2014: 1).[3]

A few ethnomusicologists in SEM's founding generation were involved in applied projects during the 1960s and 1970s, yet they did not call it applied ethnomusicology. No doubt they thought of these as proper activities for an ethnomusicologist, but to my knowledge they did not think of them as part of a subfield where research was directed toward the public interest. Some, most prominently SEM founder David McAllester, took an advocacy role in educating music teachers and broadening the kindergarten-through-high school curricula to include examples of the musics of the world's peoples. McAllester worked through the Music Educators' National Conference to accomplish this goal, and he advised several graduate students in the Wesleyan University world music program who went in this direction, among them Patricia Shehan Campbell (see her Chapter 3, coauthored with Lee Higgins, in this volume). Another prominent ethnomusicologist in the founding generation, Mantle Hood, undertook applied ethnomusicology projects in Indonesia. He related the story of his successful intervention to revive Javanese gamelan gong-making (for the large gong *ageng*), which had nearly gone extinct. However, he also reported that his intervention resulted in some unintended, negative consequences. He offered another example, when he was called on for suggestions to improve gamelan educational practice—what innovations would he recommend? But here he stepped back from applied ethnomusicology and refused to interfere, thinking that Western influence would not be good for the tradition (Hood, 1971: 358–371). His major work on ethnomusicology ends with a section on cultural exchange through music and the arts as part of a program to further international understanding—putting ethnomusicological knowledge to practical use for a clear and intended social benefit.

Thus it could be fairly said that SEM's founding generation concentrated their US efforts in two areas: first, on research in order to increase knowledge about music and to circulate it among scholars; and second, to secure an institutional base for ethnomusicology within the academic world. In the latter, they were more successful in the music divisions of the universities and colleges (variously called music departments, schools of music, conservatories, and the like) than in anthropology departments. Growth within music divisions allied the discipline more closely with musicology than anthropology, and although the SEM founders envisioned a broadly interdisciplinary field with a new emphasis on the cultural study of music—and achieved this at SEM conferences and to some extent in the SEM journal, *Ethnomusicology*—the institutional growth of the discipline favored the musicologically oriented scholars.

Ironically, however, it was not by positioning ethnomusicology as a research science that institutional growth was achieved; rather, in the last half of the twentieth century ethnomusicology benefited from a combination of external circumstances that the founding generation did not foresee. The most important of these were, first, the meteoric rise in the popularity of world music among the general public, and especially the young, which began in the 1960s. Second was the reversal, in US cultural mythology, from the idea that the nation was a melting pot that produced a single American type, to the acceptance of cultural diversity and pluralism, which in the field of education broke the Eurocentric hold on curricula and opened it to a variety of minority voices in the humanities: literature, fine arts, music, and history. Youth cultures became deeply involved in alternative musics, including folk music, blues, and bluegrass. World music began to enjoy widespread popularity, as George Harrison of the Beatles studied sitar in India, and Hindustani musicians Ali Akbar Khan and Ravi Shankar went on extended annual tours throughout the United States. Recording companies such as Nonesuch released world music recordings and targeted both indigenous as well as Asian art musics to an appreciative public. Young men and women turned to world music as one of many paths toward personal growth. Fueled by the rising popularity of world music, master musicians from Ghana, North and South India, the Arab world, China, Japan, and Indonesia soon were in residence as world music performance ensemble directors at American colleges and universities where ethnomusicologists were already teaching. Performance was attracting students into the field. Mantle Hood, director of the Ethnomusicology Institute at UCLA, spearheaded this movement, advocating on behalf of what he called bi-musicality. Just as serious study of a foreign language could turn a person bilingual, so serious study of a foreign music could make one bi-musical and impart a knowledge of that music that was otherwise unavailable. Some senior ethnomusicologists tempered their enthusiasm for world music performance ensembles, however, and for decades they were conspicuously absent at the University of Illinois and Indiana University. Nonetheless, the possibility that world music might be learned intrigued many, and some went on to enroll in graduate programs in ethnomusicology, resulting in more degrees, professors, and programs. By 1970 it was possible to study ethnomusicology and obtain the doctorate by studying with Hood at UCLA, Fredric Lieberman at Brown, George List and Merriam at Indiana, Nettl at Illinois, Robert Garfias at Washington, William Malm at Michigan, and McAllester at Wesleyan, among other universities. Moreover, those with doctoral training in ethnomusicology had begun teaching at other colleges and universities, and SEM's US membership had increased.

Diversification and expansion of the US college and university music curriculum created a demand for professors who could teach the new courses. Within music divisions, this meant the end of the near-complete domination of Western art music (or classical music, as the American public calls it). Now popular music, jazz, and the music of the world's peoples took their place among the course offerings. Gradually, ethnomusicologists began to realize that they could take a proactive role and convince university administrators that one way to accomplish their goal of affirmative action toward so-called American minority groups (something which ethnomusicologists by and large supported) was through greater diversity of music offerings, which would also mean more ethnomusicology hires. As programs and departments were established in African American studies, Native American studies, Asian American studies, Hispanic American studies, and the like, it became apparent that the music of American minorities, along with world music, had an important role to play in the expanded curricula. Of course, ethnomusicologists were far from the only ones to benefit from diversity, cultural pluralism, and affirmative action in the academic world; but while the popularity of world music has ebbed and flowed since the 1960s, the movement toward greater cultural diversity within US higher education has been persistent.

The folk music revival, rising popularity of world music, and the positive value now attached to ethnic roots and cultural pluralism brought about a renewed emphasis in applied ethnomusicology outside the academic world before it had much impact inside it. Because Alan Lomax embodied this public work in applied ethnomusicology—not only as a collector, writer, and promoter, but also as an advocate for cultural democracy and musical pluralism—it is instructive to ponder his encounter with none other than George Herzog, who also believed in the value of musical diversity and had devoted his life to the study of folk and "primitive" music. Herzog, as noted, embodied comparative musicology in the United States during the 1930s and 1940s. After Lomax had been "Assistant in Charge" of the Archive of American Folk Song at the Library of Congress for several years—field-collecting, acquiring from others, and curating recordings—he decided to move his base of operations, from February through June of 1939, to Manhattan to obtain "more systematic academic training in anthropology and in the anthropological approach to primitive and folk music." He hoped to study with Herzog and other anthropologists at Columbia, and also "to study music with private instructors" (Cohen 2010: 115). A recently published collection of Lomax's correspondence reveals the encounter with Herzog—from Lomax's viewpoint, of course—to have been less than successful. Herzog would not let Lomax into his course, insisting that he must take his two courses in sequence—primitive music (offered in the fall) followed by folk music (in the spring). Herzog would not budge from the requirement. To Harold Spivacke, his supervisor at the Library of Congress, Lomax then wrote, "I met a very much surprised Dr. Herzog at Columbia this morning, a Dr. Herzog who told me that I had made a great mistake in coming to school to take his course this term, that I should have come next term, should have come next year and for a whole year. Such a neurotic little academic man you never saw before" (Cohen 2010: 121). Although Lomax had a marvelous ear, outstanding musical taste, and broad knowledge of folk music, he had little formal musical education and could be regarded as a well-meaning amateur in search of professional training. In some scientific disciplines, such as ornithology and astronomy, serious work by amateur researchers is highly valued; and in the early history of science, the majority of natural historians and natural philosophers were amateurs and proud of it. But Herzog was wary of amateur music research. Their confrontation, exacerbated by their prickly personalities and strong convictions, can be understood as a sign of incompatibility between public and academic ethnomusicologies in an earlier era; today, as mentioned earlier, more practitioners of applied ethnomusicology are employed within academia than outside it.

Indeed, the growth of US applied ethnomusicology from the 1960s through the 1980s owed much to Alan Lomax's continuing influence, his call for cultural equity, the work of public folklorists, and the establishment of government institutions that supported cultural pluralism within the arts. At the federal level were the Office of Folklife Studies at the Smithsonian Institution, the Folk Arts program of the National Endowment for the Arts, and the Archive of Folk Culture at the Library of Congress, enlarged from the former Archive of American Folk Song, which Lomax had directed, and under the aegis of a new Library division, the American Folklife Center. Regional, state, and, in some cases, city arts councils also were established, funded in part by the National Endowment for the Arts, and by the end of the 1980s most of the state arts councils employed at least one folklorist and a few employed ethnomusicologists (see Murphy, Chapter 5 of this volume). Folklore in the United States, while conservative in the academic world, enjoyed a tradition of populist activism outside it. Each of these government agencies employed scholars as consultants, and some employed them as arts and humanities administrators; thus, a large public outreach and concern for the health of expressive culture within various US communities was put in place, with a growing number of ethnomusicologists involved in public folklore, most often as consultants, but sometimes as advocates and collaborators, doing applied work. Several ethnomusicologists worked as presenters at folk festivals, their prior fieldwork having identified and documented some of the musicians who performed there. Music was the most prominent among the arts singled out by public folklorists for identification, documentation, and presentation. As arts administrators, ethnomusicologists were employed by the Smithsonian Institution (Thomas Vennum, Charlotte Heth) and by the Folk Arts Division of the National Endowment for the Arts (NEA; Daniel Sheehy), which also hired numerous ethnomusicologists as consultants to sit on panels recommending funding for various community music projects as well as for apprenticeships and heritage awards (see Titon, Chapter 5 of Volume 1). Bess Lomax Hawes held an informal session at the SEM conference most years during the 1980s to inform ethnomusicologists of the opportunities for submitting applied ethnomusicology project proposals to the NEA. This activity, known in the 1970s and 1980s as public-sector folklore, in the 1990s became known simply as "public folklore," and influenced the course of applied ethnomusicology in the United States profoundly.

Academic ethnomusicologists involved in public folklore thus began to think of their work as applied ethnomusicology, but SEM remained chiefly an organization devoted to communicating research among scholars. It was not until most of the founding generation aged and gradually relinquished leadership that applied ethnomusicology was able to enter SEM in a significant way. But it was not merely a changing of the generations. A significant change within academia resulted from the growing critique of science, fomented by post-structuralist and critical cultural theory, and culminating in the so-called "science wars" of the 1980s. North American graduate students in ethnomusicology during this period—beginning in the late 1960s—could not help being affected, as were cultural anthropologists and folklorists. The result, particularly among those attracted to the study of music as culture, was a turn in ethnomusicology from science toward cultural critique, from the musical object to the musical experience, from analysis to interpretation, from explanation to understanding. As a result, US ethnomusicology took a humanistic turn, and the cultural study of music moved to the forefront until, by the end of the 1980s, ethnomusicology had assimilated the humanistic cultural anthropology of Clifford Geertz, Dennis Tedlock, James Clifford, George Marcus,

Vincent Crapanzano, Paul Rabinow, and others, a far cry from the empirical anthropology Herzog had championed. Much of this ethnomusicological humanism eventually achieved theoretical expression in the "new fieldwork" (Barz and Cooley, 1996) of reflexivity, reciprocity, and advocacy. Meanwhile, the scientific ethnomusicologists were in gradual retreat. A review of the essays in *Ethnomusicology* since about 1976 shows the balance point moving in the direction of music as culture rather than as form and structure. In 2010 the musicological ethnomusicologists came together outside SEM to form their own scholarly association (Analytical Approaches to World Music) with its own journal.[4]

Ethnomusicology's humanistic turn led a growing number of North American ethnomusicologists toward applied ethnomusicology in one form or another—advocating on behalf of individual musicians, musical communities, and musical life in particular places. The new fieldwork had become experience-centered, with ethnomusicological monographs such as those by Berliner (1978) and Keil (1979) reflecting this first-person turn to reflexivity. Kenneth Gourlay's 1982 essay in SEM's journal, "Towards a Humanizing Ethnomusicology," offered a theoretical basis for the new direction, along with a strongly worded critique of Merriam's insistence on science (Gourlay, 1982). In that same issue of *Ethnomusicology*, Charles Keil's essay, "Applied Ethnomusicology and a Rebirth of Music from the Spirit of Tragedy," charted a path toward work that "can make a difference" through "an insistence on putting music into play wherever people are resisting their oppression" (Keil, 1982: 407). Keil's 1982 essay caught the spirit of the postcolonialism that was central to cultural critique in the new anthropology, and to critical theory in cultural studies. And because applied ethnomusicology did not become a movement until the era of decolonization, it could (and did) oppose colonialism, orientalism, and other manifestations of the arrogance of Western power, while answering (if not avoiding) the critiques of colonialism that were being (and that continue to be) leveled at applied anthropology. Meanwhile, an ever-increasing number of US ethnomusicologists were becoming involved in public folklore and were realizing that there was much good work to be done for music in the public arena.

A humanized ethnomusicology thus made it possible for a resurgence of a postcolonial applied ethnomusicology, manifesting itself not only in a new fieldwork based in reciprocity leading to advocacy, but also through institutional gains within SEM. Applied ethnomusicology went mainstream within SEM during the 1990s. As the program chair for the 1989 SEM conference, I invited colleagues from my years in the early 1980s as a consultant for the NEA Folk Arts Program to present papers on a pre-planned panel. Entitled "From Perspective to Practice in 'Applied Ethnomusicology,'" the panel included the following presenters and papers: Robert Garfias, "What an Ethnomusicologist Can Do in Public Sector Arts"; Daniel Sheehy, "Applied Ethnomusicology as a State of Mind"; Charlotte Heth, "Getting It Right and Passing It On: The Ethnomusicologist and Cultural Transmission"; and Bess Lomax Hawes, "Practice Makes Perfect: Lessons in Active Ethnomusicology." When in 1990 I became editor of *Ethnomusicology*, this panel formed the starting point for a special issue entitled "Ethnomusicology and the Public Interest," which featured articles by Daniel Sheehy, Bess Lomax Hawes, Martha Ellen

Davis, and Anthony Seeger. This was the first time that applied ethnomusicology was featured in the SEM journal. In my introductory article for that special issue, I wrote that ethnomusicology in the public interest "is work whose immediate end is not research and the flow of knowledge inside intellectual communities but, rather, practical action in the world outside of archives and universities" and that "as a way of knowing and doing, fieldwork [which is constitutive of ethnomusicology] at its best is based on a model of friendship between people rather than on a model involving antagonism, surveillance, the observation of physical objects, or the contemplation of abstract ideas" (Titon, 1992a: 315, 321). Sheehy's article there began the process of constructing an alternative history for ethnomusicology in the United States, one in which applied work was more central (Sheehy, 1992). Hawes was invited to give the plenary Seeger Lecture at the 1993 SEM conference, and this autobiographical talk, meant in part to attract listeners to applied work as a calling, was published two years later in *Ethnomusicology* (Hawes, 1995). In 1998 Keil, continuing in the vein of postcolonial critique, called in the SEM journal for an "applied sociomusicology" that, by reclaiming participatory music-making "for the vast majority," would help engender a revolution in consciousness that would overturn the global corporate capitalist world order and reverse the coming eco-catastrophe as we move toward "sustainable futures" (Keil, 1998: 304).

At the 1998 SEM Conference, Doris Dyen and Martha Ellen Davis convened a meeting to assess interest in proposing a standing Committee on Applied Ethnomusicology to the SEM Board. Until that meeting, a single name for this activity had not yet risen to the surface; among those in circulation then were "applied," "active," "action," "practice," "public," and "public sector" (Titon, 1992a: 320–321). As applied ethnomusicologists themselves, with experience in the public sector and in the academic world, Davis and Dyen felt the time was opportune for organizing something more formal to bring together those with common interests in working for the benefit of musical communities in the public sphere. Thirty-eight hopeful founders (the editors of this volume among them) attended, their proposal was accepted by the SEM Board, and the Committee was established, with a variety of definitions of applied ethnomusicology. In 2000, Dyen and Davis, who had taken on the role of chairs of the Committee, appointed a deputy chair, Tom Van Buren, and successfully petitioned the Board to recognize the group as the Applied Ethnomusicology Section. Dyen and Davis stood aside in 2002 while appointing co-chairs Ric Alviso and Miriam Gerberg to join Van Buren, who stepped down in 2004 in favor of Mark Puryear. Alviso was succeeded in 2008 by Jeff Todd Titon, Gerberg in 2009 by Kathleen Noss Van Buren, Puryear in 2010 by Maureen Loughran, Noss Van Buren in 2014 by Michael Bakan, and Loughran in 2015 by Erica Haskell.

During the Committee and Section's first decade, the co-chairs worked to make the group a comfortable space within SEM for ethnomusicologists employed outside of the academic world. To that end, they organized practical panels on non-academic careers for ethnomusicologists, such as the "Ethnomusicologists at Work" series, organized by Gerberg; and on strategies for survival both inside and outside official institutions. Co-chairs Gerberg, Puryear, and Alviso established Section prizes for outstanding presentations at SEM, and awards for travel grants to the conference. In the new millennium, as applied ethnomusicology has become increasingly popular among graduate students and welcomed inside academic institutions, the Section has become an SEM meeting-place and platform for applied ethnomusicologists based both within and outside academia. Most recently, the Section has sponsored panels involving themes such as music and politics, community advocacy, activism and "giving back," conflict resolution, ethics, repatriation of artifacts from archives and museums, medicine, the environment, and social justice. It also sponsors presentations from guests who do not normally attend the SEM conferences but who have worked in applied ethnomusicology either independently or in extra-academic institutions. For example, at the 2011 conference, Debora Kodish, public folklorist and director of the Philadelphia Folklore Project, led a Section-sponsored discussion among traditional music and dance activists and community scholar-practitioners from the African-American and Asian-American communities in Philadelphia, showcasing a model for ethnomusicologists seeking strategies for work in community-based institutions. With approximately 300 members, Applied Ethnomusicology is now one of the largest and most active among the SEM Sections, exceeded in membership only by the student and the popular music Sections.

As might be expected of a practical endeavor, theorization of applied ethnomusicology lagged behind practice, but recent years have witnessed an increasing number of publications and events centered on applied ethnomusicology itself. These included an international conference on applied ethnomusicology organized by Erica Haskell and Maureen Loughran, at Brown University (Invested in Community 2003), a special issue of *Folklore Forum* devoted to applied ethnomusicology (Fenn, 2003), a section devoted to applied ethnomusicology in an issue of *Ethnomusicology Review* (2012), and a book of essays, *Applied Ethnomusicology: Historical and Contemporary Approaches* (Harrison, Mackinlay, and Pettan, 2010). Rebecca Dirksen authored an excellent overview of contemporary practice, with an emphasis on work by US-based ethnomusicologists, while Timothy Rice's book-length "very short introduction" to the discipline devotes the last two of nine chapters to what is in effect applied ethnomusicology (Dirksen, 2012; Rice, 2014). This *Oxford Handbook,* first published in a one-volume clothbound edition in 2015, continued in this vein, offering a cross-section of contemporary international work in the field. In 2017, one entire day's programming of the annual SEM conference was devoted to public, public-sector, and applied ethnomusicology. In response to the continued use of those three terms (public, public sector, and applied), Klisala Harrison argued that "applied" was the covering term, particularly in the international context; and that "public" and "public sector" were best understood as sub-areas of "applied" that made sense only in certain national contexts (Harrison, 2017).

Concluding this sketch of applied ethnomusicology in the United States, I do not mean to dismiss entirely the critique that applied ethnomusicology may be used for undesirable ends. Knowledge is not innocent; cultural information has a long history of being put to use for military purposes and colonial conquest. Music used in the service of a social or musical benefit may turn out to have negative consequences, or what looks like a benefit to one political entity may be a harm to another. Merriam's charge that applied ethnomusicologists are engaged in "manipulating people's destinies" is one way of looking at missionary work, for example, and it is a fact that missionaries have put their knowledge of music to use for that purpose for many centuries. Today, faith-based organizations such as SIL put ethnomusicological knowledge to use in aiding local artists in indigenous communities, with the goal of a "better future: one of justice, peace, joy, physical safety, social continuity and spiritual wholeness" (SIL). Other forces are intervening: corporations, governments, technology, the law, and so forth. Social responsibility requires social justice, cultural equity, and decolonization. I believe there is no self-correcting "invisible hand" in the marketplace or anywhere else that would permit scholars the luxury of research without social responsibility. Nor would scholars be well advised to accumulate knowledge and then supply it to those who in their ignorance would put it to use.

SEM had been slow to adopt a more active role, but recognition of the need for the organization to enter the larger political sphere has gradually come. For many years, SEM took the position that while ethnomusicologists were of course free to express their personal political views, the organization itself must not take a public political stand. But in 1976 the SEM *Newsletter* editor refused to print an employment advertisement from a university representing a government that practiced apartheid, an early harbinger of change. Not long afterward, SEM began endorsing resolutions supporting the rights of scholars detained by governments for political reasons, and the rights of musicians to travel freely internationally. It has passed position statements on rights and discrimination, copyright ownership and sound recordings, and ethical considerations. Finally, in 2007, in response to a request from the SEM Ethics Committee, the SEM Board of Directors approved a "Position Statement against the Use of Music as Torture." Arising in response to numerous reports of music as part of the torture arsenal employed by US military and intelligence agencies and their allies against suspected terrorist detainees, it reads in part that the Society for Ethnomusicology "calls for full disclosure of US government-sanctioned and funded programs that design the means of delivering music as torture; condemns the use of music as an instrument of torture; and demands that the US government and its agencies cease using music as an instrument of physical and psychological torture" (SEM Torture). The position statement on music as torture was a significant step in SEM's evolution. It recognizes that ethnomusicologists are citizens of the world with social responsibilities, and that our professional organization has not only the right but also the duty to represent the profession's ethical beliefs and act upon them.

During the second decade of the twenty-first century, the SEM leadership's recognition of the ethnomusicologist's social responsibility continued to grow, fueled by increased interest in applied ethnomusicology among graduate students, many of whom were contemplating careers outside the academic world. At the University of Limerick, Ireland, in the same year that the clothbound, one-volume edition of this *Oxford Handbook of Applied Ethnomusicology* was published (2015), SEM and ICTM sponsored a joint, three-day Forum on the subject of an activist, community-engaged ethnomusicology, attended by more than 100 ethnomusicologists from all over the world, at which the editors of this volume were among the keynote speakers.[5] A book of essays from that Forum is in preparation under the editorship of forum conveners Beverley Diamond and Salwa El Shawan Castelo-Branco; upon publication it will move both SEM and ICTM further in the direction of *Transforming Ethnomusicology* (forthcoming) in an applied direction.

Notes

1. Its recognition was signaled in 1992 when the Journal of the Society for Ethnomusicology devoted a special issue to the subject (*Ethnomusicology* 36[2]).
2. In Kunst's definition ethnomusicology was chiefly a new name for the discipline of comparative musicology. But as we shall soon see, US cultural anthropologists interested in music saw opportunity in the new name, founded the international Society for Ethnomusicology in 1955, and were prominent among its leaders. Thus by 1955 ethnomusicology could be described as a new and interdisciplinary field, not just a new name for an older academic discipline.
3. In a 2013 interview he characterized as one of four "new, or newish developments in ethnomusicology" a "widespread concern with the need to do things that benefit the peoples whose music and musical culture are studied" (Nettl 2014: 1).
4. In the new millennium, science is making a small comeback as music theory and comparative studies are applied in these analytical approaches to structural features of world musics. Science is manifest also in a growing interest among ethnomusicologists in neuroscience and music psychology, and questions concerning music and human evolution.
5. The Forum was titled Transforming Ethnomusicological Practice Through Activism and Community Engagement, and was held in Limerick City, Ireland, from September 13–16, 2015. Further information about it may be found at https://www.ictmusic.org/joint-sem-ictm-forum-2015.

SECTION 2

APPLIED ETHNOMUSICOLOGY IN THE GLOBAL ARENA

SVANIBOR PETTAN

An Introductory Vignette

In 1975, a documentary film about hunting, *Ultime grida dalla savana* (internationally known as *Savage Man Savage Beast*) was released. The authors intended to document the phenomenon of hunting in different spatial and cultural contexts. The viewers can see not only animals hunting animals and humans hunting animals, but also animals hunting humans, and finally, humans hunting humans. The scenes in which lions eat a tourist and in which humans mutilate the bodies of caught humans were received with particular controversy. The filmmakers Antonio Climati and Mario Morra were filming all the scenes with the clear attitude of detached observers, documenting the multifaceted footage in the domain of their professional interest and showing no intention whatsoever to intervene. The basic symbolic standpoint of this film brings up a number of useful questions concerning the attitudes in the field of ethnomusicology in its both temporal and spatial contexts, and highlights the stance of intervention in positioning applied ethnomusicology.[1]

The stance of the above-mentioned filmmakers reflects the attitude prevalent in the ethnomusicological mainstream within the past decades, which can be summarized in the following way: studying music as it is, not as a researcher or anybody else would want it to be. I vividly recall an example from my doctoral studies at the University of Maryland Baltimore County, in which the professor pointed out a music producer of an African music CD, who insisted on removal of those parts from the musical instrument that were responsible for the production of a buzzing sound. The producer's opinion was that the recording without them would be more pleasing to the ears of international audiences, which would consequently increase the profit expected from the final product. Of course, such an uninformed and disrespectful intervention into the aesthetics of the musicians invoked laughter and criticism among the students, with no need for further discussion.

The question, which I considered essential, that is, whether "those who know" (us, the ethnomusicologists) would actually consider making a step beyond the level of an academic debate and try to intervene, by providing the ignorant producer who misused his power over the musicians with arguments against his action, was left unanswered.

The two cases (the film and the CD producer), extreme as they are, raise at least two useful points:

a. The decision whether to intervene or not has moral implications.
b. In order to be successful, intervention has to be based on knowledge, understanding, and skills.

What Is Applied Ethnomusicology, and What Isn't It?

As will be discussed later, definitions may vary according to the parameters such as time, place, research tradition, and individual preference, but the essence is captured in the wording created and accepted at the 39th World Conference of the International Council for Traditional Music (ICTM) in Vienna in 2007, suggesting that "[a]pplied ethnomusicology is the approach guided by principles of social responsibility, which extends the usual academic goal of broadening and deepening knowledge and understanding toward solving concrete problems and toward working both inside and beyond typical academic contexts." Characterization of the ICTM Study Group on Applied Ethnomusicology that follows provides further clarification, suggesting that it "advocates the use of ethnomusicological knowledge in influencing social interaction and course of cultural change."

The introduction to the book *Applied Ethnomusicology: Historical and Contemporary Approaches* (Harrison, Mackinlay, and Pettan, 2010) analyzes this definition part by part and also addresses three common misconceptions about applied ethnomusicology, which are worth mentioning in this context:

1. Applied ethnomusicology does *not* stand in opposition to the academic domain, but should be viewed as its extension and complement.[2]
2. Applied ethnomusicology is *not* an opposition to the theoretical (philosophical, intellectual) domain, but its extension and complement.[3]
3. Applied ethnomusicology is *not* an opposition to ethnographic, artistic, and scientific research, but their extension and complement.[4]

The introductory article to the above-mentioned volume ends with a quotation of Michael Birenbaum Quintero: "Apply your ethnomusicology or someone else will apply it for you," which once again points to intervention as a key notion.

There is a rich myriad of opinions about applied ethnomusicology among ethnomusicologists worldwide, from those who claim that all ethnomusicology is in fact applied, to those who feel that applied ethnomusicology does not enjoy necessary respect within the academic discipline and therefore should not be discussed at all. It is easy to agree with Daniel Sheehy's belief that "all ethnomusicologists have at one time or another been applied ethnomusicologists" (Sheehy, 1992: 323). But "applied ethnomusicology as a *conscious practice*," says Sheehy, "begins with a sense of purpose, a purpose larger than the advancement of knowledge about the music of the world's peoples" (ibid.). This is why I started my part of this Introduction with the crucial question of *intervention*, or in other words, with the conscious decision-making of a researcher whether or not to step beyond the mere study of the selected phenomenon and affect the researched circumstances. It is the sense of purpose, rather than any specific topic, that defines applied ethnomusicology. There are "sensitive" topics, such as, for instance, the roles of music in the Israeli/Palestinian divide, in which the author of the book (for whatever reason) does not mention applied ethnomusicology (see Brinner, 2009); and there are seemingly "neutral" topics, for instance the lullabies in Slovenia, which are from their initial conceptualization framed as "applied" by the author (see Juvančič, 2010).

There are many more or less known individuals, organizations, projects, and publications known for promoting the use of music for the betterment of human condition. Their work, though inspiring, if not rooted in ethnomusicological research should not be considered "applied ethnomusicology." Venezuelan musician, activist, economist, and politician José Antonio Abreu and his El Sistema, Argentinian/Israeli/German pianist and conductor Daniel Barenboim and his West-Eastern Divan Orchestra, Irish musicians and activists Bob Geldof (Live Aid) and Bono (ONE Campaign), Musicians Without Borders, Young at Heart, Studio MC Pavarotti, most articles in the journals such as *Music and Arts in Action* and *Sounds in Europe* are just a few examples, among many more.

Some ethnomusicologists express concern about the power imbalance in projects that fit within the realm of applied ethnomusicology (e.g., Hofman, 2010). The title of my first conference paper on the topic, presented in 1995, started exactly with the same notion: "Ethnomusicologist as a Power Holder?" The sentence with the question mark looks even more bizarre in the light of Deborah Wong's reminder that "[e]thnomusicology is marginalized in most music departments because its radical relativism challenges logocentric thinking about music" (2013: 348). In my conference presentation, based on the work with Bosnian refugees in Norway (see below), I addressed the issue of power share with the participants in, to the extent possible, equal, horizontal terms. The (later) article by Samuel Araújo and members of the Grupo Musicultura (2006), inspired by Paolo Freire's dialogical pedagogy (1970), is a good example of the same intention. There is, however, the other side of the coin, which should not be overlooked. If a certain kind of knowledge and/or access to power holders in a society for the benefit of the people in need is the comparative advantage of an ethnomusicologist, and there is a consensus between the interlocutors and the ethnomusicologist that he or she should use it, I can hardly think of counterarguments. This is how Anthony Seeger benefited the Suyá community in Brazil and Ursula Hemetek the Roma people in Austria. In Harris M. Berger's words, one should be aware of the dual nature of power:

> Power is, in one sense, the power to act, the ability to bring forth events in the world. But because our action is always social—always something we achieve because of and with others, past, present, future—the potential for domination is inherent, even ripe, in the entirety of social life, and even the most mundane, equitable, or convivial practice is informed by larger social contexts and the legacies of domination that they entail. This is as true of practices of music making, teaching, research or public sector work as it is of any other kind of activity. Seeing the social life of music as a domain of coordinated practice that is inherently, rather than contingently, political is one way of coming to terms with these difficult issues.
>
> (Berger, 2014: 319).

A Personal Stance

Just as Salwa El-Shawan Castelo-Branco did in her Epilogue to the seminal volume *Music and Conflict* (O'Connell and Castelo-Branco, 2010), let me add to this Introduction a personal stance that should define my own position.

In my opinion, every scholar should be free to decide whether to make a step beyond the usual goal of deepening and broadening knowledge, understanding and skills, and consciously intervene into the human and cultural environment of his or her research interest. While doing fieldwork in the 1980s on the East African islands of Zanzibar and Pemba for my B.A. thesis (University of Zagreb, Croatia) and in Egypt for my M.A. thesis (University of Ljubljana, Slovenia), my clear intention was to affect the self-focused folk music research in what was Yugoslavia at the time and to relate it to the much larger international community of ethnomusicologists, which I was learning about mainly from the periodicals (*Yearbook for Traditional Music, Ethnomusicology, the world of music*). My goal was clearly not the mere scholarly work based on the data from elsewhere in the world, but the conscious intervention into the essence of the discipline as it was understood in my home country at that time.

Between my B.A. and M.A. studies, I was obliged to serve for a year in the Yugoslav People's Army. Following my research interests, I asked the military authorities in Croatia to be sent to serve in the multicultural city of Prizren in far-away Kosovo, which was the most politically unstable part of what was Yugoslavia in the early 1980s. After becoming the instructor for cultural affairs, I came to the position not only to conduct fieldwork (by using a military tape recorder), but also to take it a step further: to bring regularly together youngsters from different ethnic communities and fellow soldiers into a choir. Obviously, research was beneficial to the work with the choir, and contacts established through the choir activities had a positive impact on my research.

Following the end of my doctoral studies (University of Maryland) in 1992, I was faced with the dilemma of whether to try to find a position in the safety of American academia or to return to my disintegrating, war-torn country. I decided once again to cross the boundary of intervention and use my capacities not only to study "music and war at home," but also to explore whether my knowledge, understanding, and skills could in any way confront the growing hatred and help reducing the suffering of the people affected by the war. My interlocutors in Croatia were highly unusual for any type of ethnomusicological inquiry known to me at that time: they included refugees and internally displaced people, soldiers, people in shelters, representatives of nongovernmental organizations (NGOs), radio editors, producers and sellers of music cassettes under both official and black market circumstances, members of the diasporas, and nonetheless musicians—amateur and professional, representatives of diverse musical genres and with diverse political orientations. Popular music was at the forefront, but my research encompassed folk and art music, as well. What was the essence of my intervention beyond the limits of research? My ethnomusicology students in both Zagreb and Ljubljana received assignments to work on joint performances with refugees in refugee camps in order to develop a sense of compassion and togetherness, and their seminar projects— for instance, one about music in various local religious communities at the time of political calls for unification (one ethnicity, one religion, one language, one territory)— clearly aimed for more than a mere broadening and deepening of knowledge.

Invited to teach for a term at the University of Oslo in Norway in the mid-1990s, I took the opportunity to implement a project, together with my senior host Professor Kjell Skyllstad. A few years earlier he envisioned and carried out a project named *The Resonant Community* (Skyllstad, 1993), the first case in my experience that had all elements of an applied ethnomusicology project. In the period from 1989 to 1992 music of various origins (African, Asian, European, and Latin American) had been successfully used in some elementary schools in Norway in order to foster "interracial understanding." Included and affected by this project were the teachers, pupils, and their parents, for whom teaching kits were created; some of the best musicians from four continents shared their arts with them. The evaluated and confirmed impact of *The Resonant Community* inspired us to put together the Azra project, an innovative proactive attempt, with the focus on Bosnian refugee musicians and Norwegian music students, which has been already presented elsewhere (e.g., Pettan, 1996; Skyllstad, 1997; Pettan, 2010), and thus not need to be described here. Therefore, I will dedicate just a few words to its methodological aspects.

I believe the Azra project fits into what Sheehy refers to as "conscious practice" and "sense of purpose." It is a "horizontal" (not "top-down") project, driven by the clear wish for intervention by well-intended scholars and their collaborators who together, in Angosino's words, "had a concern for using their knowledge for the betterment of the human condition" (Angrosino, 1990: 106). The goals of the project were as follows: (1) strengthening Bosnian cultural identity among the refugees from Bosnia-Herzegovina in Norway, and (2) stimulating mutually beneficial cross-cultural communication between the Bosnians and the Norwegians involved. The project was envisioned as a triangle consisting of three principal domains: research, education, and music-making. Its realization was carried on in four stages: (1) recognition of the problem and definition of the goals and basic strategies; (2) collection and analysis of data, plus refinement of the strategies; (3) intervention; and (4) evaluation of the results.

Work on this project made me aware of two distinctive types of mediation, which I termed *indirect* and *direct*. *Indirect mediation* means that the scholar gives the results of his or her research to those in a position to apply them. *Direct mediation* means that scholar himself or herself actively participates in the application of scholarly knowledge, understanding, and skills. Skyllstad and I used both categories in the Azra project. While mediating indirectly through conference papers, lectures, articles, and interviews, using the synthesis of empirical fieldwork and relevant literature to encourage other people to act, we reached the limits with no insight into the consequences of our involvement. Direct mediation proved to be more useful and far-reaching. For instance, within the Azra project, Skyllstad and I were able to shape its goals and contents, observe its flow and modify it when needed, and evaluate all its stages, including the final results.

My series of publications in different formats (books, articles, CD-ROM, film), accompanied by proactive lectures and picture exhibitions—all dedicated to Roma people, largely silenced victims of the war in Kosovo in the 1990s—can be seen as yet another application of ethnomusicological knowledge, understanding, and skills. The publications include those with scholarly rigor and those aimed at communication with general audiences (more in Pettan, 2010). One of the professional involvements that I highly value, but have never written an article about, is my role in the advisory committee at the Slovenian annual state review titled "Let's sing, let's play musical instruments, let's dance" for children and youngsters with special needs.

To summarize, like many other fellow ethnomusicologists, I am involved in projects of public interest. Not everything I do in ethnomusicology has an applied extension. In my invited lectures on applied ethnomusicology, I often encourage scholars in the audience to think of research that goes beyond the broadening and deepening of knowledge in the direction of benefiting the people they study. Some become inspired, while others simply do not want to think in these terms. And it is right to be so. For me, this is the clear line between ethnomusicology and applied ethnomusicology.

"Applied" in Other Disciplines

It is a common practice that scientific and scholarly disciplines have their applied domains. To mention just some, there are applied mathematics, applied physics, applied biology, applied geography, applied sociology, applied anthropology, and then (surprisingly seldom) applied musicology, partly substituted by the category of applied music. If hydrology, for instance, is the study of water and encompasses "the interrelationships of geologic materials and processes of water" (Fetter, 2001: 3), then "applied hydrogeologists are problem solvers and decision makers. They identify a problem, define the data needs, design a field program for collection of data, propose alternative solutions to the problem, and implement the preferred solutions" (ibid., 11). Applied sociology refers to "any use of the sociological perspective and/or its tools in the understanding of, intervention in, and/or enhancement human social life" (Price and Steele, 2004), while applied anthropology refers to "any use of anthropological knowledge to influence social interaction, to maintain or change social institutions, or to direct the course of cultural change" (Spradley and McCurdy, 2000: 355).

Curiously, neither the International Musicological Society nor the American Musicological Society have sections focused on applied musicology. UCLA musicologist Elisabeth Le Guin points out that the reason might be that "in the institutional structure of the discipline's most prestigious academic society,[5] a stigma lingers around the idea of 'putting music to use', as the SEM describes applied ethnomusicology: a ghost of the old idea, coeval in its origins with my undergraduates' obdurately anti-verbal Romanticism, that music should amount to something more than its use-value" (LeGuin 2012).

A recent book with applied musicology in its title refers to "using zygonic theory to inform music education, therapy, and psychology research" (Ockelford, 2013). According to *The Oxford Companion to Music*, applied music is an American term for a study course in performance, as opposed to theory.

It is worth inquiring about the independent scientific and scholarly societies that have the adjective "applied" in their names, which implies that they have already answered the "ultimate aim" in Merriam's terms, that is, whether "one is searching out knowledge for its own sake, or is attempting to provide solutions to practical applied problems" (Merriam, 1964: 42–43) in favor of the latter. In general, "applied societies" are international and are far from being small outfits of the main disciplinary bodies; some count their members in the thousands.[6] Although the aims of these societies are defined in the disciplinarily determined ways, the great majority of them make clear that they promote the outcomes of their disciplines with the intention that the public benefits from their efforts.[7] This is particularly clearly emphasized by the Society for Applied Anthropology, active since 1941, whose "unifying factor is a commitment to making an impact on the quality of life in the world" (www.sfaa.net).

A Brief Worldwide Overview

It is quite fascinating to observe engaged scholarship within the Australian ethnomusicological realm, from Catherine Ellis (1985) to the studies of Grace Koch (2013), Catherine Grant (2014), Huib Schippers and Catherine Grant (2016), Aaron Corn, Muriel Swijghuisen Reigersberg, Sally Treloyn and several others. High ethical stands and participatory work promoted by the research institutions focused on indigenous people of Australia, such as Australian Institute of Aboriginal and Torres Strait Islander Studies (AIATSIS), as well as the active/activist involvement in Aboriginal rights issue by several leading Australian ethnomusicologists, provide inspiring lessons for applied ethnomusicologists worldwide (see Newsome, 2008).

The contributions by Dan Bendrups and Huib Schippers in Volume 1 and by Elizabeth Mackinlay in Volume 2 make a strong Australian contribution to the applied work with the Aborigines, other minorities, and carriers of music cultures in various parts of the globe.

"The practice of ethnomusicology has been central in the professional lives of ethnomusicologists in Southeast Asia," claims Tan Sooi Beng in her article about activism in Southeast Asian ethnomusicology, pointing to a project of empowerment of youth in Penang, Malaysia, to revitalize traditions and bridge cultural barriers (2008: 69). For her, and for many colleagues elsewhere in Asia, to be an ethnomusicologist means not only involvement in scholarly activities such as teaching, documenting, publishing, and organizing conferences, but also application of the ethnomusicological knowledge toward solving particular cultural problems "so as to bring about change in their respective societies" (ibid.: 70). Terada Yoshitaka provides yet another good example of sensitive work in various formats (e.g., 2005, 2008, 2010, 2011), and so do Weiya Lin, Pamela Onishi, Mayco Santaella and several others. Zhang Boyu in this volume of the *Handbook* and Tan Sooi Beng in Volume 1 present Asian views and approaches from within, while John Morgan O'Connell in this volume, Joshua Pilzer in Volume 1 and Zoe Sherinian in Volume 2 complement them from outside, covering at least some other parts of the world's largest continent.

Practical aspects of ethnomusicology are very much present in Africa, too, from indigenous teaching approaches to music education, preservation of cultural roots, building of musical instruments, to diverse uses of music against xenophobia and prejudices related to HIV/AIDS. The works of Daniel Avorgbedor (1992), Angela Impey (2002), Bernhard Bleibinger (2010), Kathleen Van Burren (2010), along with Andrew Tracey, David Dargie, Diane Thram and Patricia Opondo, to mention just a few, point to a rich diversity of approaches. In Volume 2, Jeffrey Summitt and Brian Schrag provide their own views and experiences in applied ethnomusicology in Africa.

South America is certainly the site of some of the major ongoing developments in applied ethnomusicology. This is the case thanks to two extraordinary thinkers in the field, Brazilian Samuel Araújo and US-based Anthony Seeger, whose particularly important work and scholarly formation is related to Brazil. Araújo intends "to highlight the political substance and epistemological consequences of new research contexts and roles as one area with potentially ground-breaking contributions toward the emergence of a more balanced social world, i.e. one in which knowledge will hopefully emerge from a truly horizontal, intercultural dialogue and not through top-to-bottom neo-colonial systems of validation" (Araújo, 2008: 14). Seeger's work could justifiably be discussed in any geographic context, as his articles and keynote addresses resound on all continents (2006, 2008). In Volume 2, Holly Wissler demonstrates how applied ethnomusicological projects affect two South American communities, one in the Andes, and the other in the Amazon.

Following Daniel Sheehy (1992) and Anthony Seeger (2006), Maureen Loughran (2008) noted that some leading ethnomusicologists in the North American context, such as Alan P. Merriam (1964), Mantle Hood (1971), and Bruno Nettl (1964, 1983) largely ignored the work of applied ethnomusicologists while presenting the major developments within the discipline.[8] The co-editor of this volume, Jeff Todd Titon, has presented in Section 1 of this Introduction the history of ethnomusicology in North America from his perspective, as he lived and lives it, adding previously unknown aspects and enriching the general understanding of the discipline. Besides him, several other authors in the *Handbook* refer in various respects to applied ethnomusicology in North America, including Susan Oehler Herrick, Patricia Shehan Campbell, Clifford Murphy, and Alan Williams in this volume, Klisala Harrison in Volume 1 and Michael Bakan in Volume 2.

My own firsthand experiences are largely linked to Europe, where I was born and where I live and practice ethnomusicology. This is why the following section will be about Europe. The authors linked in various ways to Europe in the *Handbook* include Lee Higgins and Dan Lundberg in this volume, Erica Haskell and Britta Sweers in Volume 1, and Ursula Hemetek in Volume 2.

Some European Views: Ethnomusicologies

The fact that there is no single, ultimate definition of ethnomusicology suggests that we may consider the coexistence of ethnomusicologies, not only in different parts of the world, but also within a single, no matter how small, location. For instance, while I may find the definition proposed by my US colleague Jeff Todd Titon ("the study of people making music") acceptable, my Slovenian colleague, folklorist Marko Terseglav, defines it very differently, as "a discipline, researching spontaneous folk vocal and instrumental music, its characteristics and development" (Terseglav, 2004: 124).

In a sharp contrast to Vienna in neighboring Austria, which figures as one of the two cradles of comparative musicology[9] and is at the same time home to the lasting legacy of folk music research, ethnomusicology in Slovenia is rooted exclusively in folk music research. Table I.1 points to the major distinctions between the two and relates them to the current ethnomusicological mainstream.[10]

Table I.1. Comparative Musicology, Folk Music Research, and Ethnomusicology

	Comparative Musicology	Folk Music Research	Ethnomusicology
When?	1885–1950s	From late 18th century	From 1950s
What?	Musics of "primitive peoples" and "high Oriental cultures"	Peasant music	People making music
How?	"Armchair"	Collecting; fieldwork (short-term)	Fieldwork (long-term)
Who?	"Other" people	"Own" people	Any people
Where?	Elsewhere	Within own ethnic/national realm	Anywhere
Why?	Knowledge	National duty	Understanding

In an article, in which she compares the features of comparative musicology and folk music research in Vienna in the early twentieth century, Ursula Hemetek points to some other important distinctions, for instance, recording with phonograph by the former and notation by ear by the latter; music as text with no context versus music as text with context; interdisciplinarity related mainly to natural sciences versus interdisciplinarity related mainly to humanities; and (particularly important in this context) the association of comparative musicology with the academia-based "ivory tower" versus folk music research's "highly motivated volunteers outside academia" and application of (research) results (Hemetek, 2009: 62).

The multitude of languages and nation-state ideologies affected research within the European space differently than in North America and Australia. By far, not all of the European countries came under the umbrella of comparative musicology, but all contributed to the legacy of folk music research. Distinctive developments of the discipline in politically, geographically, historically, demographically, economically, linguistically, religiously, and nevertheless culturally diverse national contexts within Europe inspired studies that testify primarily about the specifics of European ethnomusicologies; put together, they enable comparisons and insights into common features. Interestingly, with a few exceptions (e.g., Clausen, Hemetek, and Saether, 2009; Ling, 1999), Europe was encompassed as a whole primarily by ethnomusicologists from North America (e.g., in Bohlman, 1996, 2004; Rice, Porter, and Goertzen, 2000). Some authors discussed them within the theoretical frame of nationalism (e.g., Bohlman, 2011), some pointed to the shared developmental periods (e.g., Elschek, 1991); yet others inverted the historical trends by placing those seen in Europe a century ago as the inferior Others (Roma and Jews; comp. Wallaschek, 1893) to the forefront of contemporary Europe by naming them "transnational ethnic groups" (Rice, Porter, and Goertzen, 2000).

In the post–Cold War Europe of the 1990s, national ethnomusicologies received considerable attention, including those of Denmark (Koudal et al., 1993), Finland (Moisala et al., 1994), Latvia (Boiko, 1994), Italy (Giuriati, 1995), Spain (Marti, 1997), Croatia (Pettan et al., 1998), and many more. This research trend continued in the 2000s, as reflected in the symposium on National Ethnomusicologies: The European Perspective (Cardiff University, 2007) and the plenary roundtable under the same name at the ICTM World Conference (Vienna, 2007), both organized by one of the authors in this volume of this *Handbook*, John Morgan O'Connell, and in subsequent studies.[11]

Let us now take a closer look at the micro-plan of Croatia and Slovenia, since 1992 two neighboring independent European countries, which spent the period of the formation of ethnomusicology first as the parts of the multiethnic Austro-Hungarian Empire (1867–1918), and then as the constituent parts of what later became known as Yugoslavia. As in many other parts of Europe, ethnomusicology in Croatia and Slovenia grew from the national awakening of the nineteenth century and the sense of importance of a nation's "own" folk song for the creation and affirmation of national identity. The characteristic procedure, through the first half of the twentieth century, included extensive fieldwork, notation and analysis of the collected songs, publishing collections, and writing syntheses based on the analysis of collected materials. The aim was to define specific national features, different from those of the neighboring peoples, which would in turn provide the basis for the development of national culture. In Croatia, the key figures, such as Franjo Kuhač (1834–1911) and Božidar Širola (1889–1956), were musicians, to whom the novelties in the field of comparative musicology were known. Kuhač was interested in collecting and writing about folk songs of South Slavs (not exclusively Croats), comparing their features with those of non-Slavs (Germans, Italians, Turks). Širola, himself a composer, even earned a doctorate under the mentorship of comparative musicologist Robert Lach in Vienna, and used comparative methodological procedures in dealing with Croatian folk music. In the Slovenian cultural space, at about the same time, the initiative was taken by two widely trained linguists with Viennese doctorates and an interest in ethnology: Karel Štrekelj (1859–1912) and Matija Murko (1861–1952). Just like their predecessors, as far back as the late eighteenth century, they focused primarily on language in the folk songs. In contrast to Štrekelj's emphasis on Slovenian repertoire, Murko did research (with phonograph), for example, of sung epic poetry in Bosnia, as well.

The next generations of principal researchers included Vinko Žganec (1890–1976) and Jerko Bezić (1929–2010) in Croatia, and France Marolt (1891–1952) and Zmaga Kumer (1924–2008) in Slovenia. Žganec, doctor of law and musician, and Marolt, himself a musician, were typical representatives of folk music research in a cultural historic sense, who institutionalized the discipline in Croatia and Slovenia, respectively. Kumer and Bezić earned their doctorates within the discipline. In contrast to Kumer, who became one of Europe's best and latest representatives of the folk music research domain, Bezić was systematically broadening the scope of ethnomusicology in Croatia by opening the space for research of urban music phenomena and in general of influences from abroad. Thanks to the interaction with his multidisciplinary institutional colleagues in Zagreb, influenced by both American (e.g., Alan Dundes, Dan Ben Amos) and Russian (Kiril Chistov) folklorists, he defined the subject of ethnomusicology as the so-called "folklore music," referring to musical communication in small groups (more in Marošević, 1998). The next (current) generation of ethnomusicologists in both countries is actively involved in what can be called mainstream ethnomusicology.

Within what was Yugoslavia, practically each constituent republic had its own "school of ethnomusicology," with unquestionable commonalities, but also distinctive features. Each of these "schools" was thematically focused primarily on the material from within its own political unit and its own people in the ethnic sense. While the folk music research paradigm was the unquestionable basis, each "school" had a different stance toward the developments of ethnomusicology elsewhere and used the results of the "mainstream" at different paces.

Aware of the discrepancy caused by the lack of comparative musicology at home and even more by the lack of their own interest in studying the Others, Serbian ethnomusicologists decided to translate, with a considerable delay, two books rooted in comparative musicology. The translation of Fritz Bose's *Musikalische Völkerkunde* (1953) was published in 1975, and Curt Sachs's *The Rise of Music in the Ancient World*

East and West (1943) as late as 1980 (Saks 1980).[12] These books became a window to "folk music from other parts of the world" for generations of students of ethnomusicology in Serbia. The translation of John Blacking's *How Musical Is Man?* (1973) was intended to be a contribution to/from the Sarajevo "school" in Bosnia-Herzegovina (Bleking, 1992).[13] In Slovenia, the translations include Curt Sachs's *Eine Weltgeschichte des Tanzes* (1933) in 1996, Roberto Leydi's *L'altra musica* (1991) in 1995, and Alan P. Merriam's *The Anthropology of Music* (1964) in 2000. The other "schools" felt self-sufficient and did not translate any foreign books with a wider scope of the discipline.

According to Bohlman, "Folk music and folk song as objects have not disappeared from the practices of European musicians and scholars, but have instead provided them with complex ways of connecting tradition to modernity, and of emblematizing the past in the present" (1996: 106). Elschek suggests that in this process, "cooperation with anthropology and ethnology has been more successful than with historical musicology" (1991: 101).

Applied Ethnomusicologies

One could argue whether various colonial expositions and other showcases involving comparative musicologists should be identified as a part of the early history of applied ethnomusicology and to what extent comparative musicology in general contributed to the "public sector" of the discipline.[14] At the same time, it is clear that the other branch of European ethnomusicology—folk music research—was throughout the previous century linked to the applied domain. The principal goal of many folk music researchers, that of protection of their national heritage, implied practical application of their findings. Besides scholarly procedures that usually included field research, transcription, analysis, archiving, and publication, they often actively engaged in the popularization of folk music and dance. Important channels for this were state-sponsored folklore ensembles in Eastern Europe and less formalized revival ensembles in Western Europe. Ethnomusicologists assumed various roles in these processes: providing the ensembles with musics and dances collected in the field, writing musical arrangements and/or choreographies, singing, playing instruments and/or dancing, leading the ensembles, and touring with them.

An increasing influx of immigrants in Western Europe in the second half of the twentieth century gradually raised interest in their musical cultures among ethnomusicologists. In addition to important studies on immigrant musics (e.g., Ronström, 1991) and cultural policies (Baumann, 1991), several ethnomusicologists, particularly in Sweden, became involved in applied projects such as the *Ethno* camp for young musicians in Falun and music-making within the ensembles such as the *Orientexpressen*.[15] In Norway, Kjell Skyllstad initiated the above-mentioned three-year project named *The Resonant Community* in several elementary schools in the Oslo area in 1989, bringing together ethnomusicology and music education in paving the way to better appreciation between Norwegians and the immigrants from Africa, Asia, and Latin America through their respective musics (Skyllstad, 1993). Multicultural education, which in the United States "grew out of the ferment of the civil rights movement of the 1960s" (Banks and McGee Banks, 2001: 5), gradually became recognized and also debated in Europe. Krister Malm was actively involved in two relevant events in the 1990s: the European Music Council's conference Aspects on Music and Multiculturalism in Falun in 1995 (Malm et al., 1995)[16] and in the first world conference on music and censorship in Copenhagen in 1998, where the organization Freemuse was established (Korpe and Reitov, 1998). Ursula Hemetek was beginning applied work with various minorities in Austria (Hemetek, 1996), which would later lead to official political recognition of the Romani people in Austria (Hemetek, 2006). My applied work with refugees from Bosnia-Herzegovina in Norway, Croatia, and Slovenia, with the internally displaced victims of the war in Croatia, and with Romani victims of the war in Kosovo has been presented earlier.

In 2003 Italian ethnomusicologists organized the ninth international seminar in ethnomusicology in Venice, titled Applied Ethnomusicology: Perspectives and Problems. While recognizing that "setting up museums, service within administration of colonial empires, organization of concerts, divulgence by means of publication of writings and recordings"... were part of the professional profile of comparative musicologists at the beginnings of the 20th century, they also noticed recent "significant developments" and pointed to issues such as intercultural education, music in relation to diaspora, immigration, and refugees, "spectacularization" of traditional music, and cultural cooperation projects.[17] One of the curiosities of this seminar is the absence of folk music research.

The further conference-related developments of applied ethnomusicology in Europe are largely linked to the framework of the International Council for Traditional Music (ICTM). They will be systematically presented later in this text.

Let us now, just as in the previous section, turn our attention to the micro-plan of Croatia and Slovenia in order to discuss the stances of the most representative Croatian and Slovenian researchers toward application. Certainly, the publication of national folk song collections was not the final aim of the researchers. Either the early musically trained researchers themselves or other musicians harmonized (e.g., Kuhač) or otherwise "improved" the songs in order to create nationally distinctive art music. Marolt was known for arranging the collected songs for his acclaimed choir and for adjusting the collected dances for the staged performances by his own and other folklore ensembles. Application was somehow seen as a natural extension of research by many of these early ethnomusicologists. In fact, Jerko Bezić in Croatia and Zmaga Kumer in Slovenia were the first ones who restrained from applications, trying "to affirm ethnomusicology as an autonomous discipline based on fieldwork, theorizing, evidence and debate, detaching it from requisite utilitarity" (the original quotation is referring to Bezić only; Ceribašić, 2004: 6).[18] Today's ethnomusicologists in both countries complement their research activities by serving in juries at the reviews of folklore performances at local, regional, and national levels; serving in the organization of festivals, symposia, and other discipline-related events; Croatians are involved in the UNESCO's Intangible Cultural Heritage agendas..

Staff at the research institutes in both Zagreb and Ljubljana comprises specialists in several disciplines, including ethnochoreologists. Inspired by the developments in applied ethnomusicology, at least one researcher, Tvrtko Zebec, theorizes about applied ethnochoreology (Zebec, 2007). Joško Ćaleta, an ethnomusicologist in Zagreb, in whose work research and performing applications are closely intertwined, claims that applied activities are often paying his research activities (interview, July 14, 2014), which is a meaningful point to be taken into consideration.

This section ends with a complementing view from the other side of Europe, from the United Kingdom. In the words of Kathleen Van Buren, "Ethnomusicologists need to think more deeply about how to serve others, not just ourselves, through our work. This means listening to people within communities where we live and work, allowing their perspectives to help guide our choice of our topics and activities, trying to collaborate and respond to their needs when we can, and empowering them rather than ourselves" (2010: 219).

The International Council for Traditional Music

Perhaps the most efficient access to applied ethnomusicology in the global arena is through the principal international association of ethnomusicologists, which is the International Council for Traditional Music (ICTM), with current representation in more than 120 countries and regions on all continents. The association was established in London in 1947 under the name International Folk Music Council (IFMC). We should keep in mind that the establishment of IFMC precedes Kunst's book *Musicologica: A Study of the Nature of Ethno-musicology, Its Problems, Methods, and Representative Personalities* (1950) and the wide acceptance of the term *ethnomusicology* that followed.[19] It was an era of comparative musicology and folk music research paradigms, which were affecting each other in various ways and to various extents in various places.

IFMC's roots are clearly in the folk music research paradigm, which is evident from the following description:

> In her capacity as Honourable Secretary of the International (Advisory) Folk Dance Council, Maud Karpeles (1885–1976) organized the International Conference on Folk Song and Folk Dance, held at the Belgian Institute in London, 22–27 September 1947. Delegates from twenty-eight countries participated, mostly appointed by the governments of their respective nations, as well as a UNESCO representative.... On the afternoon of Monday, 22 September 1947, the Vice Chairman of the conference, Stuart Wilson (1889–1966), proposed "that an International Folk Music Council be formed."
>
> (www.ictmusic.org; see also Karpeles, 1971).

The article in which Karpeles offered her reflections on the 21 years of existence of the Council says a lot about its intellectual climate, including the sentences "In all parts of the world the traditional practice of folk music is disappearing—gradually in some regions and rapidly in others—and if we are to save our musical heritage for the benefit of our own and future generations, it is necessary to act quickly. Collecting activities are, of course, being carried on, but these must be intensified if precious material is not to be lost. As the saying goes, 'It is later than we think'" (Karpeles, 1971: 29). The attitudes of this kind were later largely discredited in the mainstream of the discipline as "salvage ethnomusicology," pointing to "romanticism, paternalism, and hegemony" (see also Grant, 2014: 80). Cultural relativism and the absence of value judgments became, at different paces in different parts of the world, the *sine qua non* of modern ethnomusicology.[20]

The objectives of IFMC were the following: (1) to assist in the preservation, dissemination, and practice of the folk music of all countries; (2) to further the comparative study of folk music; and (3) to promote understanding and friendship between nations through the common interest of folk music.[21] What matters particularly from the point of view of applied ethnomusicology, besides the applied overtones in the presented objectives, is the envisioned work of the newly established Council. The list of proposals included "the holding of conferences and festivals; the publication of a catalogue of recordings, bibliographies, a manual for collectors, and an international collection of folk songs; the promotion of national and international archives; the institution of a general method of dance notations; and the development of a guide to the classification of folk tunes" (Karpeles, 1971: 17). In the course of 1950s and 1960s, IFMC indeed published several catalogues, bibliographies, dictionaries, manuals, collections, statements, and songbooks. In order to accomplish these aims, the structure of IFMC included not only National Committees, but also the Radio Committee, Folk Dance Committee, and more, the names being subject to change from time to time.

The intention of the IFMC in the post–World War II years was to bring together composers, researchers, and other specialists interested in folk music and dance into a truly international association; even the intention to be related to UNESCO was there from the very inception of the Council. Maud Karpeles's principal source of inspiration was Cecil Sharp, the founding father of the folklore revival in England in the beginning of the twentieth century. Within the newly established Council she became secretary under the presidency of Ralph Vaughn Williams, renowned art music composer and English folk song collector. Members of the first Executive Board likewise included various specialists—by far, not all of them researchers—each from a different country. While referring to legacies of the previous editors, the new editor of the *Yearbook of the IFMC*, Bruno Nettl, noted their determination to "present scholarship of the highest quality and to exhibit samples of what was emanating from research carried on in all parts of the world" and that "[s]cholars from the many nations and cultures of the world do not always think, study, and write in the same style, and the editor of an international publication must tread the thin line between rigid standardization and chaotic diversity" (Nettl, 1974: 7). He intended to broaden the coverage of research to those parts of the world that had not been represented in the *Yearbook* and its predecessor the *Journal of IFMC* thus far.

A particularly important shift was the change of the name of the Council after more than three decades of its existence, strongly argued within a heated discussion by the new Secretary General Dieter Christensen at the 26th World Conference in Seoul, Republic of Korea, in 1981. Erich Stockmann recalls the consequences of this change: "It worked like magic and opened up doors in regions where the word 'folk music' had a somewhat pejorative ring" (Stockmann, 1988: 8).[22] The immediate result was new members in countries on all continents (see also H. M., 1983: 3).

The current official presentation of ICTM ends up with the sentence significant for this Introduction: "By means of its wide international representation and the activities of its Study Groups, the International Council for Traditional Music acts as a bond among peoples of different cultures and thus serves the peace of humankind." The year 1947 marked the start of both the Council and the Cold War period. Until the end of the Cold War in 1991, ICTM was actively involved in crossing the political, administrative, economic, lingual, cultural, and other boundaries set by the two military alliances, while also including in its framework those countries that proclaimed themselves "neutral" and "nonaligned." The Council authorities, including the Presidents, were from any of these politically delineated territories, and the World Conferences, Study Group Symposia, and Colloquia were intentionally taking place in all four of them (NATO, the Warsaw Pact, Neutral, Nonaligned).

Let me document this practice with two extraordinary examples.[23] The first of them takes us to a symposium on Traditional Music in Asian Countries, organized as a joint venture with the International Music Council in 1983. The symposium took place in Pyongyang, DPR Korea, and was attended by scholars from Afghanistan, China, India, Indonesia, Japan, DPR Korea, Mongolia, Pakistan, Papua New Guinea, the Philippines, the USSR, and PR Yemen. The second example refers to the 28th World Conference, hosted jointly by Stockholm (Sweden) and Helsinki (Finland). Its closing ceremony took place on the other side of the Iron Curtain, in Leningrad (USSR; today's St. Petersburg in Russia). The older members of the Council are aware of this legacy and for a good reason proud of it.

Out of the total of 44 World Conferences, 18 took place outside Europe: two in Africa (Ghana, South Africa), seven in Asia (Israel, Republic of Korea, Hong Kong, Japan, twice in China, Kazakhstan), five in North America (three in the US, two in Canada), one in Central America (Jamaica), two in South America (Brazil), and one in Australia. Of those taking place in Europe, four took place in the countries on the Eastern side of the Iron Curtain (Romania, Czechoslovakia, Hungary, German Democratic Republic), one in the nonaligned Yugoslavia, and six in the neutral countries Switzerland, Austria (three times), Finland and Sweden (jointly), and Ireland. The sites of smaller-size IFMC/ICTM gatherings, such as the Colloquia, Symposia of the Study Groups, and from 2015 on also Fora, point to the inclusion of many more countries from the world's political spectrum (e.g., Cuba, Oman, Vietnam). Serving as a communicational channel across any boundaries continues to be the conscious strategy of the Council, which justifies the view that the Council itself is a project in applied ethnomusicology. The ongoing enlargement of the ICTM World Network is a part of the same frame of thought.

The International Council for Traditional Music and Applied Ethnomusicology

Despite its international aspirations, IFMC was for a long time considered a primarily European association. Europe was the place of its foundation and residence, and Europe was home to most of its members, conferences,[24] and publications[25]—even "folk music" in its name was largely seen as a European marker. As suggested earlier, the name change from "folk" (IFMC) to "traditional" (ICTM) broadened the acceptability of the Council worldwide in the 1980s. The current frame of interests within the ICTM clearly exceeds "traditional" music, but the name of the Council remains the same, for better or worse.[26]

Search for the first mention of applied ethnomusicology in any ICTM context led to the 27th World Conference in 1983 in New York, where Ghanaian ethnomusicologist Daniel Avorgbedor presented a paper titled "The Effects of Rural-Urban Migration on a Village Musical Culture: Some Implications for Applied Ethnomusicology."[27] The next instance took place six years later, at the 30th World Conference in 1989 in Schladming (Austria), where German ethnomusicologist Artur Simon presented his paper "The Borneo Music Documentation Project (Northern Nigeria). Aspects of Documentation, Field Research in Africa, and Applied Ethnomusicology."

The author of the first mention of applied ethnomusicology in the *Bulletin of the ICTM* was John Baily. In his report on the UK National Committee, he included the following, published in April 1988:

> Members of ICTM UK have a particular interest in music in the multi- (or inter-) cultural school curriculum, and we have established a sub-committee to look into the question of teaching resources available in the UK. . . . With the same objectives we are represented on the UK Council for Music Education and Training, which is in the process of setting up a standing committee to look into the place of non-Western music in our education system. . . . Ethnomusicologists, like all other academics in contemporary Britain, have to look to their "performance indicators"; and seek to justify their existence, in part, through this form of applied ethnomusicology.

The next instances were my report on ethnomusicology in Croatia (*Bulletin of the ICTM* #90 from April 1997), in which applied ethnomusicology was related to organization of folklore festivals and amateur musical life; and Cynthia Tse Kimberlin's and

Pirkko Moisala's "In Memoriam" (*Bulletin of the ICTM* #91 from October 1997), where they indicated applied ethnomusicology as one of the areas of interests of Marcia Herndon.

The first article with applied ethnomusicology in its title published in the *Yearbook for Traditional Music* was authored by the Austrian scholar Ursula Hemetek: "Applied Ethnomusicology in the Process of the Political Recognition of a Minority: A Case Study of the Austrian Roma" (*Yearbook for Traditional Music*, vol. 38, 2006). The next major development was the special section, with a group of eight authors, on Music and Poverty, put together by the Finish/Canadian ethnomusicologist Klisala Harrison (*Yearbook for Traditional Music*, vol. 45, 2013). One should of course be aware that the lack of the wording "applied ethnomusicology" does not imply the absence of the articles relevant for the current discussion in the earlier years, with Angela Impey's 2002 essay "Culture, Conservation and Community Reconstruction: Explorations in Advocacy Ethnomusicology and Action Research in Northern KwaZulu" serving as a convincing evidence.

As far as the ICTM scholarly gatherings are concerned, the 15th Colloquium, titled *Discord: Identifying Conflict within Music, Resolving Conflict Through Music*, organized by John Morgan O'Connell in Limerick, Ireland, in 2004 can be interpreted as anticipation of what is to follow. Although music and conflict make a suitable ethnomusicological topic and applied ethnomusicology was not particularly emphasized in the colloquium documents, several presentations pointed to "ethnomusicology as an approach to conflict resolution." The articles developed from this event form the representative ethnomusicological volume on music and conflict (O'Connell and Castelo-Branco, 2010).

The 38th World Conference of the ICTM that took place in Sheffield, England, in 2005 featured applied ethnomusicology and ethnochoreology as one of the themes, pointing to "situations in which scholars put their knowledge and understanding to creative use to stimulate concern and awareness about the people they study."[28] Presenters were invited to consider issues of advocacy, canonicity, musical literacy, cultural property rights, cultural imperialism, majority-minority relations, application of technologies such as the Internet and their effects on music and dance. One plenary session explicitly featured applied ethnomusicology,[29] and yet another plenary session considered it among the other subjects.[30]

A symposium titled Ethnomusicology and Ethnochoreology in Education: Issues in Applied Scholarship took place in Ljubljana, Slovenia, in 2006. The members of the ICTM's Executive Board, who came to Ljubljana for their regular annual meeting, and the other invited scholars presented and evaluated their immediate experiences and visions of the efficient transfer of scholarly knowledge into educational domains. Presentations from contexts around the globe discussed modalities of connections between theory and practice, methods of promoting, teaching, and learning of traditional music and dance, and the strategies of preparing textbooks, recordings, and other materials for various stages of educational processes (see the report by Kovačič and Šivic, 2007).

The ICTM's 39th World Conference in Vienna in 2007 featured two important events: a double panel, The Politics of Applied Ethnomusicology: New Perspectives, with six participants, each from a different continent,[31] and a meeting at which 44 members agreed to establish a study group with a focus on applied ethnomusicology.[32] Following the adoption of the definition and mission statement, the Study Group on Applied Ethnomusicology was approved at the Executive Board's meeting in Vienna on July 12, 2007.

The next year, in 2008, Ljubljana hosted the first symposium of the newly established Study Group on Applied Ethnomusicology, which was well attended by scholars from all continents. Anthony Seeger delivered the keynote address. This event featured the history of the idea and understandings of applied ethnomusicology in worldwide contexts; presentation and evaluation of individual projects, with an emphasis on theory and method; and applied ethnomusicology in situations of conflict. It is worth mentioning the use of the Native American "talking circles" as one of the means of communication within this Study Group.

The international intentions of the Study Group continued at the symposia in 2010 in Hanoi, Vietnam (2010), Nicosia, Cyprus (2012), East London—Hogsback—Grahamstown, South Africa (2014), Cape Breton, Canada (2016), and Beijing, China (2018).[33]

Thematic frames of the symposia are trustworthy indicators of the dynamics of the Study Group and, to a smaller extent, of the interests of local organizers. In Hanoi, where the joint symposium with the Study Group on Music and Minorities took place, the emphasis was on definitions and approaches to applied work in various geographical contexts; on proactive roles that ethnomusicology can play in contributing to the sustainability of performing arts through archiving, disseminating, contributing to policies, understanding socioeconomic factors, developing audiences and markets, and empowering communities to forge their own futures; and on performing arts in building peace, negotiating power relationships, and strengthening identities through formal and informal education. Note that the use of the term "performing arts" is a manner of paying respect to the perspective, which is widely shared in Southeast Asia.

The symposium in Nicosia featured applied ethnomusicology in the contexts of social activism, censorship, and state control; in relation to various types of disability, pointing to human rights and the making of disability politics and including disability research, special education, and music therapy; and in relation to diverse social configurations of conflict, including interpersonal and intergroup, interethnic, interreligious, and interclass, with emphasis on the divided island of Cyprus.

The symposium on three locations in South Africa opened up the question of institutions, usually associated with formal and informal rules, procedures, and norms, from schools and festivals to large international bodies such as UNESCO, including instituting and institutionalization issues; and the question of media and their social, political, and cultural impacts on applied work.

The symposium in Cape Breton related music to labor and exchange, opening the floor for socio-economic agendas. Intangible cultural heritage was linked to sustainable development and tourism. Pedagogical issues found their place next to research networking at the time of intensified migrations, and methodological agendas with emphasis on collaboration and criticality.

The symposium in Beijing called for the attention to power structures that affect musical practices and their carriers, to formal and informal learning, and to reflections on how we approach cultural sustainability and on the methods we use. This was a joint symposium with the new ICTM Study Group on Music, Education and Social Inclusion.

As far as the publications related to ICTM are concerned, four of them are at disposal to the readers. First, the earlier mentioned double panel that took place at the ICTM World Conference in Vienna in 2007 inspired the creation of the thematic issue of the *Muzikološki zbornik/Musicological Annual*, 46(2), entirely dedicated to applied ethnomusicology (Pettan, 2008).[34] Five ethnomusicologists reflect on their experiences linked to Brazil, Australia, the United States, Malaysia, and former Yugoslavia; the volume also serves as a Festschrift on the 80th birthday of the aforementioned Norwegian scholar Kjell Skyllstad, an important early thinker in applied ethnomusicology.

The second edited volume resulted from the inaugural Study Group's symposium in Ljubljana and is titled *Applied Ethnomusicology: Historical and Contemporary Approaches* (Harrison, Mackinlay, and Pettan, 2010). Its 13 essays, by authors from Africa, Australia, Europe, and North America, are widely used and quoted, in this volume as well, so no additional presentation is needed here.

The third is a special thematic section on Music and Poverty in the *Yearbook for Traditional Music* 45 (Harrison, 2013). Its seven articles address various aspects of this important and largely neglected problem in the diverse contexts of Brazil, Canada, Haiti, India, Nepal, and USA.

The fourth publication is the Finnish journal *COLLeGIUM*. Its volume 21 is entirely dedicated to the theme Applied Ethnomusicology in Institutional Policy and Practice (Harrison, 2016). Based on some of the best presentations from the Study Group Symposia in 2010, 2012, and 2014, the volume features case studies from Australia, China, Germany, the Seychelles, South Africa, United Kingdom, United States, and Zimbabwe.

INDIVIDUAL VIEWS

How else could ICTM contribute to better comprehension of the emerging field? By means of its wide international representation, it can provide us with the perspectives from different geographic and cultural environments. The answers to my five essential questions were provided by five ethnomusicologists, each from a different continent.[35] Some of them are more inclined to applied ethnomusicology than the others, but together, they provide a useful global myriad of perspectives about the field. I asked for anonymous, individual views, therefore they are indicated as "A view from Australia," "A view from Asia," and so on.

1. How would you define applied ethnomusicology, or at least what is its essence in your opinion?

A view from Australia: The application of ethnomusicological method and theory to addressing practical issues.

A view from Asia: If we define applied ethnomusicology as research activities with social conscience and political involvement, I think whatever we do as ethnomusicologists should be applied ethnomusicology at least in some ways.

A view from South America: I can only see a matter of degree in its definition, acknowledging an aspect, which is inherent to any research, namely its potential to be applied to different purposes. However, in most of what has been termed as such in the humanities one finds embedded ideals of social justice and equity, sometimes of reparation and/or reconciliation, all of which also subject to different and even contradictory perspectives.

A view from Africa: Generally, how our practical work in the field is applied in an academic environment. Music is not taught in an European or abstract way, that is, by explaining music with words, but holistically, by doing—listening, imitating, and playing. Based on that experience we teach African music theory practically on instruments. It is much more appropriate and easier for people to understand musical concepts doing it that way.

A view from Europe: I do not subscribe to the term "applied ethnomusicology," although I understand why it is necessary. I think the engagement of scholars with the communities they work with should be/is a given.

2. Have you done any project(s) that would fit into your notion of applied ethnomusicology?

Australia: Preparing indigenous people's land claim is the obvious example, that is, applying knowledge of their musical culture to demonstrate rights over land using an indigenous conceptual system. I was one of three researchers (with an anthropologist and a linguist) who prepared one of the largest such claims. During the hearing of the case (by a Supreme Court judge) songs and dances were performed to demonstrate ownership of the land according to their own system of land ownership.

Asia: Following what I mentioned above, I would like to think all my projects are within the realm of applied ethnomusicology.

South America: They have ranged from short-term documentation projects related to safeguarding and revitalizing traditions perceived to be vanishing to long-term horizontal collaborations with grassroot organizations, forming research groups working on music and social justice among residents of areas affected by patterns of injustice and inequity.

Africa: We also understand applied ethnomusicology as offering of our expertise to people in order to develop a musical environment. This can be in form of workshops, teaching in schools, music projects, community outreach, and curriculum development, which takes the background of people and local needs into consideration. In our current curriculum African music components are compulsory. We just brought new streams and modules to respond to local needs; for instance the course Basic Music Literacy for students from villages who have problems with music theory and music literacy, and the streams Music Technologies and Production and Music and Arts Administration. The two streams aim at providing students with practical skills which make them more employable, and which enable them to start their own business within the music industry. We hope that these two new streams will in the future help to improve the musical infrastructure in the region.

Europe: I was involved in the application of projects to the UNESCO representative list of Intangible Cultural Heritage and served on an advisory committee to the Ministry of Culture on ICH matters. For over 20 years, I also promoted the founding of a national sound archive. Finally, I consider the publication of an encyclopedia—an all-encompassing research project with a wide outreach among musicians, cultural politicians and scholars—as "applied ethnomusicology."

3. *Is the distinction between "academic" and "applied" work present in your working environment? If so, how is the "applied" domain valued compared to the "academic" one?*

Australia: When I worked at the institute it was required of researchers to demonstrate the benefit of the proposed research to the community. This resulted in a blending of scholarly and applied research. Later, when I was working in the university environment, there was much more emphasis on scholarship for its own sake, and the application of research results was not highly valued.

Asia: There are theorists so to speak who are mainly concerned with the refinement of theoretical explorations. I respect such endeavors as long as they have applicable dimension. The "applied" domain has been treated unfairly as activities conducted by less qualified/serious scholars, partly because of the narrow definition of the "academic" domain, but also due to the inability on the part of "applied" ethnomusicologists to advance a new vision of theory construction.

South America: No.

Africa: A distinction between academic and applied work is still there (for instance when you have to teach different research methodologies or history of ethnomusicology), but the boundaries are quite blurred. A lot of our academic research is based on applied work and—as explained earlier—theory is thought practically (which is the direct application of knowledge obtained in the field).

Europe: I try to avoid making this distinction. But, in my institution we have many projects that can be classified as applied: museum expositions, digitization, community work, projects in schools, etc. I would say 40% applied.

4. Is the "applied" domain present in your teaching curricula?

Australia: I always tried to show the relationship between applied and theoretical ethnomusicology.

Asia: Whenever I teach I emphasize the importance of socially engaged research activities.

South America: Yes, in the obligatory bibliographies of both undergraduate and graduate courses as well as in systematic outreach and research programs.

Africa: We do not offer a degree program or specific modules on applied ethnomusicology. Yet, as already explained, indigenous music is compulsory, theory is taught practically, and articles on applied ethnomusicology are discussed in class. Thus, although not formalized in terms of specific modules, applied ethnomusicology is a reality here.

Europe: In my seminars, I discuss researchers' social responsibilities and the many spheres of ethnomusicological work. But, we do not have a course on "applied ethnomusicology."

5. Do you know of any university offering a course in applied ethnomusicology or applied ethnochoreology?

Australia: No.

Asia: There may be, but not that I know of.

South America: No, but I know several universities that offer opportunities to both graduate and undergraduate students to engage in applied research in the sense I outlined before, as well as portions of their curricular components devoted to applied approaches.

Africa: This is a tricky question. Applied approaches differ from institution to institution, and the motives and conditions are hardly comparable. Unlike other universities in the country, our Music Department had hardly any resources. We had to build up from zero, which means that applied ethnomusicology was a necessity and therefore a reality. At another university, applied ethnomusicology was simply understood as building up an African ensemble. Elsewhere, there was some teaching of indigenous instruments, but not applied ethnomusicology in our understanding. At Kwazulu Natal you find a completely different situation with Patricia Opondo, who is a very focused and an internationally trained academic. Applied ethnomusicology is officially part of the curriculum.

Europe: No.

What can we make of the replies of these five ethnomusicologists? All of them are well established as professionals and work in either university or research institute settings. Their representativeness is balanced in terms of geography and gender, as well, but none of them belongs to a young generation of scholars, which is seeking for more radical solutions, such as active involvement in applied projects as a part of the study curricula. At this point I would like to add that a course in applied ethnomusicology, which counts to the obligatory master level courses, exists since 2012 at the Department of Musicology of the University of Ljubljana.

The International Council for Traditional Music and the Society for Ethnomusicology

In contrast to the eight years younger Society for Ethnomusicology (SEM), which is defined as "a U.S.-based organization with an international membership" (www.ethnomusicology.org), IFMC/ICTM was envisioned in international terms in all respects. Its Secretariat moves its base periodically from one country to another; it has so far been based in the United Kingdom, Denmark, Canada, the United States, Australia, and Slovenia. Both past and current membership figures suggest that SEM, which is the US National Committee of ICTM, is larger than ICTM, but also that the single country with the largest number of members in ICTM is the United States. The two societies have distinctive intellectual histories and the resulting theoretical and methodological paradigms. In words of Dieter Christensen,

> SEM and ICTM are both unique in their roles, and they complement each other; SEM as the regional organization in North America that represents the interests of professional, academic ethnomusicologists in the USA and Canada, and at the same time serves the field of ethnomusicology world-wide through its publications; and the ICTM as the international organization in the domain of traditional music including ethnomusicology that serves scholarship with an emphasis on the mutual recognition and understanding of diverse inquiring minds.
>
> (Christensen, 1988:17)

IFMC/ICTM cherished various languages in its scholarly publications until 1985, when the last article so far in a language other than English was published in the *Yearbook for Traditional Music*. From 2006 on, the *Yearbook*'s general editor Don Niles reintroduced the practice of adding abstracts in native languages of those people who are the principal subjects of the articles. This practice was originally introduced in the 1980s, following Yoshihiko Tokumaru's proposal.

Jeff Todd Titon has described in Section 1 of this Introduction how the four founders of SEM, led by Alan P. Merriam, rejected Maud Karpeles's invitation to join IFMC and instead decided to keep SEM as an independent society. IFMC reported about the new society in the following manner in its 11th *Bulletin* from 1957: "On November 18th, 1955, at the 54th Annual Meeting of the American Anthropological Association in Boston, the Society for Ethnomusicology was founded for the purpose of establishing communication among persons in primitive, folk, and oriental music, and for furthering research and scholarship in these fields. The Society plans to continue publication of the Ethno-Musicology Newsletter three times yearly, to meet annually in conjunction with societies of anthropologists, folklorists and musicologists, and to engage in other activities of benefit to members" (Anon., 1957: 6).

According to Erich Stockmann, one of the Presidents of the Council, Maud Karpeles was sensitive to occasional criticisms and used to ask him anxiously several times in the course of the 1950s: "Are we really not 'scientific' enough? She knew my answer" (Stockman, 1988: 5). Dieter Christensen, Secretary General of the Council for 20 years, noted that the "American issue" and the "scientific issue" were clearly related (Christensen, 1988: 14).

There are several important connections between the two societies that should be mentioned here. At the inauguration of IFMC in 1947, seven US "correspondents" were identified, among them Curt Sachs, Percy Grainger, and Alan Lomax. The "Liaison officer" (single national representative) of the United States in the IFMC for 10 years (1952–1962) was Charles Seeger, one of the SEM's founding fathers. Following Seeger's mandate, the United States was uninterruptedly represented in the IFMC/ICTM by the "National Committee" until 1999, starting with Charles Haywood and ending with Ricardo Trimillos. After a five-year break, Timothy Rice, then the SEM President, re-established the connection and SEM became officially recognized as the ICTM's US National Committee.

The first SEM President, Willard Rhodes, later became ICTM's fourth President, while councillor in the first SEM nomenclature Bruno Nettl later served in a variety of roles in both societies, as did (and still do) many other scholars, from the United States and from the other countries.

It is appropriate to complete this section of the Introduction by pointing to a joint Forum that took place in September 2015 in Limerick, bringing together the two major ethnomusicological associations—ICTM and SEM—around the theme of importance for applied ethnomusicology: Transforming Ethnomusicological Praxis through Activism and Community Engagement. This historical event, the first such collaboration between ICTM and SEM, was co-chaired by the SEM President Beverley Diamond and the ICTM President Salwa El-Shawan Castelo-Branco.

> The Forum will focus on ethnomusicological praxis and collaborative strategies in different international contexts and political situations. While there is now a long history in ethnomusicology of initiatives that have sought to address problems of inequality, disparity and oppression, and a shorter history pertaining to such matters as health and environmental change, the symposium will focus, not on the problems per se, but on the methodologies that could best enable our work to have greater social impact. We are interested in critically assessing and finding strategies and best practices of collaboration, communication and policy formulation.
>
> (from the Call for papers)

This joint event convincingly testifies about the current intellectual climate in both major associations of ethnomusicologists, which is very much in tune with the ideas presented in the *Handbook*.

Notes

1. Controversy over the genre of exploitation documentary, so-called *mondo films* such as this one, suggesting that the genuine documentary footage is sometimes mixed with staged sequences, does not impact the film's symbolic standpoint.
2. The practitioners are scholars whose professional positioning may vary from universities and other schools, research institutes, archives, museums, media, and nongovernmental organizations, to freelance status.
3. Applied ethnomusicology is about how musical practice can inform relevant theory, and about how theory can inform musical practice. Knowledge of data, theories, and methods of ethnomusicology, as much as ethical concerns, are essential.
4. There is a need for increased critical reflection on political agendas, moral philosophies, and ideologies of applied ethnomusicology projects, as well as on the role of personal agency in applied ethnomusicological work.
5. Here she refers to the American Musicological Society.
6. For instance, the Society for Applied Spectroscopy, founded in 1958, has more than 2,000 members worldwide.
7. The aim of the Society for Applied Microbiology is to advance for the benefit of the public the science of microbiology in its application to the environment, human and animal health, agriculture and industry. The aim of the Society for Applied Philosophy is to promote philosophical study and research that has a direct bearing on areas of practical concern, such as law, politics, economics, science, technology, medicine, and education.
8. Timothy Rice's book *Ethnomusicology: A Very Short Introduction*, to the opposite, ends with the chapter titled "Public Service" and points to the fact that "[e]thnomusicologists are increasingly asking themselves the question 'Ethnomusicology for what purpose?'" (2014: 120). It is my hope that this *Handbook* will encourage ethnomusicologists to seek answers to this question, both inside themselves and in the world that surrounds them.
9. The other being Berlin.
10. For some useful current views on comparative musicology, see Schneider (2006), thematic issue of the Polish journal *Muzyka* 1 (2009), and the website http://www.compmus.org.
11. By scholars such as Naila Ceribašić, Marija Dumnić, Adriana Helbig, Ana Hofman, Jelena Jovanović, Ivona Opetčeska-Tatarčevska, Selena Rakočević, Velika Stojkova Serafimovska, Jasmina Talam, Ljerka Vidić Rasmussen and Dave Wilson.
12. In case of Sachs, the German version titled *Die Musik der Alten Welt in Ost und West* (1968) served as the source for translation.
13. The translator Ljerka Vidić Rasmussen used to study there under the mentorship of Blacking's former doctoral student Ankica Petrović. Petrović was widely regarded the first representative of "mainstream ethnomusicology" in what was Yugoslavia. Introduction of new disciplinary paradigms met many obstacles in the intellectual environment rooted in the strong folk music research school established by Cvjetko Rihtman.
14. This section uses parts of one of my earlier articles (Pettan 2008) and provides updates.
15. For instance, Dan Lundberg, Owe Ronström.
16. The proceedings contain articles by Kristof Tamas, Max Peter Baumann, Mark Slobin, and Krister Malm.

17. This seminar took place just a month prior to the conference *Invested in Community: Ethnomusicology and Musical Advocacy*, which took place at Brown University in Providence, Rhode Island, featuring "applied ethnomusicologists (who) work as musical and cultural advocates, using skills and knowledge gained within academia to serve the public at large. They help communities identify, document, preserve, develop, present and celebrate the musical traditions they hold dear."
18. This does not count for their institutional colleagues, who continued to supply the arrangements for musicians and choreographies for the dancers in folklore ensembles.
19. The Ukrainian/Soviet folk music researcher Kliment Kvitka (1880–1953) proposed and described the term as early as 1928 (see Lukanyuk, 2006). Interestingly, the second, enlarged edition of Kunst's book was published in 1955 under the auspices of IFMC.
20. See Chapter 2 by Harrison in Volume 1, calling for a reconsideration of this issue.
21. The third objective clearly referred to "recognition of the painful fact that the Second World War had created deep rifts between nations and peoples" (Stockmann, 1988: 2).
22. Paul Rovsing Olsen, the Council's President at that time, provided the following comment: ". . . we hope to have found a name which, much better than the original one, explains what our Council stands for in the world of scholarship—and in the world of international organizations. The IFMC has been concerned, from its beginnings, with all kinds of traditional music, not only with 'folk music'. This has not always been understood by outsiders" (Rovsing Olsen, 1981: 2).
23. Don Niles and Krister Malm respectfully shared the details of these events with me.
24. The first IFMC conference took place in Basel, Switzerland, in 1948.
25. The first issue of the *Journal of the International Folk Music Council* (predecessor of the *Yearbook of the International Folk Music Council* from 1969 and of the *Yearbook of the International Council for Traditional Music* from 1981) was published in 1949. The other publication was the *Bulletin of the International Folk Music Council*, starting in 1948.
26. In the forthcoming part of this section I gratefully acknowledge the assistance of ICTM's Executive Assistant Carlos Yoder.
27. A later version was published in 1992 in the journal *African Music*.
28. Applied ethnomusicology (and ethnochoreology) became one of the conference themes 22 years after Avorgbedor first mentioned it in his ICTM conference paper.
29. *Applied Ethnomusicology and Studies on Music and Minorities—The Convergence of Theory and Practice* with Ursula Hemetek, John O'Connell, Adelaida Reyes, and Stephen Wild.
30. Including war and revitalization in Croatia of the 1990s and early 2000s. The session was organized by Naila Ceribašić.
31. Organized by Samuel Araújo (South America) and me (Europe); the other panelists were Maureen Loughran (North America), Jennifer Newsome (Australia), Patricia Opondo (Africa), and Tan Sooi Beng (Asia).
32. I initiated the Study Group and became its first Chair; Klisala Harrison became Vice-Chair, and Eric Martin Usner became Secretary. As I became Secretary General of ICTM in 2011, Klisala Harrison assumed the duties of the Study Group's Chair, Samuel Araújo became Vice-Chair, and Britta Sweers became Secretary. In 2019, Huib Schippers serves as Chair, Adriana Helbig as Vice-Chair, and Weiya Lin as Secretary.
33. The Symposia were hosted by Svanibor Pettan, Le Van Toan, Panicos Giorgoudes, Bernhard Bleibinger, Marcia Ostashewski, and Zhang Boyu, respectively.
34. Scholarly journal, published by the Department of Musicology of the University of Ljubljana. It is available at (http://revije.ff.uni-lj.si/MuzikoloskiZbornik/issue/archive).
35. Section 1 of the Introduction, by co-editor Jeff Todd Titon, covers North America, so I did not include it here.

SECTION 3

AN INTRODUCTION TO THE CHAPTERS

JEFF TODD TITON AND SVANIBOR PETTAN

IN the Introduction we have identified several activities of contemporary applied ethnomusicologists. The chapters in this volume illustrate a range of these. Cultural policy interventions are a theme in all of the volumes in this *Handbook*. UNESCO's initiatives in safeguarding intangible cultural heritage have had a mixed record of success that is leading applied ethnomusicologists to agree that the best outcomes occur in small-scale projects resulting from long-term partnerships and mutual goals. Local and regional cultural differences require that policies adapt to varying conditions. Top-down, bureaucratic solutions are apt to be less successful and more likely to have negative consequences. Such best practices have characterized most, if not all, successful applied ethnomusicology projects, whether cultural policy interventions or not. In this volume, cultural policies interventions are discussed by Zhang as he reviews the role of government agencies, NGOs, and the arts in China. His Chapter 6 offers a lively discussion of cultural policies surrounding traditional music in China. Properly balancing the inheritance, protection, development, and utilization of Chinese traditional music has been the subject of discussion among Chinese scholars for a long period of time. This has led to increased attention and effort from government at all levels, a development that reflects the distinctive nature of applied ethnomusicology. His chapter addresses the application of ethnomusicology in China from the perspective of ethnomusicology's social practices (the macro level) and personal practices (the micro level).

Education is a concern of many of the contributors to this volume. Herrick, in Chapter 1, discusses strategies for success in educational institutions where partnerships with cultural organizations require collaborative decision-making for successful outcomes that link formal instruction to daily life. Strategies negotiated among collaborative decision-makers may most effectively apply ethnomusicology in horizontal pathways that dialogically engage and respond to varied social communities, particularly in areas where large, urban public school districts face substantial challenges. The context of Cleveland, Ohio, provides an example, where partnerships for arts education in the city's public schools date to 1915, and twenty-first-century programs for arts integration have drawn national attention. Her argument asserts that strategic process is central to both definitions of applied ethnomusicology and educators' efforts to link formal instruction to music in daily life. Murphy's review of applied ethnomusicologists working in the world of public folklore also includes partnerships among educational and cultural institutions to provide community "artists in the schools" and broaden the educational curriculum to include the music of local ethnic groups. In Chapter 3, Campbell and Higgins extend educational applications into college and conservatory levels of instruction, and also to a practice in "community music," a specialized terminology not to be confused with the looser way in which applied ethnomusicologists utilize the phrase to describe music among a group that shares commonalities. They address ways in which ethnomusicologists blend musical and cultural understanding into educational practice, and they describe cases that illustrate facets of their linkages into, and facilitation of, community music activity as these are relevant to learning and teaching—with particular attention paid to North American and United Kingdom–based circumstances, settings, and sensibilities. O'Connell, in Chapter 2, develops a hermeneutic approach to music education by exploring the relationship between music and humanity, based on the Aga Khan Humanities Project educational program in Central Asia. Following a precedent in ecology, the Project recognized music as a sustainable art in its balanced promotion of economic development and ecological conservation. O'Connell envisions the space for applied ethnomusicology in particular under war-affected circumstances, when music furnishes a humanistic locus for understanding conflict and a "humane-istic" focus for promoting conflict resolution. Lundberg (Chapter 4) recognizes the traditional relation of archives to education and the newer role that archives can play in activism.

Nationalism is yet another phenomenon that applied ethnomusicologists have to consider. In this volume, Lundberg (Chapter 4) discusses its formative aspects and its impact on research and documentation, with the Folk Music Committee's value scale, which many of us would easily recognize in a number of different national contexts.

A short-term, temporary form of migration, tourism, has offered a major opportunity and challenge for applied ethnomusicologists. As Murphy points out (Chapter 5), many have been employed as consultants and culture workers in bringing traditional music to an audience extrinsic to the musical community. Music plays an important role in cultural tourism, which many think can be a driver of local and regional economies while it also sustains older layers of music that are in danger of losing, or have lost, their original cultural contexts. Tourism often has followed UNESCO's safeguarding initiatives, which single out particular musical communities for preservation efforts. Musical tourism is thought to constitute a creative economy, but here the applied ethnomusicologist has played the role of critic as well as consultant and advocate, for ethnomusicological knowledge is sometimes at odds with the kinds of publicity that attracts tourists, while it may also be incomplete and unreliable, as occurred when the Chinese *guqin* tradition was designated as a masterpiece of intangible cultural heritage (Yung, 2009). Related to the tourist industry is music as commercial product in general, which has had an unsavory reputation among ethnomusicologists who traffic in authenticity. It has also led to an important branch of applied ethnomusicology involving music and law, forensic ethnomusicology. Commodification is anathema to those ethnomusicologists who believe that music has a cultural and artistic value that must remain beyond price. But, as Williams argues in Chapter 7, properly utilized it can be a valuable ally for the applied ethnomusicologist seeking to create social and economic capital for underserved communities.

Finally, sustainability is a theme that unites most of the chapters in this *Handbook*. Musical, and sometimes also cultural, sustainability is a goal of many arts and cultural agencies today (see Zhang, Chapter 6, this volume, and Murphy, Chapter 5). Values from the humanities provide an appropriate context for thinking about sustainability in many contexts (see O'Connell, Chapter 2). Sustainability is often one of the ends of advocacy, and has long been one of the chief reasons for music education. Indeed, in transmitting knowledge, skills, and values, education is a cornerstone of cultural continuity and sustainability. Outside the formal structures of the national schools, applied ethnomusicologists encourage traditional methods of musical education and transmission within diverse social groups and ethnic communities. Within more formal structures of education, applied ethnomusicologists contribute to the schools on the local, regional, and national levels, by expanding the reach of curricula, performing groups, and methods of instruction to reflect the strength and variety of diverse musical and cultural traditions. At the same time, however, applied ethnomusicologists pay attention to the broader economic and social forces that impact communities, sometimes negatively, and partner with community leaders in their efforts to move confidently into musical futures of their own choosing.

REFERENCES

Angrosino, Michael V. (1990). *The Essentials of Anthropology*. Piscataway, NJ: Research and Educational Association.
Anon. (1957). "Society for Ethnomusicology." *Bulletin of the IFMC* 11: 6.
Araújo, Samuel. (2008). "From Neutrality to Praxis: The Shifting Politics of Ethnomusicology in the Contemporary World." *Muzikološki Zbornik/Musicological Annual* 44(1): 13–30.
Araújo, Samuel. (2009). "Ethnomusicologists Researching Towns They Live in: Theoretical and Methodological Queries for a Renewed Discipline." *Muzikologija* 9: 33–50.
Araújo, Samuel. (2010). "Sound Praxis: Music, Politics, and Violence in Brazil." In *Music and Conflict*, edited by John Morgan O'Connell and Salwa El-Shawan Castelo Branco, pp. 217–231. Urbana-Champaign: University of Illinois Press.
Araújo, Samuel, and members of the Grupo Musicultura. (2006). "Conflict and Violence as Theoretical Tools in Present-Day Ethnomusicology: Notes on a Dialogic Ethnography of Sound Practices in Rio de Janeiro." *Ethnomusicology* 50(2): 287–313.
Avorgbedor, Daniel. (1992). "The Impact of Rural-Urban Migration on a Village Music Culture: Some Implications for Applied Ethnomusicology." *African Music* 7(2): 45–57.
Banks, James A., and Cherry A. McGee Banks. (2001). *Multicultural Education: Issues & Perspectives*. New York: John Willey & Sons.
Baumann, Max Peter, ed. (1991). *Music in the Dialogue of Cultures. Traditional Music and Cultural Policy*. Wilhelmshaven: Florian Noetzel Verlag.

Berliner, Paul. (1978). *The Soul of Mbira*. Chicago: University of Chicago Press.
Berger, Harris M. (2014). "New Directions for Ethnomusicological Research into the Politics of Music and Culture: Issues, Projects, and Programs." *Ethnomusicology* 58(2): 315–320.
Blacking, John. (1973). *How Musical Is Man?* Seattle: University of Washington Press.
Bleibinger, Bernhard. (2010). "Solving Conflicts: Applied Ethnomusicology at the Music Department of the University of Fort Hare, South Africa, and in the Context of IMOHP." In *Applied Ethnomusicology: Historical and Contemporary Approaches*, edited by Klisala Harrison, Elizabeth Mackinlay, and Svanibor Pettan, pp. 36–50. Newcastle upon Tyne, UK: Cambridge Scholars Publishing.
Bleking, Džon. (1992). *Pojam muzikalnosti*. Beograd: Nolit.
Boas, Franz. (1888). "On Certain Songs and Dances of the Kwakiutl of British Columbia." *Journal of American Folklore* 1(1): 49–64.
Bohlman, Philip V. (1996). *Central European Folk Music*. New York: Garland.
Bohlman, Philip V. (1988). "Traditional Music and Cultural Identity: Persistent Paradigm in the History of Ethnomusicology." *Yearbook for Traditional Music* 20: 26–42.
Bohlman, Philip V. (2004). *The Music of European Nationalism: Cultural Identity and Modern History*. Santa Barbara, CA: ABC-CLIO.
Bohlman, Philip V. (2011). *Focus: Music, Nationalism, and the Making of the New Europe*. New York: Routledge.
Boiko, Martin. (1994). "Latvian Ethnomusicology: Past and Present." *Yearbook for Traditional Music* 26: 47–65.
Bose, Fritz. (1953). *Musikalische Völkerkunde*. Freiburg in Breislau: Atlantis.
Bose, Fritz. (1975). *Etnomuzikologija*. Belgrade: Univerzitet umetnosti u Beogradu.
Brinner, Benjamin. (2009). *Playing across a Divide: Israeli-Palestinian Musical Encounters*. Oxford: Oxford University Press.
Castelo-Branco, Salwa El-Shawan, ed. (2010). *Enciclopédia da Música em Portugal no Século XX*. Lisbon: Círculo de Leitores/Campo das LEtras.
Ceribašić, Naila. (2004). "Double Standards: Negotiating the Place for Ethnomusicologists in Croatia." Conference paper.
Christensen, Dieter. (1988). "The International Folk Music Council and the Americans: On the Effects of Stereotypes on the Institutionalization of Ethnomusicology." *Yearbook for Traditional Music* 20: 11–18.
Clausen, Bernd, Ursula Hemetek, Eva Saether, eds. (2009). *Music in Motion: Diversity and Dialogue in Europe*. New Brunswick, NJ, and London: Transaction Publishers.
Climati, Antonio, and Mario Morra. (1975). *Ultime grida dalla savanna*. Rome: Titanus. (film)
Cohen, Ronald D., ed. (2010). *Alan Lomax, Assistant in Charge: The Library of Congress Letters, 1935-1945*. Jackson, MS: University of Mississippi Press.
Diamond, Beverley, and Salwa El Shawan Castelo-Branco, eds. (forthcoming). *Transforming Ethnomusicology*. New York, NY: Oxford University Press.
Dirksen, Rebecca. (2012). "Reconsidering Theory and Practice in Ethnomusicology: Applying, Advocating and Engaging Beyond Academia." *Ethnomusicology Review* 17. http://ethnomusicologyreview.ucla.edu/journal/volume/17/piece/602 (accessed July 1, 2014).
Ellis, Catherine. (1985). *Aboriginal Music: Education for Living. Cross-cultural Experiences from South Australia*. St. Lucia: University of Queensland Press.
Elschek, Oskar. (1991). "Ideas, Principles, Motivations, and Results in Eastern European Folk-Music Research." In *Comparative Musicology and Anthropology of Music*. edited by Bruno Nettl and Philip V. Bohlman, pp. 91–111. Chicago: University of Chicago Press.

Fenn, John, ed. (2003). *Folklore Forum* (Special issue on applied ethnomusicology) 34(1–2): 119–131.
Fetter, C. V. (2001). *Applied Hydrogeology*. Upper Saddle River, NJ: Prentice Hall.
Fletcher, Alice C., with the assistance of Frances La Flesche. (1994 [1893]). *A Study of Omaha Indian Music*. Lincoln, NE: Bison Books.
Freire, Paulo. (1970). *Pedagogy of the Oppressed*. New York: Herder and Herder.
Grant, Catherine. (2014). *Music Endangerment: How Language Maintenance Can Help*. Oxford: Oxford University Press.
Giuriati, Giovanni. (1995). "Italian Ethnomusicology." *Yearbook for Traditional Music* 27: 104–131.
Gourlay, Kenneth. (1982). "Towards a Humanizing Ethnomusicology." *Ethnomusicology* 26(3): 411–420.
H. M. (Hahn, Man-young). (1983). "Preface." *Yearbook for Traditional Music* 15: 3.
Harrison, Klisala. (2012). "Epistemologies of Applied Ethnomusicology." *Ethnomusicology* 56(3): 505–529.
Harrison, Klisala. (2013). "Music, Health, and Socio-Economic Status: A Perspective on Urban Poverty in Canada." *Yearbook for Traditional Music* 45: 58–73.
Harrison, Klisala. (2017). "Why Applied Ethnomusicology?" COLLeGIUM 21:1–17. https://helda.helsinki.fi/bitstream/handle/10138/167843/Collegium%20Vol%2021%20Introduction.pdf?sequence=1
Harrison, Klisala, Elisabeth Mackinlay, and Svanibor Pettan, eds. (2010). *Applied Ethnomusicology: Historical and Contemporary Approaches*. Newcastle upon Tyne, UK: Cambridge Scholars Publishing.
Hawes, Bess Lomax. (1995). "Reminiscences and Exhortations: Growing Up in American Folk Music." *Ethnomusicology* 39(2): 179–192.
Haydon, Glen. (1941). *Introduction to Musicology*. New York: Prentice-Hall.
Hemetek, Ursula, ed. (1996). *Echo der Vielfalt/Echoes of Diversity. Traditionelle Musik von Minderheiten—ethnischen Gruppen/Traditional Music of Ethnic Groups—Minorities*. Wien: Böhlau Verlag.
Hemetek, Ursula. (2006). "Applied Ethnomusicology in the Process of the Political Recognition of a Minority: A Case Study of the Austrian Roma." *Yearbook for Traditional Music* 38: 35–57.
Hemetek, Ursula. (2009). "The Past and the Present: Ethnomusicology in Vienna. Some Considerations." *Muzyka* 1(212): 57–68.
Herzog, George. (1936). "Primitive Music." *Bulletin of the American Musicological Society* 1: 2–3.
Hofman, Ana. (2010). "Maintaining the Distance, Othering the Subaltern: Rethinking Ethnomusicologists' Engagement in Advocacy and Social Justice." In *Applied Ethnomusicology: Historical and Contemporary Approaches*, edited by Klisala Harrison, Elizabeth Mackinlay, and Svanibor Pettan, pp. 22–35. Newcastle upon Tyne, UK: Cambridge Scholars Publishing.
Hood, Mantle. (1971). *The Ethnomusicologist*. New York: McGraw-Hill.
Impey, Angela. (2002). "Culture, Conservation and Community Reconstruction: Explorations in Advocacy Ethnomusicology and Action Research in Northern KwaZulu." *Yearbook for Traditional Music* 34: 9–24.
Invested in Community: Ethnomusicology and Musical Advocacy. (2003). Conference on Applied Ethnomusicology, Brown University, March 8–9. Videotapes of presentations by applied ethnomusicologists and community scholars from Europe, the United States,

and Native North America may be viewed at http://library.brown.edu/cds/invested_in_community/.

Jordan, Judith V. (2001). "A Relational-Cultural Model: Healing Through Mutual Empathy." *Bulletin of the Menninger Clinic* 65: 92–103.

Juvančič, Katarina. (2010). "Singing from the Dark: Applied Ethnomusicology and the Study of Lullabies." In *Applied Ethnomusicology: Historical and Contemporary Approaches*, edited by Klisala Harrison, Elizabeth Mackinlay, and Svanibor Pettan, pp. 116–132. Newcastle upon Tyne, UK: Cambridge Scholars Publishing.

Karpeles, Maud. (1971). "The International Folk Music Council: Twenty-One Years." *Yearbook of the International Folk Music Council* 1: 14–32.

Keil, Charles. (1978). *Tiv Song*. Chicago: University of Chicago Press.

Keil, Charles. (1982). "Applied Ethnomusicology and a Rebirth of Music from the Spirit of Tragedy." *Ethnomusicology* 26(3): 407–411.

Keil, Charles. (1998). "Applied Sociomusicology and Performance Studies." *Ethnomusicology* 42(2): 303–312.

Kerman, Joseph. (1986). *Contemplating Music: Challenges to Musicology*. Cambridge, MA: Harvard University Press.

Kirshenblatt-Gimblett, Barbara. (1988). "Mistaken Dichotomies." *Journal of American Folklore* 101(400): 140–155.

Koch, Grace. (2013). *We Have the Song, So We Have the Land: Song and Ceremony as Proof of Ownership in Aboriginal and Torres Strait Islander Land Claims*. Canberra: Australian Institute of Aboriginal and Torres Strait Islander Studies, Research Discussion Paper No. 33.

Korpe, Maria, and Ole Reitov, eds. (1998). *1st World Conference on Music and Censorship*. Copenhagen: Freemuse.

Koudal, Jens Henrik, et al. (1993). "[Three articles by different authors (Koudal, Torp and Giurchescu, Hauser) on selected ethnomusicological issues in Denmark]." *Yearbook for Traditional Music* 25: 100–147.

Kovačič, Mojca, and Urša Šivic. (2007). "Ethnomusicology and Ethnochoreology in Education: Issues in Applied Scholarship, Ljubljana, September 21–25, 2006." *Bulletin of the International Council for Traditional Music* 110 (April): 67–69.

Kunst, Jaap. (1950). *Musicologica: A Study of the Nature of Ethno-musicology, Its Problems, Methods, and Representative Personalities*. The Hague: Martinus Nijhoff.

Leydi, Roberto. (1991). *L'altra musica*. Giunti: Ricordi.

Leydi, Roberto. (1995). *Druga godba: Etnomuzikologija*. Ljubljana: Studia Humanitatis.

Ling, Jan. (1999). *A History of European Folk Music*. Rochester, NY: University of Rochester Press.

Lomax, Alan. (1972). "Appeal for Cultural Equity." *the world of music* 14(2): 3–17.

Loughran, Maureen. (2008). "But what if they call the police—Applied Ethnomusicology and Urban Activism in the United States." *Muzikološki Zbornik/Musicological Annual* 44(1): 51–67.

Lukanyuk, Bohdan. (2006). "Do Istorii termina etnomuzikologija" (On the History of the Term Ethnomusicology). *Visnyk Lviv Univ.* 37: 257–275.

Malm, Krister, et al. (1995). *Aspects on Music and Multiculturalism*. Stockholm: The Royal Swedish Academy of Music.

Marošević, Grozdana. (1998). "The Encounter Between Folklore Studies and Anthropology in Croatian Ethnomusicology." *the world of music* 40(3): 51–82.

Marti, Josep. (1997). "Folk Music Studies and Ethnomusicology in Spain." *Yearbook for Traditional Music* 29: 107–140.

Matthews, Washington. (1888). "The Prayer of a Navajo Shaman." *American Anthropologist*, 1(2): 148–171.

McAllester, David. (1989). Unpublished videotape of seminar at Brown University, transcribed by Lisa Lawson. Accessible from the author, and from the American Folklife Center, Archive of Folk Culture, Library of Congress, Washington, DC.

McLean, Mervyn. (2006). *Pioneers of Ethnomusicology*. Mamaroneck, NY: Aeon Books.

Merriam, Alan. (1963a). Review of Henry Weman, "African Music and the Church in Africa." *Ethnomusicology* 7(2): 135.

Merriam, Alan. (1963b). "Purposes of Ethnomusicology: An Anthropological View." *Ethnomusicology* 7(3): 207.

Merriam, Alan. (1964). *The Anthropology of Music*. Evanston, IL: Northwestern University Press.

Merriam, Alan. (1977). "Definitions of 'Comparative Musicology' and 'Ethnomusicology': An Historical-Theoretical Perspective." *Ethnomusicology* 21(2):189–204.

Merriam, Alan. (2000). *Antropologija glasbe*. Ljubljana: Znanstveno in publicistično središče.

Moisala, Pirkko, ed. (1994). "Ethnomusicology in Finland (eight articles by different authors)." *Ethnomusicology* 38(3): 399–422.

Nettl, Bruno. (1956). *Music in Primitive Culture*. Cambridge, MA: Harvard University Press.

Nettl, Bruno. (1964). *Theory and Method in Ethnomusicology*. Glencoe, IL: Free Press.

Nettl, Bruno. (1974). "Editor's Preface." *Yearbook of the International Folk Music Council* 6: 7–8.

Nettl, Bruno. (1983). *The Study of Ethnomusicology: Twenty-nine Issues and Concepts*. Urbana: University of Illinois Press.

Nettl, Bruno. (1988). "The IFMC/ICTM and the Development of Ethnomusicology in the United States." *Yearbook for Traditional Music* 20: 19–25.

Nettl, Bruno. (2002). *Encounters in Ethnomusicology: A Memoir*. Warren, MI: Harmonie Park Press.

Nettl, Bruno. (2005). *The Study of Ethnomusicology: Thirty-one Issues and Concepts*. New edition. Urbana: University of Illinois Press.

Nettl, Bruno. (2006). "We're on the Map: Reflections on SEM in 1955 and 2005." *Journal of the Society for Ethnomusicology* 50(2): 179–189.

Nettl, Bruno. (2010). *Nettl's Elephant: On the History of Ethnomusicology*. Urbana: University of Illinois Press.

Nettl, Bruno. (2013). *Becoming an Ethnomusicologist: A Miscellany of Influences*. Lanham, MD: Scarecrow Press.

Nettl, Bruno. (2014). "Fifty Years of Changes and Challenges in the Ethnomusicological Field." Interview by Héctor Fouce. *El oído pensante* 2(1): 1–11. http://ppct.caicyt.gov.ar/index.php/oidopensante (accessed March 16, 2014).

Nettl, Bruno, and Philip V. Bohlman, eds. (1991). *Comparative Musicology and Anthropology of Music*. Chicago: University of Chicago Press.

Newsome, Jennifer. (2008). "From Researched to Centrestage: A Case Study." *Muzikološki Zbornik/Musicological Annual* 44(1): 31–49.

Ockelford, Adam. (2013). *Using Zygonic Theory to Inform Music Education, Therapy, and Psychology Research*. New York: Oxford University Press.

O'Connell, John Morgan, and Salwa El-Shawan Castelo-Branco. (2010). *Music and Conflict*. Urbana: University of Illinois Press.

Pettan, Svanibor. (1996). "Making the Refugee Experience Different: *Azra* and the Bosnians in Norway." In *War, Exile, Everyday Life: Cultural Perspectives*, edited by Renata Jambrešić Kirin and Maja Povrzanović, pp. 245–255. Zagreb: Institute of Ethnology and Folklore Research.

Pettan, Svanibor, guest ed. (1998). *The World of Music* 40(3) (*Music and Music Research in Croatia*). Berlin: Verlag für Wissenschaft und Bildung.

Pettan, Svanibor. (2008). "Applied Ethnomusicology and Empowerment Strategies: Views from across the Atlantic." *Muzikološki Zbornik/Musicological Annual* 44(1): 85–99.

Pettan, Svanibor. (2010). "Music in War, Music for Peace: Experiences in Applied Ethnomusicology." In *Music and Conflict*, edited by John Morgan O'Connell and Salwa El-Shawan Castelo-Branco, pp. 177–192. Urbana-Champaign: University of Illinois Press.

Price, Jammie, and Steve Steele. (2004). *Applied Sociology—Terms, Topics, Tools and Tasks*. Boston: Cengage Learning.

Redfield, Robert. (1947). "The Folk Society." *American Journal of Sociology* 52(4): 293–308.

Rice, Timothy. (2014). *Ethnomusicology: A Very Short Introduction*. New York: Oxford University Press.

Rice, Timothy, James Porter, and Chris Goertzen, eds. (2000). *Garland Encyclopaedia of World Music*, Vol. 8: *Europe*. London: Routledge.

Ronström, Owe. (1991). "Folklore: Staged Folk Music and Folk Dance Performances of Yugoslavs in Stockholm." *Yearbook for Traditional Music* 23: 69–77.

Rovsing Olsen, Poul. (1981). "Summing Up the Conference." *Bulletin of the International Council for Traditional Music* 59: 2.

Sachs, Curt. (1933). *Eine Weltgeschichte des Tanzes*. Berlin: Dietrich Reimer/Ernst Vohsen.

Sachs, Curt. (1943). *The Rise of Music in the Ancient World East and West*. New York: Norton.

Sachs, Curt. (1968). *Die Musik der Alten Welt in Ost und West*. Berlin: Akademie-Verlag.

Sachs, Curt. (1997). *Svetovna zgodovina plesa*. Ljubljana: Znanstveno in publicistično središče.

Saks, Kurt. (1980). *Muzika starog sveta*. Belgrade: Univerzitet umetnosti u Beogradu.

Schippers, Huib, and Catherine Grant, eds. (2016). *Sustainable Futures for Music Cultures: An Ecological Perspective*. New York: Oxford University Press.

Schneider, Albrecht. (2006). "Comparative and Systematic Musicology in Relation to Ethnomusicology: A Historical and Methodological Survey." *Ethnomusicology* 50(2): 236–258.

Seeger, Anthony. (1992). "Ethnomusicology and Music Law." *Ethnomusicology*, 36(3): 345–359.

Seeger, Anthony. (2006). "Lost Lineages and Neglected Peers: Ethnomusicologists outside Academia." *Ethnomusicology* 50(2): 215–235.

Seeger, Anthony. (2008). "Theories Forged in the Crucible of Action: The Joys, Dangers, and Potentials of Advocacy and Fieldwork." In *Shadows in the Field: New Perspectives for Fieldwork in Ethnomusicology*, edited by Gregory Barz and Timothy J. Cooley, pp. 271–288. Oxford: Oxford University Press.

SEM Torture. Society for Ethnomusicology Position Statement on Torture. http://www.ethnomusicology.org/?PS_Torture (accessed July 1, 2014).

Sheehy, Daniel. (1992). "A Few Notions about Philosophy and Strategy in Applied Ethnomusicology." *Ethnomusicology* 36(3): 323–336.

SIL International. SIL International is a US-based, international Christian missionary organization. Formerly the Summer Institute of Linguistics. http://www.sil.org/arts-ethnomusicology (accessed July 1, 2014).

Skyllstad, Kjell. (1993). *The Resonant Community. Fostering Interracial Understanding Through Music*. Oslo: University of Oslo.

Skyllstad, Kjell. (1997). "Music in Conflict Management—A Multicultural Approach." *International Journal of Music Education* 29: 73–80.

Smithsonian: Fletcher. Foreword to "Camping with the Sioux: The Fieldwork Diary of Alice Cunningham Fletcher." Smithsonian Institution, Department of Anthropology. Online exhibit at http://anthropology.si.edu/naa/exhibits/fletcher/foreword.htm (accessed July 1, 2014).

Spradley, James, and David W. McCurdy, eds. (2000). *Conformity and Conflict: Readings in Cultural Anthropology*. Boston: Allyn and Bacon.

Stockmann, Erich. (1988). "The International Folk Music Council/International Council for Traditional Music—Forty Years." *Yearbook for Traditional Music* 20: 1–10.

Tan, Sooi Beng. (2008). "Activism in Southeast Asian Ethnomusicology: Empowering Youths to Revitalize Traditions and Bridge Cultural Barriers." *Muzikološki Zbornik/Musicological Annual* 44(1): 69–83.

Terada, Yoshitaka. (2005). *Drumming out a Message: Eisa and the Okinawan Diaspora in Japan* (film).

Terada, Yoshitaka. (2008). "Angry Drummers and Buraku Identity: The Ikari Taiko Group in Osaka, Japan." In *The Human World and Musical Diversity: Proceedings from the Fourth Meeting of the ICTM Study Group 'Music and Minorities' in Varna, Bulgaria 2006*, edited by Rosemary Statelova, Angela Rodel, Lozanka Peycheva, Ivanka Vlaeva, and Ventsislav Dimov, pp. 309–315, 401. Sofia: Bulgarian Academy of Science, Institute of Art Studies.

Terada, Yoshitaka, (2010). *Angry Drummers: A Taiko Group from Osaka, Japan* (film).

Terada, Yoshitaka, (2011). "Rooted as Banyan Trees: Eisa and the Okinawan Diaspora in Japan." In *Ethnomusicological Encounters with Music and Musicians: Essays in Honor of Robert Garfias*, edited by Timothy Rice, pp. 233–247. Surrey, UK: Ashgate.

Terseglav, Marko. (2004). "Etnomuzikologija." In *Slovenski etnološki leksikon*. Ljubljana: Mladinska knjiga.

Titon, Jeff Todd. (1984). *Worlds of Music: An Introduction to the Music of the World's Peoples*. New York: Schirmer Books.

Titon, Jeff Todd. (1989). "Ethnomusicology as the Study of People Making Music." Paper delivered at the annual conference of the Society for Ethnomusicology, Northeast Chapter, Hartford, CT, April 22.

Titon, Jeff Todd. (1992a). "Music, the Public Interest, and the Practice of Ethnomusicology." *Ethnomusicology* 36(2): 315–322.

Titon, Jeff Todd. (1992b). "Preface." In *Worlds of Music*, general editor Jeff Todd Titon. New York: Schirmer Books.

Titon, Jeff Todd. (2003). "A Conversation with Jeff Todd Titon." Edited and conducted by John Fenn. Special issue on applied ethnomusicology. *Folklore Forum* 34(1–2): 119–131.

Titon, Jeff Todd. (2009a). "Economy, Ecology and Music: An Introduction." *the world of music* 51(1): 5–16.

Titon, Jeff Todd. (2009b). "Music and Sustainability: An Ecological Viewpoint." *the world of music* 51(1): 119–138.

Van Buren, Kathleen J. (2010). "Applied Ethnomusicology and HIV and AIDS: Responsibility, Ability and Action." *Ethnomusicology* 54(2): 202–223.

Van Willigen, John. (2002). *Applied Anthropology* (3rd ed.). New York: Praeger.

Wallaschek, Richard. (1893). *Primitive Musik. An Inquiry Into the Origin and Development of Music, Songs, Instruments, Dances and Pantomimes of Savage Races*. London: Longmans, Green and Co.

Weintraub, Andrew, and Bell Yung, eds. (2009). *Music and Cultural Rights*. Urbana: University of Illinois Press.

Wengle, John. (1988). *Ethnographers in the Field: The Psychology of Research*. Tuscaloosa: University of Alabama Press.

Wong, Deborah. (2014). "Sound, Silence, Music: Power." *Ethnomusicology* 58(2): 347–353.

Yung, Bell. (2009). "UNESCO and China's *Qin* Music in the Twenty-first Century." In *Music and Cultural Rights*, edited by Andrew Weintraub and Bell Yung, pp. 140–168. Urbana: University of Illinois Press.

Zebec, Tvrtko. (2007). "Experiences and Dilemmas of Applied Ethnochoreology." *Narodna umjetnost* 44(1): 7–25.

PART II

EDUCATION

CHAPTER 1

STRATEGIES AND OPPORTUNITIES IN THE EDUCATION SECTOR FOR APPLIED ETHNOMUSICOLOGY

SUSAN E. OEHLER HERRICK

Introduction

THE process of becoming a culturally competent musician represents an enduring interest in ethnomusicology. Building musical capacities for expression is part of socialization, through which humans interpret cultural actions and fashion meaningful identities. Individuals can learn musical culture through formal schooling and traditional or self-directed studies, which increase avenues for musical participation and expression. As people learn through music, their interactions often stretch beyond any single institution and reflect the influence of a range of social groups.

Partnerships among institutions for formal education, cultural organizations, and professional musicians working as "teaching-artists" have long provided resources to supplement and enrich schooling (Myers, 2003; Richerme et al., 2012). Such partnerships represent streams of institutional interchanges that may bridge distinctive classrooms, communities, and pedagogical methods while enhancing access to diverse cultural and social musical practices. The site represents a rich opportunity to apply ethnomusicology to support learning through music[1] in the education sector, a web of interrelated—though not necessarily connected—institutions and community groups. Such work may inform scholarship in both music education research and the ethnomusicology of music acquisition.

This chapter identifies strategies for applied ethnomusicology that may serve opportunities in the education sector, where partnerships among music specialists substantially contribute to the learning experiences of youth in local primary and secondary schools (typically serving 4- or 5-year-olds through 18-year-olds). The chapter aims to link the analysis of strategies for applied ethnomusicology to the instructional contexts led by music-makers, teachers, and educational program administrators. The focus here is the United States in the scope of one urban region, particularly music programs for the preschool through twelfth grade level (PK–12) in the pluralistic communities of Cleveland, Ohio, and its environs. Cleveland is a Midwestern city on the south shore of Lake Erie, expanded by industrial manufacturing through much of the twentieth century.

Strategies of academically trained ethnomusicologists based in nonprofits, government agencies, or universities often have informed approaches to educational initiatives, within which any theories, methods, or resources of both ethnomusicology and music education must effectively cooperate to engender meaningful educational impact. The analysis foregrounds a micro-level perspective, examining what people do with music to foster learning in social contexts. Implicitly, the approach assumes that ethnomusicologists anticipate an integral and dynamic relationship between music and social contexts. Examples illustrate strategies of social interactions in education, seeking to reveal ways that arts educators, including ethnomusicologists, may engage learners in activities through music. It reflects a theoretical orientation to ethnomusicology centered on the social processes of musical practice,[2] and constructivist philosophies of education. The chapter demonstrates that decisions of collaborative strategizing lie at the center of what defines applied work in the cross-institutional education sector. I contend that effective strategies for applied ethnomusicology grow dialogically and contextually in reference to identified educational needs of learners in a specific instructional setting, which remain linked to larger social and cultural frames.

Applying ethnomusicology in education-sector partnerships may reveal and respond to the multifaceted, dynamic worlds of music in ways that reflect the aims both of the partners and those bearing the tools of ethnomusicology. Such outcomes promise value to discussion of theory and practice in "applied ethnomusicology," as well as broader discourse anchored in the academy and the professional field of education. For those students, however, whose learning seems deeper when they engage with music, such outcomes may assist in fostering profound personal transformations.

In the United States, contemporary educational trends in the twenty-first century—particularly those that value music as a practice connected to daily life—have proven compatible with ethnomusicological approaches, which foundationally associate music with lived human experience in social context. Many PK–12 schools have forged partnerships with music organizations in their larger community to augment resources for arts education. Music education for PK–12 students often grows within a stream of programs offered by schools and colleges, cultural organizations, museums, and religious and other community groups. In such necessarily pluralistic contexts, decision-makers who shape learning through music must navigate crosscurrents of beliefs regarding what constitutes music and what makes learning meaningful for young music-makers. Identifying useful strategies for applied ethnomusicology that emerge in the contexts of complex musical cross-talk and practice may inform the development of pedagogies for culturally responsive teaching[3] or multicultural education.

Since 2004 I have applied ethnomusicology in the education sector as a mid-level employee at nonprofit organizations in and around Cleveland, Ohio, beginning as the Education Programs Manager at the Rock and Roll Hall of Fame and Museum (2004–2008). Much of my work has involved developing and implementing pedagogies for integrating popular music into PK–12 teaching,[4] most often across humanities disciplines. These experiences inform the chapter.

Frames for Learning Through Music across Institutions

With widespread economic challenges related to the "Great Recession" and systems for funding public schools in the United States, the significance of cross-institutional partnerships for formal instruction through music has magnified (Richerme et al., 2012). This is the case even though music instruction has remained more prevalent in PK–12 schools than other arts disciplines (Parsad and Spiegelman, 2012). Discourse around the social contexts of public education in the United States notes shifts signaling cultural change, such as the rising presence of English language learners in many schools and the growth of populations designated as minority groups in US school populations. Many educators seek resources for pedagogical methods or materials that acknowledge the dynamic cultural diversity of the classrooms in which they teach.

Coinciding with these contexts in the early twenty-first century are efforts in public schools to foster learning through music in ways that develop every student's ability for meaningful self-expression, while fostering core skills for successful schooling and living (Deasy, 2002; National Association for Music Education, 2007). The federal government has designated the arts as a core subject area for instruction, specifying music as one of several arts disciplines (Richerme et al., 2012). Among students of low socioeconomic status, those who were exposed to the arts in the lower grades were far more likely than those with little or no arts exposure to pursue higher-level courses and extracurricular opportunities and to complete their high-school educations (Iyengar, 2012). These findings speak volumes in light of the increasing demand to transform educational systems across the nation that serve, but too often fail, students living in neighborhoods with highly concentrated rates of poverty (Emerging Arts Leaders Symposium, 2012; Iyengar, 2012). The goal is a matter of equity in public education.

Within initiatives to develop music education pedagogy and the professional training of teachers, educators have aimed to better connect musical activities to the life experiences of students and others in their immediate and extended communities. Some pedagogical frameworks that link music and daily life seek to expand or deepen students' experiences with musical genres or traditions beyond Western European art music. Instruction may center on repertoire popularized through the commercial music industry or anchored in broadly influential American styles such as jazz, gospel, or musical theater; it may add ethnic or regional traditions from the school's locality, increase students' interaction with professional musicians in their community or with contemporary music technologies, enhance culturally relevant instructional approaches, and/ or broaden their understanding of music in global perspective (Burton and Dunbar-Hall, 2002; Campbell et al., 2008; Clements, 2010; Dunbar-Hall, 2005; Music-in-Education National Consortium, 2013; Myers, 2003; Oehler and Hanley, 2009; Schmidt, 2009).

Pedagogy that infuses music into "non-arts disciplines" such as English/language arts, history and social studies, and STEM subjects (science, technology, engineering, and math) tends to be taught by instructors who are not certified to teach music. Schools with arts integration methods at their core may foster a "third space" in which students, teachers, and visiting artists create and respond together. Arts integration methods teach to goals in an arts discipline (i.e., dance) and a non-arts discipline (i.e., history) through instructional methods that engage students actively in relevant skills and concepts in each discipline. When a learning community experiences authentic self-expression in a "third space," it may add relevance and effectiveness to students' perspectives of schooling and its purposes (Stevenson and Deasy, 2005).

The research suggests an explanation for a truism known by educators and ethnomusicologists: that music sometimes causes connections to blossom in people in ways that other approaches do not. The phenomenon has been explored in ethnomusicological studies of the acquisition of musical culture (including cognition), music-making in childhood, music as a recurring means for lifelong human growth, or music education in schooling and teacher training (Bakan et al., 2008; Blacking, 1967; Campbell, 1998; Campbell et al., 2008; Fujita, 2006; Nettl, 1995; Monson 1996). Music therapists and educational neuroscientists have also discussed it as one reflection of how the brain and the human psyche both access and process music (Koen et al., 2008; Lane, 2012; Sousa, 2006a, 2006b, 2011). Lauren Stevenson and Richard Deasy characterize "openings" fostered through a transformational "third space" around an empowering artistry in educational terms:

> A large body of research on the effects of the arts in schools has looked at what is called *transfer*—how a particular intellectual or social skill developed by participation in the arts prepares students for learning and success in another area of school or life. The changes that we saw in the schools [of the case study] were more fundamental and more powerful than these one-to-one transfer associations. By forging new relationships between artists, students, and teachers, the arts created powerful contexts and conditions for learning in which students played active and meaningful roles in their own education and through which a sense of community was formed within and around the schools. We began to see that the lessons offered by these schools address not only public concerns about how well students learn but how schools can promote the principles and practices of a democratic society.
>
> (2005: 9–10, authors' emphasis)

A focus on collaborative process is particularly important when education is understood in a constructivist framework,[5] where teaching facilitates the ability to make connections that actively grow and shape learners' knowledge, understanding, self-expression, and ability to control their surroundings. Music-making, whether engaging learners in listening, performing sounds and movements, interpreting, or finding and applying musical meaning, may readily foster approaches to student-centered knowledge-building and expression. In education, any achievement requires engagement and growth by the participants. Efforts to shape planning, policy, and practice with theoretical, methodological, or research-driven tools must therefore keep the experiences of learners in the fore.

Decisions among a Network of Partners: Examples from Cleveland

Educators ideally look to the varied experiences of students to assess the effectiveness of strategies for learning based on evidence of students' increased understanding and abilities around targeted concepts or skills. Decision-making processes in effective educational partnerships reveal examples of strategies for learning through music and desired outcomes for students that may resonate with approaches of ethnomusicology. The network of Cleveland decision-makers interviewed for this chapter represents this nexus. Their perspectives provide examples of a practicing network of colleagues in arts administration, where I applied ethnomusicology to educational aims for PK–12 learners. This premise is also supported by the work of Joan L. Zaretti, who designed and managed educational programs for music and global studies at Carnegie Hall. Her dissertation (2006) analyzes, in terms of ethnomusicology, the decisions of arts administrators who provide music programs through a "nonprofit niche" in New York City.

The interviews, which the author conducted in 2012, dialogically inform assertions about strategies for applied ethnomusicology in education sector partnerships in the contexts of specific learning communities. Six professionals based in the Cleveland area with years of experience serving PK–12 students in northeast Ohio provided 30–60-minute interviews on a voluntary basis.[6] Each interviewee has partnered with the Education staff of a local cultural landmark, the Rock and Roll Hall of Fame and Museum (also known as the Rock Hall), to serve learners in the greater Cleveland area:

- Deforia Lane, Ph.D., MT-BC, Associate Director and Director of Art and Music Therapy, Seidman Cancer Center, University Hospitals–Case Medical Center;
- Lauren Onkey, Ph.D., Vice President of Education and Public Programs, Rock and Roll Hall of Fame and Museum;

- Santina Protopapa, Ed.M., Founder and Executive Director, Progressive Arts Alliance;
- Dianna Richardson, Orchestra Director and Music Department Chair, Cleveland School of the Arts, Cleveland Metropolitan School District;
- Judith Ryder, Manager, Cleveland Arts Education Consortium, Cleveland State University and Music Director of the chamber ensemble Red Campion; formerly the Founding Director of Cleveland Opera on Tour, the education and outreach program of the Cleveland Opera;
- Tony F. Sias, M.F.A., Director of Arts Education, Cleveland Metropolitan School District and Artistic Director, Cleveland School of the Arts.

Glimpses of the informal professional relationships among the above demonstrate how a web of decision-making partners may inform opportunities for learning through music in an urban center's education sector. A sketch of the partnerships that the interviewees have sustained in the region illustrates their significance to arts education in the greater Cleveland area, where the largest K–12 public school district is the Cleveland Metropolitan School District (CMSD) of the City of Cleveland.

The Cleveland Metropolitan School District is the largest public school system in Cuyahoga County and the second largest in the state of Ohio (State Impact Ohio, 2013). Among its successes are the Cleveland School of the Arts, which boasts an excellent rate of graduation and college acceptance among its high school level students. In the Cleveland area, public schools of several cities face a paradox of declining funding and a rising concentration of poverty among families whose children are served by public schools (Alaprantis et al., 2013; Exner, 2010; Nelson, 2008: 45; Schweitzer, 2007). Education research finds that concentrated poverty in school populations is among the greatest challenges to students' success in school (Kahlenberg, 2013; Kennedy, 1986; Poverty and Race Research Action Council, n.d.; US Department of Housing and Urban Development, 2011).[7]

Even as the growth of healthcare industries of Cleveland has countered aspects of postindustrial decline in the late twentieth century, challenges persist. In Ohio, as in many states, public school funding generates from local taxes tied to property values. Suburbs have grown as the population in the City of Cleveland has declined, historically fed by "white flight" from racial desegregation, exacerbated by biased policies in lending, including "red-lining" and subprime loans. Numerous American cities have navigated similar structural social economic challenges and their legacies, often aided by philanthropic partners. Programs for PK–12 arts education in greater Cleveland benefit from the proximity of vibrant local music scenes and world class arts institutions: an internationally lauded symphony, large theater district, and one of the nation's few museums devoted solely to the history of popular music, among others.

The examples of partnerships for learning through music examined here operate within a larger, more multifaceted network of cross-institutional arts education with deep roots. CMSD schools' official partnerships date to 1915 (CMSD Department of Arts Education, 2008: 2). CMSD is one among many districts carrying out a strategic plan for district-wide academic transformation to ensure that all students are provided with opportunities for a high-quality education. Arts partnerships are crucial to the CMSD plan. As of September 2007, certified fine-arts and other classroom teachers engaged CMSD students in educational partner programs with over 40 northeast Ohio music, visual arts, theater, dance, film, and literary organizations (CMSD Department of Arts Education, Strategic Plan: 30; Sias, 2012). These have included the Tri-C Jazz Fest of Cuyahoga Community College, the Cleveland Orchestra, GroundWorks Dance Theater, the Baldwin Wallace University Conservatory, and the Cleveland Institute of Music, as well as the Cleveland Music School Settlement and the renowned Karamu House theater (2008 CMSD Arts Strategic Plan: 30). The latter two organizations represent legacies of the settlement movement of the early twentieth century, which encouraged artistry in city neighborhoods with higher concentrations of poverty and, at the time, many newcomers who had moved to Cleveland from Europe or from black communities in the segregated South (*The Encyclopedia of Cleveland History*; Witchey and Vacha, 1994).

Like many large cultural organizations in the City of Cleveland, the Rock Hall's Education Department has prioritized partnerships with CMSD. The District's director of arts education, Tony Sias, a frequent Rock Hall advisor, suggested that I interview a classroom music teacher, Dianna Richardson, to augment his perspective of partnering. Where Sias administers arts education at the district level, Richardson's collaborations with partners are oriented primarily to daily instructional goals at the classroom and departmental level. As students engage in the resulting programs, she identifies best practices and shares them with fellow CMSD string teachers (Richardson 2012; Sias, 2012).

As the director of an arts education nonprofit serving schools in the greater Cleveland area, Santina Protopapa works among many CMSD teachers, their administrators, and teaching-artists trained by the Progressive Arts Alliance (PAA). PAA operates largely through school residency programs that often have served CMSD K–8 level schools, and Protopapa has facilitated partnerships with the Museum, Tri-C, and other large cultural organizations. PAA has demonstrated best practices for effectively teaching with rap music and hip-hop culture, as well as documentary filmmaking, in short-term out-of-school programs and summer camps.

Deforia Lane's partnerships with the Rock Hall date to 1999, when it enlisted her to lead music therapists in developing a "music-based outreach/education program for underserved preschoolers, their parents, caregivers and teachers... to promote positive interaction... and increase the children's academic, social, communication and music skills" (Rock and Roll Hall of Fame and Museum, 2013). A pilot study found that children spending six weeks in the resulting Toddler Rock program improved 72% in maintaining behavior considered "on-task" for three-to-five-year-olds and reduced "off-task behavior to only 12 times per hour" (Rock and Roll Hall of Fame and Museum, 2013). Lane has remained an active leader in Toddler Rock, which explicitly frames music therapy as a "research-based profession" that applies music:

> Skilled music therapists design music interventions aimed at enhancing the pre-academic skills that have been shown to be most indicative of later success in school, including letter recognition, rhyming and alliteration, all important for the acquisition of reading skills.... The music therapist's education and training equips them to apply music to accomplish non-musical goals.
>
> (Rock and Roll Hall of Fame and Museum, 2013)

Lane's connection to learning through music also has included supervising music therapy interns pursuing board certification in programs such as the Cleveland Music Therapy Consortium. Her partnerships typically involve outreach to apply music therapy to needs in the greater Cleveland area outside the walls of her employer, University Hospitals, an affiliate of the Medical School of Case Western Reserve University.

Since 1999, the Cleveland Arts Education Consortium (CAEC) has brought together local cultural organization administrators to coordinate programs, research, and information-sharing. CAEC hired Judith Ryder in 2008, whose leadership in arts education began in 1976 at the Cleveland Opera; Ryder oversees the Consortium office at the Center for Arts and Innovation at Cleveland State University. CAEC meetings regularly convene "large and small organizations" from across Cuyahoga County for presentations by regional, state-level, and sometimes national specialists in arts education, including representatives of philanthropic foundations. Topics discussed include "program evaluation, advocacy in the current economic landscape, funding issues, best practices in management, effective arts marketing, and new education initiatives" (Cleveland Arts Education Consortium, 2013).

CAEC has helped to facilitate large scale cross-institutional participation in citywide arts education initiatives such as the Art Is Education partnership with the Cleveland Metropolitan School District led by Young Audiences of Northeast Ohio (YANEO). Since 2010, YANEO has facilitated teaching-artist residencies in more than 140 schools in Cuyahoga County, which encompasses the greater Cleveland area, and in 17 additional counties in Ohio (Young Audiences of Northeast Ohio, 2013b). YANEO's Art Is Education project received support of major funders, the Cleveland Foundation and the Ford Foundation, among others. The project drew national attention to the efforts by dozens of partnering museums (including the Rock Hall), cultural organizations, and teaching-artists to align offerings with the district's instructional goals for K–8 literacy and learning in the arts (Dobrzynski et al., 2007; Ohio Arts Council et al., 2007; YANEO, 2013a). These partnerships helped to raise discussion about methods of infusing the arts into formal instruction and promoted pedagogy of arts integration, in addition to ongoing approaches that exposed learners to the arts as performers, audiences, and critical thinkers. The discourse in Cleveland has reflected national trends in education policy, pedagogy, and related research.

Foundations for Pedagogy for Music in Daily Life and Connections to Ethnomusicology

The application of ethnomusicology in the education sector benefits from attending to pedagogical strategies, their philosophical foundations, and the field's ongoing contributions to formal music education. In particular, pedagogy for teaching music across the curriculum through partnerships seems compatible with approaches that understand music as a social process in human life. Also significant are approaches that position students' engagement in music to illuminate its integration in daily life, as opposed to an isolated practice.

Cross-institutional partnerships have often augmented school musical experiences offered to students as arts education or a kind of educational enrichment (Myers, 2003). Typical professional roles in US programs of this kind are of three types:

1. Certified music teachers employed by schools;
2. Arts educators based in cultural organizations (symphonies, museums, etc.) or programs for community members, including after-school offerings;
3. Established musical performers, who also teach individual or group music lessons or serve as artists-in-residence.

Growing numbers of teachers who are not necessarily certified in arts education, but ideally teach in collaboration with certified arts educators, have embraced the arts as instructional resources, often fueled by early twenty-first-century education research suggesting that arts engagement supports student-driven interest in schooling and achievement gains (Stevenson and Deasy, 2005). Teachers certified to teach music may have encountered models for collaboration with non-music teachers and/or teaching-artists as pre-service teachers. A number of music education textbooks, for example, discuss sample instructional units that thread in or unite musical learning activities with concepts aligned to other subject areas (Campbell et al., 2006: 359–370).

Arts Integration

Approaches to arts integration as pedagogical methods for lessons, project-based learning activities, and curricular frames for schools have expanded interest among teachers in infusing arts across disciplines or embracing partnerships that bring expert, active artists into schools. "Concept-based arts integration"—in its fullest realization—aims for students to achieve goals for learning in both an arts and a non-arts discipline through one unit of study[8] (Kennedy Center, 2013b; Southeast Center for Education in the Arts, 2013). Some school systems have faced increasing financial challenges, and partnerships sometimes have become appealing, stop-gap responses to funding cuts for arts education (Richerme et al., 2012).[9] In theory, all students may learn through effective arts experiences during instruction led either by general classroom teachers at the elementary level, or specialists in English/language arts, history and social studies, or mathematics and sciences at the secondary level. As leading music education organizations and others have pointed out, however, students may not achieve widely held expectations for learning in music if they have less time to study under the direct guidance of a certified music teacher, who typically holds an undergraduate- or graduate-level degree in music (Myers, 2003; Richerme et al., 2012). Within this political climate, music teachers in public schools may be encouraged to design music instruction that reinforces school-wide efforts to build literacy, numeracy, and other skills critical to student success and state evaluation of school performance. Advocates of arts education increasingly tout evidence that learning in the creative arts fosters valuable, transferable skills that may further student success in academic, social, and emotional terms. Others caution that banking the value of the arts on its role in supporting growth in other subject areas may detract from the intrinsic value of learning in arts disciplines.

Many approaches of arts integration align with an ethnomusicological approach that contextualizes music in human life. In a philosophical sense, arts integration relies on reminding teachers and learners that each holds the potential for creative expression simply because they are human beings,[10] as discussed by a collective of self-defined Canadian "a/r/tographers" of visual artists and writers based largely in Vancouver, British Columbia. Its members, who also specialize in higher education, identify as

> artists, researchers, and teachers, who, by working in complementary and multiplicious, but supportive ways, have ... [entered] into inquiry... to live artfully in all of the many facets of our lives and, in particular, re-imaging a more holistic view of facilitating integration of the arts in schools and classrooms.
>
> (Weibe, 2007: 264)

Implicitly, being a teaching-artist is part of fulfilling artful living that connects artistry with a multifaceted life, a perspective concordant with musical artistry. The goal, they remind their fellow educators, is "to teach students how to embody living practice, to teach students how to sustain life-long learning, and to teach students how to appreciate the joy of creativity through self-motivation" (2007: 269). This assertion in *The Journal of Educational Thought* may read as a statement of the obvious, but the need for this articulation makes more sense in the context of a climate where accountability for particular areas of student achievement (often measured by test scores) have become central concerns of classroom teachers and administrators. An ideal of arts integration concerns more than students achieving discrete benchmarks across disciplines. It embraces both the need for maintaining academic rigor with the introduction of musicking into a social studies unit, for example. It affirms the perspective that education is enhanced when teachers "see their students as creative beings—able to connect, link, cause growth, and develop learning through multiple artful means. . . . This newness will be different for each student and thus is the dominant means of learning and transformation" (Weibe, 2007: 269). It reflects that creativity in art forms, such as poetry performed in the twenty-first century, may traverse across instructional disciplines, incorporating meters and rhetorical characteristics informed by popular music styles, intertextual references to printed and multimedia works, intoned dramatic characterizations, and so forth (Harris, 2006).

The assertion is echoed in the research-based advocacy of the National Task Force on the Arts in Education. The group's final report (2009), for which ethnomusicologist Lester P. Monts served as steering committee chair, calls on The College Board to help lead a paradigm shift in education by placing a "new curricular model with the arts at the core, integrating many subjects and types of learning in order to give them context and meaning" to better serve K–16 students (kindergarten through undergraduate college) and "provide a more effective learning environment that would induce the creative thinking needed for the 21st-century global society" (2009: 5). The report outlines recommendations for arts integration as one of eight suggestions.

Multicultural Music Education and Culturally Responsive Approaches

Given advocacy for multicultural music education as well as methods of arts integration, agencies within the education sector have often furthered relationships among school-employed music teachers and their students with performing musicians whose expertise is anchored elsewhere in the community. These agencies may connect public, private, and nonprofit/ nongovernmental resources and funding requests, missions and program goals, and staffs. When partnerships include performers whose music is "traditional" or "popular," as well as that of long-established "classical" or "highbrow" arenas,[11] students gain more opportunities to draw connections between learning about music in school and experiencing music in daily life.

This aim has long been incorporated in discussions of the purposes of music education, whether connections are intended to provide a moral foundation, inculcate canonical works, build new music professionals and their audiences, or foster students' creativity and critical thinking skills through multiple intelligences (Jorgensen, 2002). Ethnomusicological contributions include expanding the cultural scope of music scholarship and illuminating ways in which people integrate music-making with creative expressions that also represent other ways of knowing (Seeger, 1996). Patricia Shehan

Campbell's textbook *Music in Childhood* (2006), for example, orients users to a foundational assumption: that children begin learning music in relation to their parents/caregivers and early musical encounters. The book's final chapters demonstrate that the school curriculum must engage students in the realities of a world of multifaceted musical experiences, purposes, and cultural associations. Throughout Campbell's *Musician and Teacher* (2008), case studies foster a global perspective for the intended audience of pre-service music teachers, describing music teaching and learning in varied contexts in the United States and also in other countries (Gault, 2008: 213–214). Bryan Burton and Peter Dunbar-Hall (2002), among others, discuss what could be framed as culturally responsive music education for Native American learners.

Historically, partnerships for music education have created opportunities for K–12 students to examine modes of music-making that figure prominently in daily life, yet lie beyond the scope of music courses or the professional expertise of K–12 music educators. Ethnomusicologists in cross-institutional partnerships at times have sought to counter the marginalization of vernacular, regional, ethnic, religious, or other musical traditions (Seeger, 1996). Under the auspices of national, state, and local agencies in domains now embraced as "applied ethnomusicology," "public sector folklore," "public history," and/ or "multicultural music education," specialists have worked to grow culturally diverse music education in formal and/ or informal settings, advance knowledge of traditional musics and their transmission, and preserve and exhibit musical history in regional, ethnic, popular, or other performance settings, among other initiatives (Campbell et al., 1991, 2006; Hawes 1992; Maultsby 1988; Maultsby with Dunlap, 1990; Reagon 1996–2003; Reagon et al., 1994; Seeger, 1996, 2006; Sheehy 1992; Zaretti, 2006, 1998, 2002, 2003, 2004). Programs and educational resources in this vein have facilitated teachers' relationships with community tradition-bearers—whether shaped-note singers, hip-hop deejays, or symphony section leaders—and music researchers or other trained specialists, who may help teachers prepare students and artists.

Formal learning through music is associated with a larger process of acquiring, developing, and applying musicality over time (Fujita, 2006; Green, 2001, 2008; Szego, 2002). These sustained interests in ethnomusicological inquiry and theory also remain central processes in the core methodology of field research, as well as the cultivation of any musical performer's development. Related literature addresses the social matter of how and why people learn music, including processes of identity formation, enculturation, intercultural exchange, and the construction of tradition (Blacking, 1967; Burnim 1985a; Campbell et al., 2006; Campbell, 1998, 1996; Del Negro and Berger, 2004; Feld, 1990; Fujita, 2006; Kingsbury, 1988; Nettl, 1995). Since the early 1990s, the number of resources for teaching ethnomusicology—particularly those designed for undergraduates and graduate students—has grown dramatically, illustrating a zeitgeist of educational interest.[12] The resulting pedagogy, curricula, instructional resources, and related institutional development reflects an ongoing ebb and flow in the field and, of course, larger issues in education. Within the Society for Ethnomusicology (SEM), the Sections for Education and Applied Ethnomusicology each foster discussion and networking among members.

Specialists collecting and archiving US music represented as "folk," "traditional," "ethnic," or "national," as evident in catalogues of Smithsonian Folkways or the holdings of the Archive of Folk Culture of the Library of Congress, have facilitated research and teaching about widespread, commercially popularized, or intergenerationally valued styles of music. A number of music archives for popular music, based in public libraries and universities, have provided public access for researching local sites of performance and the frequently obscured studio recording process. Related materials may reveal aims of music-makers, audiences, and their social networks, which US adolescents and young adults have often shaped after 1945.[13]

Ethnomusicological scholarship has affirmed the value of music as a lifelong practice involving more than discrete performers or compositions. Books such as *My Music: Explorations of Music in Daily Life* (Crafts et al., 1993) and Daniel Cavicchi's study of rock fandom, *Tramps Like Us: Music and Meaning among Springsteen Fans* (1998), have helped to reveal the significance of ways of knowing music in the quotidian of the digital era—representing frequent routes through which most Americans gain musical knowledge and interpret what music means. Gospel scholar Mellonee V. Burnim (1985a) and jazz scholar Ingrid Monson (1996), among others, bring understanding to elusive communicative and transformational experiences that help put in words the powerful qualities of live jazz or gospel events, where responsive improvisational performances resonate philosophical or metaphysical awareness among participants. Recent medical ethnomusicology studies identify connections between music, as an expressive way of knowing, and its application in promoting healing and health in the United States among individual children and their caregivers (Koen et al., 2008).

Opportunities for Applying Ethnomusicology in the Cross-Institutional Education Sector

Applications of ethnomusicological practice may assist certified teachers in connecting PK–12 students with musicians, who extend or augment the instructors' resources in a given school. The processes of ethnomusicology, or the field's approaches, also may assist in navigating distinctive social or cultural contexts for "musicking" in schooling, among community tradition-bearers or other specialists, and within the daily experiences of those teaching and learning together (Small, 1998). Decisions of partners in music programs for PK–12 learners in Cleveland describe a range of opportunities for applying ethnomusicology to further effective learning through music in a specific context. Selected examples reveal aims, approaches, and valued educational outcomes at the crux of learning through music in these cases.

Expanding Instructional Access to Musical Traditions in Formal Schooling

Increasing students' access to exemplary musical performance, as learners who perform and also make up audiences, may support goals for effective learning. Cleveland is characterized by thriving musical communities that include the established traditions embraced in institutions of higher education and a more widely varied range of musics. Like many Northern cities fueled by early twentieth-century industrial growth, the population of the Cleveland area includes many families who connect their distant or recent history to immigration or large scale rural-to-urban migrations in the twentieth century. Such regional and ethnic identities have flavored the soundscape of Cleveland.

In order to provide all CMSD students with high-quality educational opportunities for music-related career and college readiness, it seems critical for students to learn through music that dominates college-level degree programs. CMSD programming helps facilitate students' access to supplemental after-school instruction at no or low cost (i.e., private lessons, community youth ensembles), which historically have served as a key component in the preparation of college-level students in the arts (Richardson, 2012). The relevance of this approach is affirmed by a report published by the Ohio Department of Education (2013) that measures a 100% poverty rate among CMSD students based on data drawn from the US Census and US Department of Education.

The role of music in culturally responsive education may also support students' social and emotional development; they may value belonging to a musical group, discover that the arts open routes for success in school, or find connections to school and community through music that they identify with home communities (outside school). The fact that "the majority, 69%, of CMSD students are African-American" (State Impact Ohio, 2013) may bear significance in considering what constitutes culturally relevant pedagogies in this context.

When CMSD students are viewed as potential members of the Cleveland area arts scene (as adult residents are often assumed to be), "music in daily life" becomes a very rich tapestry. The City of Cleveland is home to both the Cleveland Orchestra—a world-renowned symphony orchestra with residencies in Miami, Florida, and Vienna, Austria—and the Playhouse Square theaters, each maintaining landmark architectural sites as performance venues. In the early twenty-first century the greater Cleveland area has been celebrated as the anchor of music superstars, such as the O'Jays and other commercially successful recording artists of the recent past. Cleveland's music scenes include nightclubs featuring R&B vocalists and rock clubs showcasing metal guitarists. Repertoire explores the standards of straight-ahead jazz, electronic architecture of industrial rock, or the avant-garde edge to noise music. Community grows in the live battles of rappers and the exchange of downloaded music videos. Cleveland's sounds are shaped by choirs, cantors, dance teams, bugle corps, drum lines, mariachi ensembles, polka bands, pow-wows, classical recitals, and performances by the local School of Rock. In addition to the Tri-C Jazz Fest, the city hosts crowd-drawing annual music celebrations, whether to honor an international pool of competitive concert pianists or a gathering of students and gurus of South Indian music.

As Stephen Blum notes, when music-making "in the public sphere" is viewed in historical perspective, "the conflicts that have been most audible and visible in the musical life of the United States are linked to our [sic] long history of injustice toward so-called peoples of color" (2010: 232). Such a historical legacy bears particular weight in the context of the 43,000 students served by Cleveland's public schools, in which 85% of students identify as "minorities," according to demographic reports of the Ohio Department of Education (2013). Among the city's resident population in 2010 of around 396,814, the US Census Bureau (2010) counted 53.3% as African American or Black, 33.4% as "White alone," and 10% as Hispanic or Latino. Court battles over racial desegregation of the Cleveland public schools persisted into the early 1980s (*Encyclopedia of Cleveland History*, n.d.).

In contradistinction to the Rock and Roll Hall of Fame and Museum, few large cultural institutions in northeast Ohio represent a sustained, cultural contribution from African-American music-makers, though many such organizations offer a range of resources to explore African-American history in specialized programs or events.[14] Northeast Ohio, however, is home to numerous networks of African-American musicians who have sustained music for wide audiences, from the local to the global in scale. Local school ensembles are rooted in traditions of Western European art music, jazz maintains institutional presence, many high school–level choral groups have a strong gospel repertoire,[15] and teaching-artists have fostered musical experiences with a broad range of styles and traditions.

There may be particular value in the opportunity for young people in schools to learn in partnership with expert musicians whose cultural frames of reference do not require college and university programs for certification as a music teacher or other degree in music. The musicians also may gain skills as teaching-artists that could enhance opportunities to partner with music educators or other classroom teachers. Cleveland's Progressive Arts Alliance (PAA), for example, trains teaching-artists to lead residencies or workshops. The residencies (10–12 weeks) place PAA teaching-artists in a classroom or across a grade level in a K–8 level school, and after-school workshops typically involve teaching fourth through eighth graders. The instructional methods of PAA teaching-artists have engaged students in music anchored in various styles of jazz, works for symphonic orchestra, rock and roll, rap music, hip-hop deejaying and dance, and West African and Afro-Cuban drumming. Santina Protopapa notes that some PAA teaching-artists "don't have a background in music education, because what they do with music is so unique that you couldn't go to a conservatory" (2012). PAA provides professional development to its teaching-artists around curricula and pedagogical strategies for K–12 instruction through music.[16] Protopapa explains that PAA coaches teaching-artists to consider the relationships between their professional practice and their role as partnering educators in schools:

> It's been [a question of] how can we get teaching-artists to think bigger and broader, and hip-hop artists to see themselves... as music educators.... It's finding ways for music students in the conservatory to understand their roles as an artist in the community, and the... various contexts [beyond] a concert hall [or]... jazz club.... What does your work look like outside of performing? And the teaching might not be your studio practice. Many of the artists we work with, who are now partners to public schools, said, "I would have never imagined myself having a significant source of income teaching social studies and jazz at a public, inner-city Cleveland school. But now I love it, and I [want] this to... be a part of everything else I do." So how do we give exposure to the different ways that they can do that?
>
> (2012)

Classroom teachers may learn from teaching-artists' musical approaches or may validate new pedagogical approaches for engaging students through music. "We're building the capacity of classroom teachers as well," says Protopapa, who contends that teaching-artists and the curricula they have created during PAA residencies have inspired certified music teachers to adapt the resulting instructional materials for ongoing use. "The values of artists who are in the community and are pushing their art... are doing that in the classroom. They're not going in this [classroom] and turning off their values" (2012).

Similarly, Protopapa ascribes opportunities for mutual influence with the large cultural organizations with which PAA has partnered on a long-term basis, such as the Recording Arts and Technology Program at Tri-C and the education division of Playhouse Square; PAA is provided the use of equipment for digital sound production and recording and venues for after-school programs and summer day camps. According to Protopapa, PAA staff has assisted other larger partners over time (2012).

Toddler Rock: Learning Through Music as a Social Process

Music therapist Deforia Lane's approach to partnerships emphasizes the value of a dialogic process. Lane makes decisions about programs like Toddler Rock by considering, for example, the objectives for serving targeted individuals in relation to their caregivers, who may include parents and other family members, teachers, or health-care providers. Weekly Toddler Rock sessions at the Rock and Roll Hall of Fame and Museum must suit the educational objectives mandated for Greater Cleveland Head Start[17] programs and must successfully engage the participating children, who are accompanied by their Head Start teachers. School administrators' priorities, mandated educational standards, and partners' aims are also factors. Lane works expressly to develop and model varied approaches for involving students in activities with musical sound, timing, movements, and technology that Head Start teachers may use again with students back in their own classrooms; Head Start teachers' comfort level in leading musical activities does vary. Lane designs interventions for the needs of a diverse student population, as well as those of the teachers and caregivers who may reinforce Toddler Rock activities. Lane explains that she gives the Head Start instructors

> formal and informal instruction on the integration of music in the classroom. Techniques focus on engaging the youngsters in listening, associating sounds with letters or words, recall and recognition of concepts, problem-solving, and sequencing. Interventions for these purposes integrate song, chant, rhythm and movement in group activities.
>
> (2013)

A team of music therapists first models the specially designed activities held inside the Rock Hall before the museum opens its doors to the public. Interventions engage the students and caregivers with provided resources; some therapists use iPads or listening stations to access audio or video recordings. Given the expectation that all present will actively participate, the Head Start teachers learn musical activities as their students do. Prompted by the music therapists, Head Start teachers model participation for their classes and positively reinforce on-task behavior designed to foster cognitive and social-emotional growth. They may repeat or adapt the session's activities in their regular classrooms or devise similar music-based activities. Newsletters that describe Toddler Rock lessons or themes are sent home with students, inviting parents or caregivers to reinforce skills, too.

Lane expects partnerships to encompass learning through music for all involved.

> Because music is so diffusely processed in the brain, it can address many issues—cognitive, social, physical, psychological and spiritual issues—I can't think of an area where music cannot have an impact. But the person with whom I am collaborating or partnering may not be aware of that. So I think part of my role is to educate; part of it is to inspire; and part of it is [creative development].
>
> (Lane, 2012)

As Lane collaborates with partners, she anticipates a creative process of "learning as you go and experiencing those brilliant 'Ah ha! Moments'" and avoids a "cookie cutter approach." She adds, "I believe part of learning is exploration. How can we do what we do better? And when we find what works, sharing those successes with teachers and children so they will reap the benefits is key" (Lane, 2013).

"Musicking" a Public Voice

A dialogic approach to Cleveland-area partnerships for learning through music points to another important outcome. Santina Protopapa, like many other arts educators, emphasizes that students' musical expression provides them with opportunities not only to develop musical interest and skills, but also to voice ideas through a performance form that has the potential to reach a larger audience. In 2013, for example, with the guidance of PAA teaching-artists, two teams of students collaboratively created a song as part of "What's Going On... NOW," the Kennedy Center for the Performing Arts' national "digital youth arts and media campaign" (2013a) in which students from around the United States responded to creative works via digital media. The theme references Marvin Gaye's 1971 album, *What's Going On*.

One team at CMSD's East Technical High School created their song in a voluntary after-school program. The high school draws students from Cleveland's Central neighborhood, where highly concentrated poverty has sparked a community transformation initiative to support children's success in schooling through building community and social support services in the neighborhood. The other student group, the PAA All-Stars, submitted the song "Think Cleveland," which was selected for the "What's Going On... NOW" Youth Showcase at the Kennedy Center in Washington, D.C. (2013a). The PAA All-Stars is a select ensemble of student MCs (rappers), deejays, and dancers from the Cleveland area who have attended the PAA's annual RHAPSODY Hip-Hop Summer Arts Camp (grades 6–12).

Both the East Tech group and the PAA All-Stars wrote songs that "were really heady" as students considered problems faced by Clevelanders and the messages of the 1971 album, Protopapa explained (2012). The program

> challenged students to create new work based on music and social issues that Marvin Gaye was examining in that album. As they were talking about that, they were using quotes and metaphors that you hear in some of the songs in *What's Going On*, and it was a really creative way to tie it all together.... The Kennedy Center had this online platform, where you could submit your work, and then everybody gets to see it. Even if they weren't going to the Kennedy Center to perform, there was all this back-and-forth with kids exchanging work.
>
> (2012)

According to Protopapa, the PAA All-Stars saw the campaign as a vehicle to position their song as "part of a bigger platform" (2012). The group periodically performs by invitation at museums and community events, but Protopapa says the students viewed the national event differently:

> [Going] to D.C. and perform[ing] at the Kennedy Center amidst other groups around the country expanded our students' view of . . . the music they created. It wasn't just a page on a band [concert] program. It was, "I own this, and I'm going to present this to . . . people who don't know me, aren't my parents, aren't my fellow classmates, aren't from Cleveland." It was a really, unbelievably positive experience. They got invited to a second performance . . . to do another song, ["We're Here"] . . . . It gave them a vehicle to open the possibilities to what a professional career could be like.
>
> (2012)

Protopapa describes the role of PAA teaching-artists in supporting students' projects and how students' ownership emerged collaboratively:

> They started examining the media: "What does Cleveland report about Cleveland? What trends do you see? Do you think these trends are accurate? What else do you see that's not being recorded or that's being reported too much?"
>
> It was interesting. Poverty is really high in Cleveland. Not all these kids lived in poverty-stricken neighborhoods, but they experience it or have friends.... The last line of the song is, "Think bigger than yourself: think Cleveland.".... The students were like, ... "This [line] encapsulates everything we were trying to do."... They decided how many measures everyone would have; who was going to be the person responsible for the refrain [and] the order. (2012)

The PAA All-Stars' experiences in Washington, D.C., brought them face-to-face with selected peers from around the country who digitally submitted recorded songs, videos, short films, and poetry readings. The culminating Youth Showcase intertwined students' recorded media and live performances of the digital submissions. In addition to witnessing the positive reception of a larger audience, the PAA All-Stars experienced membership in a larger arts community that affirmed their style of expression, acknowledged their maturity extended beyond expectations for "a kids' group," and sparked growth. Protopapa recounts that

> [o]ne of the students said, "I've never been in a situation where everybody is into the same kind of things I'm into, and they respect my work. And they want to know more about it and were talking really deeply about music."
>
> And I said, "Well, go to college, and you'll have that. Be a music major in college."
>
> [He continued,] "Some people are better and are really pushing me [to be] the greatest I could possibly be? And it's all over music!"
>
> It just really blew his mind.... It ended up being a huge validation. It's not just that PAA thinks you're cool.... Other people, kids from D.C., from the Bay Area [are saying], "This is the real thing."
>
> (2012)

In a time when young people expect to use digital platforms to gain, share, and comment on information, partnerships like "What's Going On... NOW" [18] provide an opportunity for engaging students appropriately through educator-facilitated interfaces of arts communities and the internet that foster a forum resounding with student voices to address matters of both civics and culture.

Deepening a Sense of Belonging

Music therapist Deforia Lane affirms the idea that learning on location in a museum like the Rock Hall helps children to internalize the notion that public institutions for the arts in Cleveland belong to them, which builds a kind of confidence (2012, 2013). Lane views Toddler Rock as "an opportunity to invite children who seldom get to experience this place of elegance and rich history in the Rock Hall to make it a world they can call their own.... Toddler Rock [engages] the mind, body, and spirit of a child with the art and science of music" (2013). During class activities, the children "confidently put on earphones, listen to music as far back as Mahalia [Jackson] and Billie Holiday, and go away [with] more... school readiness" (Lane, 2012). They use museum technology, are able to "identify the guitar of Les Paul, or dance the twist when they hear Chubby Checker" (Lane, 2013). According to Lane, parents have proudly shared their surprise when toddlers have recalled the names of artists like Jerry Lee Lewis or B. B. King to identify the letters in their names (2012, 2013).

Effective programming in the education sector also involves intergenerational connections. Judith Ryder, in her former position as Founding Director of Cleveland Opera on Tour, intentionally began in 1995 to involve senior citizens and other adult volunteers as trained assistants for the opera's educational programs for residencies in schools, teacher professional development, and educational opera productions. As lifelong learners, the trained volunteers would support operatic vocalists in residencies with primary-level students in the greater Cleveland area. The objectives of instruction remained focused on the students, but often the volunteers would witness the program's educational impacts, a lesson valuable for taxpayers and advocates for public funding of arts education.

In 2012, for example, City of Cleveland voters approved the first levy in 16 years to increase property taxes and fund CMSD's Academic Transformation Plan (2010) for dramatically improving the performance of the city's public schools (Anderson, 2012; O'Donnell, 2012a). This vote was of particular significance to sustaining instruction in the arts, which had been reduced or eliminated from most K–8 schools in 2012 due to district budget cuts.[19] Even as the City of Cleveland has addressed these challenges, many children still face what was termed an "arts opportunity gap" by US Secretary of Education Arne Duncan in 2012 (quoted in Richerme et al., 2012: 2). To sustain PK–12 arts education, it may be crucial for adults to cultivate a sense that northeast Ohioans belong to the CMSD community.

Teaching and learning approaches develop through an emergent process within the context of distinctive but interrelated learning communities. This fact may resonate with ethnomusicologists, who often build musical understanding through intensive engagement in field research or apprenticeship to master performers, while navigating powerful social dynamics.

Strategies for Applied Ethnomusicology: A Contextualized Definition

Given the contexts through which arts administrators approach partnerships for learning through music, the notion of "applied ethnomusicology" may be most valuable as an orientation to strategies for thinking about music and what people do with it, where strategies relate musical knowledge to social actions undertaken through music. These assumptions reflect a philosophical investment in pragmatism and the phenomenological significance of human social experience. In "A Few Notions about Philosophy and Strategy in Applied Ethnomusicology" (1992), Daniel Sheehy describes "applied ethnomusicology" as conscious, purposeful professional practice that

> shapes our action into concrete lines of strategy that are not preconceived or predetermined by an absolute idea of what these actions should be. . . . On the part of its practitioners, applied ethnomusicology is perhaps most observable as an implacable tendency first to see opportunities for a better life for others through the use of music knowledge, and then immediately to begin devising cultural strategies to achieve those ends.
>
> (1992: 323)

Strategies are framed by ongoing musical experiences for pragmatic aims. In the education sector, this may involve collaborating to create educational programs and events or pedagogical tools and frameworks. Applied ethnomusicology strategies connect ideas about music with social actions through music.

In the context of navigating partnerships for education, it seems problematic to center frames for the motivations of educators or ethnomusicologists around terms that seek to lift up or speak for others. Even if unintended by the author, such language may resonate with a moral altruism. If altruism functions as a definitive motivation for action, the power of "others" may be diminished, as the spotlight remains on the power of the educator or the perspective of the applier of music to generate change on behalf of someone else. Nonetheless, I certainly agree with Sheehy and others: strategies in applied ethnomusicology typically aim to further ameliorative changes that assist individuals and groups. An ethnomusicologist may join efforts to navigate challenges or solve problems, as other characterizations of applied ethnomusicology have emphasized (Pettan, 2008; Titon, 1992a). Surely numerous schoolteachers and ethnomusicologists may also ascribe ameliorative motives to work, even if their academic research and publications are not considered to be "applied ethnomusicology."

It seems pragmatic to leave the matter of social amelioration outside the core of the definition of "applied ethnomusicology," centering instead on the action's processes and relationships. Within Sheehy's conceptualization in terms of "purpose, strategy, techniques, and evaluation" (1992: 324), strategies are "the ways to solve a particular problem" and most often

> are aimed at affecting the community of origin of a given music. . . [by] (1) developing new "frames" for musical performance, (2) "feeding back" musical models to the communities that created them, (3) providing community members access to strategic models and conservation techniques, and (4) developing broad, structural solutions to broad problems.
>
> (1992: 330–331)

As illustrated by Portia Maultsby's discussion of applied ethnomusicology in an interview with Delia Alexander published in 2003, the purpose of applied work may center on process and audience in different contexts and roles (Alexander, 2003: 9–11, 13). Maultsby was teaching a two-part graduate level course, "Ethnomusicology and the Public Sector," in Indiana University's Department of Folklore and Ethnomusicology. In Maultsby's eyes,

> [p]ublic sector and academic work represent different sides of the same coin. My academic work provides content for public sector projects and the research conducted for these projects feeds back into my own work and teaching. I expose students to the latest perspectives on issues drawing from my discussions with scholars of various disciplines. Another point—public sector work has made my research accessible to broad audiences and in different formats.
>
> (Alexander, 2003: 11)

Maultsby provides examples of the range of roles, nature of tasks, and special opportunities to influence "public spaces" through applied work:

> I have applied my knowledge as an ethnomusicologist in a variety of contexts, including public sector institutions, where I have worked as a researcher, presenter, consultant, author, co-curator, and program designer in museums; consultant for companies specializing in museum soundtrack and multimedia productions; and consultant/ advisor for PBS and NPR/PRI documentaries. Working part- or full-time in public sector institutions enables ethnomusicologists to influence the presentation and representation of American ethnic minorities and world cultures in public spaces.
>
> (Alexander, 2003: 9)

This statement emphasizes the collaborative work process and possibly a kind of shared responsibility in the perceived impacts of the resulting projects. The form of the projects and their routes of dissemination may broadly influence the perceptions and experiences of people in public spaces in ways that extend Maultsby's scholarly fueled understandings of the history of African-American music and culture beyond typical academic audiences. Strategies for applied ethnomusicology in this vein are a potential route for ethnomusicological participation in creating resources with the potential to broadly communicate, if not foster, self-directed learning through music. Communications may engage the media, mass/ popular culture, well-funded educational websites, or networks to localities and communities. The process may expand or open access to the authoritative production of knowledge, in this case, influencing how "American ethnic minorities and world cultures" are represented in public and ways that the tools of ethnomusicology may inform other means for examining music and its significance.

Maultsby focuses on the importance of "negotiation" in a way that distinguishes it as a kind of collaborative core strategy for applied work:

Negotiation is central to collaborative work and important to debating ideological positions regarding institutional traditions and practices. Working as music consultant for *Eyes on the Prize II*, for example, I negotiated the use of songs that contained lyrics, a practice contrary to traditions of documentary filmmaking [at the time]. In most cases, lyrics are avoided because of their potential to editorialize or influence the interpretation of content. Even though this potential does exist, I believe that song lyrics, if strategically placed in appropriate scenes, can help reinforce important issues introduced in the narrative. Through several discussions supported by a rationale, the producers eventually gave in to my position, which in turn influenced changes in perspectives on the role of music documentaries.

(Alexander, 2003: 14)

This strategy, according to Maultsby, enhanced the opportunity for songs in the film to function as a primary source within "multimedia narratives on African American history and culture" in a culturally relevant way:

This is significant because. . . vocal and instrumental music is central to African American community life. It expresses a range of emotions and reveals the level of resilience and creativity of African Americans under changing social conditions and as a marginalized group in society. . . . [E]thnomusicologists can influence changes in long-standing practices and perspectives of public sector institutions in ways that contribute to effective presentations and appropriate representation of cultures. . . .

(Alexander, 2003: 14)

The documentary's embrace of recorded songs, as well as reinterpretations by artists anchored in the tradition of freedom songs and related styles of congregational singing, adds more African-American voices to the historical narrative. The documentary series features, for the most part, excerpts from oral historical interviews with movement leaders and eyewitnesses, historical stills and moving images, and a narrator's voiceover. By including audible lyrics in the documentary film's quilt of selected historical memories, the multivalent messages of music performed by black communities and civil rights activists are represented. Music is documented as a tool of the grassroots nonviolent Civil Rights movement and a valuable mode of expression, not merely a soundscape.

In contrast to Maultsby's successful negotiation, where an ethnomusicologist applies ideas about music in cultural context to influence an approach to decision-making about a project, collaborative work also may involve negotiations that limit the ethnomusicologist's influence. Contracts may restrict ownership of intellectual property, the right to disseminate information to the public, or to speak on behalf of the organization.

Strategies in applied ethnomusicology must function in light of the potentially conflicting expectations of partnering individuals, organizations, and those they aim to serve (Loughran, 2008; Seeger, 1992). When ethnomusicologists cultivate dialogic relationships around music with community members, more avenues for negotiation may open, regardless of the ethnomusicologists' level of perceived influence or contracted role. Community members' requests, requirements, and directions are sought in addition to those generated or controlled by the partnering ethnomusicologist(s) (Araújo, 2006: 298–309).

The empowerment of the ethnomusicologist cannot be denied (Pettan, 2008: 90–91), nor the need for methods that base research on sustained, intensive dialogic relationships negotiated by the both the researcher and the music community in order to foster a "new knowledge-producing praxis" (Araújo, 2008: 28).[20] In the context of the Cleveland area, dialogic relationships for learning through music navigate social characteristics that profoundly shape the experiences of schoolchildren and their families. Partnerships for learning that welcome lived definitions of music-making benefit from strategies that seek horizontal pathways for understanding music among people oriented to differing social positions, cultural frameworks, and community networks.[21]

When ethnomusicologists join together with arts educators, their negotiations with other individuals in planning and designing educational programs, resources, or events are framed by a larger web of institutional policies, communal practices, cultural preferences, and related values for music-making and learning. In the ideal, the policies and practices of PK–12 schools and their partners in arts education serve the needs of students in ways valued by their families and larger communities. Strategies for applied ethnomusicology in the PK–12 education sector benefit when collaborative efforts to design and implement instruction through music ultimately center on the needs of students in specific learning contexts, where guidelines for navigating a school's web of expectations typically are articulated. Here strategies approach a specific community of learners in dialogue with partners, where teachers (not only educators) in the learning community play a leading role. Ultimately, how may students' current understandings of music in daily life be connected to music in school and also expanded, in order to support particular goals for learning?

Navigating Social Barriers and Building Access in Cleveland

In the Cleveland area, social positions related to race, socioeconomic status, and social mobility are relevant to dialogic relationships. At some level, school partners will navigate such social realities, whether they are overtly acknowledged or not. This includes positions related to identities of the ethnomusicologist and other decision-making partners.[22] Strategies for applied ethnomusicology may benefit from understandings of ways that schools serving K–12 learners aim to navigate structural barriers while providing music education.

Some navigation is literally a logistical concern. It is an ongoing challenge to provide all Cleveland students access to musical experiences in daily life in ways that foster reflection, participation, and understanding. While foundations and wealthy individuals may fund cultural organizations' on-site programs, fees for bus transportation to these events are increasingly considered "incidentals" that are not covered by grant awards. Tony Sias explains a paradoxical challenge in a "music-rich community" facing limited transportation funds and rising transportation costs:

> One of the barriers is bus transportation... to the various venues.... I think it's great to bring programming into the schools, but there's nothing like going to Severance Hall and experiencing The Cleveland Orchestra in that acoustically brilliant and magnificent edifice of a music hall. *Nothing* like it. There's nothing like seeing something at Playhouse Square, [which] has done a phenomenal job of making transportation a priority in terms of fund development on behalf of Cleveland [CMSD] schools.
>
> (2012)

Sias emphasizes, like many music educators, that the CMSD Department of Arts Education insists that a high-quality music education should provide all students opportunities to both perform and think critically about performances by accomplished artists in their professional settings.

The significance of providing access to such experiences in schools in the region is magnified by the fact that nine Cuyahoga County public school districts indicate levels of "very high student poverty" or "high student poverty" (38%–88%), according to the Ohio Department of Education (2013). Nearly one-third of City of Cleveland residents live in poverty (US Census, 2010), a statistic exceeding poverty rates of most other US cities of its size (Alaprantis et al., 2013, Exner, 2010; Nelson, 2008: 45; Schweitzer, 2007).

The District navigates institutional matters involving curriculum and instruction as well as the bottom line of funding. To offer a high-quality arts education for all students in the District, the 2008 Strategic Plan authored by the district's Department of Arts Education aims to embrace external partnerships that support goals for the arts in the CMSD Transformation Plan. The goal is to spread across the District practices integral to the "proven success" of the Cleveland School of the Arts and arts-focused schools benefiting from collaborative partnerships. It notes the past role of awards from national and local philanthropic foundations in arts-focused schools (2008: 3).

The Cleveland School of the Arts serves students in grades 6–12 on two campuses, who gained admission through an audition process. In addition to intensive study in arts disciplines, project-based learning that integrates the arts across core subject areas has infused school culture. The high school campus boasts an exceptional rate of graduation (96% in 2013), and 100% of graduates in 2013 matriculated to college and universities. Through the district's anticipated PASS program (Premier Arts Specialty System), additional PK–8 schools in the district may embrace innovative, high-quality curricula for "arts-focused learning" with "national best practices as benchmarks," according to the CMSD Department of Arts Education's Strategic Plan (2008: 3, 4).

Given the likelihood that most CMSD students face economic barriers to visiting large cultural organizations and encountering expert performers in Cleveland's professional venues, Sias praises opportunities that permit CMSD students to enter cultural organizations situated geographically within the bounds of the City of Cleveland. One partner, the Rock and Roll Hall of Fame and Museum, has helped the district's certified music teachers, student ensembles, and students' families explore the history of selected Inductees of the Rock and Roll Hall of Fame at no cost. Sias describes how an annual event of 12 years, the Rock Your World Festival, has drawn large numbers of students in the district's musical ensembles and their families to culminating performances that represent students' year-long study in music:

> [Over] 6,000 Clevelanders attend the festival. We usually have around 2,000 students who participate, and the balance of the guests are parents, community, and family members.... On that day we have access to the Rock Hall [for CMSD student performers and their audiences].... One of our agreements with the Rock Hall is that teachers will select music to be performed: at least one selection by a Rock Hall Inductee.
>
> (2012)

As part of study of concert repertoire in the district's music education curriculum, student performers come to know a song that represents an honored musician's contribution to the history of rock and roll music, as defined by the Museum and their teachers. At a venue that entices larger turnouts than a typical school auditorium, students perform for large audiences of their peers and family, as well as other museum visitors.

Sias values experiences that connect students with college campuses. The Museum's Library and Archive is available to Cleveland School of the Arts students for specialized research projects for the Senior Recital and Exhibition requirement, for which "students [write] a research paper about the artist he or she will present, as a part of their repertoire and performance" (2012). The partnership provides multiple opportunities to increase familiarity with educational opportunities in music through a library housed at Cuyahoga Community College.

Dianna Richardson acknowledges the traditional roles of after-school, family-funded ensembles, and private individual instruction in fostering high-level achievements in musical technique critical for admission to college-level music study and many professional opportunities in music. To enrich the string orchestra she directs at the Cleveland School of the Arts, Richardson has built partnerships with her alma mater, the Cleveland Institute of Music (which operates in cooperation with Case Western Reserve University) in Cleveland's University Circle district, and the Baldwin Wallace University Conservatory of Music, located just south of the City of Cleveland in Berea. Richardson hires and guides college music majors eligible for work-study positions to provide regularly scheduled, individual lessons for CSA students during the orchestra class she teaches. Richardson also seeks opportunities for her students to watch top-level performers, such as those affiliated with the Cleveland Orchestra, who present chamber music at the school, at times just feet away from high school students. The partnerships also grow into mentoring relationships with students. Richardson sketches a school day in her classroom:

> I am working with a group, but I've got three private lessons happening in [other] rooms. Then some days... there's a quartet performance [by Cleveland Institute of Music students] right in front of us. And it's amazing. Think about it: that college student is not that far away in age from you.... In a way, you can't be what you don't see.
>
> (2012)

Richardson herself helps connect CMSD strings students with out-of-school enrichment offered by the district and pre-college experiences on community college and university campuses; Richardson's involvement in several music programs of this nature allows her to keep CMSD strings teachers informed about offerings that may support district goals. Richardson leads the district's All-City Orchestra, which pulls students from across the district for after-school and weekend rehearsals, culminating in a public performance; summertime All-City Arts programs take place on the Tri-C campus. Baldwin Wallace University hosts an annual summer String Camp made affordable to secondary level students with financial need, where Richardson is one of several conductors.

Music education in the district aims to build in ensemble experiences and individualized enrichment by linking in-school and after-school programs without adding financial burdens for families. Tony Sias values such partnerships that bring college-affiliated and active musicians into direct contact with students during and after school, which he credits as promoting readiness for college and generating mentoring relationships for career-readiness (Richardson, 2012; Sias, 2012).

Many families of students enrolled in CMSD schools face structural challenges of poverty and inequality (Avery, 1989; Campbell, 2010). The state of Ohio has wrestled for years over inequitable systems for funding local public schools through property taxes; the funding systems were declared unconstitutional by the Ohio Supreme Court in 1997 (Pittner et al., 2010). Within Cuyahoga County, wealthier suburban neighborhoods outside the City of Cleveland are composed of separately governed municipalities, and none shares responsibility for providing schooling, or other public services, to City of Cleveland residents. In contrast to greater concentrations of poverty in the City of Cleveland and several of its "inner ring" suburbs (City of Cleveland, 2011; Piiparinen and Coulten, 2012), a number of "outer ring" suburbs thrive with a growing population and economy.

Within and without the City of Cleveland, racial segregation in law and custom—in addition to social gatekeeping—has erected barriers in neighborhoods, business networks, and political factions that reinforce the significance of race, religious affiliation, ethnicity and nationality, and socioeconomic class, even as labor unions and social justice organizations such as the NAACP have countered and resisted these barriers. School populations reflect these realities.

As of 2013, the Ohio Department of Education draws on data from the 2010 US Census and the US Department of Education to quantify "shared demographic and geographic characteristics" of school districts across the state, and the report designates 10 urban school districts in the greater Cleveland area of Cuyahoga County, including CMSD, with "very high" or "high" rates of student poverty. For research purposes, the report also assigns a percentage of students classified as "minority" populations for each school district. Eight of the 10 "large" or "very large" districts with "high" or "very high" poverty have student populations of more than a quarter designated as minorities; six of the eight districts include a majority population comprising students identified as minorities (59%–100%). Yet 2012 estimates report that 60.9% of Cuyahoga County residents are classified as White, 30.2% as Black, 5.1% as Hispanic or Latino, 2.9% as either Asian or Native Hawaiian or Pacific Islander, and less than .3% as Native American; an additional 1.9% identified with more than one of the categories (US Census, 2010).[23] The typology lists 21 other Cuyahoga County Districts as "suburban" areas with "low poverty" (rates ranging from 10% to 61%) or "very low poverty" (rates ranging from 9% to 32%). Only four school districts in the county show both lower rates of poverty and a majority of students who are identified as minority group populations.

Urban planning policy, combined with effectual internal policing by neighborhood residents, has historically exacerbated geographic features that section Cleveland and its inner-ring suburbs into an "East" and "West" side. Larger Black and Jewish communities were originally established on the East Side than on the West (*Encyclopedia of Cleveland History*). Within these East-West sectors of Cleveland, many neighborhoods are associated with working-class, union-affiliated, and/ or professional residents, whose place of work is—or historically was—a nearby factory, hospital, or a city's public services division (i.e., law enforcement, fire protection, etc.) Strongly influential and distinctive Jewish communities in Cleveland and surrounding suburbs anchored in the East Side have also exerted national influence on Jewish religious and social institutions (*Encyclopedia of Cleveland History*). Catholics have outnumbered Protestants in Cleveland, and many diocesan schools hold high status in the region.

A number of communities in the Cleveland area link identity to the cultural heritage of recent or distant immigrants, their historical neighborhoods, and social organizations that may foster spoken and written languages and the musical arts from areas including Western and Eastern Europe, Palestine, Brazil, East and Southeast Asia, and Pakistan. Waves of migrants from rural southern and Appalachian regions and Puerto Rico also settled in Cleveland, despite an overall population decline in northeastern Ohio since the late twentieth century (Grabowski, n.d.). Traditional neighborhoods are changing as residents of the City of Cleveland and some inner-ring suburbs continue to move to suburban areas (Smith, 2011).

Demographic statistics of the City of Cleveland and its environs reveal another pattern evident in many Northern industrial centers in the Great Lakes region. People who identify as Black or Hispanic disproportionately live in neighborhoods with the highest rates of poverty, and the incomes of families headed by people who identify as Black or Hispanic disproportionately fall below the federal poverty line (City of Cleveland,

2013). Socially constructed race matters at a structural level despite past successes of Civil Rights–era leaders in Cleveland and their continued advocacy. This is the case despite the prominence of African-American and Hispanic leaders in business, politics, philanthropies, and other influential nonprofits.

Ethnomusicological literature often anticipates that understandings of music grow in relation to the social ebb and flow of communities and ways that people identify themselves within them—both in terms of partially shared and more unique experiences, including those arising from specially valued roles or positions of power. A dialogic approach to strategies for applied ethnomusicology that attend to the micro-level of relationships among a specific learning community to support decision-making may navigate social routes and barriers relevant to schooling. Critics may question where the functional starting place in the process may be found; indeed, music lessons alone are unlikely to quickly achieve massive structural social change. Perhaps an effective beginning is to aim to open K–12 students' experiences for exploring their identity and their connections to groups on their own terms.[24]

For music therapist Deforia Lane, effective interventions may activate an individual's pre-existing positive associations or familiarity with musicians, but may also help to expand them. In the Toddler Rock program, in addition to evidence of cognitive growth and expanded sense of belonging, Lane has observed students' personal connections to musicians celebrated in the Rock Hall (2012)

> There are famous people in the Rock Hall who look like them, who have contributed in ways that are honored and are valued. Just think of the impact that such an iconic place can have that reflects people with whom they can identify: to watch the excitement in the eyes of a child when they recognize Michael Jackson's glove and say, "I'm going to wear that some day," or to see the girls admire a sequined gown of the Supremes. Mary Wilson [of the Supremes] was a guest at Toddler Rock, and the children proudly sang and performed, "Stop in the Name of Love," and "taught" her the dance moves. Just think of a 3-year old teaching Mary Wilson how to dance and sing.
>
> I don't think children forget that. Those little moments can be very significant and remembered for years. And when we can learn in an engaging, positive way, in a beautiful environment among accomplished and talented people—what a privilege! We're building skills, teaching concepts, all within the context of music.
>
> (Lane, 2013)

In addition to the interventions gained through word work, improving motor skills and time-on-task that promote preschoolers' readiness for learning in K–12 schools, Lane's observations suggest that many preschoolers may build self-awareness and experience a sense of connection to celebrated historical figures as they learn together through music. Students who come to the Museum for Toddler Rock from Head Start centers around the greater Cleveland area may identify with and/or forge new social connections with one another, the staff, figures in popular music history, and sometimes visiting Inductees. Through developmentally appropriate stories about contributions made to the history of rock and roll music, such as Chuck Berry's popularization of the duck walk or Aretha Franklin's recognition as the "Queen of Soul" (Lane, 2012), the Toddler Rock program teaches Head Start students and teachers a bit more about expert musicians than that represented through mass media.

Ethnomusicological discourse often positions an understanding of music within frames suited to the complexity of social life and ways people weave musical expression throughout it. Building children's readiness for schooling may theoretically occur anywhere, but the partnerships of the Toddler Rock program may foster additional levels of culturally responsive and/ or social-emotional connections in a resource-rich environment through music.

Judith Ryder agrees, drawing on a 30-year scope of ways that students in Cleveland can be drawn into the theatrical music and dramatic characters of opera, if logistical and social barriers are reduced. When directing education programs for the Cleveland Opera, Ryder had to champion the value of dedicating both time and financial resources to allow learners to explore cultural sites in ways that forged relationships with Cleveland's arts community:

> For many years I struggled with funders, who were saying, "You've got to do the opera projects in the schools; the field trips have got to stop." And I said, "Without them, the students don't know about their [larger] community. They have got to know and experience a museum. They have got to experience walking through the doors of a theater to know that they are welcome there. [Without these experiences], how are they going to feel comfortable doing that later in their lives?" That's our job to introduce kids to all aspects of life in a community and being a part of that life [through active participation in the arts].
>
> (Ryder, 2012)

To know creative life, students must experience being part of it (not just visiting it), a point that resonates with Diana Richardson's rationale for intertwining accomplished professional string players into the Cleveland School of the Arts through educational partnerships.

At Cleveland Opera, Ryder offered a scaffolded series of in-school and on-site experiences to help make of many facets of an opera performance more visible for students and teachers by placing students in the opera-making community in Cleveland. Materials guided classroom teachers and students in a preliminary examination of key moments in an opera's plot through reading or acting out scenes, and visiting teaching-artists demonstrated techniques of singing and staging. Next the Cleveland Opera would welcome student audiences to the theater for a full opera performance with curtains held back throughout, simultaneously revealing the backstage movement of characters and props. Some teachers then pursued extended projects, where students created an original opera in their classrooms (Stevenson and Deasy, 2005: 60–61) or performed an abbreviated version of an opera alongside teaching-artists (Ryder 2013). Ryder (2013) offers anecdotal evidence of genuine interest in the form among students a year or more after their intensive participation culminated. Cleveland Opera teaching-artists returned to a high school they had visited in the previous academic year. As they entered the building, students recognized opera staff, a student asked about the opera season, and Ryder reports, "They *all* wanted tickets; they all wanted to come to the theater" (Ryder, 2012).

Empowering students' exploration of identity and relationships in their communities is of great value. Systemic interventions in Cleveland are massive efforts that require large-scale partnerships, including funders. Before children engage in effective experiences for learning through music that draw on cross-institutional resources, individuals have negotiated to set goals, locate the necessary funds, and logistically deliver appropriate programs of quality. Like many sizable cities in the United States, Cleveland benefits from initiatives of large philanthropic foundations that offer substantial financial support to nonprofit and publicly funded agencies that meet residents' central needs, furthering their education, health, and quality of life.[25] Foundations, ideally, offer the potential of collective financial power to spark or sustain structural changes or advocate for collective buy-ins for initiatives that promise growth.

When momentum builds among influential funders, large arts education organizations, and the Cleveland Metropolitan School District, initiatives may shape educational practice broadly. For example, the Cleveland Foundation, Young Audiences of Northeast Ohio (YANEO), and CMSD leadership played key roles in the development of Art Is Education, an initiative supported in part by major federal grants and sustained largely with the support of Cleveland's primary philanthropic foundations. The project fostered collaborative sharing of instructional goals for literacy, best-practices for arts-integrated programs, and critical components in the scope and sequence of literacy instruction in designated K–8 CMSD schools. The Ford Foundation, a major funder, identified Cleveland in 2004 as one of nine model sites for improving urban public education through arts integration programs. The project was assisted by networks of an earlier program, ICARE, first created by the Cleveland Arts Consortium to facilitate artists-in-residence at CMSD schools (YANEO, 2008: 5; YANEO, 2013a).

YANEO project leaders for Art Is Education coordinated dozens of educational managers of programs in varied art forms housed in Cleveland-area cultural organizations; collaborative committees created new resources for arts-infused instruction and mounted an advocacy campaign. The Art Is Education Curriculum Committee, for example, convened in workshops led by a nationally noted consultant in arts integration to collaboratively design arts activities for CMSD classroom teachers in alignment with the district's scope and sequence of third grade literacy instruction. The relatively time-intensive partnership provided a deeper understanding of goals and needs of CMSD educators and their students at the grade level, local colleagues' approaches to arts education, and, in my case, opportunities to enhance Rock Hall programming targeted for K–4 level learners. Examples of resulting best practices for teaching and outcomes for selected Cleveland cultural organizations participating intensively in Art Is Education were discussed before an invited national audience during the Arts Education Partnership's 2007 Fall Forum pre-conference presentations and breakout sessions

(Oehler, 2007). Art is Education Project leaders shared elements of the planning, design, and outcomes of the multiyear project, including substantial challenges that arose with a change in CMSD leadership (Dobrzynski et al., 2007).

Partnerships for learning through music in the Cleveland context both reflect and inform ways in which teachers and other administrators of educational programs and institutions engage children in musical experiences across institutional bounds to explore music within the bounds of formal schooling and beyond them. Ethnomusicologists who prepare to encounter music in the education sector as a site of cultural negotiation seem particularly skilled to navigate the complex institutional, cultural, and pedagogical cross-talk required for effective collaboration that fosters effective, meaningful, and musically differentiated PK–12 learning experiences. In the United States the field affords perspectives of musical sound and messages that may help connect a pluralistic representation of music in daily life to learning in schools. To further pragmatic aims for fostering learning through music in the education sector, it seems useful to examine strategies for partnerships in the Cleveland context through the lens of applied ethnomusicology.

Formulating Contextualized Strategies for Partnerships for Learning Through Music

It seems clear that decision-making about PK–12 music education in Cleveland's education sector navigates complex histories and contemporary positions informed by the social dynamics of race and class. For this reason, useful strategies for applied ethnomusicology in this context overtly maintain awareness of the continual significance of power relations in approaching interaction with musical communities. Samuel Araújo's discussion of his intentionally counterhegemonic, collaborative ethnomusicological projects in a Brazilian context (2008) provides an example of this approach in applied ethnomusicology.

Power Relations and the Decisions of Ethnomusicologists

The significance of power relations is undergirded by ongoing discourse concerning the role of ethnomusicologists in building relationships with, and partially representing, people who have provided access to musical understandings in the domains of "academic" and "applied" work. Mellonee Burnim (1985b), Jeff Titon (1985), and Maureen Loughran (2008) address the topic in terms of negotiating identities and roles during field research, an emphasis represented in the collection *Shadows in the Field* (Barz and Cooley, 1997). Though less frequently the focal point of peer-reviewed publications, ethnomusicological roles that afford access to musical understandings also develop through routine work in the course of ongoing professional networks or collegial relationships—whether or not they are conceptualized as occurring in the midst of the distinctive power dynamic of field work (Burnim, 1985b; Davis, 1992; Feld, 1990; Jackson, 2006, 2012; Loughran, 2008; Shelemay, 1994). When constructing histories of the discipline, ethnomusicologists often turn to narratives that describe those relationships, networks, and institutions in oral histories, personal reflections, personal communications, and institutional archives that document the output of ethnomusicologists at work (Aracena, 2006; Diamond, 2006; Frisbie, 1991, 2006; Jackson, 2006; Nettl, 2006; Seeger, 2006; Stone, 2002; Wade, 2006; Wong, 2006). Strategizing in collaborative work is often routine for applied ethnomusicologists in nonprofit groups serving the education sector, in contrast to infrequent, if not rare, opportunities to undertake formal field research or other academic modes of inquiry. Applied ethnomusicology takes place inside or outside the frame of research in a web of internal work relationships and external institutional partnerships that resonate with Klisala Harrison's notion of "epistemological communities" (2012).

Collaborative strategizing among ethnomusicologists and their partners resonates with several of Harrison's characterizations. In addition to "knowledge-based experts," Harrison specifies partners in applied ethnomusicology also include "people with working and authoritative claims to knowledge." She asserts, "Both have roles to play in articulating the cause-and-effect relationships of complex problems that involve music, and in working toward their solution through action and research" (2012: 522).

Many arts education administrators, in my experience, seem to hold authoritative claims to an expert working knowledge forged through dialogue and written communication, though few consider themselves scholars or ethnomusicologists. They write narratives that discuss the aims and rationale for work with music and present them to specialized local, regional, and national audiences. They disseminate grant proposals and submit program evaluations, publish instructional guides with reference materials, and communicate via websites, blogs, conferences, and printed media. Communications may address governmental, philanthropic, and arts initiatives, as well as the philosophies that infuse them and the financial enterprises that help fund them.

In applying ethnomusicology in the Cleveland context, it seems crucial to seek dialogically constituted "rationales for social actions, understandings of involved practices, and analysis of results" (Harrison, 2012: 522) in order to further goals in schools where authorization to partner for the purposes of learning through music—or any subject—comes with a high stakes commitment. In many cases, a partner must deliver on promises to use school resources, including class time, to significantly advance learners' progress toward achieving measurable standards for learning and/ or test outcomes. Harrison's discussion of epistemic communities as a site of negotiation is applicable:

> Analyses of epistemic communities and epistemologies including ideologies involved in applications of music can serve as bases for analyses of ethics of

applications of music and ethnomusicological research (Whose welfare? How is welfare defined?). The notion also importantly puts a focus on shared approaches around which practice and discourse can cohere. Epistemic communities result in knowledge as well as action.

(2012: 522)

In the web-like network of formal and informal partnerships for arts education, personal dialogue among trusted colleagues may often spread best practices or reveal rationales driving overarching goals for learning through music. Public presentations often highlight a project's clearest successes, reserving the fuller backstory of challenges and related problem-solving for internal discussion. Strategies for applied ethnomusicology that build relationships to prioritize trust among partners, while maintaining the capacity to move independently between "multiple epistemic communities" (Harrison, 2012: 523), may grow resources for problem-solving in partnerships for learning through music.

Partnerships, in my experience in Cleveland, seem grounded in expectations for lateral flows in relationships, even as participating institutions and individuals often hold differing motivations for their decisions or operate from hierarchically distinct positions of influence. When I enter dialogues about a specialized musical style with people who consider it their own, it often has helped open relationships when I reveal understandings of music that value cultural frames for performance, in addition to knowledge of relevant recording history or other discrete facts. Academic specialization in the history of African American music and culture with an ethnomusicological approach centered around music in daily life has routinely empowered me to contribute efforts for learning through music in ways valued by partners. But relationships that build partnerships take place with knowledge attached to whole people, amidst the confluence of our multiple identities, and in light of the significance of how people may perceive us and accord us privilege, or not. Classroom teachers, for instance, often value my background as a public high school history teacher and current college-level instructor; for some, revealing this fact seems to visibly reduce skepticism about my way of knowing teaching.

An ethnomusicologist may "aim toward an equality of representation," as suggested by Maureen Loughran (2008), but strategies must be fashioned for flexible relationships, rather than stability. Strategizing collaboratively along laterally flowing pathways may support applied ethnomusicologists who work in nonprofit or for-profit businesses or under contract. Their actions may be supervised internally through a chain of decision-makers. The intellectual property that results from their work may be owned by the contracting organization, rather than the partnering ethnomusicologist.

In this context, Samuel Araújo's assertion in "From Neutrality to Praxis: The Shifting Politics of Ethnomusicology in the Contemporary World" (2008) seems very useful. "Musical processes and products are permanently mediated by power relations," Araújo writes, "demanding constant action/ reflection" (2008: 28), where the ethnomusicologist and other partners "negotiate from the start the... focuses and goals" as well as the desired results of the partnership and how it will be documented and shared (2008: 15). Araújo demonstrates ways to "build a new knowledge-producing praxis" (2008: 28) through pedagogical approaches and research projects in the vein of Paulo Friere's participatory action, from which "knowledge will hopefully emerge from a truly horizontal, intercultural dialogue and not through top-to-bottom neo-colonial systems of validation" (2008: 14). Strategies to navigate across epistemological communities for purposes of applied ethnomusicology may support the construction of a new praxis for knowledge in the education sector. In the context of the institutional characteristics of most decision-makers described in this article, however, a full embrace of strategies for sustaining horizontal relationships for the collaborative construction of knowledge may not truly upend a "top-to-bottom" system. Nevertheless, the pragmatic reality does not prohibit individuals from choosing an oppositional stance challenging inequitable structures within their respective spheres of influence.

Summary and Suggestions

Opportunities for ethnomusicologists accompany partnerships supporting arts education, which contribute acutely significant resources for public schools, particularly those serving students living in areas of high concentrations of poverty. Ethnomusicologists seem primed to work in settings that require the maintenance of social relationships in cross-institutional collaborative partnership. Also likely is the ethnomusicologist's capacity for operating from a heterophonic appreciation for differing musical ideas and practices that may strongly characterize cultural life of diverse communities.

Strategies for collaborative work and pedagogies that place learners in direct contact with people of varied musical backgrounds may be cultivated in ethnomusicological methods and research, in addition to specialized scholarship and collegial discussions focused on methods of applied ethnomusicology and pedagogical approaches of ethnomusicology. From these sources, frames for strategies in collaborative ethnomusicological work may grow from research-based expectations about how one learns or gains an understanding of music.

Examples of collaborative cross-institutional partnerships for learning through music reveal that the decisions and approaches of those involved—the students, their instructors, audiences, educational institutions, and partnering artists and arts organizations—offer students a range of opportunities. Through music and performance, students may gain increased access to communal, creative expression. Processes of creating ideas through and about music-making may open an opportunity for schoolchildren to voice their ideas, successfully participate or flourish in the classroom and larger community in new ways, or develop a persuasive presentation of their point of view to advocate for an idea shared with others locally and virtually. Students may discuss social concerns, further their imaginative fantasies, and create a space for hoping and dreaming. Experiencing professional musical events as part of a diverse community may foster learners' appreciation for and interest in becoming audiences, pursing musical training, or considering musical careers.

Partnering may offer a vehicle that empowers students (and their teachers) to bridge classroom learning with musical activities and related cultural knowledge that connect ways of knowing valued by students to that gained through traditional classroom sites, approaches, resources, and formally acknowledged centers of knowledge. This, in turn, may contribute to acknowledgment of the value of new or different musical forms from those traditionally featured by established institutions. As institutions embrace learning through music that serves multifaceted needs of children and their caregivers in support of educational strategies set by educational leaders and classroom teachers, they further relationships that go beyond the notion of audience-building and outreach. Partners must negotiate aims with a focus on what learners will know, do, own, discover, make, voice, or give as a result of a musical activity.

The examples from the contexts of cross-institutional partnerships in Cleveland illustrated in this chapter suggest that partners routinely negotiate routes for learning through music that tap into what could be considered multiple epistemological communities around music. Applications of ethnomusicology may be valuable in strategizing horizontal pathways that recognize and respond to music as a result of a dialogic process of understanding music in relation to diverse musical lives and dynamic social experiences—what people expect music to be and what people do with it.

To this end, ethnomusicological strategies will ideally emerge through collaboration in context to achieve effective partnerships for learning through music. Several foundational issues and theoretical assumptions about music, which are debated in academic ethnomusicological discourse, may provide an orienting touchstone from which strategizing may grow, a place of reflection on the theoretical side of praxis. Three notions about music relevant to the contexts of Cleveland represented in this chapter provide an example:

1. **Music-making is a human experience often woven into daily life.** The study of music, systems for its transmission, and life stories of music-makers benefit from exploring music not only as repertoire or aesthetic form, but also in social contexts. These contexts may include memory, individual and group identities, schooling and informal learning, social history, work and its product, and avenues for exerting power.
2. **Learning about music involves negotiating, understanding, and sharing collaborative experiences with people making music—whether as a listener, performer, social analyst, or classroom teacher.** Ways of talking about music, as well as performing and experiencing its meanings, reflect cultural expectations for music within which individual preferences and social affiliations may operate. Part of learning to collaborate with partners may involve learning how to refer to music, call it into being, or prohibit disrespectful associations with an iconic musical form or musician, tradition, or spiritually empowered action. Approaching collaborative work may require acknowledging that many young people experience music as an entertainment commodity that exists in digital media, from

audio downloads and film soundtracks to do-it-yourself YouTube videos; live performance may not be closely related to a centering on the digital reality of sound. When encountering live performances that augment, rather than devalue, such an orientation, students may access a larger frame of reference for defining, analyzing, discussing, or differentiating among musical sounds, actions, and ideas.

3. **Hierarchies informed by social position, cultural aesthetics, and other evaluative frames enter into decisions about what kinds of musical experiences are appropriate for schooling.** Inquiring about historical and cultural frames for how people come to know music may shed light on relevant orientations for learning through music. These may include experiences within and without school buildings and content embedded in music curricula, explored across subject areas, or encountered in project-based learning. Music resources may flow from teacher to students or vice versa; interchanges among peers may take place during formal activities in class, during after-school events, or as a result of informal interactions of students' social life.

As ethnomusicologists partner to apply orientations such as these and negotiate strategies for learning through music in ways effective for the students at hand, continual opportunities to contribute to the growth of musical communities arise, both within and without the education sector as well as academia.

If a strategy of applied ethnomusicology for learning through music must necessarily be collaborative in order to promise effective work in the education sector, where partnering is an essential mechanism for music education, an ethnomusicologist's strategies should function around decision-making in process, as partners form and apply the strategies. If teaching occurs in a constructivist framework, plans for learning through music must keep students' choices and actions at the center, for their engagement with music is the crucible in which theory and practice either successfully spark effective teaching and learning, or fail.

Acknowledgments

The author acknowledges research assistance provided by the Cleveland Public Library, Cuyahoga County Public Library, and Lakeland Community College Library, and the detailed feedback of Deforia Lane, Judith Ryder, and Katherine Harper.

Notes

1. In this chapter, "learning through music" refers to any learning experience engaging in musical sounds, ideas, or actions of music-making or related processes to build understanding or ways of knowing in any area of human experience. The use of the term here does not distinguish between those educational engagements with music for student mastery of educational standards in music or those for other disciplines, such as English

language arts, science, etc., though many make such distinctions with terminology of "learning in the arts"/"learning in music" (studies in the arts discipline) versus "learning through music" (where music serves students' studies of subjects not considered arts disciplines, such as biology). As used in this chapter, the phrase, "learning through music," intentionally references "learning through the arts," a notion encouraged by advocates, such as the Arts Education Partnership, of the value of a "high-quality arts education" for all learners in arts disciplines but also across disciplines, as stated in the mission of the Arts Education Partnership on its website in 2013. The National Endowment for the Arts—a federal agency which established the Arts Education Partnership in 1995 with the US Department of Education in association with organizations of state level education and arts leaders—has also embraced the phrase to conceptualize arts education (2002).

2. Following phenomenological and performance-centered approaches (Stone, 1988; Berger, 1999; Monson, 1996; Small, 1998; Blacking, [1969] 1995; Stokes, 1997), I locate "music" in experiences that emerge in the process of performance and shape the construction of musical meaning, including contexts where people engage with musical ideas, actions, sounds beyond the bounds of a live performance event (Oehler, 2001).

3. See Geneva Gay's *Culturally Responsive Teaching: Theory, Research, and Practice* (2010) as an example of multicultural educational praxis created in dialogue with dynamic, group preferences for communication, styles of social interaction, and other valued qualities associated with "ethnicity and culture" (p. 11) for the purposes of forwarding pedagogical efforts that may assist in closing achievement gaps for marginalized school populations in the United States (pp. xvii–21).

4. See Oehler and Hanley (2009) on our approaches to popular music pedagogy at the Rock and Roll Hall of Fame and Museum.

5. The appeal of constructivist approaches and the rise of studies of cognition may accompany interest in applications of research on the brain to pedagogy for arts integration (Sousa, 2011; Kennedy Center, 2013a) and educators' embrace of work that affirms students' differentiated routes of learning and expression, as in Howard Gardener's *Frames of Mind: The Theory of Multiple Intelligences* (2011), first published in the late 1980s.

6. I also interviewed Fernando Jones, the Chicago-based blues musician and educator, to gain the perspective of a teaching-artist, who is asked to provide a single, brief learning experience without the opportunity for sustained interactions. Jones, for example, has delivered one-hour workshops for teachers at the Rock and Roll Hall of Fame and Museum in the mid-2000s. Jones directs The Blues Kids Foundation, instructs the Blues Ensemble course at Columbia College Chicago, and was a voluntary participation in my ethnographic field research of the Chicago blues scenes in the late 1990s (Oehler, 2001).

7. For statistical approaches relevant to federal measurement of "educational progress" in the United States, see National Center for Education Statistics (2012).

8. A unit of study is a series of related lessons with activities designed for students' mastery of a central concept or deeper understanding of a topic.

9. Although music is defined as a core subject by the federal No Child Left Behind Act (2002), classroom music teachers and their supervisors in the US increasingly have incorporated advocacy and community engagement in fashioning and sustaining effective curriculum and the requisite resources it. See Arts for All (2013). A focus on student achievement in literacy and mathematics means state and federal level agencies monitor test scores and other markers related to these areas of study, but student achievements in music classes

are not similarly prioritized; school investments in staffing and resources for arts subjects consequently may fall in the priorities of a district.
10. Music education includes all students, including hearing impaired and deaf learners. See Darrow (1989) and Hash (2001).
11. The problematic modifiers of "traditional," "popular," and "classical" reflect common conceptualizations of broad musical styles and communities, which bear hegemonic weight (Kassabian, 1999). Vernacular conversation frequently includes the three terms, nonetheless, in referencing music in daily life in the United States and arts education. "Highbrow" is borrowed from Lawrence Levine's usage for music embraced in or ascribed to elite cultural hierarchy (1988), and I extend the term to describe music routinely framed as "the fine arts."
12. For example, consider the expansion of more comprehensive texts and handbooks first published between 1990 and 2010, such as the Garland series of encyclopedias (Garland *Encyclopedia of World Music*, first volume published 2001) and undergraduate level textbooks on music in global perspective (Campbell, 1991; Shelemay, 2006; Titon, 1992b; Wade, 2009) or in the United States (Alviso, 2011; Lornell and Rasmussen, 1997), and on ethnomusicological approaches to the history of African-American music and culture (Burnim and Maultsby, 2006), among other areas.
13. Examples include the Chicago Public Library's Blues Archive, the Rock and Roll Hall of Fame and Museum Library and Archives at Tri-C, and Indiana University's Archives of Traditional Music and Culture and Archives of African American Music and Culture, among others. Each institution reflects distinctive missions for providing access to the public at large and scholarly researchers.
14. Discourse regarding the accurate representation of African-American cultural contributions in the history of rock and roll, as well as what constitutes "rock and roll," remains contested by historians, music industry insiders, and fans (Associated Press, 2014; Maultsby, 2012; Onkey, 2010). Nonetheless, arts educators and other large museums and cultural organizations have approached the Rock and Roll Hall of Fame and Museum Education staff as a resource for representing a racially diverse story about the history of twentieth-century American culture.
15. The history of jazz, gospel music, and related styles in the greater Cleveland area includes community performances as well as scenes of influential artists, ensembles, broadcasts, festivals or special events, and recordings over decades (Mosbrook, 2003; Williams, 2006).
16. See Myers's (2003) discussion of a similar concept applied at Georgia State University through its Center for Educational Partnerships in Music. University students in music education and music performance, as well as members of the Atlanta Symphony Orchestra who work as teaching-artists, partner with certified music teachers in public schools.
17. The federal Head Start Program of the US Department of Health and Human Services "promotes the school readiness of children [birth to five years of age] from low-income families" by enhancing learning environments to grow language, literacy, and physical, social, and emotional development, while supporting parents' involvement, according to websites of the Office of Head Start (2014) and the Council for Economic Opportunities in Greater Cleveland (2014).
18. The Rock Hall's Voice Your Choice project allows any teacher to submit students' work that persuasively argues for the induction of artists who are not currently in the Rock and Roll Hall of Fame. Selected projects are displayed on the Museum's website (Onkey, 2012).

19. District finances had forced cuts in staffing and programming following negotiations with local leaders of teachers' unions. By May 2012, Patrick O'Donnell (2012b) reported that the cuts had shortened the length of the school day and eliminated hundreds of teaching positions, and reduced planning time, professional development, and employee benefits including pay and healthcare. Eric Gordon, CEO of the Cleveland Metropolitan School District, clarified the urgency of gaining funds to restore this loss in a June 1 presentation to leaders in the arts sponsored by the Community Partnership for Arts and Culture (Gordon, 2012).
20. Relevant to Araújo's position is also education foundations literature, which applies critical pedagogy in the vein of Paulo Freire to critique hegemonic dominance in schooling, such as Antonio Darder's *Culture and Power in the Classroom* (2012).
21. See discussions of the significance of social positions of ethnomusicologists' relationships (Araújo, 2008; Loughran, 2008: 58) and the teaching of music by teaching-artist Jamie Topper (2011) and ethnomusicologist Cheryl Keyes (2009).
22. "Position" refers to "power relationships negotiated by persons in reference to particular social contexts, identities, and purposes" that, in this context, acknowledge the social construction of race, gender, and culture (Oehler, 2001: xi). I discuss my identity as a white, middle-class woman in relation to ethnographic field research in my dissertation (Oehler, 2001: xv–xxv, 284–287, 310–317). On the significance of scholars' racial, gendered, and other partially shared identities to ethnographic and cultural research in the United States, see also bell hooks (2004), Mellonee Burnim (1985b), and Charles Gallagher (2004).
23. The typology designates minorities based on the percentages of "African American, Hispanic, Native American, Pacific Islander, or multiracial students" in a district, according to the Ohio Department of Education's 2013 School District Typology Methodology and Descriptors available on its website (2013).
24. On the significance of identity development in pedagogy that confronts histories marked by mass violence and/ or struggles for social justice in pluralistic societies see Gay (2010), Derman-Sparks and Ramsey (2011), Cole and Barsalou (2006), and Sears (2008).
25. The Cleveland Foundation, established in 1914, is the nation's oldest community foundation and the nation's third largest as of January 2010, according to the *Encyclopedia of Cleveland History*.

References

Alaprantis, Dionissi, Kyle Fee, and Nelson Oliver. (2013). "The Concentration of Poverty within Metropolitan Areas—Economic Commentary." *Federal Reserve Bank of Cleveland*. http://www.clevelandfed.org/research/commentary/2013/2013-01.cfm (accessed July 15, 2013).

Alexander, Delia, interviewer. (2003). "A Conversation with Portia K. Maultsby." *Folklore Forum*. Special Issue on Applied Ethnomusicology guest edited by John Fenn 34 (1–2): 9–15.

Alviso, Ric. (2011). *Multicultural Music in America: An Introduction to Our Musical Heritage*. Dubuque, IA: Kendall Hunt Publishing.

Anderson, David I., videographer. (2012). "Cleveland School Levy Passes Issue 107—A 15 Mil School Levy." *The Plain Dealer*, posted November 7. http://www.cleveland.com/education/index.ssf/2012/11/cleveland_passes_issue_107_a_1.html (accessed August 5, 2013).

Aracena, Beth K. (2006). "Latin American Music in the History of SEM." *Ethnomusicology*. Special 50th Anniversary Commemorative Issue, co-guest edited by Ellen Koskoff and R. Anderson Sutton, 50(2): 314–323.

Araújo, Samuel. (2006). "Conflict and Violence as Theoretical Tools in Present-Day Ethnomusicology: Notes on a Dialogic Ethnography of Sound Practices in Rio de Janero." *Ethnomusicology*. Special 50th Anniversary Commemorative Issue co-guest edited by Ellen Koskoff and R. Anderson Sutton, 50(2): 287–313.

Araújo, Samuel. (2008). "From Neutrality to Praxis: The Shifting Politics of Ethnomusicology in the Contemporary World." *Musicological Annual* 44(1): 13–30.

Arts for All. (2013). "For Schools & Classrooms." *Arts for All: Empowering L.A. County Schools to Prepare Students for the Workforce of Tomorrow*. http://www.lacountyartsforall.org/for-schools-classrooms/ (accessed August 5, 2013).

Associated Press. (2014). "Chubby Checker Upset Rock and Roll Hall of Fame Has Left Him Twisting in the Wind." June 6. *Cleveland.com*. http://www.cleveland.com/music/index.ssf/2014/06/chubby_checker_upset_rock_and.html (accessed July 11, 2014).

Avery, Robert B. (1989). "Making Judgments about Mortgage Lending Patterns." Economic Commentary (newsletter). Cleveland, OH: Federal Reserve Bank of Cleveland. http://www.clevelandfed.org/research/commentary/1989/econcomm19891215.pdf?WT.oss=cleveland%20history%20of%20red%20lining&WT.oss_r=81 (accessed July 15, 2013).

Bakan, Michael B., et al. (2008). "Saying Something Else: Improvisation and Music-Play Facilitation in a Medical Ethnomusicology Program for Children on the Autism Spectrum." *College Music Symposium* 48: 1–30.

Barz, Gregory F., and Timothy J. Cooley, eds. (1997). *Shadows in the Field: New Perspectives for Fieldwork in Ethnomusicology*. New York: Oxford University Press.

Berger, Harris M. (1999). *Metal, Rock, and Jazz: Perception and the Phenomenology of Musical Experience*. Hanover, NH: Wesleyan University Press.

Blacking, John. (1995 [1967]). *Venda Children's Songs: A Study in Ethnomusicological Analysis*. Chicago: University of Chicago.

Blacking, John. (1995 [1969]). "Expressing Human Experience Through Music. Music, Culture, and Experience." In *Music, Culture, and Experience: Selected Papers of John Blacking*, edited and with an introduction by Reginald Byron, pp. 31–53. Chicago: The University of Chicago Press.

Blum, Stephen. (2010). "Musical Enactment of Attitudes toward Conflict in the United States." In *Music and Conflict*, edited by John Morgan O'Connell and Salwa El-Shawan Castelo-Branco, pp. 232–242. Champaign: University of Illinois Press.

Burnim, Mellonee V. (1985a). "The Black Gospel Music Tradition: A Complex of Ideology, Aesthetic and Behavior." In *More Than Dancing: Essays on Afro-American Music and Musicians*, edited by Irene V. Jackson, pp. 146–167. Contributions in Afro-American and African Studies, No. 83. Westport, CT: Greenwood Press.

Burnim, Mellonee V. (1985b). "Culture Bearer and Tradition Bearer: An Ethnomusicologist's Research on Gospel Music." *Ethnomusicology* 29(3): 432–446.

Burnim, Mellonee V., and Portia K. Maultsby, eds. (2006). *African American Music: An Introduction*. New York: Routledge.

Burton, Bryan, and Peter Dunbar-Hall. (2002). "Teaching About and Through Native American Musics: An Excursion into the Cultural Politics of Music Education." *Research Studies in Music Education* 19: 56–64.

Campbell, Doug. (2010). "The Role of Social Effects in Subprime Lending (CR Report)." Federal Reserve Bank of Cleveland. http://www.clevelandfed.org/community_development/publications/crreport/2010_fall/index.cfm (accessed July 12, 2013).

Campbell, Patricia Shehan. (1991). *Lessons from the World: A Cross-Cultural Guide to Music Teaching and Learning.* New York: Schirmer Books.

Campbell, Patricia Shehan. (1996). *Music in Cultural Context: Eight Views on World Music Education.* Reston, VA: MENC (Music Educators National Conference).

Campbell, Patricia Shehan. (1998). *Songs in Their Heads: Music and Its Meaning in Children's Lives.* New York: Oxford University Press.

Campbell, Patricia Shehan, Carol Scott-Kassner, and Kirt Kassner. (2006). *Music in Childhood: From Preschool through Elementary Grades* (3rd ed.). Belmont, CA: Thomson Schirmer.

Campbell, Patricia Shehan, with contributions from Steven M. Demorest and Steven J. Morrison. (2008). *Musician and Teacher: An Orientation to Music Education.* New York: W. W. Norton.

Cavicchi, Daniel. (1998). *Tramps Like Us: Music and Meaning among Springsteen Fans.* New York: Oxford University Press.

City of Cleveland. (2011). "City Planning Commission—Cleveland Neighborhood Fact Sheets." City of Cleveland. http://planning.city.cleveland.oh.us/census/factsheets/cpc.html (accessed July 15, 2013).

Clements, Ann C., ed. (2010). *Alternative Approaches in Music Education: Case Studies from the Field.* Lanfield, MD: MENC—The National Association for Music Education and Rowman and Littlefield Education.

Cleveland Arts Education Consortium. (2013). "About Us—Cleveland Arts Education Consortium." *College of Liberal Arts and Social Sciences, Cleveland State University.* http://www.csuohio.edu/class/caec/aboutus.html (accessed August 14, 2013).

"The Cleveland Foundation." (n.d.). *The Encyclopedia of Cleveland History.* Last updated January 2010. Case Western Reserve University and the Western Reserve Historical Society. http://ech.case.edu/cgi/article.pl?id=CF (accessed July 7, 2013).

Cleveland Metropolitan School District. (2010). "Academic Transformation Plan: A Strategic Development Initiative." Last updated February 22. *Cleveland Metropolitan School District.* http://cmsdnet.net/AboutCMSD/~/media/Files/About/Transformation/Plan/CMSD_TransformationRevised2-23-10.ashx (accessed August 4, 2013).

Cleveland Metropolitan School District, Department of Arts Education. (2008). *Strategic Plan, 2008–2013.* Booklet.

"The Cleveland Music School Settlement." (n.d.) *The Encyclopedia of Cleveland History.* Case Western Reserve University and the Western Reserve Historical Society. http://ech.case.edu/cgi/article.pl?id=CMSS (accessed June 27, 2013).

Cole, Elizabeth A., and Judy Barsalou. (2006). "Unite or Divide? The Challenges of Teaching History in Societies Emerging from Violent Conflict." Special Report, June 1. United States Institute of Peace.

The College Board, National Task Force on Arts and Education. (2009). *Arts at the Core: Recommendations for Advancing the State of Arts Education in the 21st Century.* http://advocacy.collegeboard.org/preparation-access/arts-core (accessed via *The College Board Advocacy & Policy Center*, December 22, 2013).

Council for Economic Opportunities in Greater Cleveland. "Head Start Services." *CEOGC: Council for Economic Opportunities in Greater Cleveland.* http://www.ceogc.org/programs/head-start-services (accessed June 2, 2014).

Crafts, Susan D., Daniel Cavicchi, and Charles Keil. (1993). *My Music: Explorations of Music in Daily Life*. Middletown, CT: Wesleyan University Press.

Darrow, Alice-Ann. (2007 [1989]). "Music and the Hearing Impaired: A Review of Research with Implications for Music Educators." *Update: Applications of Research in Music Education* 7(2):10–12. doi: 10.1177/875512338900700205.

Davis, Martha Ellen. (1992). "Careers, 'Alternative Careers', and the Unity between Theory and Practice in Ethnomusicology." *Ethnomusicology*. Special Issue: Music and the Public Interest 36(3): 361–387.

Deasy, Richard J., ed. (2002). *Critical Links: Learning in the Arts and Student Academic and Social Development*. Washington, DC: Arts Education Partnership.

Del Negro, Giovanna P., and Harris M. Berger. (2004). "New Directions in the Study of Everyday Life: Expressive Culture and the Interpretation of Practice." In *Identity and Everyday Life: Essays in the Study of Folklore, Music, and Popular Culture*, pp. 3–22. Middletown, CT: Wesleyan University Press.

Derman-Sparks, Louise, and Patricia G. Ramsey. (2011). *What if All the Kids Are White?: Anti-Bias Multicultural Education with Young Children and Families*. New York: Teachers College Press.

Diamond, Beverley. (2006). "Canadian Reflections on Palindromes, Inversions, and Other Challenges to Ethnomusicology's Coherence." *Ethnomusicology*. Special 50th Anniversary Commemorative Issue co-guest edited by Ellen Koskoff and R. Anderson Sutton, 50(2): 324–336.

Dobrzynski, Marsha, et al. (2007). "Cleveland Integrated Arts Collaborative." Arts Integration: Theory, Practice, and Lessons Learned. Fall Forum of the Arts Education Partnership. Cleveland, Ohio. September 27.

Dunbar-Hall, Peter. (2005). "Colliding Perspectives? Music Curriculum as Cultural Studies." *Music Educators Journal* 91(4): 33–37.

Emerging Arts Leaders Symposium. (2012). "Arts Advocacy Receives Research Gift," blog post by Jennie Sue, April 4. *American University Arts Management Program*. http://emergingartsleaders.wordpress.com/2012/04/04/arts-advocacy-receives-research-gift/ (accessed August 4, 2013).

Exner, Rich. (2010). "Cleveland's Poverty Is Second among Big Cities; Gap Between Rich and Poor Grows Nationally." *The Plain Dealer*, September 28. http://www.cleveland.com/data-central/index.ssf/2010/09/clevelands_poverty_is_second_a.html (accessed July 15, 2013).

Feld, Steven. (1990). *Sound and Sentiment: Birds, Weeping, Poetics, and Song in Kaluli Expression* (2nd ed.). Philadelphia: University of Pennsylvania Press.

Frisbie, Charlotte J. (1991). "Women and the Society for Ethnomusicology: Roles and Contributions from Formulation through Incorporation." In *Comparative Musicology and Anthropology of Music: Essays on the History of Ethnomusicology*, edited by Bruno Nettl and Philip V. Bohlman, pp. 244–265. Chicago: University of Chicago Press.

Frisbie, Charlotte J. (2006). "A View of Ethnomusicology from the 1960s." *Ethnomusicology*. Special 50th Anniversary Commemorative Issue co-guest edited by Ellen Koskoff and R. Anderson Sutton, 50(2): 204–213.

Fujita, Fumiko. (2006). "Musicality in Early Childhood: A Case from Japan." *The Musical Human: Rethinking John Blacking's Ethnomusicology in the Twenty-First Century* edited by Suzel Ana Reily, pp. 87–106. Burlington, VT: Ashgate Publishing.

Gallagher, Charles A. (2004). "White Like Me? Methods, Meaning, and Manipulation in the Field of White Studies." *Approaches to Qualitative Research: A Reader on Theory and Practice,* edited by Sharlene Nagy Hesse-Biber and Patricia Leavy, pp. 203–223. New York: Oxford University Press.

Gault, Brent. (2008). Review of *Musician and Teacher: An Orientation to Music Education* by Patricia Shehan Campbell with Steven M. Demorest and Steven J. Morrison. *Philosophy of Music Education Review* 16(2): 213–216.

Gay, Geneva. (2010). *Culturally Responsive Teaching: Theory, Research, and Practice* (2nd ed.). New York: Teachers College Press.

Gordon, Eric, presenter. (2012). Arts and Education Roundtable. Community Partnership for Arts and Culture. Cudell Recreation Center, Cleveland, Ohio. June 1.

Grabowski, John J. (n.d.). "Immigrants and Migrants." *The Encyclopedia of Cleveland History*. Case Western Reserve University and the Western Reserve Historical Society. http://ech.case.edu/cgi/article.pl?id=IAM (accessed July 7, 2013).

Green, Lucy. (2001). *How Popular Musicians Learn: A Way Ahead for Music Education*. Burlington, VT: Ashgate.

Green, Lucy. (2008). *Music, Informal Learning and the School: A New Classroom Pedagogy*. Burlington, VT: Ashgate.

Harris, Kelly A. (2006). "Young Poets' Society: Playhouse Square Program Cultivates Teens' Voices." *Cleveland Magazine*, June. http://www.clevelandmagazine.com/ME2/dirmod.asp?sid=E73ABD6180B44874871A91F6BA5C249C&nm=Arts+%26+Entertainemnt&type=Publishing&mod=Publications%3A%3AArticle&mid=1578600D80804596A22259366932-1019&tier=4&id=3D01CFABEF994C8080CB2CBB75441B16 (accessed July 15, 2013).

Harrison, Klisala. (2012). "Epistemologies of Applied Ethnomusicology." *Ethnomusicology* 56(3): 505–529.

Hash, Philip M. (2001). "Teaching Instrumental Music to Deaf and Hard of Hearing Students." *Research and Issues in Music Education* 1(1). http://www.stthomas.edu/rimeonline/vol1/hash.htm (accessed July 12, 2013).

Hawes, Bess Lomax. (1992). "Practice Makes Perfect: Lessons in Active Ethnomusicology." *Ethnomusicology*. Special Issue: Music and the Public Interest, 36(3): 337–343.

hooks, bell. (2004). "Culture to Culture: Ethnography and Cultural Studies as Critical Intervention." *Approaches to Qualitative Research: A Reader on Theory and Practice*, edited by Sharlene Nagy Hesse-Biber and Patricia Leavy, pp. 149–158. New York: Oxford University Press.

Iyengar, Sunil. (2012). "Taking Note: Reviewing the Official Numbers on Arts Education." *Art Works: The Official Blog of the National Endowment for the Arts*, April 2. http://artworks.arts.gov/?p=12535 (accessed August 4, 2013).

Jackson, Travis A. (2006). "Rearticulating Ethnomusicology: Privilege, Ambivalence, and Twelve Years in SEM." *Ethnomusicology*. Special 50th Anniversary Commemorative Issue co-guest edited by Ellen Koskoff and R. Anderson Sutton, 50(2): 280–286.

Jackson, Travis A. (2012). *Blowin' the Blues Away: Performance and Meaning on the New York Jazz Scene*. Berkeley: University of California Press.

Jorgensen, Estelle R. (2002). "The Aims of Music Education: A Preliminary Excursion." *Journal of Aesthetic Education* 36(1): 31–49.

"Karamu House." (n.d.). *The Encyclopedia of Cleveland History*. Case Western Reserve University and the Western Reserve Historical Society. http://ech.case.edu/cgi/article.pl?id=KH (accessed June 27, 2013).

Kahlenberg, Richard D. (2013). "From All Walks of Life: New Hope for School Integration." Reprinted from *American Educator* Winter: 2–14, 40. http://www.aft.org/periodical/american-educator/winter-2012-2013/all-walks-life (accessed February 8, 2015).

Kassabian, Anahid. (1999). "Popular." In *Key Terms in Popular Music and Culture*, edited by Bruce Horner and Thomas Swiss, pp. 13–23. Maiden, MA: Wiley-Blackwell.

Kennedy Center for the Performing Arts. (2013a). "What's Going on... NOW Youth Showcase—Past Performances, May 2 and May 3, 2013." *Kennedy Center for the Performing Arts*. http://www.kennedy-center.org/explorer/artists/?entity_id=85637&source_type=B (accessed August 15, 2013).

Kennedy Center for the Performing Arts. (2013b). "Why Arts Integration? Relevant Literature." *ArtsEdge*. http://artsedge.kennedy-center.org/educators/how-to/arts-integration-beta/why-arts-integration-beta/why-relevant-literature-beta.aspx#the-case (accessed July 12, 2013).

Kennedy, Mary M., et al. (1986). "Poverty, Achievement and the Distribution of Compensatory Education Services: An Interim Report from the National Assessment of Chapter 1." Washington, DC: Office of Educational Research and Improvement.

Keyes, Cheryl L. (2009). "Sound, Voice, and Spirit: Teaching in the Black Music Vernacular." *Black Music Research Journal* 29(1): 11–24.

Kingsbury, Henry. (1988). *Music, Talent, and Performance: A Conservatory Cultural System*. Philadelphia: Temple University Press.

Koen, Benjamin D., Michael B. Bakan, Fred Kobylarz, Lindee Morgan, Rachel Goff, Sally Kahn, and Megan Bakan. (2008). "Personhood Consciousness: A Child-Ability-Centered Approach to Sociomusical Healing and Autism Spectrum Disorders." In *The Oxford Handbook of Medical Ethnomusicology*, edited by Benjamin D. Koen et al., pp. 461–481. New York: Oxford University Press.

Lane, Deforia. (2012). Interview with the author. Cleveland, Ohio. October 18.

Lane, Deforia. (2013). Personal communication with the author. September 7.

Levine, Lawrence W. (1998). *Highbrow/Lowbrow: The Emergence of Cultural Hierarchy in the United States*. Cambridge, MA: Harvard University Press.

Lornell, Kip, and Anne Rasmussen, eds. (1997). *Musics of Multicultural America: A Study of Twelve Musical Communities*. New York: Schirmer Books.

Loughran, Maureen. (2008). "'But what if they call the police?' Applied Ethnomusicology and Urban Activism in the United States." *Musicological Annual* 44(1): 51–67.

Maultsby, Portia K., advisor. (1988). *That Rhythm & Those Blues*, produced and directed by George T. Nierenburg. Broadcast in *The American Experience* series by PBS. Alexandria, VA: PBS Video.

Maultsby, Portia K., with Lillian Rae Dunlap, music consultants. (1990). "The Time Has Come (1964–66), Power! (1966–68), Ain't Gonna Shuffle No More (1964–72), A Nation of Law? (1968–71), and Back to the Movement (1979–83)." In *Eyes on the Prize II: America at the Racial Crossroads*, by Henry Hampton, Judith Vecchione, Steve Fayer, Orlando Bagwell, Callie Crossley, James A. DeVinney, Madison Davis Lacy, et al. [Alexandria, Va.]: PBS Video.

Maultsby, Portia K. (2012). "'Everybody Wanna Sing My Blues... Nobody Wanna Live My Blues': Deconstructing Narratives of Race, Culture and Power in African American Music Scholarship." Charles Seeger Lecture, Annual Meeting of the Society for Ethnomusicology, New Orleans, Louisiana. November 2. Archived video recording. http://www.ethnomusicology.org/?page=Conf_Video (accessed November 2012).

Monson, Ingrid. (1996). *Saying Something: Jazz Improvisation and Interaction*. Chicago: The University of Chicago Press.

Mosbrook, Joe. 2003. *Cleveland Jazz History*. Cleveland, OH: Northeast Ohio Jazz Society.

Music-in-Education National Consortium (MiENC). (2013). "Initiatives and Information." *MiENC*. http://music-in-education.org/about/ (accessed August 4, 2013).

Myers, David E. (2003). "Quest for Excellence: The Transforming Role of University-Community Collaboration in Music Teaching and Learning." *Arts Education Policy Review* 105(1): 5–12.

National Association for Music Education. (2007). "Why Music Education?" *National Association for Music Education.* http://musiced.nafme.org/resources/why-music-education-2007/ (accessed August 4, 2013).

National Center for Education Statistics. (2012). *Improving the Measurement of Socioeconomic Status for the National Assessment of Education Progress: A Theoretical Foundation.* US Department of Education. http://nces.ed.gov/nationsreportcard/pdf/researchcenter/Socioeconomic_Factors.pdf (accessed July 13, 2013).

National Endowment for the Arts. (2002). *Learning Through the Arts: A Guide to the National Endowment for the Arts and Arts Education.* Washington, DC: NEA.

Nelson, Lisa. (2008). "Case Study: Cleveland, Ohio: The Central Neighborhood." In *The Enduring Challenge of Concentrated Poverty in America: Case Studies from Communities Across the U.S.*, edited by David Erickson, Carolina Reid, Lisa Nelson, Anne O'Shaughnessy, and Alan Berube. Federal Reserve System and the Brookings Institution. Richmond, Virginia: Federal Reserve Bank of Richmond. http://www.frbsf.org/community-development/files/cp_fullreport.pdf (accessed February 8, 2015).

Nettl, Bruno. (1995). *Heartland Excursions: Ethnomusicological Reflection on Schools of Music.* Urbana: University of Illinois Press.

Nettl, Bruno. (2006). "We're on the Map: Reflections on SEM in 1955 and 2005." *Ethnomusicology.* Special 50th Anniversary Commemorative Issue co-guest edited by Ellen Koskoff and R. Anderson Sutton, 50(2): 179–189.

O'Donnell, Patrick. (2012a). "Cleveland School Levy Sails to Apparent Victory." *The Plain Dealer*, November 7. http://www.cleveland.com/open/index.ssf/2012/11/cleveland_school_levy_sails_to.html (accessed August 5, 2013).

O'Donnell, Patrick. (2012b). "Layoffs, Other Cuts, Extra Money Reduce Cleveland Schools' Deficit." *The Plain Dealer*, May 11. http://www.cleveland.com/metro/index.ssf/2012/05/layoffs_other_cuts_extra_money.html. (accessed August 17, 2012).

Oehler, Susan E. (2001). "Aesthetics and Meaning in Professional Blues Performance: An Ethnographic Examination of an African American Music in Intercultural Context." Doctoral dissertation. Indiana University-Bloomington.

Oehler, Susan E., presenter. (2007). Preconference. Arts Education Partnership Fall Forum: Arts Integration—Theory, Practice, and Lessons Learned? Cleveland, Ohio. September 26.

Oehler, Susan E., and Jason Hanley. (2009). "Perspectives of Popular Music Pedagogy in Practice." *Journal of Popular Music Studies.* Special Issue on Popular Music Pedagogy co-guest edited by Jason Hanley and Susan Oehler, 21(1): 2–19.

Ohio Arts Council and the Ohio Department of Education. (2007). "National Forum Held in Cleveland." *Links and Threads: An Arts Learning Resource* October. http://linksandthreads.com/aep-clevelandpres.html (accessed June 2, 2012).

Ohio Department of Education. (2013). "Typology of Ohio School Districts." *Ohio Department of Education.* http://education.ohio.gov/Topics/Data/Frequently-Requested-Data/Typology-of-Ohio-School-Districts (accessed July 12, 2013).

Onkey, Lauren. (2012). Interview with the author. Cleveland, Ohio. November 30.

Onkey, Lauren. (2010). A Response to "Why No Yes in the Rock Hall." Blog post, January 13. Rock and Roll Hall of Fame and Museum website. http://rockhall.com/blog/post/5442_a-response-to-why-no-yes-in-t/ (accessed July 11, 2014).

Parsad, B., and M. Spiegelman. (2012). *Arts Education in Public Elementary and Secondary Schools: 1999-2000 and 2009-10* (NCES 2012-014). Washington, DC: National Center for Education Statistics, Institute of Education Sciences, US Department of Education.

Pettan, Svanibor. (2008). "Applied Ethnomusicology and Empowerment Strategies: Views from across the Atlantic." *Musicological Annual* 44(1): 85-99.

Piiparinen, Richey, and Claudia Coulten. (2012). "The Changing Face of Poverty in Northeast Ohio." Research Summary in *Briefly Stated*, January (12-01). *The Center on Urban Poverty and Development, Mandel School of Applied Social Sciences, Case Western Reserve University.* http://blog.case.edu/msass/2012/01/23/Briefly%20Stated%20%2012-01%20-%20Changing%20Face%20of%20Poverty%20Jan2012.pdf (accessed July 15, 2013).

Pittner, Nicholas A., Melissa M. Carleton, and Cassandra Casto. (2010). "School Funding in Ohio: From DeRolph to the Evidence-Based Model (EBM) and Beyond." *Journal of Education Finance* 36(2): 111-142.

Poverty and Race Research Action Council. (n.d.). "Annotated Bibliography: The Impact of School-Based Poverty Concentration on Academic Achievement and Student Outcomes." http://www.prrac.org (accessed July 11, 2014).

Protopapa, Santina. (2012). Interview with the author. Cleveland, Ohio. November 9.

Reagon, Bernice Johnson, exhibition organizer. (1996-2003). *Wade in the Water: African American Sacred Music Traditions*. Washington, DC: Smithsonian Institution Traveling Exhibition Service.

Reagon, Bernice Johnson, Tonya Bolden, Lisa Pertillar-Brevard, and Judi Moore Latta, writers. (1994). *Wade in the Water: African American Sacred Music Traditions*, educators guide, edited by Michaelle Scanlon. Based on the NPR radio series, *Wade in the Water: African American Sacred Music Traditions* by Bernice Johnson Reagon, Curator, Smithsonian Institution. Washington, DC: National Public Radio.

Richardson, Dianna. (2012). Interview with the author. Cleveland, Ohio. November 16.

Richerme, Lauren Kapalka, Scott C. Shuler, Marcia McCaffrey, with Debora Hansen and Lynn Tuttle. (2012). *Roles of Certified Arts Educators, Certified Non-Arts Educators, & Providers of Supplemental Arts Instruction*. SAEDAE Arts Education White Paper, June 22. Dover, DE: The State Education Agency Directors of Arts Education (SEADAE). http://www.seadae.org/.

Rock and Roll Hall of Fame and Museum. (2013). "Toddler Rock." *Rock and Roll Hall of Fame and Museum*. http://rockhall.com/events/toddler-rock/ (accessed August 15, 2013).

Ryder, Judith. (2012). Interview with the author. Shaker Heights, Ohio. November 2.

Ryder, Judith. (2013). Personal communication with the author. September 4.

Schmidt, Margaret, ed. (2009). *Collaborative Action for Change: Selected Proceedings from the 2007 Symposium on Music Teacher Education*. Lanham, MD: MENC—The National Association for Music Education and Rowman & Littlefield Education.

Schweitzer, Mark E. (2007). "A Closer Look at Cleveland's Latest Poverty Ranking—Economic Commentary." *Federal Reserve Bank of Cleveland*. http://www.clevelandfed.org/research/commentary/2007/021507.cfm (accessed July 15, 2013).

Sears, Alan. (2008). Review of *Teaching the Violent Past: History Education and Reconciliation*, edited by Elizabeth A. Cole. *British Journal of Educational Studies* 56(4): 488-490. *Academic Search Premier*, EBSCO*host* (accessed July 12, 2014).

Seeger, Anthony. (1992). "Ethnomusicology and Music Law." *Ethnomusicology*, Special Issue: Music and the Public Interest, 36(3): 345-359.

Seeger, Anthony. (1996). Foreword to *Multicultural Perspectives in Music Education* (2nd ed. with compact disc), edited by William Anderson and Patricia Shehan Campbell. Reston, VA: MENC (Music Educators National Conference).

Seeger, Anthony. (2006). "Lost Lineages and Neglected Peers: Ethnomusicologists outside Academia." *Ethnomusicology*, 50th Anniversary Commemorative Issue guest co-edited by Ellen Koskoff and R. Anderson Sutton, 50(2): 214–235.

Sheehy, Daniel. (1992). "A Few Notions about Philosophy and Strategy in Applied Ethnomusicology." *Ethnomusicology*. Special Issue: Music and the Public Interest, 36(3): 323–336.

Shelemay, Kay Kaufman. (1994). *A Song of Longing: An Ethiopian Journey*. Urbana: University of Illinois Press.

Shelemay, Kay Kaufman. (2006). *Soundscapes: Exploring Music in a Changing World* (2nd ed.). New York: W. W. Norton and Co.

Sias, Tony F. (2012). Interview with the author. Cleveland Heights, Ohio. October 19.

Small, Christopher. (1998). *Musicking: The Meanings of Performing and Listening*. Hanover, NH, and London: Wesleyan University Press/ University Press of New England.

Smith, Robert L. (2011). "Census Data Reveal New Migration Pattern as Black Families Leave Cleveland." *The Plain Dealer*, March 28. http://blog.cleveland.com/metro/2011/03/census_data_reveals_new_migrat.html (accessed July 12, 2013).

Sousa, David A. (2006a). "The Brain and The Arts." *The Jossey-Bass Reader on the Brain and Learning*, pp. 331–358. San Francisco: John Wiley & Sons.

Sousa, David A. (2006b). "How the Arts Develop the Young Brain." *The School Administrator*, December. *The American Association of School Administrators* http://www.aasa.org/SchoolAdministratorArticle.aspx?id=7378 (accessed August 5, 2013).

Sousa, David A. (2011). *How the Brain Learns* (4th ed.). Thousand Oaks, CA: Corwin Press.

Southeast Center for Education in the Arts. (2013). "Concept-based Arts Integration." *Southeast Center for Education in the Arts, University of Tennessee-Chattanooga*. http://www.utc.edu/Outreach/SCEA/artsintegration.php (accessed July 12, 2013).

State Impact Ohio. (2013). "What You Need to Know about the Cleveland School District." *National Public Radio*. http://stateimpact.npr.org/ohio/tag/cleveland-metropolitan-school-district/ (accessed July 12, 2013).

Stevenson, Lauren M., and Richard J. Deasy. (2005). *Third Space: When Learning Matters*. Washington, DC: Arts Education Partnership.

Stokes, Martin. (1997). "Introductions: Ethnicity, Identity, and Music." In *Ethnicity, Identity, and Music: The Musical Construction of Place* (2nd ed.), edited by Martin Stokes, pp. 1–27. Oxford and Providence, RI: Berg Publishers.

Stone, Ruth M., ed. (2002). *The World's Music: General Perspectives and Reference Tools, The Garland Encyclopedia of World Music*, Vol. 10. New York: Garland.

Stone, Ruth M. (1988). *Let the Inside Be Sweet: The Interpretation of Music Event among the Kpelle of Liberia*. Bloomington: Indiana University Press.

Szego, C. K. (2002). "Music Transmission and Learning: A Conspectus of Ethnographic Research in Ethnomusicology and Music Education." In *The New Handbook on Research in Music Teaching and Learning*, edited by Richard Colwell and Carol P. Richardson, pp. 707–729. New York: Oxford University Press.

Titon, Jeff Todd. (1985). "Stance, Role, and Identity in Fieldwork among Folk Baptists and Pentecostals." *American Music* 3(1): 16–24.

Titon, Jeff Todd. (1992a). "Music, the Public Interest, and the Practice of Ethnomusicology." *Ethnomusicology*. Special Issue: Music and the Public Interest, 36(3): 315–322.

Titon, Jeff Todd, general editor. (1992b). *Worlds of Music: An Introduction to the Music of the World's Peoples*. New York: Schirmer Books.

Topper, Jamie. (2011). "Collaborative Ethnomusicology: Thoughts and Projects in Community Music." *Teaching-Artist Journal*, posted December 13, 2011. http://tajournal.com/2011/12/13/collaborative-ethnomusicology-thoughts-and-projects-in community-music/.

US Census Bureau. (2010). "Cleveland, Ohio—State and County QuickFacts." *US Department of Commerce*. http://quickfacts.census.gov/qfd/states/39/3916000.html (accessed August 3, 2013).

US Department of Health and Human Services. (2014). "Office of Head Start." *U.S. Department of Health and Human Services*. http://www.acf.hhs.gov/programs/ohs/about/haed-start (accessed June 2, 2014).

US Department of Housing and Urban Development. (2011). "Understanding Neighborhood Effects of Concentrated Poverty." *Evidence Matters*, edited by Rachel Levitt. Winter. http://www.huduser.org/portal/periodicals/em/winter11/highlight2.html (accessed July 11, 2014).

Wade, Bonnie C. (2006). "Fifty Years of SEM in the United States: A Retrospective." *Ethnomusicology*. Special 50th Anniversary Commemorative Issue co-guest edited by Ellen Koskoff and R. Anderson Sutton, 50(2): 190–198.

Wade, Bonnie C. (2009). *Thinking Musically: Experiencing Music, Expressing Culture* (2nd ed.). Global Music Series, co-edited by Bonnie Wade and Patricia Shehan Campbell. New York: Oxford University Press.

Weibe, Sean, Pauline Shameshima, Rita Irwin, Carl Leggo, Peter Gouzouasis, and Kit Grauer. (2007). "Re-imagining Arts Integration: Rhizomatic Relations of the Everyday." *Journal of Educational Thought* 41(3): 263–280.

Williams, Regennia M. (2006). "Praying Grounds: Introduction" (essay and video). Praying Grounds: African American Faith Communities collection. *The Cleveland Memory Project*. Cleveland State University Libraries. http://images.ulib.csuohio.edu/cdm/landingpage/collection/praying (accessed August 23, 2013).

Witchey, Holly Rarick, and John Vacha. (1994). *Fine Arts in Cleveland: An Illustrated History*. Bloomington: Indiana University Press.

Wong, Deborah. (2006). "Ethnomusicology and Difference." *Ethnomusicology*. Special 50th Anniversary Commemorative Issue, co-edited by Ellen Koskoff and R. Anderson Sutton, 50(2): 259–279.

Young Audiences of Northeast Ohio (YANEO). (2008). "ICARE—Celebrating Ten Years of the Arts in Cleveland Schools." *The Sun* (Winter): 5.

Young Audiences of Northeast Ohio (YANEO). (2013a). "History." *Art Is Education*. http://www.artiseducationcleveland.org/aboutus.php (accessed September 4, 2013).

Young Audiences of Northeast Ohio (YANEO). (2013b). "Who We Are—About Us." *Young Audiences of Northeast Ohio*. http://www.yaneo.org/who/who.html (accessed August 14, 2013).

Zaretti, Joan L. (1998). "Multicultural Music Education: An Ethnography of Process in Teaching and Learning." Master's thesis, Indiana University–Bloomington.

Zaretti, Joan L. (2002). *Global Encounters: Sounds along the Silk Road, 2001–2002 Teacher's Guide*. New York: Carnegie Hall Education Department.

Zaretti, Joan L. (2003). *Global Encounters: South African Sounds, 2002–2003 Teacher's Guide.* New York: Carnegie Hall Education Department.

Zaretti, Joan L. (2004). *Global Encounters: Sounds of Brazil, 2003–2004 Teacher's Guide.* New York: *The Weill Music Institute at Carnegie Hall.*

Zaretti, Joan L. (2006). The Nonprofit Niche: Managing Music Education in Arts Organizations. Ph.D. dissertation, Indiana University–Bloomington.

CHAPTER 2

SOUNDS HUMANE

Music and Humanism in the Aga Khan Humanities Project

JOHN MORGAN O'CONNELL

APPLIED ethnomusicology has come a long way.[1] It has been more than 20 years since the special issue entitled "Music and the Public Interest" was published in *Ethnomusicology* (see Titon, ed., 1992). Since then the field has flourished, being represented in significant international conferences (such as Vienna, 2007) and in important scholarly outputs (such as Pettan, ed., 2008). It has also been represented in ancillary study groups (such as Music and Minorities) and in related subject areas (such as medical ethnomusicology). Although an applied dimension in ethnomusicology is not new, especially in the areas of cultural conservation and government policy (see Dirksen, 2012), I was present at the first meetings of the new field called "applied ethnomusicology" in the United States (hosted by Brown University in 2003) and in Europe (hosted by Ljubljana University in 2006), where distinctive versions of applied ethnomusicology emerged, one based on a folkloric model and the other following an anthropological precedent.

Has applied ethnomusicology come far enough? Today, the discipline considers an eclectic array of interests—ranging from education to legislation, disability to sustainability—and directions that encompass advocacy and activism, responsibility and citizenry. Increasingly, the field is self-reflexive, as scholars (like Barz, 2012) find ways to mediate through collaboration and not to meddle without consultation (see Araújo and Grupo Musicultura, 2010). Significantly, many scholars are concerned with conflict, seeking justice at a national level (see Seeger, 2010) or critiquing war at an international level (see Sugarman, 2010). However, applied ethnomusicology still strives to find a unified voice, be it in terms of disciplinary definition or philosophical aspiration. Of course, Harrison (2012) has attempted to formulate a theoretical solution to accommodate this intradisciplinary fragmentation. By recognizing interdisciplinary collaboration in terms of epistemic association, she in fact highlights the epistemological divisions in applied ethnomusicology that exist between the United States and Europe, divisions that are related to distinctive intellectual traditions and different institutional structures.

Perhaps Pettan (2008: 90) has come closest to defining an applied ethnomusicology. Adapting a taxonomy from cultural anthropology (see Spradley and McCurdy, eds., 2000), Pettan distinguishes between four key areas: first, action ethnomusicology (that deploys musical knowledge); second, adjustment ethnomusicology (that nurtures social interaction); third, administrative ethnomusicology (that activates external change); and fourth, advocate ethnomusicology (that fosters individual agency). Pettan (with Harrison) also provides a negative definition of the discipline (see Harrison and Pettan, 2010: 16–17). According to them, applied ethnomusicology is not a field that stands in opposition to an academic ethnomusicology; it is not a field that is opposed to the consideration of philosophical reflection or theoretical criticism, or a field that is antagonistic toward ethnographic research and artistic expression. Critical here is the distinction between the applied and the pure. That is, Pettan questions the false dichotomy between applied research and academic inquiry. Significantly, he proposes a cohesive discipline in which applied ethnomusicology is an integral part of academic ethnomusicology (see also Titon, 2011).

Of course, Pettan is essentially interested in the practical. Although theory is recognized in his negative definition of applied ethnomusicology, Pettan is not primarily concerned with the theoretical or the philosophical. Here, he is not alone. For example, Titon (1992) questions the significance of theoretical discourse in his groundbreaking study of music and the public interest. In this article, Titon interrogates the truth claims of theoreticians and philosophers who are sponsored by the scholarly community. Invoking Rorty (1979), he distinguishes between a theoretical aspiration toward Truth and a practical disclosure of truths. Interestingly, Titon advocates a reflexive theory of practice that promotes action and that denigrates inaction both within and outside the academy. In this matter, he sets an important precedent (see, for example, Araújo, 2008). Yet, Titon's critique of philosophy is remarkably philosophical. Not only is he conversant with contemporary issues in philosophical discourse, but he also reveals a remarkable philosophical insight into his own "being in the world musically" (1992: 319).[2]

Should applied ethnomusicology subscribe to philosophical reflection? I think so. Where some scholars are rightly concerned with pragmatic issues, they need to distinguish between "the how" and "the why," between the practical and the theoretical. Further, they need to interrogate their own intentions and aspirations. True, some scholars are now reflexive, questioning an individual positionality with respect to motive and ambition (see, for example, Seeger, 2010). However, few scholars ask the fundamental question: Why do I engage in applied ethnomusicology? If the question is obvious, the answer is not. Looking over the extensive literature in the field, the themes of tolerance and empathy are stated. The notions of intercultural dialogue and interethnic accord are explicit. Yet, when speaking about a better life in a better world, many scholars resort to the relative concepts of social responsibility and civic duty, two themes that are informed by a particular intellectual tradition and a specific cultural worldview.

True, the issues of human welfare (especially in the realm of education) and human well-being (especially in the arena of health) feature prominently in the current literature. True, too, the respect for human value and the desire for human benefit are sometimes mentioned. Yet, the twin ideals of human justice and human rights are often quoted but rarely interrogated. When cited, they usually reflect a specific humanist tradition with its own historical trajectory. What is missing in the discussion is this: to be human is to be part of humanity. That is, the human condition is universal. Here, human understanding is possible precisely because human values are shared. To paraphrase Morrison (1988) in his hermeneutic consideration of empathy, "I am you." Although Morrison unravels the asymmetric relationship between the "I" and the "you" in his innovative approach to intersubjective understanding, the title of his book (*I Am You*) provokes an alternative reading of empathy: that is, "I could be you."

Is this notion of empathy (the "I could be you") an overriding principle in applied ethnomusicology? Are the aims of applied ethnomusicology consistent with the humanistic goals of intersubjective understanding? What is the role of music and musicians? What can academics and activists contribute? This chapter addresses such issues. From a humanist position, the chapter evaluates the significance of a Muslim version of humanism as it relates to an educational program in Central Asia (the Aga Khan Humanities Project). It also explores the relationship between music and humanity by developing a hermeneutic approach to music education and music research. Significantly, it adopts a reflexive methodology organized around the principal tenets of hermeneutics (namely, experience, reflection, and interpretation). Central to this method is a moment of "distantiation," a period of reflection that arises from an episode of experience. That is, it advances a specific reading of interpretation, one that recognizes music as an integral component of the human condition.

Applied Ethnomusicology: A Hermeneutic Method

Sounds Human

Is it possible to be human without music? This is a question I ask my students. Is music an integral part of the human condition, as Arendt (1958) might argue? Or, is music just an aberration of human evolution, as Pinker (1997) would contend? Is music a special behavior that is essential to the survival of the human species? On this issue, Blacking (1977) would probably agree. Or, is music a distinctive intelligence necessary for human progress? Such an argument Gardner (1983) might proffer. Yet, there are uncertainties. Music is specific to humans. I suspect that some zoomusicologists and biomusicologists might dispute this assertion.[3] Music is a discrete human activity. However, music often intersects with language. Again, music frequently overlaps with dance (see Figure 2.1).

FIGURE 2.1. A professional dancer at a wedding in Bartang

While such coincidences call into question the conceptual integrity of music as a human category, it is evident that the definition of music is relative but that the practice of music is universal.

Music provides an ideal platform for studying humanity. It enables the examination of music theories as human ideas. It allows for the conceptualization of musical instruments as human artifacts. It even enables the interrogation of musical activity as a human behavior that is learned and performed according to the communal interests and the symbolic constructions of culture. Music can be viewed as a human event that is configured sonically and practiced socially in a specific time and place. Music is a way of being human, a lifestyle reflected in the social relations, the economic activities, the ideological formations and the aesthetic values of society. In this way, music can be understood as a human endeavor in which musical concepts as human knowledge, musical materials as human technology, musical activities as human action, and musical contexts as human event intersect in different ways to help us make sense of our world. In short, music helps us to be human.

Music is not a medium for studying humanity in isolation. As an expression of culture, music intersects with (yet is distinguished from) other artistic media (see, for example, Feld, 1988). In this respect, music is an art form using abstract structures (musical sounds) and physical materials (musical instruments) to configure and to deploy respectively musical elements that are perceived by humans to have aesthetic value. Music is an art process. It invites participation in a deeply felt shared experience (see Keil, 1987). Music is an art event. It has a functional significance for culture, and it has a significant place in culture. Music is part of an art world (see O'Connell, 1996). It operates as a locus for experiencing, reflecting upon, and interpreting culture beyond (but not limited to) traditional explanations of the human condition. It is a productive medium for identity formation, as it discloses unique ways of "being in the world," or *Dasein* (Heidegger, 1927).

Music is humanistic. As an expressive art, music offers a unique insight into taste and beauty, especially from the perspectives of class and ideology, respectively. As a social art, music presents an alternative medium for expressing social accomplishment and for displaying social status. As a learned art, music is another way of training good citizens to engage in civil society. Here, the relationship between music and humanism needs clarification. In a secular humanism, music provides an ideal focus for analyzing and adapting scientific principles and natural laws. In a sacred humanism, music allows for the interrogation of human beliefs and human emotions freed from (yet consistent with) religious norms. In both traditions, music is a unique expression of human creativity, another way of speaking eloquently and another means of communicating effectively. As Sharpe argues (2000: 179), music is a valued expression of human interest, enabling humans to make sense of the lives they live.

Music is also humane. As an expert in humane education, Weil (2004) argues that music offers an important means of exciting curiosity and of nurturing creativity. While her claim that music is civilizing is probably overstated, Weil argues that an education in the musical is consistent with a training in the humane, especially with respect to reverence, respect, and responsibility when humans are confronted with challenge. Weil is not only speaking about humanity. She is also speaking about a humane approach to animals and to nature. Central to her holistic approach to education is the concept of sustainability, where humans live ethically and peaceably with humans and non-humans. Her notion of sustainability also encompasses the symbiotic relationship between the animate and the inanimate, the issues of animal protection and environmental stewardship being central concerns of a humane education. For Weil, music must go beyond the humanistic. It must become "humaneistic" (my term).

Music affords a bridge between the humanistic and the "humaneistic." On this bridge, applied ethnomusicology might find its voice. This is especially significant in the realm of sustainability (see Titon, 2011). Either musical practices are no longer salvaged but are now sustained (see Schippers, 2010), or musical materials are no longer conserved but are now managed (see Impey, 2002). Following a precedent in ecology, applied ethnomusicology might have advocated a harmonic equilibrium in the world or a dynamic equilibrium with the world. Invoking this precedent, the Aga Khan Humanities Project recognized music as a sustainable art in its balanced promotion of economic development and ecological conservation. At the time, however, the intersection between the musical and the sustainable was only an aspiration. More concrete was the role of music in threatened communities that had suffered from the trauma of annihilation consequent to the terror of war. Here, the art of music furnished a humanistic locus for understanding conflict and a "humaneistic" focus for promoting conflict resolution.

Music as art presents a structured framework for realizing a human solution to a humane endeavor. That is, music is an art form, an art process, an art event, and an art world. Music also permits a hermeneutic methodology to uncover the significance of expressive culture for humanity. That is, music is a locus for experiencing, reflecting upon, and interpreting culture. Music is also a mediating category between the self and the other, allowing for a fusion of horizons between one and another (see Rice, 1994). Music provides an ideal locus for intercultural understanding since it promotes a dialogue between humans, both sonically and socially. Critical here is a moment of "distantiation." That is, music enables a detour into the other, an instance of auditory dislocation that challenges and yet nourishes the audible self. Music allows me to hear myself through the sounds of others. Music is the crossroads where my understanding becomes self-understanding (Ricoeur, cited in Reynhout, 2013: 178).

Understanding

Music is a defining characteristic of my humanity. As a form of human knowledge, music operates as a lens for distilling my experience at a local level and at a global level. In the former, my training in music at home enabled me to acquire the materials and the practices of a "Western" tradition. In the latter, my education abroad in anthropology allowed me to analyze the materials and to interpret the practices of a non-"Western" tradition. For this reason, I was drawn to ethnomusicology, a subject that allowed me to combine my knowledge of music and anthropology, and that equipped me with the skills to teach in a "Western" institution and to research in a non-"Western" context. In this sense, music is my way of "being in the world," since my economic means, my social activities, my ideological biases, and my aesthetic preferences are engaged with a community of musicians influential upon yet implicated in my life.

Two moments in my life are especially significant. The first is my encounter with the musical traditions of the Middle East. Here, Ali Jihad Racy at UCLA was a major influence. Although I had conducted preliminary research on immigrant musics in Berlin and resident musicians in Istanbul, it was with Racy that I began to understand the relevant traditions. In his ensemble, I began to experience the music of the Middle East as a place for ethnography. In his research seminar, I started to analyze the music of the Middle East as a context for reflection. I completed the hermeneutic cycle by taking theoretical classes in ethnomusicology (among others) as sites for interpretation. Central to this hermeneutic process was a moment of "distantiation,"[4] a critical moment of learning new music and of meeting new musicians. Significantly, Racy welcomed a diverse group of followers. It was his way of promoting interdenominational tolerance and intercultural understanding through music.

The second was my encounter with the musical traditions of Central Asia. Here, Rafique Keshavjee of the Aga Khan Humanities Project was an important inspiration. In contrast to my studies with Racy, my meeting with Keshavjee was accidental. At a conference in Florida, we literally bumped into each other. At the time he was promoting his project in the humanities that was based in Dushanbe (Tajikistan). Since he had heard my presentation on a hermeneutic approach to musical instruction in Turkey, he was interested in discussing my wider interests in music and humanism. At first, I was circumspect. However, Keshavjee needed a music specialist to supplement his team of academic advisors, scholars who were especially selected to supervise and to design a humanities curriculum. Since music was to be a key component in this endeavor (see "Music" below), I would be in an ideal position to fill an important lacuna. How could I refuse his invitation?

This was my first time in Central Asia.[5] This was also my first time studying the musical traditions of Central Asia.[6] In preparation, I listened to relevant recordings and I studied pertinent publications. I found that music helped make sense of cultural diversity in a vast heartland. In this respect, cultural difference is disclosed in the structure, the technology, the practice, the context, and the life of music. It is also expressed in language, where ethnic difference is broadly classified along Turkic and Persian lines. This linguistic division between a Turkic domain and a Persian world is found in music. It is revealed in the melodic scales (five note vs. seven note), the rhythmic structures (asymmetric vs. symmetric), and the poetic meters (quantitative vs. qualitative) respectively. The linguistic distinction is evident in music technology, where the morphology of musical instruments (especially long-necked lutes) conforms to the dualistic taxonomy.

The linguistic divide between a Turkic domain and a Persian realm is apparent in musical practice. Musical transmission (oral vs. literate), musical performance (solo vs. group), and musical choreography (no dance vs. dance) are classified accordingly. So, too, are musical contexts where musicians in the Turkic domain live in rural areas, play at informal gatherings, and (sometimes) function as religious leaders. By contrast, musicians in the Persian realm live in urban centers, perform in formal contexts, and (usually) operate as secular professionals. In sum, the significance of music for the human condition in Central Asia is not only revealed in the characteristics of its structure, its technology, its practice, and its context, but it is also exposed in the world of musicians, where the social organization, the political system, the economic activity, and the aesthetic disposition of individual groups (broadly speaking) confirm the division of the region into distinctive cultural spheres defined according to fundamental linguistic differences.

This is what I learned in theory. It was not what I experienced in practice. When I arrived in Tajikistan, I had to revise my reading of music and humanity. Tajik

FIGURE 2.2. A professional musician at home in Khorog

musicians (who speak a dialect of Persian) often performed folk genres and lived in rural areas reminiscent of the Turkic domain described above (see Figure 2.2). By contrast, Uzbek musicians (who speak a Turkic language) played classical styles and lived in urban centers reminiscent of the Persian realm described above. The musical geography was complicated by a colonial legacy, especially a Russian inheritance (by way of the Soviet Union) that controlled musical production in terms of institutions (such as conservatories) and policies (such as collectivization). The Soviet register was also evident in the continued patronage of "Western" art music and in the widespread dissemination of "Western" popular music. Further, ethnic minorities (especially in Badakhshan) had their own languages and their own musics.[7]

My critical revision of music provoked a critical reading of humanity. With the collapse of the Soviet Union, Tajikistan was thrust into an extended civil war (1992–1997). On the one hand, Uzbeks in the north wanted to secede from the Tajiks in the south. On the other hand, Badakhshan sought independence from Tajikistan.[8] Some estimates put the death toll at 100,000. Even when I arrived (2001), there was sporadic fighting in the capital, and there were warring militias in the hinterland. Perhaps, music was more indicative of inhumanity, a sonic inscription of cultural difference that reinforced competing identities. Was I experiencing another critical moment of "distantiation"? Would I discover that music in fact unveiled an inhuman condition? Keshavjee taught me otherwise. Though the humanities project, I had a moment of ontology, an instance of self-understanding. Under his leadership, I understood that music can indeed be humane and that music can promote humanism.

APPLIED ETHNOMUSICOLOGY: A HUMANIST THEORY

Humanism

The standard account of humanism is decidedly Eurocentric. Generally considered to have been an intellectual movement that developed in Italy during the Renaissance, humanism (It., *umanesimo*) questioned the pragmatic focus of Medieval scholasticism (which prepared university graduates for professional careers) and offered instead a new curriculum founded upon the twin tenets of spoken eloquence and written ability. In a drive to forge a new "man of letters," contemporary advocates of humanism looked to the ancients, where the study of grammar and the examination of text allowed for the rediscovery of classical writings. With a keen interest in philology, humanists began to interrogate sacred as well as secular sources, derived from Christian and non-Christian traditions. It was not long before a schism between reason and religion led to a resurgence in scientific inquiry (by way of Galileo) and to a questioning of theological veracity (by way of Erasmus). The stage was now set for a new era of humanism, a "religion of humanity."

The eighteenth century witnessed the second age of humanism. In contrast to the Renaissance, when citizens were educated to engage in civic life within the context of a sacred order, the age of Enlightenment beheld the rise of a secular humanism in which individuals were endowed with agency freed from the debilitating strictures of religious dogma and despotic control. In the contexts of a bloody Reformation (initiated in Germany) and an even bloodier revolution (erupting in France), humanism and nationalism coalesced in a vitriolic assertion of human supremacy, reason and justice now determining the pathway of human salvation. While the philanthropic potential of humanism was not underdeveloped, the "deification" of humanity involved the cult of atheism. Following Comte, a ritualized humanism was founded to discredit the religious establishment and to espouse a humane altruism. In this way, humanists set a precedent for the separation of church and state as the guiding principle in "Western" democracy.

Yet, humanism had its darker side. Could the philanthropic become misanthropic? For example, the civilizing ideals of evangelism can be viewed as part of the colonizing objectives of imperialism. Here, altruism could be said to disguise egotism. When does the emancipation of humanity become the subjugation of humans? Inspired by the humanistic principles of freedom and brotherhood, Napoleon conquered much of Europe, promising liberty from tyranny yet practicing tyranny without liberty. Even under the Code Napoléon, equality was clearly relative (see Adamczyk, 1995: 204–208). At its ugliest, humanism became embroiled with fascism by providing a philosophical basis for supporting a German reading of humanity. Heidegger was a principal exponent. Although the philosopher advocated an anti-humanist position after World War II (see Heidegger, 1947), he was actually countering a humanist outlook that he had originally employed to validate National Socialism. Indeed, Heidegger became a member of the Nazi Party (1933), an affiliation for which he was chastised but for which he never apologized.

Critics of humanism have highlighted such paradoxes. They have also emphasized the ineffectual character of international bodies where humanists have thrived, noting, for example, how exponents of humanism in the League of Nations were unsuccessful at halting the rise of fascism and preventing the onset of war. Yet, such critics have themselves failed to provide a solution to the pressing issue of improving the human condition. Perhaps, their search for truth by way of reason was itself informed by the central principles of secular humanism, a philosophical position that denied the supernatural but advanced the natural. Here lies the problem. Humanists and anti-humanists employ the same terms of reference to advance distinctive viewpoints. Further, they both deny the sacral origins of humanism, especially the desire to educate citizens in the humanities and to create a civil society in ecclesiastical states. As Partner (1979) argues, humanistic belief and religious conviction were complementary during the Renaissance.

Christians were not alone in espousing this version of humanism. For many centuries, Muslims had looked to the ancients for inspiration in the realms of science and society. Like the humanists in Europe, they translated the works of Aristotle and Plato (among others) to develop rational solutions to the issues of divine causality and human agency. Like humanists in the Renaissance, they endeavored to highlight human creativity in the academic and the artistic realms by emphasizing the distinction between philosophy and theology, even proposing an ethical state that was ruled by a philosopher king (al-Fārābī) or a single God that was deduced by way of pure reason (al-Bīrūnī). These humanists of the "East" influenced the humanists of the "West," especially in the realms of astronomy (al-Bīrūnī), medicine (Ibn Sīnā), and mathematics (al-Kindī) among many others. Invoking the naturism of antiquity, they initiated a renaissance in the Muslim world long before the Renaissance in the Christian world.[9]

However, this golden age of Islamic humanism was not to persist. The rise of the "West" marked the decline of the "East," especially after 1492, when a "new" world was discovered (from Iberia) and an old world was recovered (in Iberia). The period also witnessed the demise of the Muslim heartland, which was devastated by successive incursions of Turkic hordes from Central Asia. The certainties of their past were replaced by the uncertainties of their present, rational thought now being inadequate to explain irrational activity. Broadly speaking, Muslims developed two strategies. First, they resorted to a literal reading of the Qur'an, a dogmatic reaction to reasoned action that today has a contemporary relevance. Second, they adopted an esoteric interpretation of Islam, a mystical version of their religion, which allowed for a subjective response to an objective reality. Where the first strategy was anti-humanist, the second strategy was humanist, a different conception of humanism in which mystical experience took precedence over mental explanation.[10]

Perhaps, this humanism should be rendered more correctly as "humaneism." Although the rational underpinnings of humanism are not foregrounded, the anthropocentric focus in the Muslim version of humanism is. So, too, are the humanistic attributes of tolerance and inclusion. Non-Muslims as well as Muslims were accepted as human equals. Like their counterparts in the Renaissance, humanists were trained in the humanities; the "man of letters" represented the "ideal man" who was eloquent in speech and expert in writing, and who was knowledgeable about prose and conversant with poetry. Mystical adepts were trained in language and literature, often translating texts from different languages to advance esoteric wisdom. They were also philologists. While the rationalist philosophy of some sophists was side-lined (such as Plato), the metaphysical philosophy of others (such as Plotinus) was not. In other words, philology played a significant role in the development of gnostic thought among mystics in Islam.

Music

Music transcended the divide between humanism and "humaneism." As an expression of humanism, music was an object worthy of rational scrutiny. That is, it could be observed, analyzed and explained as a natural phenomenon. In the Muslim world, music was studied scientifically. Either, a theory of music was developed from performance practice, al-Kindī invoking Pythagorean principles (such as the tetrachord) to represent finger positions on a musical instrument. Or, a theory of music was informed by philosophical reflection, al-Fārābī also invoking Pythagorean principles (such as a fixed gamut of pitches) to explain cosmic order and the human spirit. Both theorists drew upon a scientific study of classical antiquity to provide two readings of music theory, the philosophers presenting either a material explanation or a metaphysical interpretation of music practice. The science of music reached its climax with Safi al-Dīn, who synthesized the theories of al-Kindī and al-Fārābī to present a systematic treatment of musical modes (*maqāmāt*).

In the Christian world, music was also studied scientifically as an expression of the humanist project. During the Renaissance, theorists consulted Greek treatises to recreate classical conceptions of beauty in music. Greek notions of consonance and dissonance informed a new approach to counterpoint in which the third and the sixth acquired a new status in music composition. Allied to this, Greek concepts of intonation enabled the fixity of particular intervals and the development of just intonation, where simple ratios were devised to create perfect intervals. Here, temperament reflected an empirical study of contemporary practice, rather than a slavish adherence to historic principles.

The democratic impulse was not ignored. Music was liberated from the despotic rule of the *cantus firmus*. Rather, polyphonic textures attested to a new equality between voices, whose range and number expanded in the context of *a cappella* ensemble. The Greek legacy covered other issues related to music and emotion, music and modality, and even music and declamation.

Yet, here the similarity ends. Where humanism in the Christian world would evolve into a secular guise, "humaneism" in the Muslim world would revert back into a metaphysical form. As the humanist impulse in the "West" developed the idea of music as a universal language (see Sharpe, 2000; Higgins, 2012), the "humaneist" drive in the "East" re-envisaged music as a divine expression. Critical here were the writings of al-Ghazzālī. Responding to a contemporary debate about the acceptability of music in Islam (called "the *semāʿ* polemic"), al-Ghazzālī advocated the benefits of music and dance for promoting ecstasy in religious rituals. Although he was cautious about the time and the place of such ecstatic moments, al-Ghazzālī recovers the theological status of music, arguing in particular that song, like poetry, was merely an embellishment of speech. Accordingly, it was lawful. Further, song is the work of God since it is merely another embellishment of nature (Goodman, 2003: 42).

However, al-Ghazzālī was critical of errant philosophy (*falsafah*). In part, he disapproved of those philosophers who were non-Muslim, especially the great thinkers of classical antiquity. Further, he was a virulent opponent of neoplatonism, questioning its monotheistic credentials with mathematical abstraction. It took another sophist to balance the equation. Ibn al-ʿArabī employed neoplatonic ideas to ground his revolutionary notion of "unity of being" (*waḥdat al-wujūd*). That is, al-ʿArabī melded the distinction between the creator and the created. Differentiating between a divine essence and a cosmological emanation, he argued that the cosmos represented different manifestations of God's qualities. For al-ʿArabī, the world was both one and many, both divine and mundane. To experience God, it was necessary to uncover the divine within the humane. That is, each human had the potential of being able to experience God since each person was simply a microcosm of a divine reality. Predictably, al-ʿArabī is celebrated by mystical Islam and shunned by orthodox Islam.

Music played a key role in this ontology. For al-ʿArabī, music occupies a liminal space (*barzakh*) between heaven and earth. Music is one means by which God is revealed to humans. Another is dance. By combining music and dance, humans can achieve a state of enlightened ecstasy as each person unveils the divine within. Musical instruments may have a similar function. Many instruments are anthropomorphic. For example, the end-blown reed flute in Turkey (called *ney*) is believed to symbolize man, its nine holes representing the nine orifices of man. Music results from the breath of God passing through the vessel of man. In this way, it reveals sonically the unification of God with man. For example again, the short-necked lute in Badakhshan (called *rubab*) has a human form, being endowed with bodily attributes (such as a face and a rib cage). The musician (*madahkhan*) performs poetry (*madah*)

FIGURE 2.3. A praise singer or *madahkhan* in Khorog

in praise of God (see Figure 2.3). The instrument is believed to have mystical as well as magical properties.

The two examples described above come from two distant corners of Asia. However, they represent two manifestations of a singular ideal. In Turkey, the *ney* is intimately associated with the Mevlevî dervishes, a mystical order founded by the thirteenth-century Sufi saint, Jalāl al-Dīn Rumi. Mevlevî adepts (*semazen*) emulate in their ritual (*sema*) the neoplatonic constellation of cosmic order. Here, each participant represents a planet rotating around an axis (*qutb*) symbolizing the sun (or "the perfect man"). In Tajikistan, the *madahkhan* performs *madah* to accompany ecstatic dance, often employing poetry written by the eleventh-century Sufi mystic, Nasir Khusraw. Following a neoplatonic precedent, music making reveals the hidden meaning (*batin*) within the apparent meaning (*zaher*). Interestingly, both examples involve choreographic representations of the solar system in the context of mortuary rituals. Both examples, too, involve neoplatonic philosophers, one who left Tajikistan (namely, Rumi), the other who came to Tajikistan (namely, Khusraw).

The choreographic connection is especially significant. Rumi was the pupil of Shams-eTabrīzī (also called Shams al-Dīn) in Tabriz, with whom he had a close relationship. The Mevlevî *sema* commemorates Rumi's inconsolable sorrow at Tabrīzī's death (see Figure 2.4), when the mystic was murdered by rival adepts who were jealous of the intimacy between teacher and student. The *sema* is remarkably similar in concept to the mortuary dances associated with the *madah* (see Figure 2.5). Interestingly, some mystic groups believe that Tabrīzī was a religious missionary (daʿī) of the Ismaʿili branch of Shiʿaism.[11] More remarkable, some Ismaʿilis believe that Tabrīzī was actually the twenty-eighth Imām, Imām Shams al-Dīn Muhammad. What is interesting is this: both Rumi and Tabrīzī were profoundly influenced by neoplatonic philosophy, each mystic being connected to a place (Tajikistan) and a sect (Ismaʿilism) where music and dance were utilized to uncover the divine within.[12] In this respect, music making is intimately associated with the creation of "the perfect man," a veritable supernatural version of humanism.

FIGURE 2.4. A Mevlevî *Sema* in Turkey ca. 1890

FIGURE 2.5. Janbaz Dushanbiyev performing a mortuary dance in Khorog

Applied Ethnomusicology: A Humanitarian Project

Man

For Ismaʿilis, man is at the center of a unified universe. Emulating a philosophical precedent set by al-ʿArabī, man is the axis of all things, a being that can approach the limits of divinity. Like al-ʿArabī too, they believe in a succession of prophets (Imām-s) who reveal divine truth, the first of whom is the "original Adam." Each Imām is believed to be "the perfect man" (*al-insān al-kāmail*) since he alone manifests divine attributes. Each

Imām is pole of the universe (*qutb*) divine in nature yet human in form, guiding mankind along the path to divine revelation. Interestingly, a comparison here with the incarnation of Jesus Christ is instructive. Further, Ismaʿilis believe in a brotherhood of man, where no distinctions are made on the basis of ethnicity or creed. In fact, Ismaʿilis advance the unity of all religions since each religion is of one essence. Love is at the heart of Ismaʿili belief, love of God and love of man.

Philanthropy is the logical outcome of philosophy. As part of his sacred remit, the Imām is expected to contribute to the well-being of both believers and non-believers. In fact, the current Imām (Aga Khan IV) is ambivalent about the term "philanthropy," believing it to be a "Western" practice that is intimately associated with sacred institutions. He considers that his benevolent contribution is the institutional responsibility of the Imām, a responsibility of his office that involves improvements to the worldly life of underprivileged communities. How was this financed? Traditionally, Ismaʿilis were required to contribute a tithe (called *dasond*, or "ten parts") to the Imām, worth 12.5% of their gross income (10% as *dasond*; 2.5% as *zakat*). Some of this income was earmarked for the upkeep of ritual structures (called *jamatkhana*-s), while the remainder was destined for charitable projects. *Dasond* also included a provision for war booty, 20% of the takings being assigned to the poor and the homeless (among others).

In the recent past, the charitable contribution has been considerable. During the reign of the previous Imām (Aga Khan III), jubilees were marked by donations that matched his weight in gold and diamonds. Since he was not a slim man and since he was not short-lived, the resulting levies were substantial. However, this Imām was a major visionary. As a politician, he played a significant role in peace negotiations that followed the two world wars, after the first in favor of Turkey, after the second in favor of India. He was also the President of the League of Nations at a critical moment in its history (1937–1938). As a radical with a socialist inclination, he believed that labor should be organized and that the subjugated should be enfranchised, especially in those continents that were colonized by European powers. In particular, he was especially critical of the British for their discriminatory policies in Africa (see Aziz, 1997–1998).

However, this Imām (Aga Khan III) was best remembered as an educator. He believed that human brotherhood could be nurtured through international education (both formal as training and informal as travel). He encouraged his followers to learn the languages and literatures of others. This was especially important at a time of civil strife between Hindus and Muslims in South Asia. Later, it would also prove important for nurturing interfaith understanding between Christians and Muslims, and for fostering interdenominational accord between Shiʿas and Sunnīs. Here, he considered health and wealth to be the guarantors of international order, education being the mechanism by which both could be achieved. In his activism on behalf of peace, he viewed literature as the hallmark of culture, a key to understanding humanity and a key to promoting deity. In particular, he considered Persian poetry, with its humanist message and its mystical ethos, to be the "voice of God speaking through the lips of man."

However, music was missing in this utopian vision of the former Imām (Aga Khan III). Perhaps this reflected the logocentric focus of Islam, in which the written word is accorded a principal position. Perhaps, it also reflected the ambivalent position afforded to music by Muslims throughout history. Yet, music plays an important part in the oral transmission of esoteric knowledge throughout the Isma'ili community. For example, *ginan*-s are devotional songs that are believed to have been transmitted by itinerant proselytizers (called *Pir*-s) during the twelfth century as they converted followers to Isma'ilism in South Asia. To suit their converts, *ginan*-s were composed in a variety of languages that encompassed local dialects (such as Gujarati) and foreign tongues (such as Persian). They are identified by two criteria: first, by the mode (here called *raga*) employed; second, by the author (usually a *Pir*) mentioned. Significantly, *ginan*-s are almost exclusively studied as an exercise in philology and not as an enterprise in ethnomusicology.

However, song texts are also missing in this utopian vision of the former Imām (Aga Khan III). In many classical traditions where Isma'ilis are resident, Persian is the language of song. Usually, lyrics are taken directly from the poetry of great figures in the Persian tradition (such as the famous poet Hāfez-e Shīrāzī). They may appear as fixed compositions (as in the *tarona* section of the Tajik-Uzbek *shashmaqam*), or they may be rendered as improvisations (as in the *āvāz* section of the Iranian *dastgāh*). The tropes of Persian poetry are more widespread, appearing in Urdu as devotional songs (such as *qawwali*-s) or in Turkish as classical compositions (such as *beste*-s). In these instances, a diverse range of musical traditions is unified around a standard vocabulary of Persian themes. Even in informal contexts, Persian is employed in vocal performance. In this respect, the *madah* is especially important. Rendered by the *madahkhan* on the *rubab* using Persian texts, *madah* is often performed to venerate the Imām-s of Isma'ilism.

The relationship between music and poetry is not lost on the current Imām (Aga Khan IV). Mindful of the philological focus of Isma'ili scholarship, he has endeavored to introduce a musicological dimension in his cultural agenda. As part of his Trust for Culture program, the present Imām has highlighted music (by way of the Aga Khan Music Initiative) as a means to preserve and disseminate folk and classical traditions in Central Asia. Not only has the initiative sponsored international performances by relevant artists (by way of the Silk Road Project), but it has also supported the transmission of relevant musics by means of the "master-apprentice" program. For example, in Tajikistan, the initiative has funded a conservatory (called "The Academy of Maqâm") for the teaching of classical music (*shashmaqam*). Directed by Abduvali Abdurashidov (see Figure 2.6), the institution now accepts around two hundred students and accommodates around one hundred experts.

Project

The Aga Khan Humanities Project is another initiative sponsored by Aga Khan IV. In contrast to the Music Initiative, which is concerned with music practice in the realms of transmission and performance, the Humanities Project is focused on curriculum development, academic instruction, and scholarly research.[13] Conceived as an educational

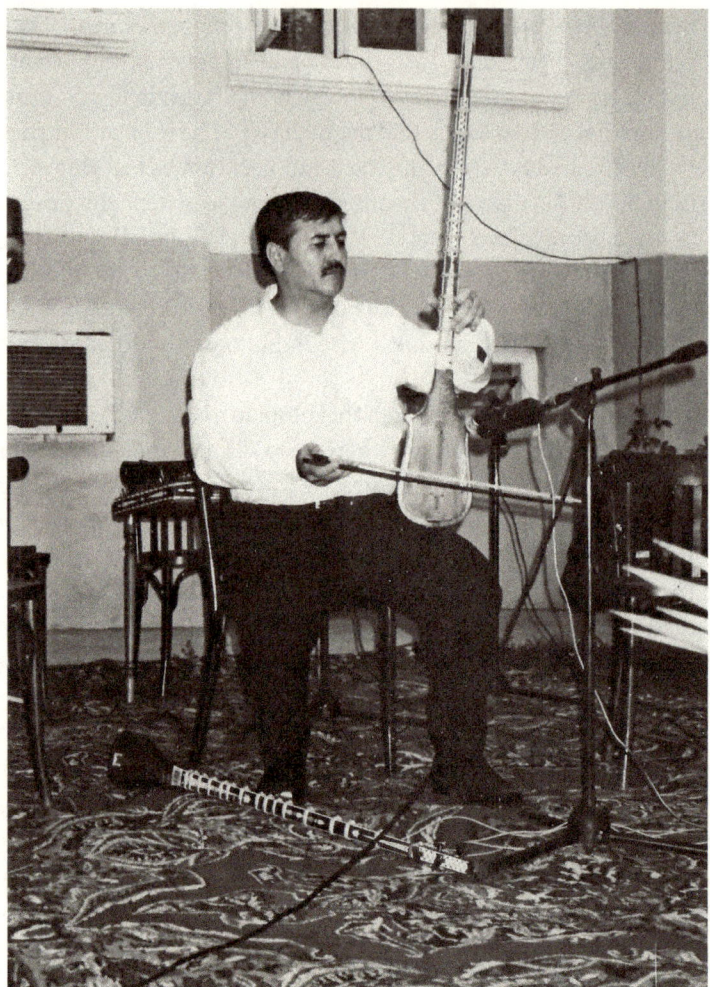

FIGURE 2.6. Abdulvali Abdurashidov playing the Sato in Dushanbe

project that serves to promote pluralism and tolerance in Central Asia, the program draws upon an international range of pedagogical sources. These encompass the cultural artifacts of world traditions that foster a new understanding of difference in the region. Critical here is the development of a civil society that is both democratic and humane in the wake of Soviet disintegration. As a way of building bridges across the region, the curriculum is now taught in more than 50 institutions. Since the syllabus involves "core texts" from around the world and the pedagogy emphasizes critical reasoning in a cross-cultural perspective, the curriculum aims to promote leadership through a humanist approach to education.

The project acknowledges music in the curriculum. As part of a wider study of expressive culture, the program views music as a human activity that serves both to embed cultural identity and to foster intercultural dialogue. In the first instance, the curriculum honors the musical traditions of Central Asia, be they of Turkic origin (such as the epic cycle called Manas in Kyrgyzstan) or Persian derivation (such as the elegiac form called *madah* in Tajikistan). The curriculum also looks at the materials of music (such as song texts) and the artifacts of music (such as instrument design). The curriculum examines the lives of musicians, tracing how each learned his or her art and how each practiced his or her tradition. This part of the curriculum draws on the work of the Music Initiative, especially the master-apprentice program now established in Afghanistan, Kazakhstan, Kyrgyzstan, Pakistan, and Tajikistan (among other countries). Significantly, musical anthologies of representative performances are available in the form of CDs and DVDs.

The musical content of the curriculum benefits from these resources. Music theory is not described as technical abstraction. Principles are related to practice, the curriculum emphasizing the relationship between the audible and visible to demonstrate the sophistication of creativity both as an expression of human cognition and as a celebration of human sensibility. Music repertoire is related to musical concepts, showing how musical performances are structured and realized. Here, music categories are viewed as cultural commodities that are shared and exchanged between distinctive traditions. True to its humanistic principles, the curriculum honors the music traditions of different denominations, vedas being representative of Indian Hinduism, chant being representative of Russian Christianity, and *shashmaqam* being representative of Bukharan Judaism. This pluralism is reflected in the representation of intradenominational difference. The Turkish *sema* honors the Sunnī tradition, and the Iranian *dastgāh* honors the Shiʻa faith. Of course, musical genres (such as *ginan* and *madah*), which are intimately associated with the Ismaʻili community, are also included.

Initially, the musical content of the curriculum was presented with other examples of expressive culture. A section on architecture examined the relationship between sound and space to study harmonic proportions in a church and a mosque. A section on art looked at the aesthetic attributes of the visible and the audible in painting and music, both in the "West" and the "East." A section on theater observed the use of music and drama in Italian opera and Iranian drama (called *taʻziyeh*). However, this productive dialogue between the arts and music was never realized. As Jonboboev (2010) recounts, music now has its own volume. Entitled "Rhythm and Movement," it examines exclusively the intersection between music and life. However, this change in the curriculum was probably unsuccessful since a new text on music in Central Asia is envisaged. Its remit is "to sustain, develop and transmit musical traditions." Here, the implicit aspiration toward the modernization of music is somewhat questionable.

The curriculum is published and taught in English and Russian. At first glance, the Russian edition might seem problematic. Given the colonial mindset of the past and the nationalist antipathy of the present, a Russian translation of the humanities project seemed doomed to failure. At second glance, however, the Russian translation is expedient. For many in Central Asia, Russian is still the lingua franca, a common currency that transcends the linguistic differences in the region. The use of Russian has another advantage. It bypasses local antagonisms in which music and language still present a volatile medium for interethnic discord. Indeed, when I was in Tajikistan, Russian was often spoken in preference to Tajik or Uzbek. In either case, it represented the cultural capital of social aspiration. Since many Tajiks wished to speak Russian rather than Tajik, I was unable to communicate using my halting knowledge of Persian. Or, it allowed Tajiks to avoid speaking Uzbek. Since I could just be understood in Uzbek by speaking Turkish, this circumvention was also difficult.

The project was not just concerned with a humanities curriculum. The project sponsored a cinema group that attained a number of international accolades. The project was also home to an Internet technology that was considered advanced in Tajikistan at the time. The project staged a series of concerts that allowed students to appreciate the musics of the locality and to engage in the techniques of scholarly research. Here, academics and technicians collaborated in recording events both to the economic advantage of musicians and to the academic benefit of the students. In this matter, an innovative approach to musical production was initiated. It employed the Internet as a means of empowering musicians by circumventing the mediating stranglehold of transnational corporations in the recording industry. This was especially effective. Most important, the project enlisted the support of volunteers from the Isma'ili community outside Tajikistan. Further, it solicited the assistance of helpers from within Tajikistan, especially Russians who now felt alienated within a newly established Tajik state.

The project has evolved in a number of phases. At its outset, international advisers collaborated with national scholars to develop a university curriculum that was both innovative and relevant. As Keshavjee (2009) states, local authorities were able to act with creativity since they were freed from the strictures of Soviet doctrine, while at the same time they were exposed to the results of Soviet disintegration. As with all projects, there were casualties over time. The project was absorbed into the emerging University of Central Asia, where its significance was eclipsed by the concerns and perspectives of the then-technically oriented staff. As a consequence, significant protagonists found other opportunities to develop similar programs outside Tajikistan. That being said, the humanities curriculum is very much alive.[14] It is now scheduled to be taught at relevant universities in East Africa and South Asia. It is now set to be a humanities program for humanity.

Applied Ethnomusicology: A Humane Application

Application

I was involved at three stages in the development of the project. In 2001, I was invited as a music specialist to participate in an induction program that involved the training of teachers and students. In 2002, I was also invited to contribute as a music educator to design and to write a volume principally devoted to expressive culture. Later in 2002,

I was finally invited as a music anthropologist to supervise research expeditions, one in the principal capital Dushanbe, the other in the provincial capital Kulob. I was also involved in the running of a pilot scheme in Bishkek (Kyrgyzstan). Further, I undertook my own research on the *madah* in Badakhshan. This was an exciting time for me. I was thrust into a musical world that was familiar yet different from my research in Turkey. It was also an exciting time for the world since it coincided with the allied invasion of Afghanistan (following 9/11) and the concomitant transformation of Tajikistan.

In stage one, I participated in the education of instructors and pupils. In this, I worked with a team of enlightened scholars (mostly from North America) who were principally involved in research-led teaching in the arts and the humanities. Although our range of expertise encompassed the fine arts and the performing arts, we were unified in our search for a humanistic approach to expressive culture. For me, this was a personal and an intellectual goal. However, our mission was not easy. Since we had all trained in the United States, our empirical method did not rest easily with the idealist tradition advocated by our wards. This was a clash of civilizations, an intellectual conflict between the inductive and the deductive, a conflict between an American and a Russian reading of intellectual endeavor. Keshavjee mediated this divide. Empowering our teachers and students with democratic agency, he solicited feedback from each. This was new for them, and they were not forgiving.

I was the target of particular rancor. In some cases, participants found my emphasis on experience over explanation problematic. Here, music specialists wished to employ the technical language of musicology to make sense of music, thereby framing all musics according to the delimiting strictures of a "Western" (albeit a Russian) mind set. In other instances, participants found my preoccupation with music in the context of a humanistic project difficult. This disclosed a variety of prejudices that ranged from a gendered to a sacralized perspective in which music was considered either to be feminine or immoral, depending upon the biases of the individual in question. The central questions were as follows: Is it possible to instruct music specialists in the humanities? Is it possible to teach non-music specialists music? This is a persistent problem in ethnomusicology. While I endeavored to train musicians in theory and non-musicians in terminology, I am not sure whether I was successful in each instance.

In stage two, these issues were again salient (see Figure 2.7). I was asked to design a lesson for the curriculum. I chose a piece that could be performed, analyzed, and interpreted according to the principles of my hermeneutic methodology. I selected a composition that was different yet familiar to the anticipated audience, a Turkish song (*şarkı*). To test my lesson plan, I organized a workshop. After saying the words, after clapping the meter, and after singing the melody, the participants managed to execute the piece with some semblance of recognition. I then asked them to analyze the metric structure of the text (–.--) and the meter (–.–|–.–). In doing so, I demonstrated the polymetric exchange between poetry and rhythm. This task was not difficult for most participants. However, the analysis of melody was. It involved identifying a descending contour that consisted of two symmetrical yet disjunct tetrachords. When I drew the descending contour on the board, they could see as well as hear.

FIGURE 2.7. Musicians from the Academy of Maqâm in a workshop

Finally, I asked them to interpret the piece. I started with the song text. Immediately, they could understand the lyrics since they employed a standard vocabulary of Persian terms that is also found in Tajik and Uzbek. For similar reasons, they could recognize the mystical topoi of Persian poetry. Here, the dialogue between the lover and the beloved was standard fare. I then asked them to clap the meter while they spoke the words. Interestingly, they felt the ways in which the metric cycle helped clarify (through emphasis) the meaning of the song text. By adding the melody, a new set of correspondences occurred, where the "I" of the lover and the "Thou" of the beloved fused momentarily in instances of ontology. Further, the symmetries in the poetry matched the symmetries in the melody. For such an audience, acquainted with the language of literature, this discovery of correspondences and symmetries was revealing, since it demonstrated the principal role of music in unveiling divine presence.

In stage three, I no longer had to convince the teachers or the students about the significance of music. I also did not have to convince members of the design team about my hermeneutic approach to the form and content of the humanities curriculum. However, I did have to show participants and specialists alike how to integrate music making into the curriculum. To do this, I organized two expeditions. In the first expedition, we visited an instrument museum (the Gurminj Museum) in Dushanbe to describe, analyze, and interpret musical artifacts. In particular, we examined the *rubab* to uncover its symbolic meanings. We also visited a music school (the Academy of Maqâm). We attended a lesson in *shashmaqam*. At once, we noted the similarities between learning a Turkish *şarkı* and a Tajik *tarona*, especially with respect to analyzing the connection between poetry and rhythm. Indeed, students at the Academy are expected simultaneously to say and to clap complex poetic meters and rhythmic patterns.

In the second expedition, we undertook field research in Kulob. In preparation for this fieldtrip, I taught an introductory seminar on methods in ethnomusicology. In contrast to the excursion in Dushanbe, I wanted to show teachers and students how to collect musical materials for a class and how to integrate music makers into a class. In the former, they employed field techniques learned in my seminars to record, both visually and audibly, musical performances that were performed inside and outside. Done properly, this would enrich the educational experience and enhance the library resources. In the latter, they tested the integration of musicians in a hypothetical classroom. Following the tripartite model, they attempted to perform, analyze, and interpret a musical item, using the musicians both as performers and interpreters. Apart from some confusion (and some sarcasm) on the part of the music practitioners, this case study proved to be successful, being both simple in conception yet dialogic in character.

Research

To teach is to learn. This is certainly true in my experience. Although invited as an instructor and as a researcher, I was profoundly indebted to the knowledge that I gleaned from the participants on the project and from the excursions organized during the project. On the one hand, this acquisition of knowledge was informal, often based on a chance encounter between lessons or after concerts. At first, it allowed me acquire a basic facility with the principal language (namely Tajik). Later, it enabled me to ask focused questions about musical practice and cultural value, be it from specialists resident on the project or from musicians invited to the project. On the other hand, this acquisition of knowledge could be formal. Like the teachers and the students, I expanded my knowledge of music technology, music transmission, and music practice on the expeditions in Dushanbe and to Kulob. Critical here was not only the successful completion of fieldwork by the participants but also the adequate preparation for field research by me.

The project afforded me a visit to the heartland of the Ismaʿili community in the mountainous region of Badakhshan. Since I was especially interested in completing research on the *madah*, relevant participants on the project provided me with introductions to prominent musicians. Since many *madahkhan*-s lived in inaccessible valleys, I was able to prepare my itinerary in advance. This was especially invaluable. Further, I was accompanied for a short time by another consultant on the project, Bill Beeman. This was an ideal combination: Bill the language expert and me the music specialist, conducting joint research on a genre that had a literary as well as a musical dimension. In the first instance, we focused our energies on prominent musicians in the capital (Khorog), recording representative performances and documenting cultural values. In particular, we benefited from the esoteric knowledge of Janbaz, a respected *madahkhan* who explained the significance of cosmological order in dance and who outlined the place of numerology in music.[15]

According to Janbaz, the instrument of the *madahkhan* (the *rubab*) has five pegs and five strings.[16] He explained that the *madah* is divided into five sections (three main and two subsidiary). The *madah* is organized into five melo-rhythmic modes and by five distinctive poetic forms (starting with a five-lined poetic genre called *mukhammas*). This numerical arrangement has a mystical dimension. Humans are endowed with 10 attributes and 10 feelings, each of which is organized into five exterior (*zaher*) and five interior (*batin*) categories. Five is found in the Badakhshani conception of space. Here, internal pillars, household shelves, and door lintels (among other elements) follow a similar layout. Further, the "rule of fives" has a wider geographical significance. Badakhshan is divided into five regions, each with its own distinct language and each nourished by a tributary of the Panjāb (meaning "Five Rivers"). Simply put, the Badakhshani conception of sound is consistent with a Badakhshani conception of space.

When Beeman departed, I was fortunate to conduct two excursions into two valleys. The first was to Bartang. There, I documented the ecstatic dance that accompanied *madah*. This dance embodies cosmic order since it involves the continuous rotation of the hands and the feet. This symbolizes the constant flux of primal elements (earth, fire, water, and air) and the continuous interaction of good and evil. Where I had found that the number five had an Islamic significance in Khorog, I found that the number four had a pre-Islamic importance in Bartang, be it in architectural construction, clothing design, or bodily movement. Four is especially important in building. It is found in the shape of the central skylight (*chahar khaneh*) (see Figure 2.8), a tangible articulation of Aryan philosophy, in which the four elements fuse together in a circular fashion and where the four seasons progress from one to another, maintaining order in the cosmos.

FIGURE 2.8. A skylight or *chahar khaneh*

The second excursion was to Wahan. There, I discovered how music reveals the centrality of man in the Isma'ili universe. Visiting a shrine (*mazar*), I discovered a musical instrument (called *maqamboland*) similar to the *rubab* but shaped like a man (see Figure 2.9). Like the *rubab*, it had another feature, a horse attached to the head of the instrument. This conflation of horse and man seemed to contradict the anthropocentric reading of music according to an Isma'ili worldview.[17] Further, ancient hieroglyphics (dating from pre-Islamic times) represent the *rubab* (with five strings) as a dancer whose hands are held out in the form of a swastika. As I traveled along the Panj River, which marked the remote border between Tajikistan and Afghanistan, I witnessed a confusing assemblage of cosmogonic patterns and symbolic systems reflective of a Central Asian, a South Asian, and a West Asian reading of cultural identity. Clearly, the "rule of fives" was just one interpretation of Badakhshani identity.[18]

FIGURE 2.9. A musician playing a Maqamboland in Wahan

How did I make sense of this complexity? At first, I was drawn to a Derridean deconstruction of Heideggerian ontology (see O'Connell, 2004). At the time, each explanation of Badakhshani music seemed to disclose a distinctive interpretation of Badakhshani identity. It was not just the juxtaposition of the five (indicative of a West Asian register) and the four (indicative of a South Asian register), it also involved the intersection of a six and a seven, representing the equal and the unequal division of twelve in music and philosophy throughout Asia.[19] It would have been easy to conclude in a colloquial fashion that the issue was simply a matter of being "at sixes and sevens."[20] But is it? Numerology is visible and audible in the music culture of Badakhshan. It is expressed in musical discourse and it is uncovered in musical practice. It is performed as music. It is embodied as dance. Perhaps, there is a larger issue at stake here.

I return to Wahan. Inevitably, the car breaks down as night is falling. Aware of the possible dangers, the Tajik driver, the Russian soldier, and I are invited to stay in the nearest Pamiri residence. As is typical, the house has five pillars, representing the five key figures of Sh'ia heterodoxy (Mohammad, Ali, Fatima, Hassan, and Hussein). It also has a variety of designs representing an Aryan influence (especially the swastika) and a Zoroastrian legacy (especially the hearth). Before we repair to a single bed in the male quarter, we are invited to a sumptuous meal, followed by a night of entertainment. Animals are removed from the house for the occasion. The *madahkhan* plays *madah* while the family members dance. The party lasts for hours. Vodka flows freely. This is a lavish gathering, yet the family is apparently destitute. Accordingly, I ask the head of the house about this extravagance. He responds without hesitation: "without music we are not human."

Sounds Humane

Music makes us human. For my host, this was his immediate way of dealing with the calamity of war and the poverty of circumstance. But was there a hidden answer? Could he have meant "without music we are not divine"? That is, music helps each man to uncover the divine within. Is this the meaning behind the one and the many, one God in many men? Could this be the reason for the different numerologies and the distinctive symbolisms in Badakhshani culture, different manifestations of the divine in sound and space? In fact, diversity in culture could be read as complexity in history, where many peoples and many faiths have inhabited this hallowed terrain located at the epicenter of Asia. Here, unity in diversity could be understood as a comfortable accommodation of cultural difference in a highly contested strategic location. Or, it could be read as an expressive inscription of pluralism where one God is to be found in every man.

This notion of pluralism is explicit in the Aga Khan Humanities Project. When I returned to Dushanbe, I asked Keshavjee about my discoveries (see Figure 2.10). On the one hand, he confirmed the pluralist agenda that underpinned the project where all faiths and all ethnicities are accorded respect and deemed equal.[21] On the other hand, he emphasized the mystical source of this humanism: to love man is to love God. Such

FIGURE 2.10. Rafique Keshavjee in Dushanbe

a rationale is quite different from the secular humanism of European Enlightenment. It does not separate the natural from the supernatural, but it uncovers the supernatural within the natural. In this sense, it searches for an empirical explanation of the mystical. That is, the knowledge of humanity is the path to the knowledge of divinity. This is why a hermeneutic approach to the humanities curriculum is appropriate since it attempts to understand through experience and reflection—where observation, analysis and interpretation provide a productive framework for uncovering (the) truth.

Should I say "the Truth" or "truths"? This is an important point that Titon (1992) makes. For him, Truth resides in the theoretical, while truths emerge from the practical. Although Titon invokes Rorty (1979) in his criticism of philosophical reflection, he is in fact reiterating a contemporary conversation in anthropology about truth claims in the social sciences. In particular, his argument is remarkably similar to that of Clifford (1986),[22] whose notion of "partial truths" provides a philosophical bridge between hermeneutics and post-structuralism, between Heidegger and Derrida. For Heidegger, there is Truth. For Derrida, there is no Truth. Clifford presents an alternative answer to this philosophical debate. By recognizing partial truths as they emerge in ethnographic inquiry, Clifford calls for "an interplay of voices" where spoken utterance is not excluded from written representation, where the observer is engaged dialogically with the observed. In fact, Clifford significantly upsets the scholarly project by suggesting that truths are spoken and lies are written.

Applied ethnomusicology is also concerned with the truths that subjects speak. It allows the subaltern to speak in an academic world where scholars are required to write. It is a field where truths emerge in practice and not a field where Truth is prescribed in theory. Yet, should applied ethnomusicology exclude theory? Should applied ethnomusicology discount philosophy? I think not. And I am not alone (see Pettan and Harrison, 2010). In applied ethnomusicology, there are excellent examples of theoretical approaches to practice (see, for example, Araújo, 2008) and philosophical reflections on practice (see, for example, Loughran, 2008). Indeed, applied ethnomusicology has an established place in the academy, where field research is a guiding principle in ethnomusicology and in its cognate disciplines (such as anthropology and folklore). What applied ethnomusicology lacks is a unifying idea, a philosophical principle to underscore its important mission. In this matter, a humane approach to humanism offers a possible solution to the pressing issue of disciplinary disarray.

What might applied ethnomusicology consider if guided by the principles of a humane humanism? Clearly, the issues of tolerance and empathy would remain. So, too, the aspirations toward conservation would continue, especially in the realms of music transmission and cultural awareness. Consistent with a humane humanism, human welfare (in the form of music education), human well-being (in the form of music therapy), and human rights (in the form of music legislation) would continue to be central concerns. Perhaps, the critique of music in conflict and the advocacy of music in conflict resolution are more complex (see O'Connell, 2011). However, the notion of sustainability should provoke further investigation. This might involve a critical appraisal of musical materials used in the mass production of musical instruments. Or, it might involve the innovative deployment of music makers in development projects that foster communal pride and promote economic wealth. Significantly, the Aga Khan Humanities Project set a precedent in both areas.[23]

In this chapter, I have explored the central contribution of music to humanity. With respect to the Aga Khan Humanities Project, I have examined the ways in which music and humanism are revealed in the methodological, the theoretical, and the applied domains, three distinctive arenas of academic inquiry that embrace the spiritual, the scholarly, and the educational realms, respectively. Rather than viewing each as exclusive, I show how these domains interconnect with an alternative reading of humanism, a religious humanism in a Muslim tradition where tolerance and pluralism are honored and respected. Here, music provides a place for uncovering the humanistic (the "I in you") and for revealing the "humaneistic" (the "I could be you"), the twin tenets of tolerance and empathy underpinning a motivation to engage in applied research. Interestingly, I never thought of myself as an applied ethnomusicologist. However, I have always been an advocate and I have sometimes been an activist. As an applied ethnomusicologist, I can also be a theoretician and a scholar.

It is more than 10 years since I was in Central Asia. Since then, war has continued to decimate the region, setting religion against religion, pitting culture against culture.

I believe that music has a central role to play in this apparent "clash of civilizations." As a human endeavor, it helps to understand human difference through the humanistic tradition of scholarly reflection. As a humane endeavor, it helps to combat human indifference through the "humaneistic" aspiration of altruistic intervention. In the first instance, music can be used to celebrate human achievement, be it a renaissance among Muslims or a Renaissance among Christians. In the second instance, it can be utilized to foster human creativity, creating new human relationships as well as new human artifacts. Of course, some might argue that the power of music to advance a humane humanism is overstated—some might even say arrogant. I contend that a humane approach to humanism through music is an obligation. It is an obligation that we as ethnomusicologists cannot ignore.

Notes

1. Research in Tajikistan was sponsored by the Aga Khan Humanities Project (AKHP) and the Institute for Ismaili Studies (IIS). A grant from the Fulbright Commission allowed me to continue this research at Brown University (2002–2003). In this respect, I am especially indebted to William Beeman (Brown University) and Rafique Keshavjee (AKHP) for supporting my application. I would also like to thank Fatima Abduraufova, Karima Kara, Azim Nanji, Samandar Pulatov, Uvaido Pulatov, Tojidin Rahimov, Munira Sharapova, John Tomarra, and Anise Waljee of the Aga Khan Foundation for their help and encouragement. In Badakhshan, I am very grateful to the musicians and their families who made field research possible. These musicians include Janbaz Dushanbiyev, Mosavar Minakov, Mamadata Tavalayev, and Haydar Tokayev. In Dushanbe, I would like to acknowledge the assistance of Abduvali Abdurashidov and Gurminj Zavkibekov. More recently, I would also like to acknowledge Rafique Keshavjee, who read and amended an earlier draft of this chapter.
2. Of course, Titon (1992) is invoking the American tradition of pragmatism here. Like Rorty (1979), he is opposed to those philosophical traditions that seek the Truth. However, he does not contend that pragmatism is in itself anti-theoretical. May I convey my sincerest thanks to Jeff Todd Titon for clarifying this significant point.
3. Dario Martinelli (2005) provides a concise introduction to the field of zoomusicology and its related fields (such as zoosemiotics and biomusicology). Arguing that zoomusicology is concerned with musical universals, he attempts to apply musical principles to the analysis of bird song and whale song. Here, the author invokes an ongoing conversation that concerns music and evolution, Pinker (1997) believing it to be a non-essential aspect and Jordania (2011) believing it to be a vital component of human evolution. See also http://www.zoosemiotics.helsinki.fi/zm/ (accessed July 19, 2014).
4. During my time at UCLA, hermeneutic philosophy was the subject of considerable interest. Inspired by the intellectual leadership of Roger Savage (currently President of the Society for Ricoeur Studies), a number of ethnomusicologists adopted a hermeneutic approach to musical inquiry. These included Timothy Rice, Sonia Seeman, and me.
5. Note on transliteration: I have attempted to provide a scientific transliteration of those words and names that are represented in Arabic and Persian sources. Where Turkish terms are found, I provide the modern Turkish spelling rather than the Ottoman transliteration.

Since no Tajik-English dictionary was extant at the time of this study, I follow the system of transliteration that is used by the Institute for Isma'ili Studies (see www.iis.ac.uk). For example, I spell the Badakhshani lute as *rubab*, not following the Persian transliteration *rubāb* or the Tajik pronunciation *rubōb*. The same holds true for other terms associated with Isma'ili practice, such as the ritual space *jamatkhana* (rather than *jamā'at khāna*) and the musical genre *madah* (rather than *maddāh*). Since the representation of plurals is problematic, I employ the English plural suffix ("-s") instead. Of course, the same concepts and the same people appear in different languages and in different forms. In this matter, it is difficult to remain consistent (for example, Jalāl al-Dīn [Rumi] in Persian, but Calaleddin[-i] Rumi in Turkish), especially when a language (such as Tajik) has employed an Arabic, a Latin, and a Cyrillic script at various moments in its recent history.

6. In preparation, I read the following sources. For an introduction to the culture and history of Central Asia, I sourced Curtis (1997), Ferdinand (1994), Manz (1994), Rashid (1994), and Soucek (2000). For a more specialist overview of minority issues in Central Asia, I studied Allworth (1973, 1982), Brower and Lazzerini (1997), Kappeler (2001), McCragg and Silver (1979), and Smith (1998). To understand musical diversity in Central Asia, I examined Baily (1988), Beliaev (1975), During (1998), Jung (1989), Levin (1996), Parkes (1994), Sakata (1983), Slobin (1976), and Żerańska-Kominek (1997).

7. In preparation, I also accessed a variety of sources that concern the history and culture of Badakhshan. These include Badakshi (1988), Grevemeyer (1982), Nurjonov (1974–1975), Rajabov (1989), and van den Berg (1997). For representative sound recordings of Badakhshani music, I listened to During (1993), Fujii and Takahashi (1997), Kasmaï (2000), and van Belle and van den Berg (1994, 1998).

8. Badakhshan is situated in the sparsely populated Pamir Mountains. With a population of around 200,000, Badakhshan is distinguished geographically (mountains vs. plain), historically, linguistically, ethnically, and theologically (Shi'a vs. Sunnī) from the rest of Tajikistan. In the everyday lives of its residents, the distinction is expressed in the special allocation of a time zone to the region (called Khorog Time), in the special restrictions governing travel to the region (a *Gbau* visa is required), and in the special use of an official language in the region (Russian is preferred to Tajik).

9. Muslims are not alone in this espousal of humanism. As Tu and Daisaku (2011) show, the Confucian concept of the unity of heaven and humanity and the Buddhist notion of the oneness of self and universe represent a humanistic impulse to promote a "dialogue between civilizations." Like the Aga Khan Humanities Project, education plays a central role in this aspiration by cultivating an individual understanding of humaneness and compassion. In this matter, China is not exceptional. Other humanistic traditions can also be found in India (by way of Hinduism) and in Iran (by way of Zoroastrianism), where human nature takes precedence over religious dogma. As I emphasize in this chapter, it is important to distinguish between a religious humanism and a secular humanism, the former finding expression in many "Eastern" religions, the latter finding voice in a number of "Western" ideologies. See Murry (2006) for a contemporary discussion of religious humanism with respect to a branch of Christianity, Unitarian Universalism.

10. Many scholars view the destruction of Baghdad (1258) as a critical moment in this transformation. This event marked the end of the Muslim renaissance that had been promoted by the 'Abbāsid Caliphate (750–1258). Conquered by Genghis Khan, many libraries in Baghdad were destroyed and many scholars in the city were killed. Critical here was the transformation of the learned men in Islam (*'ulemā'*) from enlightened scholars to

theological dogmatists, abandoning scientific interpretation for scriptural explanation. Some scholars have also viewed the proliferation of Sufism in a similar light. For them, mystical experience offered an alternative to religious doctrine, providing a distinctive pathway at a time of political instability and social upheaval. See, for example, the classic accounts of Islam and mysticism written by Trimingham (1998 [1971]) and Geoffroy (2010), among many others.

11. The Isma'ilis belong to an esoteric branch of Islam (closely related to the Druze). They recognize the spiritual power and the temporal authority of the Aga Khan, who himself is a direct descendent (in contrast to other Shi'a groups) of the Seventh Imām (Imām Isma'il). Widely dispersed through Asia, Isma'ilis trace their origins to the diaspora of Nizari-s from Egypt during the Fatimid Period (909–1171), migrating eastward through Syria and Iran and settling also in Badakhshan (Tajikistan) and in Gujarat (India). See Daftary (1990) for an authoritative history of the Isma'ilis. See Hamawi (2011 [1970]) for an in-depth study of Isma'ilism, especially from the perspectives of philosophy and theology. See Keshavjee (1998) for an anthropological investigation of religious meaning among Isma'ili communities in Iran.

12. Of course, Tajikistan did not exist at the time of Rumi or Khusraw. While most Muslims believe that Rumi was born in Balkh (in Northern Afghanistan), recent research suggests that he may have been born further north in the Vakhsk Valley (in Central Tajikistan) (personal communication with Rafique Keshavjee, January 8, 2014). What is interesting is as follows: Both Rumi and Khusraw influenced the unique development of Isma'ilism in Badakhshan, especially with respect to a religious identity founded upon the central tenets of cosmic order, universal humanism, and imamate supremacy. While the Isma'ili community in Badakhshan (like other Isma'ilis) also subscribes to the five pillars of Shi'ism (unity, prophesy, judgment, imamate, and justice), their belief system is also informed by Khusraw's mystical ideals that melded neoplatonic philosophy with a pragmatic interpretation of Islam (see also Hunsberger 2000a, 2000b).

13. Since its inception, the Aga Khan Humanities Project has published 3,700 pages of texts in eight volumes, each of which is accompanied by teachers' guides, involving print, music, and film media.

14. Concerning changes to the status of the Aga Khan Humanities Project, Keshavjee explains "Soon after the project got started, the partner faculty, mainly social scientists and philosophers, realized that they had difficulty giving what I called 'parity to both reason and imagination'. They lacked a basic educational understanding of the arts, so the project organized an intensive training program in the pedagogies of painting, architecture, music, [. . .] and fiction." He continues "The Aga Khan Humanities Project is now much better understood as an unusual and powerful program based at the University of Central Asia that offers educational outreach to state institutions in Tajikistan, Kyrgyz Republic and Kazakhstan" (personal communication with Rafique Keshavjee, February 6, 2015).

15. Numerology has a long-established tradition in Islamic thought. In this respect, music by way of numerology provides an ideal medium for exploring natural relationships and for explaining supernatural occurrences. See Meisami (1997) and Malti-Douglas (1997) for a pertinent examination of cosmic numbers in poetry and literature, respectively. See also O'Connell (2004) for a relevant study with respect to music.

16. Other scholars have noted the significance of the number five. In particular, Koen (2003) provides a similar reading of sound and space in his study of devotional music in Badakhshan. Of course, his research was published after the presentation of my findings

at the Music and Minorities Conference in Lublin (2002). It also postdates the completion and the acceptance of my original article (which was finalized in 2002 but which was not published until 2004). While Koen talks about the importance of numerology in performance, he does not explore the significance of alternative cosmogonic systems that call into question a single reading of expressive culture in Badakhshan.

17. In terms of morphology, there are some conflicting narratives about the horse's head on the *rubab*. Since the horse occupies a prominent position in the Badakhshani imagination, it may indicate a complex exchange between Siberian and Indo-Iranian cultures in the Himalayan belt during the Bronze and the Iron Ages. In other words, it may represent a North Asian register in Badakhshani culture in addition to influences from the eastern, western, and southern corners of the continent. See Francfort (1998) for an overview of different interpretations of the horse found in Central Asian petroglyphs.

18. As Hunsberger notes (2000a, 2000b), there are a number of competing cosmogonic systems in Badakhshan: systems which (broadly speaking) emphasize a fivefold (the al-Fārābī school) and a fourfold reading (the Khusraw school) of the Badakhshani cosmos. These systems demonstrate the ways in which historic conceptions of a pre-Islamic and a post-Islamic past have become re-inscribed and re-interpreted within the discursive realm. In this way, traditional practices survive the destabilizing forces of geo-political fragmentation and ideological control.

19. There is a subtle symbiotic relationship between the numbers five and seven in Badakhshan. This play has a sonic articulation in Pamiri music (in terms of pentatonic vs. heptatonic musical structures) and in Pamiri organology (compare, for instance, the fivefold character of the Pamiri *rubab* with the sevenfold character of the Pamiri *tanbur*). This sense of numerical difference may also be gendered where the materials of music occupy distinctive but interconnected male and female spaces represented by the numbers five and seven, respectively. Here, Pamiri design clearly shows an intertextual play between the numbers five and seven, especially in the layout of the Pamiri house. This numerological relationship may have a larger significance in other Islamic countries (see, for instance, Becker and Becker, 1995).

20. As Popescu-Judetz (2002: 162–167) argues, the number six has a wider significance in Asian astrology, where the alignment of the Zodiac in the Medieval period resulted in two conceptions of cosmic order: that is, the division of the Zodiac into two equal units of six and six (representing the South Asian position) and the division of the Zodiac into two unequal units of five and seven (representing the West Asian position). Such conflicting worldviews are also played out in cosmogonic readings of the *rubab*, where some authorities emphasize the sixfold (rather than the fivefold) attributes of the musical instrument.

21. Concerning pluralism, Keshavjee writes "The stress on pluralism operated at different levels in the Aga Khan Humanities Project. Firstly, there was a plurality of intellectual perspective, of which the foremost was [. . .] parity given to works of reason and those of the imagination, especially in the arts. Secondly, the project aimed at pluralism by accommodation, where the texts covered an enormous range, from Lenin, through religious texts from various traditions, to Tolstoy and Kālidāsa. Thirdly, every civilization and faith tradition was represented pluralistically. Finally, the pluralism embodied in the Islamic mystical tradition was given prominence, especially since the then-parent organization of the project, the Aga Khan Trust for Culture, emphasized gnostic thought through its

involvement in the Aga Khan Music Initiative" (personal communication with Rafique Keshavjee, February 2, 2015).
22. Although Titon (1992) was writing in the 1990s, he is in fact quoting Rorty (1979), who was writing in the 1970s. In this respect, his concern for a dialogic approach to field research draws upon Bakhtin's notion of intersubjectivity (in linguistic terms: the space between signs) where language always needs to be negotiated. Simply put, meaning can never be fixed since it is always dependent upon the context of an utterance (see Bernard-Donals, 1994). That Clifford (1986) was also critiquing the concept of absolute truth during the 1980s does not mean that the ethnomusicologist and the anthropologist were in direct communication at the times of publication. May I convey my sincerest thanks to Jeff Todd Titon for clarifying this important point.
23. Rafique Keshavjee, in association with the Christensen Fund, was later involved in a sustainability project in Turkey, which funded musicians and dramatists. He employed artists to educate communities to cope with environmental change and political instability. See also a lecture by Keshavjee in the series entitled "Sustainability Unbound" at http://www.sustainableunh.unh.edu/sustainabilityunbound (accessed July 10, 2014).

References

Adamczyk, Lawrence P. (1995). "Napoleon I (Napoleon Bonaparte)." In *Great Leaders, Great Tyrants? Contemporary Views of World Leaders Who Made History*, edited by Arnold Blumberg, pp. 204–208. Westport, CT: Greenwood Press.

Allworth, Edward. (1973). *The Nationality Question in Soviet Central Asia*. New York: Praeger Publications.

Allworth, Edward. (1982). *The End of Ethnic Integration in Southern Central Asia*. Washington, DC: The Wilson Center, Kennan Institute for Advanced Russian Studies.

Araújo, Samuel. (2008). "From Neutrality to Praxis: The Shifting Politics of Ethnomusicology in the Contemporary World." In "Applied Ethnomusicology," edited by Svanibor Pettan. *Muzikološki zbornik/Musicological Annual* 44(1): 13–30.

Araújo, Samuel, and Grupo Musicultura. (2010). "Sound Praxis: Music, Politics and Violence in Brazil." In *Music and Conflict*, edited by John M. O'Connell and Salwa El-Shawan Castelo-Branco, pp. 217–231. Urbana: The University of Illinois Press.

Arendt, Hannah. (1958). *The Human Condition*. Chicago: University of Chicago Press.

Aziz, Khursheed K., ed. (1997–1998). *Aha Khan III: Selected Speeches and Writings of Sir Sultan Muhammad Shah*. 2 vols. London: K. Paul International.

Badakshi, Mirza S., and Mirza A. Bayk. (1988). *Tarikh-i Badakshan*. Tehran: Mu'assasah-i Farhangi-i Jahangiri.

Baily, John. (1988). *Music in Afghanistan: Professional Musicians in the City of Herat*. Cambridge: Cambridge University Press.

Barz, Gregory. (2012). "Advocacy Activism: Responsibility and the Ethnomusicologist." *SEM Student News* 4(Spring/Summer): 8–9.

Becker, Alton, and Judith Becker. (1995). "A Musical Icon: Power and Meaning in Javanese Gamelan Music." In *Beyond Translation: Essays Towards a Modern Philology*, edited by Alton Becker, pp. 349–364. Ann Arbor: University of Michigan Press.

Beliaev, Vikor M. (1975). *Central Asian Music: Essays in the History of the Peoples of the U.S.S.R.*, translated and edited by Mark Slobin and Greta Slobin. Middletown, CT: Wesleyan University Press.

Berg, Gabriel van den. (1997). "Minstrel Poetry from the Pamir Mountains: A Study on the Songs and the Poems of the Isma'ilis of Tajik Badakhshan." Ph.D. dissertation, University of Leiden (Netherlands).

Bernard-Donals, Michael F. (1994). *Mikhail Bakhtin: Between Phenomenology and Marxism.* Cambridge: Cambridge University Press.

Blacking, John. (1977). *Anthropology of the Body.* London: Academic Press.

Brower, Daniel R., and Edward J. Lazzerini, eds. (1997). *Russia's Orient: Imperial Borderlands and Peoples, 1700–1917.* Bloomington: Indiana University Press.

Clifford, James. (1986). "Introduction: Partial Truths." In *Writing Culture: The Poetics and Politics of Ethnography*, edited by James Clifford and George E. Marcus. Berkeley and Los Angeles: University of California Press.

Curtis, Glenn E., eds. (1997). *Kazakhstan, Kyrgyzstan, Tajikistan, Turkmenistan and Uzbekistan: Country Studies.* Washington, DC: Federal Research Division, Library of Congress.

Daftary, Farhad. (1990). *The Isma'ilis: Their History and Doctrines.* Cambridge: Cambridge University Press.

Dirksen, Rebecca. (2012). "Reconsidering Theory and Practice in Ethnomusicology: Applying, Engaging and Advocating Beyond Academia." *Ethnomusicology Review* 17: 1–32.

During, Jean. (1998). *Musiques d'asie centrale: L'esprit d'une tradition.* Paris: Cité de la Musique, Actes Sud.

Feld, Steven. (1988). "Aesthetics as Iconicity of Style, or Lift-up-over Sounding: Getting into the Kaluli Groove." *Yearbook for Traditional Music* 20: 73–113.

Ferdinand, Peter, ed. (1994). *The New States of Central Asia and Their Neighbours.* New York: Council on Foreign Relations Press.

Francfort, Henri-Paul. (1998). "Central Asian Petroglyphs: Between Indo-Iranian and Shamanistic Interpretations." In *The Archaeology of Rock Art*, edited by Christopher Chippindale and Paul Taçon, pp. 302–318. Cambridge: Cambridge University Press.

Gardner, Howard. (1983). *Frames of Mind: The Theory of Multiple Intelligences.* New York: Basic Books.

Geoffroy, Éric. (2010). *Introduction to Sufism: The Inner Path of Islam.* Bloomington, IN: World Wisdom, Perennial Philosophical Series.

Goodman, Lenn E. (2003). *Islamic Humanism.* Oxford: Oxford University Press.

Grevemeyer, Jan-Heeren. (1982). *Herrschaft, Raub und Gegenseitigkeit: Die politische Geschichte Badakhshans 1500–1883.* Wiesbaden: In Kommission bei O. Harrassowitz.

Hamawi, S. Khodr. (2011 [1970]). *Introduction to Isma'ilism.* F.I.E.L.D.: The Heritage Society, www.ismaili.net (accessed January 8, 2014).

Harrison, Klisala. (2012). "Epistemologies of Applied Ethnomusicology." *Ethnomusicology* 56(3): 505–529.

Harrison, Klisala, and Svanibor Pettan. (2010). "Introduction." In *Applied Ethnomusicology*, edited by Klisala Harrison, Elizabeth Mackinlay, and Svanibor Pettan, pp. 1–20. Newcastle upon Tyne: Cambridge Scholars Publishing.

Heidegger, Martin. (1927). "Sein und Zeit." *Jahrbuch für Philosophie und phänomenologische Forschung* 8: 1–438.

Heidegger, Martin. (1947). *Brief über den Humanismus.* Bern: A. G. Franke.

Higgins, Kathleen M. (2012). *The Music Between Us: Is Music a Universal Language?* Chicago: University of Chicago Press.

Hunsberger, Alice. (2000a). "Nasir Khusraw: Fatimid Intellectual." In *Intellectual Traditions in Islam*, edited by Farhad Daftary, pp. 112–129. London: I.B. Tauris.

Hunsberger, Alice. (2000b). *Nasir Khusraw: The Ruby of Badakhshan*. London: I. B. Tauris.

Impey, Angela. (2002). "Culture, Conservation and Community Reconstruction: Explorations in Advocacy Ethnomusicology and Participatory Action Research in Northern Kwazulu Natal." *Yearbook for Traditional Music* 34: 9–24.

Jonboboev, Sanatullo. (2010). *Humanities in Transition: Liberation of Knowledge in Central Asia and the Potential Role of the European Union*. Giessen, Germany: Zentrum für Internationale Entwicklungs- und Umweltforschung.

Jordania, Joseph. (2011). *Why Do People Sing? Music in Human Evolution*. Tbilisi: Logos.

Jung, Angelika. (1989). *Quellen der traditionellen Kunstmusik der Usbeken und Tadshiken Mittelasiens: Untersuchung zur Entstehung und Entwicklung des sasmaqām*. Hamburg: Karl Dieter Wagner, Beiträge zur Ethnomusikologie 23.

Kappeler, Andreas. (2001). *The Russian Empire: A Multiethnic History*. Translated by Alfred Clayton. Harlow, UK: Pearson Education.

Keil, Charles. (1987). "Participatory Discrepancies and the Power of Music." *Cultural Anthropology* 2(3): 275–283.

Keshavjee, Rafique. (1998). *Mysticism and the Plurality of Meaning: The Case of the Isma'ilis of Rural Iran*. London and New York: I. B. Taurus.

Keshavjee, Rafique. (2009). "Dancing to a Different Tune." *Aga Khan University Newsletter* 10(1): 4–5.

Koen, Benjamin D. (2003). "The Spiritual Aesthetic in Badakhshani Devotional Music." *the world of music* 45(3): 77–90.

Levin, Theodore. (1996). *The Hundred Thousand Fools of God: Musical Travels in Central Asia (and Queens, New York)*. Bloomington: Indiana University Press.

Loughran, Maureen. (2008). "'But What if They Call the Police': Applied Ethnomusicology and Urban Activism in the United States." In "Applied Ethnomusicology," edited by Svanibor Pettan. *Muzikološki zbornik / Musicological Annual* 44(1): 51–68.

Malti-Douglas, Fedwa. (1997). "Playing with the Sacred: Religious Intertext in *Adab* Discourse." In *Humanism, Culture and Language in the Near East: Studies in Honor of Georg Krotkoff*, edited by Asma Afsaruddin and Mathias Zahniser, pp. 51–60. Winona Lake, IN: Eisenbrauns.

Manz, Beatrice. (1994). *Central Asia in Historical Perspective*. Boulder, CO: Westview Press.

Martinelli, Dario. (2005). "A Whale of a Song: Zoomusicology and the Question of Musical Structures." *SEED* 5(1): ISSN 1492–3157.

McCragg, William, and Brian D. Silver, eds. (1979). *Soviet Ethnic Frontiers*. New York: Pergamon Press.

Meisami, Julie S. (1997). "Cosmic Numbers: The Symbolic Design in Nizami's Haft Paykar." In *Humanism, Culture and Language in the Near East: Studies in Honor of Georg Krotkoff*, edited by Asma Afsaruddin and Mathias Zahniser, pp. 39–50. Winona Lake, IN: Eisenbrauns.

Morrison. Karl F. (1988). *I Am You: The Hermeneutics of Empathy in Western Literature, Theology and Art*. Princeton, NJ: Princeton University Press.

Murry, William R. (2006). *Reason and Reverence: Religious Humanism for the 21st Century*. Boston: Skinner House Books.

Nurjonov, Nizom. (1974–1975). *Muzykal'naia Zhizn' Sovetskogo Tadzhikistana: 1919–1945*. 2 vols. Dushanbe: Donish.

O'Connell, John M. (1996). "Alaturka Revisited: Style as History in Turkish Vocal Performance." PhD dissertation, University of California, Los Angeles.

O'Connell, John M. (2004). "Sustaining Difference: Theorizing Minority Music in Badakhshan." In *Manifold Identities: Studies on Music and Minorities*, edited by Anna Czekanowska, Ursula Hemetek, Gerda Lechleitner, and Inna Naroditskaya, pp. 1–19. Newcastle upon Tyne: Cambridge Scholars Publishing.

O'Connell, John M. (2011). "Music in War, Music for Peace: A Review Article." *Ethnomusicology* 55(1): 112–127.

Parkes, Peter. (1994). "Personal and Collective Identity in Kalasha Song Performance: The Significance of Music-Making in a Minority Enclave." In *Ethnicity, Identity and Music: The Musical Construction of Place*, edited by Martin Stokes, pp. 157–188. Oxford: Berg.

Partner, Peter. (1979). *Renaissance Rome 1500–1559: A Portrait of a Society*. Berkeley and Los Angeles: University of California Press.

Pettan, Svanibor. (2008). "Applied Ethnomusicology and Empowerment Strategies: Views from Across the Atlantic." In "Applied Ethnomusicology," edited by S. Pettan. *Muzikološki zbornik / Musicological Annual* 44(1): 85–99.

Pettan, Svanibor, ed. (2008). "Applied Ethnomusicology." *Muzikološki zbornik/Musicological Annual* 44(1).

Pinker, Steven. (1997). *How the Mind Works*. New York: W.W. Norton.

Popescu-Judetz, Eugenia. (2002). *Tanburî Küçük Artin: A Musical Treatise of the Eighteenth Century*. Istanbul: Pan Yayıncılık.

Rajabov, Askaralī. (1989). *Az Ta'rikhi Afkori Musiqii Tojik*. Dushanbe: Donish.

Rashid, Ahmed. (1994). *The Resurgence of Central Asia: Islam or Nationalism*. Karachi: Oxford University Press.

Reynhout, Kenneth A. (2013). *Interdisciplinary Interpretation: Paul Ricoeur and the Hermeneutics of Theology and Science*. Lanham, MD: Lexington Books.

Rice, Timothy. (1994). *May It Fill Your Soul: Experiencing Bulgarian Music*. Chicago: The University of Chicago Press.

Rorty, Richard. (1979). *Philosophy and the Mirror of Nature*. Princeton, NJ: Princeton University Press.

Sakata, Hiromi L. (1983). *Music in the Mind: The Concept of Music and Musician in Afghanistan*. Kent, OH: Kent State University Press.

Schippers, Huib. (2010). "Three Journeys, Five Recollections, Seven Voices: Operationalising Sustainability in Music." In *Applied Ethnomusicology*, edited by Klisala Harrison, Elizabeth Mackinlay, and Svanibor Pettan, pp. 150–160. Newcastle upon Tyne: Cambridge Scholars Publishing.

Seeger, Anthony. (2010). "The Suyá and the White Man: Forty-five Years of Music Diplomacy in Brazil." In *Music and Conflict*, edited by John M. O'Connell and Salwa El-Shawan Castelo-Branco, pp. 109–127. Urbana: The University of Illinois Press.

Sharpe, Robert. (2000). *Music and Humanism*. Oxford: Oxford University Press.

Slobin, Mark. (1976). *Music in the Culture of Northern Afghanistan*. Tucson: University of Arizona Press, Viking Fund Publications in Anthropology 54.

Smith, Dianne L. (1998). *Opening Pandora's Box: Ethnicity and Central Asian Militaries*. Carlisle Barracks, PA: Strategic Studies Institute, US Army War College.

Soucek, Svatopluk. (2000). *A History of Inner Asia*. Cambridge: Cambridge University Press.

Spradley, James, and David W. McCurdy, eds. (2000). *Conformity and Conflict: Readings in Cultural Anthropology*. Boston: Allyn & Bacon.

Sugarman, Jane C. (2010). "Kosova Calls for Peace: Song, Myth and War in an Age of Global Media." In *Music and Conflict*, edited by John M. O'Connell and Salwa El-Shawan Castelo-Branco, pp. 17–45. Urbana: The University of Illinois Press.
Titon, Jeff Todd. (1992). "Music, the Public Interest, and the Practice of Ethnomusicology." *Ethnomusicology* 36(3): 315–322.
Titon, Jeff Todd. (2011). "Sustainable Music." *The Curry Lecture: Applied Ethnomusicology.* http://sustainablemusic.blogspot.co.uk, 1–11 (accessed January 17, 2014).
Trimingham, J. Spenser. (1998 [1971]). *The Sufi Orders of Islam.* New York: Oxford University Press.
Weil, Zoe. (2004). *The Power and Promise of Humane Education.* Gabriola Island, BC: New Society Publishers.
Weiming, Tu, and Daisaku Ikeda. (2011). *New Horizons in Eastern Humanism: Buddhism, Confucianism and the Quest for Global Peace.* London: I. B. Tauris.
Żerańska-Kominek, Sławomira. (1997). *The Tale of Crazy Harman: The Musician and the Concept of Music in the Türkmen Epic Tale, Harman Däli*, translated by Jerzy Ossowski. Warsaw: DIALOG Academic Publications.

Discography

During, Jean P. (1993). *Tajik Music of Badakhshan: Musique Tadjike du Badakhshan.* Musiques et Musiciens du Monde/Musics and Musicians of the World Series. Paris: Unesco and Auvidis, D 8212.
Fujii, Tomoaki, and Akihiro Takahashi. (1997). *Afghanistan on Marco Polo's Road: The Musicians of Kunduz and Faizabad.* Barre, VT: Multicultural Media, MCM 3003.
Kasmaï, Sorour. (2000). *Badakhshan: Pamir, chants et musiques du toit du monde.* Paris: Buda Records, CD 92744.
van Belle, Jan, and Gabrielle van den Berg. (1994). *Badakhshan: Mystical Poetry and Songs from the Ismaʿilis of the Pamir Mountains.* Leiden: Pan Records, CD 2024.
van Belle, Jan, and Gabrielle van den Berg. (1998). *Madāhkhanī, Gazalkhānī, Dafsāz: Religious Music from Badakhshan.* Leiden: Pan Records, CD2036.

CHAPTER 3

INTERSECTIONS BETWEEN ETHNOMUSICOLOGY, MUSIC EDUCATION, AND COMMUNITY MUSIC

PATRICIA SHEHAN CAMPBELL AND LEE HIGGINS

THE intermingling of dynamic activist-musicians in ethnomusicology and education in recent decades has resulted in changes to curricular content and instructional process in schools, in community venues, and on university campuses. Particularly in North American communities, but also in the United Kingdom, across Europe, in Australia, New Zealand, and Singapore, diversity mandates in schools and society have prompted teachers to expand and vary the music they feature in their elementary and secondary school classrooms. Teachers in a wide variety of venues, including university professors, who seek a multicultural array of songs, instrumental pieces, dance, and listening selections are locating them in the catalogues of publishing companies with national and international distribution and on the Internet, where they are finding the results of fieldwork by ethnomusicologists to apply to their curricular practices and programs. Tertiary-level students in colleges, conservatories, and universities are increasingly enrolling in ethnomusicology and world music performance courses in their degree programs, while their professors of music (often not trained ethnomusicologists) are finding ways to diversify the content of their programs through various resources (including invitations to local community musicians and culture-bearers). Practicing teachers are participating as in-service teachers in an array of short- (and longer-) term in-service courses to fill the gaps of knowledge created by their earlier university degree programs in music education, and they are learning from collaborative teams of ethnomusicologists and educators (and following on the works of ethnomusicologists that comprise the course reading and listening lists) in honing their understandings and skills in world music pedagogy. With the rise of Community Music as a bona fide professional pathway and influential movement that emphasizes inclusion through non-formal learning, teachers are growing an ethnomusicological sense of place, an intrigue with and honoring of local communities, and a resonance with the position that music is situated within the lives of those who choose to make it—with or without musical training or extensive experience. As a field of practice, those who work in community music, or advocate for it, make distinctions between community music, music of a community, and communal music making. Music of a community identifies and labels a type of music; communal music making describes being part of, or exposed to, that music; while community music is an active intervention between a music leader or facilitator and participants and is not tied to any particular genre of music. From this perspective and serving as an illustration, samba reggae reflects particular Afro-Brazilian communities in Bahia and could be described as music of a community. With the emphasis in a different place, a music session in a local Irish bar involves musicians and participants drawn from the communities where music is made. These are communal music-making events because they strive to bind people together through performance and participation. Community music is understood as different because it is an intentional approach to engage participants in active music making and musical knowing outside formal teaching and learning environments. It involves skilled music leaders, who facilitate inclusive group music-making experiences with an emphasis on people, participation, context, equality of opportunity, and diversity. Musicians who work this way seek to create accessible music-making experiences that emphasis creative music making and self-expression. Examples of projects might include working with young people to create their own songs, running large-scale intergenerational carnival groups, facilitating a choir or popular music bands within the prison or health service, or working within a community to enable community members to tell their story through music, song, and movement. The convergence of music education practice with ethnomusicology, especially of the applied action-based work of socially responsible professionals, and with community music, is extending and deepening the potential of music to engage learners in meaningful ways in various school and out-of-school settings.

This chapter seeks to document and decipher the intersection of applied ethnomusicology and music education, as well as their affiliations with the phenomenon of community music. Formal, informal, and non-formal educational practices and policies are described and dissected as they play out in various settings and circumstances, and are recognized for the myriad ways in which specialist-musicians (again, ethnomusicologists, music educators, and community musicians) have paralleled and overlapped one another in their endeavors. An historical chronology of systemic school music education, with particular attention to US schools as well as the tertiary-level programs that train them,[1] is offered as a means of contextualizing music education as a long-standing endeavor. The realms of ethnomusicology pertinent to music teaching and learning, particularly within institutions, are noted as well, along with the interfaces of ethnomusicologists with music educators. The collaborations among them illustrate the means by which they have jointly affected change in the lives of children, youth, and other learners whose potential it is to think and behave musically. The work of ethnomusicologically conscious educationists is described, from the production of instructional materials, including books, recordings, and Internet resources, to the enfolding of culture-specific processes of music learning and teaching in clinical ways for the diversification of music in classroom and rehearsal settings. Insights are offered as to how educators with the sensibilities engendered by studies in ethnomusicology and community music (as well as with traditional artists and culture-bearers) have developed school and community projects that celebrate the local. The lens is sharpened for views of the Harlem Samba project and the Music Alive! in the Yakima Valley in order to clarify the many facets of ethnomusicological precepts in action within educational contexts. The chapter lands squarely on the meaning of applied ethnomusicology as it is relevant and useful to those committed educators in schools and communities who seek global as well as local relevance of music as a human phenomenon. It draws on the experiences of children and youth, their teachers, facilitators, and group leaders in music-making ventures, especially those whose identities are shaped by their participation as singers, players, dancers, and active listeners.

Contextualizing Music in Systemic School Education

Contemporary practices of systemic music teaching and learning emanate from a long and colorful history, and it can be argued that music education dates to the first historic instances of music's transmission from expert musician to novice. There is rich evidence of music education in churches, conservatories, and universities in medieval Europe, and music joined the curricular array of required subjects in the United States and the United Kingdom during the nineteenth-century rise of the common school of tax-supported education for all children and youth. Lowell Mason formally established music as an American curricular subject in Boston in 1838, and its song-based emphasis was heralded as an avenue to the development of children's moral and physical well-being (Pemberton, 1985). Other North American cities followed suit, even as music was also emerging as a school subject in the United Kingdom, Germany, France, and elsewhere in the world. Within a few decades the vocal music education of American elementary schools had become a way for learning to read staff notation by singing a repertoire of European-based folk songs and traditional hymns (Pemberton, 1985). Ensembles of choirs, bands, and orchestras began to appear in American secondary schools by the late nineteenth century, and performance experiences in the music of the European tradition rapidly developed for the aesthetic-expressive education of adolescents. Even as Americans were singing sacred and secular music in their communities (far beyond the realm of schools, in churches, communities, and "singing societies"), Lowell Mason and his contemporaries were asserting a musical hierarchy in which music of the German tradition was of such quality that even the "new compositions" they were writing for schoolchildren resembled the structures and sentiments of German-origin (and some Italian, French, and British) art music (Mark and Gary, 2007).

Nineteenth-century school music teachers in the United States, the United Kingdom, and continental Europe focused their efforts on singing, notational literacy, and music appreciation (Keene, 1982). Canonic works by European composers comprised the repertoire of musical study in schools, and composed works for school-age singers and instrumentalists were decidedly European and Euro-American in flavor. With the invention of the gramophone, listening lessons on the Victrola talking machine offered homage to the composers of masterworks by composers of the European Baroque, Classical, and Romantic periods, too, as music appreciation goals gained prominence in the curriculum in the opening decades of the twentieth century (Mark and Gary, 2007). Group violin lessons and school orchestras were gradually coming into being, but instrumental music study was rare in schools (especially in the US) until the end of World War I, when bandsmen from the battlefields in France and Germany were hired as music teachers in American schools to work with young wind, brass, and percussion musicians in concert and marching bands (Keene, 1982).[2] Glee clubs, mixed choirs, and instrumental ensembles spread like wildfire in the 1920s and 1930s, partly under the influence of popular touring orchestras and widely available church choirs. An increasing number of secondary schools were staffed by specialist teachers in choral and instrumental music, trained in music and eventually graduating from university programs in music education.

Distinctively original expressive forms of American cultural communities comprised urban, and even suburban and rural areas, and yet Western art music forms continued to prevail as the principal curricular content in school music classes well into the twentieth century. In the United States, teachers generally viewed folk music, including the expressions of Native Americans, African Americans, and Latin Americans, as "primitive" repertoire that was ill-suited for curricular inclusion (Volk, 1998). In fact, the designation of "folk music" inferred, often inaccurately, a minimalist or simplified expression when compared to the sophistication of European art music (Campbell, 1991). A performance by the Fisk Jubilee Singers at the Music Supervisors National Conference in 1922 was an impressive first encounter for many educators of the power and sophistication of their choral music, after which spirituals began to surface on the concert programs of school choirs (Volk, 1998). African American popular music forms were forbidden in the curriculum of that time, including blues, ragtime, and jazz, in no small part due to the climate of racial inequality that was rampant in American society of the time. Their associations with saloons and "after hours" clubs caused concerns by educators that the music itself was cheap, vulgar, and immoral and thus potentially ruinous to young people (Mark and Gary, 2007). Music of the Jazz Age was excluded from the schools, and in the 1920s neither the popular Charleston nor "the shimmies" were permitted on school grounds. Jazz was finally allowed into some schools in the 1950s as an extracurricular club activity in which students met after school to rehearse for the school dances at which they would perform, yet even then they were referred to as "dance bands" rather than jazz.

School music teachers understood folk and traditional music of a variety of origins as interesting but not fully appropriate for the enlightenment of young people for whom the benefits were greatest through experience in the expressions of high culture. From the 1920s onward, a gradual awakening of interest in the broader palette of musical styles and cultures revealed itself in classrooms where immigrant populations were prominent. Folk dancing (especially from European countries from which immigrants were arriving) was featured in community centers, "settlement houses," and local schools (Mark and Gary, 2007), and physical education classes featured "folk dances from around the world" (including US-based square- and contra-dancing, but also Irish set dances, Germanic-style polkas, circle dances of the Slavic groups, and the Italian tarantella). "Songs of many lands" surfaced in school classrooms at both elementary and secondary levels, and integrated units were developed of folk songs with geography, history, and literature content. The growth of folk music in schools was aided by the advent of recordings, so that as schools were equipped, teachers could play Irish, or German, or Italian music alongside the works of European art music (Campbell, 2004).

Largely through the Good Neighbor Policy established by the Roosevelt administration to direct cultural exchanges with the countries of Central and South America, a surge of interest in Latin American music arose in the United States in the 1930s (Volk, 1998). The State Department funded concert performances and educational residencies of artists and educators from Latin America to the United States, as American music educators traveled south to Mexico, Brazil, and Argentina. The Music Educators National Conference advocated the use of Latin American songs and listening experiences, and textbook companies responded to an urgent demand for "materials." Yet rarely was there a school orchestra that was given the opportunity to tackle a work by Mexican composer Carlos Chavez, or a band that was offered occasions to play a bolero, rhumba, or other dance form on their wind and brass instruments. American music educators often sufficed with leading their students in singing *The Mexican Hat Dance* or *La Cucaracha* as demonstration of their attention to the music of their Latin American neighbors (Volk, 1998).

A number of events were seeding music curricular change in American schools in the mid-twentieth century, not the least of which were rapid transformations in transportation and communications. With close of World War II, music educators were inspired to seek means for achieving international understanding and world peace, and music was romantically viewed as "the international language." The United Nations Educational, Scientific and Cultural Organization (UNESCO) established the International Music Council (IMC), which in turn set up the International Society for Music Education (ISME) in 1953 with the intent of bridging cultures in classroom practices by fostering the presence of world music cultures for performance and study in elementary and secondary schools, and in universities as well (Schippers and Campbell, 2013). Policy statements on music in the curriculum were advocating the importance of knowing "music of the world's peoples," and elementary school textbooks were shifting to the presentation of musical cultures through authentic field recordings.

Music educators in the United States were challenged by their professional society, the Music Educators National Conference (now the National Association for Music Education), to consider the community values of their diverse student populations, and to rethink repertoire and pedagogical approaches, particularly with the advent of multiculturalism in American society. By the 1970s, the organization recommended a shifting of policy and practice from a European-based musical content to an all-inclusive curriculum comprising popular music, jazz, and music of the world's cultures (Campbell, 2013). The rhetoric was eloquent, and some teachers were impassioned by the possibilities, but the reality is that few were prepared to know the content and method of a more global view of music. First-generation "world music educators" like William M. Anderson, Barbara Reeder Lundquist, Sally Monsour, and James Standifer served the cause by contributing to the reform of repertoire in textbooks and recordings, and modeled content and method of songs and singing, polyrhythmic percussion ensembles, folk dancing, and listening experiences that were part analysis and part participation. Their interest in diversifying the curriculum was due in no small part to their own training or professional work at universities with strong ethnomusicology programs (Anderson, Lundquist, and Standifer), or due to their own experiences as members of minority populations (Monsour, Standifer). In the heyday of "multicultural music education"—especially in the 1980s and 1990s, when district mandates were requiring secondary school band, choir, and orchestra directors as well as elementary music specialists to develop broader cultural understandings through music—the dissemination of songs, dances, and instrumental pieces was continued by a second generation of "world music educators," including some who were trained in and working at the edges of ethnomusicology, as well as through the proliferation of multicultural materials in textbooks, on recordings, and through the Internet (Schippers and Campbell, 2013). In selected schools, music educators were developing "African drumming ensembles," gospel choirs, steel bands akin to those in Trinidad, full-fledged Mexican-style mariachis, Filipino kulintangs, and floor-sized marimba bands modeled after those found in a handful of Sub-Saharan African cultures. The Folk Arts Division of the National Endowment for the Arts (NEA) was funding grants to introduce traditional artist-musicians and culture-bearers into the schools, a movement whose ideas were first fostered by ethnomusicologists and public folklorists. In the professional literature, additional labels were ascribed to the movement to diversify the school music curriculum, including "world music pedagogy," "global music education," and "cultural diversity in music education" (Campbell, 2004). Central principles were articulated: to engage students in the performance and directed listening of music in its multiple manifestations; to teach cultural understanding through the study of music, musicians, and their musical values; and to respond to the identities and interests of individual students within the school community. Ideally, and in the hands of dedicated music educators, diversity was gaining a toehold in the music curriculum.

The funding crisis in the arts that began in the late 1990s has limited the capacity of music educators to work in schools toward fully embracing the tenets of a multicultural or world-oriented curriculum. Across the United States, many schools are expending every effort to hold on to their programs, shoring up against the erosion of long-standing traditions in band, choir, orchestra, and conventional song-based elementary music programs. In the post- 9/11 period, there have been some indications of a backlash to the movement to multiculturalize the curriculum, and some music educators are drawing their attention back to the traditional "American" repertoire of standard school ensembles (Schippers and Campbell, 2013). Opportunities for professional development in selected world music cultures—especially beyond light treatment via simple songs to sing—are available but rare, as funding from institutions and public agencies has largely disappeared. Given dwindling time for music within the school-day schedule, a monocultural approach is still widely in practice to sustain the repertoire of the historical school-music culture, and experimental world music ensembles and programs of music consisting of a mix of world cultures are not as common as the rhetorical writing in the professional literature would have one believe.

Despite the obstacles, there are exemplary models of music education practice attendant to matters of musical and cultural diversity, some of them traceable to the work of ethnomusicologists and community music practitioners. The Smithsonian Folkways certification course in World Music Pedagogy is one such successful collaboration of educators, ethnomusicologists, and local artist musicians for offering participating teachers the opportunity to develop sensibilities and skills for featuring both online recordings and human resources in the experiences they build into their programs. The emergence of a community consciousness has motivated some music educators to be in touch with musicians living locally, and in this way gospel choir singers, Irish fiddlers, Puerto Rican salsa-style percussionists, Japanese koto players, and Native American singer-storytellers have served as resident artists in schools, providing up-front and personal experiences with music and musicians. While federal and state funding has largely disappeared for such programs, local organizations (such as the nationally networked parent-teacher organizations) have supported these residencies. Model programs featuring "zimarimba" ensembles based on Shona-style music of Zimbabwe, bluegrass orchestras, samba bands, mariachis-in-school (rather than as after-school clubs), and world vocal ensembles are thriving in some schools due to the work of committed teachers and supportive families. Vibrant school programs are mixing traditional music education practices with world music traditions, and a conscientious attention and abiding respect are paid to the musicians and cultures from which the music comes. In these programs, informal, non-formal, and formal learning circumstances are wedded, and students are offered personal and communal expressions of artistic, social, political, and cultural concerns from a wide span of the world's musical cultures.

Ethnomusicology in Higher Education

In addition to its place in elementary and secondary school programs (whether mono- or multicultural in nature), music is a frequent degree option in tertiary-level programs of study colleges, conservatories, and universities. Alongside performance studies of the orchestral instruments, and vocal studies for singers, there is in higher education a selection of academic programs in musicology, music theory, composition, and music education. Yet another specialized realm of study in higher education is ethnomusicology, which may be encompassed within musicology or left to stand alone as its own entity. Where available, ethnomusicology is more likely featured as a graduate degree option than as an undergraduate degree, and may appear in the guise of single undergraduate-level survey courses in world music cultures or as performance opportunities in music beyond European art music styles. Occasionally, there is a confusion of the term and concept, positing "ethnomusicology" as interchangeable with "world music" in performance, as in the case of a Javanese gamelan or an African drumming ensemble, when in fact the former is the scholarly study of music in culture for which fieldwork is central (Nettl, 1983). Ethnomusicologists on university faculties of music are educators themselves by way of the teaching of courses, applied lessons, and ensembles, and while they are more rarely involved in the education of children and youth in schools, they devote themselves to passing on the musical practices they have studied in their fieldwork.

Ethnomusicology is a relatively recent arrival to higher education. Despite its appearance in some American university settings just after World War II and in Europe under the name "comparative musicology" from the late nineteenth century, it was with the founding of the Society for Ethnomusicology in 1955 that the curiosity of university faculties of music was piqued to know the musical expressions of "the exotic other," and to find relevance in the study of music as a world phenomenon. The contributions of ethnomusicologists to university units of music expanded the palette of sonorities to which students could have access. Where multicultural mandates were in place, ethnomusicologists were hired to pay tribute to musical expressions reflecting populations on campus, in the surrounding community, nationally, and even globally. In universities where ethnomusicology programs were first established and at which education programs were already vibrant—at the University of California Los Angeles, the University of Washington, the University of Michigan, Indiana University, and the University of Illinois, the door was opening in the 1960s and 1970s to studies in the music of India, Japan, Indonesia, across the African continent, and in the Americas, and the ears of prospective music educators was opening to a wide spectrum of world music. Early in the history of ethnomusicology in higher education, gamelan "orchestras" dominated by bronze metallophones and gongs became iconic statements of tertiary-level programs seeking diversity in their content. These ensembles were exemplar of "high-art Asian music" that began to appear in courtyards or rehearsal rooms, drawing students directly into music-making experiences. At the edge of the Civil Rights era, visiting artists from Ghana and elsewhere in West Africa were invited by university music departments to form drumming ensembles and to lecture on the musical cultures of their communities. Students—including music education majors—were made aware of the *ngoma* tradition, in which singing, dancing and drumming are equally valued, even as they were learning to think and act in ways that required their keen attention to rhythmic precision, physical involvement in synchronous movement, and interactive and communal performance. Gospel choirs began to appear at universities, too, although more often within the realm of student activities rather than as a scheduled course within the music department. Latin American music began to seep into the repertoire of jazz ensembles, and Mexican mariachi became an occasional presence on selected campuses in California and Texas. While still uncommon, some students were graduating from university degree programs with the requisite sensitivity and skills for teaching music from a broader palette of expressions, largely due to the presence of ethnomusicologists on their campuses.

Of the various faculty in schools and departments of music, ethnomusicologists have continued to receive especially enthusiastic support from composers and music educators to run performance ensembles and teach courses in world music cultures that would meet multicultural mandates (Solis, 2004). Composers sought new sonic sources from ethnomusicologists who share their fieldwork recordings from far-flung places in the world, while music educators press ethnomusicologists with questions of "authentic materials" to add to the multiculturalizing of a curriculum in schools. Music majors, as well as students with little interest in music but with demands for an arts elective, are well served by ethnomusicologists through introductory academic courses in the "Music of Asia," "African Music," and "Music of the Americas." With the presence of ethnomusicologists on university faculties, a balanced diet of musical experiences is achievable in an undergraduate music program—although the reality is that most music programs remain as European-styled conservatories steeped in the study of European art music. Still, those music students seeking certification as teachers can develop their commitment to a broader palette of music expressions for the school-age students they will teach.

The Convergence of Ethnomusicology and Education

The greater convergence of ethnomusicologists and educators (especially those with their attention to school music education) began in in the 1960s, and while the development of understandings and collaborations has been gradual and uneven, the results of the forging of interests and expertise have been impressive. Some of the earliest earnest efforts to diversify the curriculum and to develop a resonance of school music education with local musical communities happened at seminars and symposia at Yale University (1963), Northwestern University (1965), and Tanglewood (1967), all think tanks of sorts to examine music practices in schools and universities, and to consider music "of quality and relevance." Set against a broader culture of change that included an increased availability of world music during the 1960s, the folk music revival, the blues revival, the concert tours of musicians such as Ali Akbar Khan and Ravi Shankar, and the rise of recordings such as the "Explorer" series from Nonesuch Records, the meeting at Tanglewood involved educators, along with musicologists and ethnomusicologists, composers, jazz and popular musicians, and community leaders for the purpose of examining tidal-wave changes in society that would necessitate music educational reform in schools. David McAllester's historic proclamation to music educators in 1967 at the Tanglewood Symposium set the tone—that "music of our time and places in the world" should be taught to children, and that the contributions of ethnomusicologists to education should be presented to teachers at conferences and workshops, in the development of materials for instructional purposes (films, recordings, and books), and in visits to schools and community settings where children and youth gather. McAllester, attuned as he was to the musical cultures of the Navajo, the Hopi, and other Native American peoples, was also an activist in support of a broader spectrum of music study by schoolchildren. His remarks at the Tanglewood meeting were observant of the beginnings of curricular change, as he noted in particular the presence in schools of songs from Israel and various African cultures and the growth of "youth music" (popular and rock music) for educational purposes. McAllester posed a question that turned the heads of participants in this historic symposium: "How then can we go on thinking of 'music' as Western European music, to the exclusion of the infinitely varied forms of musical expression in other parts of the world?" Of all the gatherings of that tumultuous decade, Tanglewood stimulated thinking at the national level as to whose music could be featured in schools.

Ethnomusicologists have notably influenced curriculum and instruction in and through music, and their advisories and models have radiated into philosophy, policy, and practice within school music education. Conferences provided venues for demonstrations, workshopping sessions, and dialogue, particularly at annual meetings of the Society for Ethnomusicology (SEM), the Music Educators National Conference (MENC), and the International Society for Music Education (ISME). In the 1970s, Charles Seeger, David McAllester, and William P. Malm were among the active participants in Education Committee workshops for teachers at annual SEM meetings that featured presentations by educators who also had trained in ethnomusicology. A banner year of cross-field discussion happened in 1984: Robert Garfias offered his vision of "thinking globally, acting locally" to teachers at the 1984 MENC meeting; a panel of ethnomusicologists and music educators (including Robert Garfias, David McAllester, Edward O'Connor, Abraham Schwadron, and Patricia Shehan) at the annual SEM meeting addressed the challenges of representing world music in authentic fashion; and the Wesleyan Symposium on Becoming Human Through Music brought together John Blacking, Charles Keil, Adrienne Kaeppler, David McAllester, Timothy Rice, and others to explore the "practical implications of research findings in other cultures for U.S. music teachers in their daily instruction." With the re-establishment and strengthening of the Education Committee by the SEM board in 1985, SEM workshops became an annual attraction for local teachers in the city in which the annual conference was held. Sessions at Rochester (1986), Ann Arbor (1987), and Cambridge (1989) were particularly memorable for their unique formats and features, and considerable length. In 1990, the efforts of MENC, the SEM, and Smithsonian Folkways were combined to develop a three-day meeting of music educators with ethnomusicologists and artist-musicians in response to questions by teachers facing multicultural mandates of whose music should be taught, and how it could be integrated into school music programs (Campbell, 1996); William M. Anderson, Han Kuo-Huang, Dale Olsen, Bernice Johnson Reagan, Anthony Seeger, Daniel Sheehy were among the featured clinicians. A considerable number of ethnomusicologists were traveling the circuit of music teachers to explain and demonstrate the possibilities of world music expressions in school classes, including Melonee Burnim, Shannon Dudley, Charlotte Heth, David Locke, Portia Maultsby, Ricardo Trimillos, and Bonnie C. Wade. Some were influential among music educators internationally, too, such as J. H. Kwabena Nketia and Bruno Nettl (who twice articulated the importance of diversifying the musical repertoire in schools in his keynote addresses to members of the International Society for Music Education in Seoul, Korea, 1994, and Beijing, China, 2010).

With clear indications that the nation and the world were forever changed by demographic shifts and efforts at globalization, instructional materials began to appear to take account of more of the musical world. Textbooks, some with recordings to accompany them, began to appear for use in tertiary-level courses: David Reck's (1976) compilation of course notes in his *Music of the Whole Earth*, Jeff Todd Titon's (1984) launch of *Worlds of Music* text and recordings, and Bruno Nettl's (1992) *Excursions in World Music*. The latter two have been highly influential through their multiple editions in offering several generations of university students an understanding of music as a world phenomenon. Other collegiate-level textbooks emerged, including Kay Kaufman Shelemay's *Soundscapes* (2001), Michael Bakan's *World Music* (2007), Michael Tenzer's *Analytical Studies in World Music* (2006), Terry E. Miller and Andrew Shahriari's *World Music: A Global Journey* (2005), and 26 small books with recordings in *The Global Music Series* edited by Bonnie C. Wade and Patricia Shehan Campbell, beginning in 2004 (Wade, 2004; Campbell, 2004).

Ethnomusicologists were invited by educators and their publishers into advisory roles in the expansion of K–8 repertoire for listening and performing, especially in American editions. Basal music textbooks (and accompanying recordings) of the 1970s were presenting art music traditions from China and Japan, and "rhythm complexes" of West African percussion ensembles for listening and performance. Fueled by the multicultural movement, *Multicultural Perspectives in Music Education* (Anderson and Campbell, 1989)[3] was published by MENC as a collaborative effort of educators working with ethnomusicologists to recommend materials and methods for infusing a broader sampling of musical cultures into the curriculum; Anthony Seeger wrote the foreword. From the late 1980s onward, books with associated recordings were churning out of the Connecticut garage of Judith Cook Tucker, editor-publisher of World Music Press, many of them the products of collaborations between educators and culture-bearers (who were often trained as ethnomusicologists, too): *Let Your Voice Be Heard* (Adzenyah, Maraire, and Tucker, 1996), *From Rice Paddies and Temple Yards* (Nguyen and Campbell, 1990), *The Lion's Roar* (Kuo-huang and Campbell, 1997), and *From Bangkok and Beyond* (Phoasavadi and Campbell, 2003). Songs, percussion pieces, choral works, and listening examples were selected for their authenticity and representation (as well as for their capacity to be performed and understood by young students), and authors were eager to ensure that the context, function, and meaning of the music were accurately represented. Recordings and video-recordings accompanied the music notation, and a standard caveat was offered: that the notation only more generally illustrates the sound, but that listening is essential to the learning process of music far from home.

For choirs of children, adolescents, and university-level singers, the launch in 2001 of *Global Voices in Song* was deemed as an important video-source of unison and choral song from the African continent, Asia, the Pacific Islands, and elsewhere, the result of work by music educator Mary Goetze and various artist musicians.[4] Even as hard-copy traditional media and materials continued to be available, the Internet soon became a go-to source of ideas by teachers for teaching world music. Especially noteworthy to educators were websites of *Smithsonian Folkways* (especially the "Tools for Teachers"),[5] the *Association for Cultural Equity* (with its lessons "For Teachers"),[6] and *Mariachi Online*,[7] all fruits of the efforts of ethnomusicologists and educators. These and other developments are opening up the channels for teaching beyond the Western European canon, not only in regard to repertoire, but also with attention to the pedagogical approaches that are evident within the various cultures.

The likelihood of the involvement by ethnomusicologists with educators appears to be directly related to the extent to which they have established themselves as recognized scholars on specific music-cultures (for example, Garfias on Japanese court orchestra [1975], McAllester on Navajo music [1973], William P. Malm on Japanese theater music [2001], Nettl on music of Iran and of the Blackfoot of Montana [1989], Wade on music of North India [1988]). Then, in their capacity as Presidents of the Society of Ethnomusicology, journal editors, and senior members with track records behind them, they have responded generously to the call for input and advice on world music for teachers. Should this pattern continue, there is then a promising future for partnership projects between ethnomusicologists and music educators.

From Transmission to Learning to Pedagogical Process

One historic topic of ethnomusicologists is the transmission of music, particularly among those whose interests concern oral tradition as verbally transmitted song, chants, folk tales, or speech (or sonically transmitted instrumental music). Learning is another topic of increasing interest in ethnomusicology, and yet with historical roots as well: Alan P. Merriam's (1964) declaration of learning as basic to understanding music-as-culture prompted some to study who teaches and who learns and how it is done. In classic fieldwork and the musical ethnographies that have resulted from it, the participant-performance approach to research has naturally placed ethnomusicologists in the position of students learning repertoire and techniques from artist-teachers of sitar and sarod, mbira, kora, and instruments such as the metallophones and gongs of the gamelan orchestra. This student perspective served to raise an awareness of the teaching-learning process, referred to ethnomusicologically as "transmission and acquisition," which is in fact akin to the "pedagogical practice" of music educators' ongoing attention. Bruno Nettl (1984) wrote of the importance of his consultants as teachers, including the Arapaho Indian, Will Shakespear, who sang a vast array of traditional melodies for him to learn and transcribe, and the Persian master, Nour Ali-Bouromand, who taught him the *radif* collection of micromelodies that are core to improvisation. Dissertations and monographs, particularly in the last quarter-century, along with journal articles, conference papers, and even films, have been important channels of information for knowing who teaches and who learns music, in which contexts music is taught and learned, and how informal learning of music occurs through enculturation processes. Other issues have been given limited attention by ethnomusicologists, too, including the politics and economics of music learning. Through these investigations, not only are specific music cultures known more fully, but a deeper understanding of the sociological features of music as human thought and behavior is thus developed (Campbell, 2011; Nettl, 2005).

Some have discussed in fine detail the instructional transactions of learning to play an instrument, or to sing or dance, within societies that are open and eager to have the musical participation of all their members, while others have described music learning within the strictures of social class, gender, or ethnicity. John Blacking (1967) wrote of the manner in which children learned the music of the Venda by positioning themselves centrally in the midst of performances and practice sessions, so that they might develop as if by osmosis into their rightful role as participants in the music-making of their egalitarian society. For John Bailey (2001), an ethnomusicologist with 30 years of study of *dutar* and *rubab*, two lutes of Afghanistan, learning to perform invites the practitioner into "the cognition of performance," the active movements and kinesthetic-spatial relationships, and the thinking processes of those at the center of musical life within a culture. Daniel Neuman's (1980) classic work on the training of classical musicians in North India is a description of the roles of teachers and students in the *gharana* system, in which music training is restricted by family status and heredity. The descriptions of Timothy Rice (1994) and Michael Bakan (1999) of their journey as cultural outsiders to learn traditional instruments of selected cultures are revealing of which skills may transfer, and which do not, from first cultures to second, adopted, cultures.

Ethnomusicologists have studied music learning in formal and informal settings, in conservatories, schools, private homes, and even in the open air (Rice, 2003). They have examined the extent of verbal and nonverbal techniques, the use of vocalization and solmization, the extent of aural and oral techniques, the use of rehearsal strategies, and the pace of the instructional delivery from the teacher to the student (Campbell, 1991, 2011). Neuman's (1980) work discussed the disciplined practice (*riaz*) in the *gharanas* of North India, in which students are expected to put in long hours of rigorous working out of their assigned drills on their instrument, and that the calluses on their hands and fingerpads are evidence of their time. In the study of the Bulgarian *gaida* (bagpipe),

Rice (1994) attends to the combination of aural, visual, and tactile means of learning the phrases that are connected to other phrases and which are later recalled in improvisation. Likewise, Bakan (1999) focused on the critical importance of combined modalities that must work in a complementary manner to ensure that skills and repertoire develop, with students observing the hands of the master while they follow closely in imitation of them. Blacking (1967, 1995) called attention to the choice of songs learned by Venda children as not necessarily appearing in a sequential order of simple-to-complex, but that they will select to learn first the songs that are most often heard over songs that are simpler in structure. In his study of jazz musicians, Paul Berliner (1994) found that many would transcribe entire solos from recordings but also use them for extracting and learning short phrases as vocabulary for improvisations to come.

The field of comparative music education is in its infancy, and yet this research by ethnomusicologists is relevant to interests by educators in knowing both diverse and common practices across cultures and systems in pedagogical processes, institutional models, and curricular structures. An understanding of aural learning, including imitation; improvisation; the presence, partial use, or complete absence of notation; and rehearsal strategies as they are found in various cultures are more than academic exercises or curious pastimes (Campbell, 1991). They are among the concerns of practicing teachers who seek the most effective means of instruction for their students, and who are buoyed by knowing of their effective use by others in the world.

Through the gradual process of ethnomusicology's convergence with the practice of musically educating students in the world's musical cultures, a phenomenon known as world music pedagogy is emerging (Campbell, 2004). Changing demographics, globalization, and mandates of multiculturalism have turned music educators toward a search for musical sources and the means by which they are transmitted, and have led them along the well-traveled pathways of ethnomusicologists, whose work has embraced music, learning, and transmission across cultures. The two streams of musical professionals have forged a focus on the pedagogy of world music, reaching beyond queries of "what" and "why" but also "how" with regard to the teaching and learning of music within cultures, and in the recontextualized settings of classrooms and rehearsal halls. Those working to evolve this pedagogy have studied with native artist-musicians, and have come to know that music can be understood through experiences that retain aspects of the culture's manner of musical learning and teaching. While "re-enactment" of a musical tradition in a new context is not the principal point, the pedagogy of world music encompasses oral/aural techniques, improvisatory methods (when pertinent), and customary behaviors during the lesson, as well as preliminary to and following the lesson. Sometimes referred to as "world music educators," those who have forged this field have ventured to the borders of their disciplines to blend the expertise and insights of ethnomusicology and education into a pedagogical system that considers culture as both "old" (original culture of the music) and "new" (instructional culture of the classroom).

Case studies of world music pedagogy are played out within classroom contexts that encompass elementary and secondary school settings, as well as university courses

(Campbell et al., 2005; Schippers, 2010). One prominent theme we hold is the belief that teachers teach effectively those genres that they themselves have learned from culture-bearers who are master musicians of their given traditions—even when they may feel compelled to recast the instruction to fit their students' needs. That non-Balinese can teach Balinese gamelan to non-Balinese children and youth is not so controversial a concept as it once was in educational circles. Still, it is a valued notion that teachers should train with culture-bearers at some point in their development of gamelan technique and repertoire, so that "the Balinese way" might deliver to students something of an inside track on musical and cultural understanding (Dunbar-Hall, 2005). In the view of those who study Indian classical music in the West, they frequently know an experience in modified transmission processes (Hamill, 2005), and yet the age-old practice of aurally learning "one phrase at a time" from a master musician appears to be essential to their internalization of ragas and their potential for improvisation. For Keith Howard (2005), who teaches SamulNori percussion ensembles at the tertiary level, his own study of the music led him to develop "encounters" rather than experiences in the mastery of the music. He described the aims of his modified SamulNori pedagogy as one that provides "entry and musical knowledge rather than cultural competence," using shortcuts and techniques that "inspire rather than frustrate." In teaching world music, then, studies with artist-musicians who bring an insider's view to the music are balanced by a belief in the importance of honoring the culture of the students.

Community Music at the Interface of the Fields

Community music as concept and term has been recently gaining popularity within the music education profession, particularly in relation to informal and non-formal learning, as well as cultural diversity in music teaching and learning. Applied ethnomusicology and community music share a common heritage and thus have overlapping interest in the social and cultural importance of music and music making (and thus music learning) within an educational context. On the whole, community musicians are committed to the idea that all people have the right and ability to make, create, and enjoy their own music—styles and expressions they prefer, that they grew up on, that they are still growing to know. Working with music, but cognizant of the social goals, those who facilitate community music activities seek to enable accessible music-making opportunities for those with whom they are working—children, adolescents, adults, and seniors. Concerned with encouraging open dialogue among different individuals with differing perspectives, musicians who work in this way strive to be conscious in developing active musical knowing while acknowledging both individual and group ownership of the music that they make. Community music happens in community centers, youth clubs, churches, senior homes, and prisons, and increasingly the community music processes are working their way into schools. Ideologically, the notion of cultural democracy is at the heart of the practice and aids as a compass in pointing toward its historical roots (Higgins, 2012a).[8]

Relevant to community music, to music education at large, and to applied ethnomusicology is the concept of cultural democracy as a tool for empowerment. As an early advocate, Charles Keil (1982) believed that beyond the scholarly pursuit and performance orientations of ethnomusicology, "applied" is another of the field's critical pursuits. He explained that applied ethnomusicology "can make a difference... (and) can intersect both the world outside and the university in more challenging and constructive ways" (407). A decade later, Jeff Todd Titon's (1992) introduction to the seminal collection of essays "Music, the Public Interest, and the Practice of Ethnomusicology" suggested that applied ethnomusicology has its awareness in practical action rather than the flow of knowledge inside intellectual communities. This concrete belief in action and agency is also true of community music, as well as activist school music educators. Somewhat differently from ethnomusicology, community music has not had a strong scholarly presence until relatively recently with the launch of the *International Journal of Community Music* in 2007. Community music has therefore been a relatively marginal subject within the academy, unlike ethnomusicology, whose anchoring can be located within university departments (Nettl, 2002). Community musicians have sought to challenge polarities that include formal/informal/non-formal, aesthetic/extra-aesthetic, and consumption/participation (Higgins, 2012a: 31). For a predominantly freelance workforce, paid opportunities to think, reflect, and write critically about the work has been rare; community musicians are looking for their next employment opportunity, rather than to engage in academic inquiry and establish a research culture.

Resonant with past practices in community music, applied ethnomusicologists have been concerned with the development of projects in the public sphere that involve and enable musicians and various musical cultures to present, represent, and affect the dispersion of music (Titon, 1992). Practice-informed theory, the development of public sector projects, and a desire to communicate ideas and findings without generating disengaged and remote scholarship are qualities that have taken precedence within the community music movement. Pedagogically in line with developments of non-formal education (Rogers, 2004), community music places emphasis on music making that supports a "bottom-up" rather than "top-down" approach to teaching, a stress on the inclusivity and participation, the encouragement of a personalized learning experience, and an understanding that the work can have an impact beyond the music making itself. Initially an "alternative" approach to formal education within developing countries, interest in non-formal education emerged from those who felt that formal education systems alone could not respond to the challenges of modern society. These included changes in the cultural, social, economic, and political landscape, such as ideas connected to globalization, government decentralization, and a growing democratization. Coming to prominence around the late 1960s, with the work of Philip Coombs (1968), non-formal education continued its growth through the 1970s within the context of development, "the idea that deliberate action can be undertaken to change society in chosen directions considered desirable" (Rogers, 2004: 13). Although the term "non-formal education" had been used prior to the 1970s, it was Coombs who claimed the first systematic study of it, laying down a number of definitional frameworks, the most refined of which states that non-formal education is "simply any organized activity with educational purposes carried on outside the highly structured framework of formal education systems as they exist today" (Coombs and Ahmed, 1974: 233). With this in mind, community musicians (as well as applied ethnomusicologists and enlightened music educators) need to have a keen understanding that they do intervene within groups and that the very nature of intervention generates issues and challenges of power within those relationships they seek to foster.

As skilled music leaders, community musicians emphasize active participation, sensitivity to context, equality of opportunity, and a commitment to diversity in their practice. Working within flexible learning, teaching, and facilitation modes, community musicians are committed to collaborative relationships, aiming for excellence in both the processes and products of music making. Learning happens in ways that fit the learners, and at their pace, and with attention to repertoire and techniques they prefer to learn. Within community music, the social well-being and personal growth of participants are as important as their musical development, and as such the framework of lifelong musical learning has been an important aspect of the work (Jones, 2009; Myers, 2007; Smilde, 2010).[9] As a common characteristic, community music facilitators are also aware of the need to include disenfranchised and disadvantaged individuals or groups, "recognizing the value of music in fostering inter-societal and inter-cultural acceptance and understanding" (Higgins and Bartleet, 2012: 496). As an example, in the United Kingdom during the late 1990s there was increased government support for community music activity through the National Foundation of Youth Music.[10] Policymakers have understood that music can play a valuable role in re-engaging young people with mainstream education, and therefore marginalized, or "at-risk," young people have benefited from increased music project funding. This has not been without criticism, as governmental cultural policy can have a negative impact on participatory music activity (Rimmer, 2009, 2012).

Applied ethnomusicology, like community music, is best understood through the work that it does rather than any attempt to describe what it is (as opposed to music education, which is so widely understood through earlier experience). Applied ethnomusicology examples that resonate with what we are describing here include Kathleen Van Buren (2010), World AIDS Day event in Sheffield, United Kingdom, Samantha Fletcher (2007) and the benefit concert she organized in support of the refugee and social justice committees at the Unitarian Church, Vancouver, Canada, Angela Impey's project (2006) that explores the operational interface between ethnomusicology, environmental conservation, and sustainable development in South Africa, Samuel Araújo's musical culture map in Brazil (2008), Tom van Buren's community cultural initiative (2006), Tina Ramnarine's collaborative project between universities and NGOs (2008), and Svanibor Pettan's advocacy work with various communities linked to the territories of former Yugoslavia (2010). Projects such as Keil's 12/8 path bands,[11] the activist street bands of the HONK! Festival (Garafalo, 2011), Maureen Loughran's (2008) community-powered resistance radio, the Seattle Fandango Project (Dudley, 2012), and Music for Change[12] all support the proposition that applied ethnomusicology intersects with the "spirit" of community music, and is considerably linked to best practices in music education. Applied ethnomusicologists and community musicians understand that music can play a vital role in community development through education, income generation, and self-esteem.

THE CASE OF HARLEM SAMBA

In 2002, music classes at the Frederick Douglass Academy (FDA) in New York City's Harlem neighborhood were not popular.[13] The band program had been in steady decline for years, and in order to get it back on its feet the school administration hired Dana Monteiro, a trumpet player and music educator from Providence, Rhode Island. After trying to develop the program for four years, Monteiro felt that he had made little progress and was faced with significant increases in class sizes and a transient student population.[14] While on vacation in Brazil, Monteiro met some local Pagode musicians and they encouraged him to visit an *escolar de samba* in the Quadra da Villa Isabel favela in Rio. It was during this trip that Monteiro had the idea that this particular form of music, with 250 drummers playing *batucada*, might just resonate with his students back in the United States. As he reflected about the school environment he was working in, he recalled that many students had been vocal in expressing that they wanted to play drums rather than brass or wind instruments. Upon his return to New York City, he decided to join a community samba group, Samba New York, and experience as a participant how the music was performed. Beginning with the cavaquinho, a small string instrument, Monteiro moved on to explore the percussion instruments such as the *surdo, tamborim, caixa*, and *repinique*. After an initial purchase of 10 drums, an after-school club was started; it eventually consumed the rest of the music program, forming what is known today as Harlem Samba.

At the FDA, over 200 students play samba every week on instruments imported from Brazil. Students learn traditional Rio-style samba and sing entire songs in Portuguese. The ensemble has now performed at Lincoln Center, the Museum of Modern Art, the Brooklyn Academy of Music, the World Cafe Live in Philadelphia, and the Broward County Performing Arts Center in Fort Lauderdale. The samba program has also been featured in the documentary film *Beyond Ipanema: Brazilian Waves in Global Music* (Barra and Dranoff, 2009). In 2007 and 2009, Harlem Samba traveled to Rio de Janeiro, and in 2012 won the Brazilian International Press Award in the category of Best Institution for the Promotion of Brazilian Culture in the United States, and Ever since Monteiro decided to introduce samba to the school, his strategy has been to create an open environment where every student is enabled to participate in a meaningful musical experience. He reinforces this by asserting that "I have almost an entire school with someone who is playing an instrument," and he further notes that "[w]hat I have made here will, I think, get more kids playing later in life than a traditional program." The students were aware of the transferable nature of the skills they were learning in the samba classes. One group of students said that learning music from a culture other than their own would help them get the most out of study abroad programs. Others described informal music-making experiences they are currently having outside school, such as playing bongos with a local street band. Many saw how their music-making experiences were providing a sense of independence and a thirst for playing beyond the school gates.

Students at the FDA listen to a lot of hip-hop, R&B, gospel, and reggae. How has playing samba influenced the students' listening? As Stephen, a student in the program, explained, "I actually have samba on my iPod and that was actually the biggest thing for me [. . .] I didn't have samba as a mind-state in my freshman year but now it is like second nature to me now." Another student, Sarah, explained, "Well. . . I've never listened to samba before," and Jay noted, "Yeah, it's like I hear more the beat and how things are played than the flow of the music—you hear different instruments inside." One of the students explained that when learning a Brazilian song in Portuguese, he listened to it 50 times a day to understand what they were saying. This sort of commitment was common with those who had become what Monteiro termed "true believers," meaning those for whom the samba program had become an important part of their life. Commenting on being given the opportunity to learn an instrument, Simon, a 16-year-old who now considered himself a *sambista*, said, "I think I'm the first person in my family to start with music so I'm probably the first one to start a generation. I'll just pass it on." Student experience as instrumentalists varied, but the majority had little or no experience in formally learning an instrument.

Described as a "dynasty" by senior students, samba at the FDA encourages not only music learning but also peer teaching. Reflecting on her music classes, Juno stated, "It's more of teamwork than competition," and Robert noted that it feels like a family, "You help each other out." In the context of the samba band, competition between students became visible between some students when they were performing, with drummers trying to outwit the other with fast triplets and inventive improvisations. This aspect of music-making was discussed among the group with friendly banter, and was described as "a healthy competition—it's not like oh I'm definitely better than you. The competition is almost like friendship—it makes you better we learn from each other." In this context, competition was a type of playfulness between musicians rather than fierce rivalry brought about by pressures of an all-state competition or jostling to get first position in an orchestra. This is a testament to how the music program has been organized, the spirit of which can be found in many community music projects (Higgins, 2012a). Monteiro embraces what could be called a cultural democracy, in which creative arts opportunities, enjoyment, and celebration become available to all. Samba was not a part of any students' cultural heritage; however, as one student notes, "not only do we have to play [the instruments, but] we have to learn about the history of the songs." As a political idea, cultural democracy advocates that people need to create culture rather than having culture made for them: "Culture isn't something you can get. You've already got it" (Graves, 2005: 15). The availability of performance footage from YouTube cannot be underestimated, either, and is an exemplar of what Schippers (2010) deems recontextualization. Monteiro goes so far as to suggest that without YouTube the advancement of the program would not have been possible because the students have immediate access to both the context and music from within their homes.

One of the most intriguing things about any world music ensemble is how the sound and form of the music reflects the local context and those who perform it. In terms of samba, this can be deliberately woven into the band's ethos or sound, such as Macumba (samba with bagpipes), Bloco Vomit (samba-punk), and Sambangra (samba and bhangra), for example. It is more common, however, that community samba bands strive for a so-called "authentic" sound, generally understood as approximating what is perceived as original and true to a Brazilian cultural setting. In the case of Harlem Samba, their sound does approximate the Rio-style quite closely but not at all costs. Monteiro's strategy has been to empower students to feel ownership of the music they make and the various samba bands they inhabit, placing an emphasis on what students can achieve with the abilities they have. This is reflected in the day-to-day running of the classes, where students take leadership roles. As a consequence there are a considerable number of graduates who return each year to play with the band. "I don't lose many," Monteiro says, "once we get past December 10th [end of Fall semester] all those college kids will be here everyday. They will play when we have a concert; there are always us and the kids who have finished college. There are kids who are 22 [years of age] who come and play." This was evident in my conversations with the budding sambistas, who all explained that after school, "I'm coming back!"

Some students in the Harlem Samba project perceived Mr. Monteiro as a friend: "Oh I'm much more of a friend to Mr. Monteiro than my other teachers in my old school [...] I could say that he is definitely more interested in the work."[15] From Monteiro's perspective, the teaching is very challenging, "because no matter what I throw at them they get it—there is a level of comprehension—I think they really get it." He also rather modestly feels that students over-value his musicianship. The musicianship is not in doubt— listening to the band, one could not help but be impressed by the quality of the samba "groove," a unified sound that was clearly well-crafted and well-understood. What then, if anything, made it distinctive from its Brazilian counterparts? In some respects there was nothing extraordinary in the sound, except if you took a close look at those who were playing. This was remarkable. It is therefore here, at the point of the participants and the context, that Harlem Samba gains its distinctiveness. There is an energy that drifts from the streets right into the rehearsal space and through the drum, a performance full of New York teenage intensity.

From a non-formal after-school club, the FDA samba program has developed to include almost every member of the school community. It seems a truism to state, as Monteiro did, that "[i]f you were to go in the hallway, if you were to take a walk around the building and 40 kids were going by and we dragged them all in they could probably play: Almost every 9–12th grader in the building knows how to play." Initially supported by a principal who believed in the power of music, the program attracted a private donor, who has now given significant amounts of money to purchase instruments and aid travel. The latest purchase is a collection of Candombe drums from Uruguay, which offers an opportunity to expand the school musical and cultural experiences. The program has given some students a stronger sense of identity, and this is reflected in the number of students who return to play after graduation. Asked about where he got his T-shirt. Stephen replied, "It's Harem Samba, yes I'm proud of it. I'm proud to be part of this." Other participants have a sense of responsibility that emulates from Monteiro's teaching strategy, which enables students to take active roles in peer teaching and in directorship. Jay stated, "I will never forget this class—I will never forget."

As a musician who has embraced ethnomusicological approaches to music learning, such as those described by Bakan (1999), Rice (1994), and Chernoff (1979), Monteiro has been visiting the Santa Marta favela and the São Clemente samba school since 2010. Prior to 2010 he visited every major samba school in Rio and Sao Paulo and schools in Tokyo, Cape Verde, London, and throughout the United States, honing his skill and consolidating relationships. Monteiro realizes now that you do not have to teach trumpet and have a traditional marching band to consider your program successful. "We can give a concert, we can do parades, so suddenly we had a marching band, a concert band, and we can do parades—all these things that at one point [the FDA] did have before it collapsed. Suddenly it was back in this form." Do you need to have choir, band, and orchestra to have a successful music program? Monteiro is emphatic: "Not at all."

The Case of Music Alive! in the Yakima Valley

It's not easy to pack up a group of university music majors for off-campus course activity for a few days, not when they're enrolled for a necessary run of multiple scheduled sessions in a semester's classes, seminars, ensembles, and studio lessons. Their professors may ask questions, and rightly so, for student absences mean make-up classes and assignments for the missing students and a temporary "tilt" and imbalance of the composition of the course for those who remain. For the ensemble directors, an absent oboist makes for a lopsided "hole-in-the-middle" sound, and the loss of three sopranos from the chamber choir can clean out the treble sonorities. It takes a very good reason to shift a carefully laid-out campus schedule, and a logically articulated rationale (passionately and persistently proffered to colleagues) is essential in the process of making it happen.

Because of the flexibility of a committed faculty, University of Washington (UW) students have been packing up for 13 years for trips across the Cascade Mountains, with the intent of "making a dent of a difference" in a place far beyond campus. They sing, they dance, and they play for schoolchildren and youth in rural Toppenish, on the high plateau of the Yakama Tribal Lands, where Yakama and Mexican-American families live side by side. When there's funding (for 10 of the 13 years in this period), the program, Music Alive! in the Yakima Valley, does well, and benefits stream in two directions: to the Toppenish community and to the music majors. The project lands at the nexus of music education, applied ethnomusicology, and community music, and its aims are multiple: to bridge the gap between privileged university music students and under-served school populations, to provide a civic engagement of music majors with children and youth of poor and rural communities, to perform for the Mexican-American and Yakama children vocally and on instruments they have never heard or seen "live," and to listen to and participate in the music made in these communities. With this last action, we sought also to validate a diversity of musical expressions that is beyond the standard university music-major repertoire (Soto, Lum, and Campbell, 2009).

Like many college music programs in North America, the University of Washington (UW) School of Music has offered programs of performance, composition, and scholarship for more than a century. In the 1920s, the School's mission expanded to include the preparation of teachers for music positions in K–12 schools.[16] With the establishment of the ethnomusicology program in the 1960s, and the development of multicultural education studies in the College of Education by late in that decade, a theme was introduced into the content of its music education programs: to approach music and teaching from multiple cultural perspectives, and to develop music teachers who could think globally and act locally, and who could respond to diversity in the schools with cultural sensitivity. Seeds were sown a half-century ago for a movement in multicultural music education where music could be a powerful means of making a pathway to cultural awareness and understanding. Whether music of the Vietnamese or the Venezuelans, the Hawaiians or the Hungarians, the Saami or the Samoans, UW students of music education have provided the model for other multiculturalists to offer song, dance, and instrumental expressions of a people as a means of knowing music and culture in a profound way.

For cultural sensitivity to develop more fully into the perspectives of music majors, firsthand interaction with culturally diverse populations has proven effective—perhaps even transformative. But how? Through short-term single cameo-visits of "culture-bearers in the classroom," in which a song is sung, an instrument is played, and a brief question-answer period ensues? Year-long residencies of artist-musicians? Field trips to a given cultural community? At the UW, we opted for a mix of these experiences through an assemblage of guest musicians to our classes and seminars, arrangements for visiting artists (from Korea, Mexico, northern Ghana, southern India, Ireland, Indonesia, Puerto Rico, Senegal, Tanzania, Afghanistan, and elsewhere) who teach their performance craft for a term or a year, and field trips through Music Alive! in the Yakima Valley (also known as "the MAYV program"). Especially with MAYV, firsthand interaction is furthered, as students travel to the field of communities that are distinguished by their location, their ethnic-cultural composition, and their socioeconomic circumstance. There, in the Yakima Valley, they have opportunities to interact with students musically and socially in the comfort of their hometown, to feel the rhythm and pace of the people of the community, and to wonder about ways in which local values are reflected in the music of the conjunto, mariachi, and pow-wow events.

There are day visits, overnights, and one week-long residency each year by University of Washington music majors in the Yakima Valley. The day-long visits are very long indeed, as sleepy-eyed students assemble with their instruments in the parking lot of the School of Music in the pre-dawn chill, fingers crossed that the mountain pass they will reach in an hour's time will be dry and ice-free. Following 10–12 hours of energetic onsite activity in elementary, secondary, and tribal schools of Toppenish, they arrive back to a dark campus, fully exhausted and ready for bed. The week-long residency transpires in January, and music majors enjoy homestays when they live in groups of three with families in town. This becomes an opportunity for music majors to quickly enter into the town's cultural environment, as they gain firsthand knowledge of what family life is like in this community, so far from Seattle's city lights. Whether for the day or the week, homestays are filled with time to talk across the boundary that distinguishes rural from urban life, poor from privileged circumstances, and minority groups of Mexican Americans and Yakama Indians (Campbell, 2010).

The experience in the Yakima Valley is undergirded with discussion sessions wrapped into the course, Ethnomusicology in the Schools, that precede and follow the trip, in order to prepare students for activity and observation and to deconstruct the cultural experience. At the top of the reading list are classic works by John Blacking (1973), Charles Keil and Steven Feld (1994), E. Thayer Gaston (1968), Christopher Small (1998), Thomas Turino (2008), and Deborah Wong (2001), all of which refer to a more musical humanity than is typically acknowledged, with emphasis on the position that all people have need for musical expression. Small refers to "musicking" as a common sociomusical practice across communities, and Keil describes all children as "born to groove"—prior to the unfortunate societal message sent out that "some are, and others never will be, musical." (Keil and Campbell, 2015 [2006]). Turino's *Music in Social Life* turns their heads in questioning why music and dance provide for profound personal and social experiences, in many times and places. Questions of sameness versus distinctions emerge in class and on-site discussion, as the students tick off the myriad ways in which the people of the Yakima Valley think and do music. Without fail, the observation arises among students that all people are anchored in music, despite variations in sound, behavior, and values (Soto, Lum, and Campbell, 2009). Students of the MAYV experience are typically music education majors, but performance, ethnomusicology, and jazz studies majors have also joined in on the course, the trips, and the discussions.

Music Alive! in the Yakima Valley is an "extra" in the lively work-a-day world of faculty and students. It works, though it has its bumps along the way, as it is not (yet) self-sustaining. There is the constant worry of where the next year's support will be coming from—for student meals, van rental, fuel, small percussion instruments and instrument-making materials, and an assistantship for a seasoned graduate student with performance chops, music education, and/or community music experience, who can negotiate and arrange for the various details of the approximately 10 trips across the academic year. Many have committed themselves to "making a dent of a difference" in the MAYV program, including graduate students of music education and ethnomusicology. Amanda Soto, originally from a Tex-Mex border town, served three years as "fieldworker" and facilitator of activities in the Yakima Valley, and her bicultural experience was extraordinary in connecting to the Mexican-American community there. Robert Pitzer worked in arranging for musical exchanges between music majors and the Yakama Nation drummers and flute players, so that give-and-take sessions could proceed in a manner that fit the school-day priorities of the Tribal School. Ethan Chessin's efforts were directed toward providing performances (and participatory events) with his campus klezmer group and with Son de Madera, the university's visiting artists of *son jarocho* music from Veracruz, Mexico. There are educators and activists in the Valley who support the effort: Robert Roybal, principal of Valley View Elementary School; Toppenish High School music teacher Nicola Mayes; Earl Lee, the blues-guitar-playing music teacher at the Yakama Nation Tribal School; Steven Meyer and John Cerna, superintendent and assistant superintendent of the Toppenish Schools; and Ricardo Valdez of Heritage College on the Yakama Tribal Lands (Campbell, 2010).

Projects like Music Alive! in the Yakima Valley are inspired by the works of others. Public sector music-activist Dan Sheehy, director of Smithsonian Folkways and the Smithsonian Center for Folklife and Cultural Heritage, is an inspirational model for making music happen in communities, for seeking ways to support the continuation of music by the people and for the people. The outpouring of energy by Charles Keil to create and sustain live music-making outside formal educational institutions—in 12/8 path bands, the East and West Coast Honk! Festivals, after-school programs, and public gatherings—is the stuff of legend, and he is always in mind (Garafalo, 2011). University administrators offered continuing moral and monetary support for our efforts. Close colleagues in music education and ethnomusicology believe in the project and help to uphold and continue it, and the School of Music calls it their "community engagement" program.

"What's in it for you?" one senior (and distinguished) faculty member from across campus once asked, in reference to the MAYV program. There is the joy that we see on the faces of children who are visibly in awe of the university students' performances on violin, or saxophone, or guitar, their eyes wide and their jaws dropped open. There is the positive energy that can be physically felt in the exchanges of university and high school students over instruments, repertoire, and the meaning of music. There is the way that university students return to classes, fired up and firm in their belief that they are destined make a difference as musicians and music teachers in their lives ahead by reaching out to the outlying communities (rural? poor? socioculturally distinctive?) they had previously never connected to. There is their increased and genuine interest in "other" musics and musicians. Finally, there are more than a few students, over the years, who have taken the pathway to teaching jobs in places beyond their own familiar and safe suburban environments, to work with children and youth far from the mainstream who deserve highly skilled and sincerely dedicated musicians in their midst (Soto, Lum, and Campbell, 2009).

In the music majors program at the University of Washington, there is strong evidence that the MAYV program has opened ears, eyes, and minds to different but equally logical ways of conceiving time and space, of thinking and doing, of musicking, learning, and transmission. For some music majors, the program is a "startle experience," an "in-their-face" event that is mildly disorienting to them in the midst of their orderly university lives. After all, there is plenty of adjustment in going from the gentle flow of campus events to the sometimes raucous and riled-up activity of a group of schoolchildren (anywhere!), and they also must adjust from a warm room in the residence hall to a cot in a family's spare (and sometimes drafty) room. There is a certain distance, both literal and figurative, between university students and the children of a culturally distinctive rural community, a crevasse that needs a bridge. For those who work with Music Alive! in the Yakima Valley, there is our continuing hope that they can help to lessen the distance, so that Seattle students and the people of the Yakima Valley might come to know "the other" through meaningful experiences in music.

Revolutionary Potentials

Over 40 years ago, John Blacking predicted that "[e]thnomusicology has the power to create a revolution in the world of music and music education" (1973: 4). This prediction has come to pass and is now realized in the broader conceptualization of music that finds its way into academic courses and applied performance experiences for students of all levels of instruction, and through the questions, frameworks, and processes of research that straddles the fields. The reverse may be just as plausible, that music education may be a means by which ethnomusicology is made more relevant, and is revolutionized. Adding to the works of music educators and ethnomusicologists is the emergence of community musicians committed to facilitating the music with which a community identifies, and which engages learners who seek to express themselves musically. Overlapping the fields, and in the two case descriptions, there appears a definitive commitment to embracing an ethnomusicological sense of people and place, to honoring the local, and to understanding that music is situated within the lives of those who choose to make it. While the future will tell the truth of this challenge, it is nonetheless reasonable now to accept this premise—that the intersection of ethnomusicology and music education, joined by the emergent field of community music, is a point at which the means for understanding music, education, and culture may be found. It is at this juncture, where these dynamic fields and their considerable histories merge, that new knowledge may be developed. From the pure to the practical, this crossroads of specializations may be critical to future insights in each of these distinctive fields, revealing facets of their shared interests in music, learning, and education.

Notes

1. The attention to American contexts is due to the extensive experience of the authors in various US programs and projects, as well as due to an extensive literature that explains and interprets American-style ethnomusicology and education. Ethnomusicology and music education activity exist in many settings worldwide, but it was deemed beyond the scope of this chapter to attempt to be all-inclusive of these perspectives globally.
2. For a wider picture of the impact of brass bands, see *Brass Bands of the World: Militarism, Colonial Legacies, and Local Music Making* (Reily and Brucher, 2013).
3. Second and third editions published in 1996 and 2010.
4. See http://www.mjpublishing.com/
5. http://www.folkways.si.edu/
6. http://www.culturalequity.org/
7. 222.youtube.com/user/MariachiOnline.
8. See also (Deane and Mullen, 2013; Rimmer, 2009; Koopman, 2007).
9. For a critique of the notion of lifelong learning in community music see (Mantie, 2012).
10. http://www.youthmusic.org.uk/
11. See http://www.128path.org/.
12. UK-based Music for Change has an emphasis on empowerment through music and runs projects in the United Kingdom, but also Africa, Asia, and Latin America. See http://www.musicforchange.org/.
13. The Frederick Douglass Academy (FDA) offers a college preparatory education for grades 6–12. Located in Harlem, in New York City, the school serves an urban population and seeks to educate young people within a diverse curriculum. Under the motto "without struggle, there is no progress," FDA prides itself in giving its students the best possible chance to be competitive in college applications (http://www.fda1.org/).
14. There are 1,700 students in the school and all of them have to do music in order to graduate. Until very recently there was only one music teacher seeing up to 50 students at a time. Another key reason was that in an urban school such as FDA the population can be transient and this makes it very difficult to cultivate a traditional US band program.
15. This is resonant of previous research. See Higgins (2012b).
16. K–12 is a designation used in the United States among other nations as the sum of elementary (primary) through secondary education.

References

Adzenyah, Abraham K., Dumisani Maraire, and Judith Cook Tucker. (1996). *Let Your Voice Be Heard*. Danbury, CT: World Music Press.

Anderson, William M., and Patricia Shehan Campbell, eds. (1989). *Multicultural Perspectives in Music Education*. Reston, Virginia: Music Educators National Conference.

Bailey, John. (2001). "Learning to Perform as a Research Technique in Ethnomusicology." *British Journal of Ethnomusicology* 10(2): 84–98.

Bakan, Michael. (2007). *World Music: Traditions and Transformations*. New York: McGraw-Hill.

Bakan, Michael, B. (1999). *Music of Death and New Creation*. Chicago: University of Chicago Press.

Barra, Gutto, and Béco Dranoff (writers). (2009). *Beyond Ipanema: Brazilian Waves in Global Music*. Los Angeles: FiGa Films.

Berliner, Paul. (1994). *Thinking in Jazz: The Infinite Art of Improvisation*. Chicago: University of Chicago Press.

Blacking, John. (1967). *Venda Children's Culture*. Johannesburg: Witswatersrand University Press.

Blacking, John. (1973). *How Musical Is Man?* London: Faber and Faber.

Blacking, John. (1995). *Venda Children's Songs: A Study in Ethnomusicological Analysis*. Chicago: University of Chicago Press.

Campbell, Patricia Shehan. (1991). *Lessons from the World*. New York: Schimer Books.

Campbell, Patricia Shehan. (1996). *Music in Cultural Context: Eight Views on World Music Education*. Reston, VA: Music Educators National Conference (MENC).

Campbell, Patricia Shehan. (2004). *Teaching Music Globally*. Oxford: Oxford University Press.

Campbell, Patricia Shehan. (2010). "Music Alive! in the Yakima Valley." *International Journal of Community Music* 3(2): 303–307.

Campbell, Patricia Shehan. (2011). "Teachers Studying Teachers: Pedagogical Practices of Artist Musicians." In *Ethnomusicological Encounters with Music and Musicians*, edited by Timothy Rice, pp. 81–96. London: Ashgate.

Campbell, Patricia Shehan. (2013). "Children, Teachers, and Ethnomusicologists: Traditions and Transformations of Music in School." In *Beyond Borders: Welt-Musick-Padagogik*, edited by Barbara Alge, pp. 13–26. Augsburg: Wissner-Verlag.

Campbell, Patricia Shehan, John Drummond, Peter Dunbar-Hall, Keith Howard, Huib Schippers, and Trevor Wiggins, eds. (2005). *Cultural Diversity in Music Education: Directions and Challenges for the 21st Century*. Brisbane: Australian Academic Press.

Chernoff, John Miller. (1979). *African Rhythm and African Sensibility*. Chicago: University of Chicago Press.

Coombs, Philip H. (1968). *The World Educational Crisis*. New York: Oxford Univ. Press.

Coombs, Philip H., and Manzoor Ahmed. (1974). *Attacking Rural Poverty: How Nonformal Education Can Help*. Baltimore, MD: John Hopkins University Press.

Deane, Kathryn, and Phil Mullen. (2013). "Community Music in the United Kingdom." In *Community Music Today*, edited by Kari K. Veblen, Stephen J. Messenger, Marissa Silverman, and David J. Elliott, pp. 25–40. Landham, MD: Rowman and Littlefield.

Dunbar-Hall, Peter. (2005). "Training, Community and Systemic Music Education: The Aesthtetics of Balinese Music in Different Pedagogic Settings." In *Cultural Diversity in Music Education: Directions and Challenges for the 21st Century*, edited by Patricia Shehan Campbell, John Drummond, Peter Dunbar-Hall, Keith Howard, Huib Schippers, and Trevor Wiggins, pp. 125–132. Brisbane: Australian Academic Press.

Fletcher, Samantha. (2007). "Good Works" with Benefits: Using Applied Ethnomusicology and Participatory Action Research in Benefit Concert Production at the Unitarian Church of Vancouver, Memorial University of Newfoundland. Thesis (M.A.) Memorial University of Newfoundland (Canada).

Garafalo, Reebee. (2011). "Not Your Parents' Marching Band: The History of HONK!, Pedagogy and Music Education." *International Journal of Community Music* 4(3): 221–236.

Garfias, Robert. (1975). *Music of a Thousand Autumns: The Togaku Style of Japanese Court Music*. Berkeley: University of California Press.

Gaston, E. Thayer. (1968). *Music in Therapy*. New York: Macmillan.

Graves, James Bau. (2005). *Cultural Democracy: The Arts, Community, and the Public*. New York: University of Illinois Press.

Hamill, Chad. (2005). "Indian Classical Music as Taught in the West: The Reshaping of Tradition?" In *Cultural Diversity in Music Education: Directions and Challenges for the 21st Century*, edited by Patricia Shehan Campbell, John Drummond, Peter Dunbar-Hall, Keith Howard, Huib Schippers, and Trevor Wiggins, pp. 143–149. Brisbane: Australian Academic Press.

Higgins, Lee. (2012a). *Community Music: In Theory and in Practice*. New York: Oxford University Press.

Higgins, Lee. (2012b). "One-to-One Encounters: Facilitators, Participants, and Friendship." *Theory into Practice* 51(3):159–166.

Higgins, Lee, and Brydie-Leigh Bartleet. (2012). "The Community Music Facilitator and School Music Education." In *The Oxford Handbook of Music Education*, edited by Gary McPherson and Graham F. Welch, pp. 495–511. New York: Oxford University Press.

Howard, Keith. (2005). "Teaching SamulNori Challenges in the Transmission of Korean Percussion." In *Cultural Diversity in Music Education: Directions and Challenges for the 21st Century*, edited by Patricia Shehan Campbell, John Drummond, Peter Dunbar-Hall, Keith Howard, Huib Schippers, and Trevor Wiggins, pp. 133–142. Brisbane: Australian Academic Press.

Impey, Angela. (2006). "Culture, Conservation, and Community Reconstruction: Explorations in Advocacy Ethnomusicology and Participatory Action Research in Northern KwaZulu Natal." In *Ethnomusicology: A Contemporary Reader*, edited by Jennifer C. Post, pp. 401–411. New York: Routledge.

Jones, Patrick. (2009). "Lifewide as Well as Lifelong: Broadening Primary and Secondary School Music Education's Service to Students' Musical Needs." *International Journal of Community Music* 2(2–3):201–214.

Keene, James A. (1982). *A History of Music Education in the United States*. Hanover, NH: University Press of New England.

Keil, Charles. (1982). "Applied Ethnomusicology and a Rebirth of Music from the Spirit of Tragedy." *Ethnomusicology* 26(3): 407–411.

Keil, Charles, and Steven Feld. (1994). *Music Grooves: Essays and Dialogues*. Chicago: University of Chicago Press.

Keil, Charles, and Patricia Shehan Campbell. (2015 [2006]). Born to Groove. www.borntogroove.com.

Koopman, Constantijn. (2007). "Community Music as Music Education: On the Educational Potential of Community Music." *International Journal of Music Education* 25: 151–163.

Kuo-huang, Han, and Patricia Shehan Campbell. (1997). *The Lion's Roar: Chinese Luogu Percussion Ensembles* (2nd ed.). Danbury, CT: World Music Press.

Loughran, Maureen E. (2008). Community Powered Resistance: Radio, Music Scenes and Musical Activism in Washington, D.C. Ph.D. Thesis. Providence, RI: Brown University.

Malm, William P. (2001). *Traditional Japanese Music and Musical Instruments*. New York: Kodansha.

Mantie, R. (2012). "Learners or Participants? The Pros and Cons of 'Lifelong Learning.'" *International Journal of Community Music* 5(3): 217–236.

Mark, Michael L., and Charles L. Gary. (2007). *A History of American Music Education*. Lanham VA: Rowman & Littlefield Education.

McAllester, David. (1973). *Enemy Way Music: A Study of Social and Esthetic Values as Seen in Navaho Music*. Milwood, NY: Kraus Reprint.

Merriam, Alan P. (1964). *The Anthropology of Music*. Illinois: Northwestern University Press.

Miller, Terry E., and Andrew Shahriari. (2005). *World Music: A Global Journey*: New York: Routledge.

Myers, David E. (2007). "Freeing Music Education from Schooling: Toward a Lifespan Perspective on Music Learning and Teaching." *International Journal of Community Music* 1(1): 49–61.

Nettl, Bruno. (1983). *The Study of Ethnomusicology*. Urbana: University of Illinois Press.

Nettl, Bruno. (1984). "In Honor of Our Principal Teachers." *Ethnomusicology* (28): 173–185.

Nettl, Bruno. (1989). *Blackfoot Musical Thought: Comparative Perspectives*. Kent, OH: Kent State University.

Nettl, Bruno. (1992). *Excursions in World Music*. Englewood Cliffs, NJ: Prentice Hall.

Nettl, Bruno. (2002). *Encounters in Ethnomusicology: A Memoir*. Warren, MI: Harmonie Park Press.

Nettl, Bruno. (2005). "An Ethnomusicological Perspective." *International Journal of Music Education* 23(2): 131–133.

Neumann, Daniel M. (1980). *The Life of Music in North India*. Detroit: Wayne State University Press.

Nguyen, Phong, and Patricia Shehan Campbell. (1990). *From Rice Paddies and Temple Yards: Traditional Music of Vietnam*. Danbury, CT: World Music Press.

Pemberton, Carol. (1985). *Lowell Mason: His Life and Work. Studies in Musicology, No. 86*. Ann Arbor, MI. UMI Research Press.

Phoasavadi, Pomprapit, and Patricia Shehan Campbell. (2003). *From Bangkok and Beyond: Tai Children's Songs, Games and Customs*. Danbury, CT: World Music Press.

Reck, David. (1976). *Music of the Whole Earth* (1st ed.). New York: Charles Scribner's Sons.

Reily, Suzel Ana, and Katherine Brucher, eds. (2013). *Brass Bands of the World: Militarism, Colonial Legacies, and Local Music Making*. Farnham, UK: Ashgate.

Rice, Timothy. (1994). *May It Fill Your Soul: Experiencing Bulgarian Music*. Chicago: University of Chicago Press.

Rice, Timothy. (2003). "Time, Place, and Metaphor in Musical Experience and Ethnography." *Ethnomusicology* 47(2): 151–179.

Rimmer, Mark. (2009). "'Instrumental' Playing? Cultural Policy and Young People's Community Music Participation." *International Journal of Cultural Policy* 15(1): 71–90.

Rimmer, Mark. (2012). "The Participation and Decision Making of 'At Risk' Youth in Community Music Projects: An Exploration of Three Case Studies." *Journal of Youth Studies* 15(3): 329–350.

Rogers, Alan. (2004). *Non-Formal Education: Flexible Schooling or Participatory Education? CERC Studies In Comparative Education*. Hong Kong: Comparative Education Research Centre, the University of Hong Kong.

Schippers, Huib. (2010). *Facing the Music: Shaping Music Education from a Global Perspective*. New York: Oxford University Press.

Schippers, Huib, and Patricia Shehan Campbell. (2013). "Cultural Diversity: Beyond 'Songs from Every Land.'" In *Oxford Handbook of Music Education*, edited by Gary McPherson and Graham Welch, pp. 87–104. New York: Oxford University Press.

Shelemay, Kay Kaufman. (2001). *Soundscapes: Exploring Music in a Changing World*. (1st ed.). New York: W. W. Norton.

Small, Christopher. (1998). *Musicking: The Meanings of Performing and Listening*. Hanover, NH: University Press.

Smilde, Rineke. (2010). "Lifelong and Lifewide Learning from a Biographical Perspective: Transformation and Transition When Coping with Performance Anxiety." *International Journal of Community Music* 3(2): 185–202.

Solis, Ted, ed. (2004). *Performing Ethnomusicology: Teaching and Representation in World Music Ensembles*. Los Angeles: University of California Press.

Soto, Amanda Christina, Chee-Hoo Lum, and Patricia Shehan Campbell. (2009). "A University-School Music Partnership for Music Education Majors in a Culturally Distinctive Community." *Journal of Research in Music Education* 56(4): 338–356.

Tenzer, Michael, ed. (2006). *Analytical Studies in World Music*. New York: Oxford University Press.

Titon, Jeff Todd. (1984). *Worlds of Music: An Introduction to the Music of the World's Peoples*. New York: Schirmer Books.

Titon, Jeff Todd. (1992). Special Issue: Music and the Public Interest. *Ethnomusicology* 36(3).

Turino, Thomas. (2008). *Music as Social Life: The Politics of Participation*. Chicago: University of Chicago Press.

Van Buren, Kathleen. (2010). "Applied Ethnomusicology and HIV and AIDS: Responsibility, Ability, and Action." *Ethnomusicology* 54(2): 202–223.

Volk, Therese M. (1998). *Music, Education, and Multiculturalism*. New York: Oxford University Press.

Wade, Bonnie C. (1988). *Music in India: The Classical Traditions*. London: Sangram Books.

Wade, Bonnie C. (2004). *Thinking Musically*. Oxford: Oxford University Press.

Wong, Deborah. (2001). *Sounding the Center: History and Aesthetics in Thai Buddhist Performance*. Chicago: The University of Chicago Press.

PART III
AGENCIES

CHAPTER 4

ARCHIVES AND APPLIED ETHNOMUSICOLOGY

DAN LUNDBERG

CAN documentation and archiving be regarded as applied ethnomusicology? That, of course, depends on what we mean, both by applied ethnomusicology and by archiving. From my perspective, applied ethnomusicology is primarily about ethnomusicological studies and research activities reaching outside the academic world and in direct interaction with the community—often with an intention to influence and change political and social structures and conditions. Archives thus can be seen as identity projects with the aim to create continuity.[1] Target groups may be groupings of various kinds and at various levels, from nations to different interest groups in society. From that perspective it can be argued that archives and museums are about democratic and human rights—the rights to your own history and your cultural identity. In the research project *Music, Media, Multiculture*, music was used as the starting point to understand and explain how social and cultural diversity is constructed and organized in modern societies.[2] The project departed from the idea that music has a twofold significance from this perspective, partly as that which needs to be explained and partly as that which explains. When viewed from this angle, people's increasing desire to invest time, energy, and money on music and dance can be understood as a consequence of the fact that these activities are in themselves the goal, aesthetically, emotionally, and socially, while at the same time being the means by which various types of messages are given shape and communicated, both individually and collectively. The music archives' documentation is an active act about selection, often with a goal beyond the musical material. The archival mission also oscillates between two poles, which in principle are constant but where the emphasis has varied over time. On the one hand, the archive is a place for orderly storage—where cultural heritage is given a secure preservation and is available for research and historiography. On the other hand, the archive plays an active part in cultural life as a source and inspiration for musicians but also as an instrument for cultural policy—as a creator of cultural heritage.

The music collecting and archiving, in earlier times as well as today, have almost always to some extent been related to both poles. But the approaches have varied, often dependent on ideology. The work of the early collectors often had an educational aim—to ensure that the public users, the musicians, or other target groups used and appreciated, in the collectors' eyes, the most valuable music. During other periods, the objectives are better described as *Volksbildung*—to increase knowledge about history and musical traditions. In some cases the goal was purely about cultural heritage "to preserve for future generations." We can also observe how the collection's significance, meaning, and value have varied over time.

It is reasonable to argue that collection works, publication of archive material, and research in the folk music area are a form of applied ethnomusicology, since the goal was not only to preserve for the future but also to interact with the music community. There is, however, an interesting distinction between the collecting work that had nationalistic aims and, for instance, the work within comparative musicology that was performed in the circles of the Berlin School by scholars as Erich von Hornbostel, Otto Abraham, and Curt Sachs.[3] When it comes to archival work, the comparative musicology had preservation for study and comparative analysis as the main goal. So there is an important difference between the national folk music archives, which had and still often has a nationalistic agenda, and comparative musicology, which most often did not. But obviously there have been ideological motives even behind the work of the Berlin School.

And What about Folk Music?

What is folk music? The question never seems to be definitively answered. And one can, of course, ask whether it is really necessary to discuss the concept of "folk music" in almost every major study on the subject. It seems as if folk music researchers consider it an obligation to take a stand on the question. The concept of folk music, however, is very complex, and its meanings vary over time and space. A general tendency in the Swedish context is that the meaning in recent years has come to emphasize *music* rather than folk—that is, folk music is in many situations seen as a family of musical styles. In earlier times, however, the emphasis was rather on *folk*, that is, the music's strong connection to the culture in which it emerged. The American ethnomusicologist Mark Slobin notes in *Folk Music: A Very Short Introduction* that his book

> [. . .] will not offer anything like a definition of "folk music," relying instead on the principle of "we know it when we hear it." Understandings of the term have varied so vividly over space and time that no single summary sentence can pin it down.[4]

Slobin's principle—that we know what folk music is, based on sound and previous understanding, indicates that folk music in a global perspective has increasingly evolved into a family of musical styles and that the link to cultural contexts has become less important.

Archives and collection work not only reflect and preserve music traditions, they also serve as an active part and re-creator of the traditions they preserve. This article describes the starting point for the early collecting work from the late 1700s onward. The emphasis is in the description of work of the Swedish *Folkmusikkommissionen* (the Folk Music Commission; FMK) during the first half of the twentieth century. The Commission created Sweden's largest collections of folk tunes but has also had a great impact on the definition of the music, in terms of repertoire, instruments, and what is today perceived as folk music.[5]

One important aim of the various national collecting projects in European countries during the nineteenth and early twentieth centuries was to create a sense of unity and continuity—to demonstrate that each nation was culturally specific. The familiar recipe reads "one country, one people, one language, one culture." An important function of archives is to provide the raw materials for a constant, ongoing reconstruction of history, and this reconstruction always reflects the collectors' and users' ideas and values. All interpretations of the past are impregnated by, and filtered through, the ideologies of their own time.

Archives

The keeping and preservation of official documents has deep roots in history. The word *archive* comes from the Late Latin term *archivum*, which means a place where one receives and retains public records and documents. The Latin word can be traced back to the Greek *arkheion* (ἀρχεῖον), which means "place of public administration." The term "archive" appears in English and in other European languages, during the 1600s. One of the most well-known historical archives is the clay tablets of the ancient city-state of Ebla, a town located in present-day Syria. Ebla had its political heyday around 2400–2250 BC. It ended when the town was conquered and destroyed by King Naram-Sin of Akkad. A second golden age occurred about 1850–1600 BC.

In 1974 a find of 40 tablets was made during excavations by Italian archaeologists. The next year another 1,000 were discovered, and some months later more than 15,000 tablets, written in an old Semitic language, were found. Nearly 20,000 tablets or fragments were recovered from Ebla. This is the most comprehensive mass of information of the political and socioeconomic situation in a society during the third millennium BC, with no comparison.

The Ebla find has been described as the discovery of the century, and thanks to its archives, the history of not only Syria but of the entire region can be written. When the Italian archaeologist Giovanni Pettinato deciphered and translated the text, it was obvious that it was really the great city-state of Ebla that had been found and that the tablets were about 4,500 years old.

> Most of the Ebla documents are written on big slabs of clay almost a foot square. There are texts that, when transliterated, fill almost more than fifty pages of thirty lines each.[6]

According to Pettinato, the information on the tablets concerned the administration of Ebla, the organization of the state, diplomatic contacts with other city-states, agricultural business, and trade. There are also word-books and documents about education and science, but very few literary texts. We know little about the organization of the archive and the tablets, since the wooden shelves that they were stored upon had been destroyed over the centuries. But there is evidence that at least some systematic criteria existed and that the content was important for the shelving, and that the tablets were marked in such a way that they could easily be found.[7]

It is important to notice that "archive" has multiple meanings. On the one hand, it addresses the building—the archive—and on the other, it refers to the content and the archiving activities. It is difficult to find a clear and unanimous definition, and we probably have to live with this double meaning.[8]

Public archives are matters of power and control over records and documents that confirm the existence of the state and its decisions. The preservation and organization of written documents is a symbolic act and a kind of legitimation and verification that ensures continuity of power; it is something to refer to when political assessors are approaching. To create archives is to exercise power—to bring signs, texts, and symbols to a limited space and to control it.[9]

The discussion above addresses the archives of national agencies and organizations, and it is in this sense that we usually mean the word. What then are the differences between this kind of archive and music archives (or other cultural heritage archives)? One important difference is of course the purpose. Music archives usually have multiple purposes—to preserve documents (in the same way as an organization's archive), but also to serve as a resource for musicians, scholars, and others. Music archives often use substantial resources to publish their collections through different channels. Another difference is that the collections of music archives often have different origins—as, for instance, donations and deposits from many sources—while the organization's archive documents for the most part consist of records and documents generated through the activities of the organization. This can, of course, also be the case for the collections in music archives, for instance when the collections are the result of the work of collectors and researchers employed by the archive institution. But the main difference, in my opinion, is the music archives' clear ambition to make their collections available to outsiders, while the archives of, for example, national agencies are not kept for these purposes in the first place. In this article, it is primarily the availability aspect of music repositories that is being dealt with, and the effects that the choices made in the processes of collecting and publishing may have on the community in which the archive is functioning.

The first music archives of greater importance in Europe were connected to the church and the monasteries and later also to the music activities at the courts. Notation of Gregorian chant can be traced back to the eighth century. An essential development—which has had decisive importance for the development of the folkloristic and later ethnomusicological archives—is the interest for folk culture that emerged in the late eighteenth century.

Following the Napoleonic wars, a strong desire for vindication grew in many countries, as it did in Sweden after the loss of Finland in 1809, and several of the country's intellectuals turned to Sweden's "glorious past" to find comfort. With renewed intensity, ancient monuments and other testimonies of the ancient Swedish significance came in focus. The Icelandic sagas, graves, megalithic graves, stone circles, and inscriptions became the subject of renewed interest. The view of the "folk" as unspoiled and pristine had been put forward by the French philosopher Jean Jacques Rousseau. According to him, man is basically good, while evil had its roots in cultural development. New ways of living had made the Europeans too civilized, if not contrived. It was among the peasants in the countryside that one could still find the original human nature.

The interest in the "folk" spread rapidly across Europe and the collection of folk epics started in many countries. The models were found in older poetry, such as the Icelandic Edda and Homer's works. The Edda became a model for Elias Lönnrot's collection work and the creation of the Finnish national epic *Kalevala*.[10] Prior to that, James MacPherson issued Ossian's songs (1760) in an attempt to present a Scottish historical national epic. MacPherson gathered his material from the Scottish Highlands, where the most original Gaelic folk culture was thought to have survived. In a sense, one can see a Nordic ideal in Ossian songs. The setting was a barren and windswept landscape with deserted moors and misty mountains, not far from an idealized Norse world, and the songs were supposed to have existed in oral tradition since the third century. The author was, according to MacPherson, the Gaelic bard Ossian. In England, the work received much attention: suddenly, the British had their own Homer. However, on closer inspection, it turned out that MacPherson had produced much of the material himself, although the ballads probably were partly modeled on Scottish folk songs.[11]

Although Macpherson's work was questionable, he was a typical representative of the craze for the "folk" that spread in Europe. Perhaps the most influential proponents of the 1800s were the German folk memory researchers Jacob and Wilhelm Grimm and their publications of German folk tales. In 1812–1815 they released *Kinder-und Hausmärchen*, which includes many well-known fairy tales, including Cinderella, Snow White, Hansel and Gretel, Little Red Riding Hood, and Sleeping Beauty. The collections became immensely popular and were translated into many languages. The Grimm brothers stressed that these tales originated in the folk tradition and that they had no known author. In this way they expressed the people's "pure" culture. The anonymization of the author became a kind of ideal and the collective creation process normative. There was also a kind of faith that the selection process of storytellers and singers was a type of filter. The individual can write poetry and compose, but it is the people who select what should be preserved. One can see this as a canonization process on a practical level, whereby the individual creation only survives if it reflects people's collective aesthetics.

The works of Macpherson, Lönnrot, the Grimm brothers and others became the foundation of European folk culture archives. The goal was to portray their own nation's history, and it is fair to say that they are part of a kind of contest. The Swedish ethnomusicologist Owe Ronström has described these ways to connect music expression, culture, and nature as the creation of cultural "manuscripts"—to canonize the description form in itself. It was envisioned, says Ronström:

> [. . .] a powerful, collective and spontaneous process of creation, sprung from a strange and magical union between nature and culture, place, and way of life. It's the folk, the race, the nation itself that is the author, "Das Volk dichtet." "Every epic has to write itself," said the famous folktale scholar Jacob Grimm.[12]

The archives became the arena where folk culture's manuscript could be performed. The nations could be presented as natural, ethnic, local, regional, and national imagined communities. Therefore, it became necessary to search for, collect, and publish expressions of these naturally given communities, and among the most important symbols were folk tales and folk music.

The Nation in a Cabinet and the Collection of the Music of Mankind: Two Fundamental Perspectives

The key issue that determines whether you can consider a cultural heritage archive as a form of applied ethnomusicology is connected to the archive's mission. The archives created as part of the national projects had as one of their major aims to present the nation as uniform and, not least, as distinctively different in relevant areas in relation to other nations. This is a pronounced applied mission. Other archives, where the collections themselves and the comparative perspective are the focus, might also have expectations of creating better conditions, for example, for culture research, but this is, in my eyes, not primarily an effort to change or influence contemporary culture or the view of a national history. Below I will present two examples: the large collection of Latvian *dainas* and the establishing of the phonogram archive in Berlin. It might be interesting to note that both these collections have been inscribed on UNESCO's Memory of the World Register.[13]

The major collecting projects that came about in the nineteenth century, as described earlier, were based on emerging nationalism in Europe. The (re-)creation of national epics, such as Kalevala, Ossian's songs, and so on, had the more or less explicit purpose of strengthening the nation as a unit—providing its residents access to a shared history with national symbols, legends, heroes, and martyrs.

At the Italian Parliament's first meeting in 1861, the politician Massimo d'Azeglio noted "L'Italia è fatta. Restano da fare gli italiani" (We have created Italy. Now we must make Italians). This quote nicely sums up the national projects. The nation-state is not given by God, it is a created entity, which emerged in the 1800s, partly as a vehicle for a new class of bourgeoisie against the old elites, partly as a means to deliver the millions of soldiers that the new modern warfare demanded. The music archives' role was to collect, organize, and present the nation's building blocks.

"The Nation in a cabinet"—that is the way the Swedish cultural historian Anders Hammarlund has described the Latvian folklorist Krišjānis Barons's (1835–1923) work.[14] Barons was born in the village of Strutele in Kurland. He studied mathematics and astronomy at Dorpat University in Tartu in present-day Estonia, and after his studies he worked as a tutor and newspaper editor. In the 1870s Barons began a grand collection and systematization project based on Latvian folk poetry. Barons was particularly interested in the dainas, traditional four-line poem stanzas. He took summer walks in the countryside, where he was looking for people who knew dainas. He also engaged friends, colleagues, and students in the gathering.

> It seemed as if the wells of folk memories, that for a long time have been regarded dried up and dehydrated, began to spring fresh and wonderful. From all parts of Latvia came letters with ancient wisdoms and memories from former times, among which the folk songs occupied a very special place.[15]

To be able to more easily compare the stanzas, he created a system in which he organized them by topics, motives, and variants. He also studied the forms of the dainas carefully, but it was not what he was primarily interested in. It was the content that fascinated Barons—the Latvianness—and his goal was a complete mapping of the content. Barons had a cabinet built to store his dainas (Figures 4.1a and 4.1b). According to Barons, the Latvian and Lithuanian folk poems showed similarities to the Homeric verses—to an original unity of poetry, music and dance. In his view, the people's language and its poetry are the highest expressions of a nation's identity, and they are simultaneously the most important tools for identity maintenance.

Barons was obviously influenced by Johann Georg Hamann and Johann Gottfried von Herder, but he was also inspired by a scientific, positivistic approach, which led him to regard and treat cultural expressions as natural phenomena. In this view the social community is an organism that should be grown in accordance with its "natural" predisposition.[16]

Barons moved to Riga in 1893, where he published the first part of *Latvju dainas* (Latvian dainas). The work was completed in 1915. The Latvju dainas consists of six volumes with 217,996 folk lyrics. In the early 1920s, the Ministry of Education ordered that a selection from the Dainas Collection be included in the Latvian school curriculum, and Barons's cabinet was placed in the Latvian National Museum. The cabinet was moved to the newly built National Library in Riga 2014. In 1983 an exact replica of the cabinet was placed in Barons's apartment in Riga, which by then had become a museum,

FIGURE 4.1. Other nations in cabinets. Variant register of FMK. In Svenskt visarkiv.

a tribute to a collector and systematist who, through popular culture, seemed to be able to reach the Latvian people's soul—the essence of the Latvian. These measures gave historical legitimacy to the new independent Latvia.

On the museum's website the collector's character and deed is described reverently:

> He was surrounded by the love of his near people at the end of his life giving them back his quietness and experience. The world of Dainas had changed the life of the Dainas collector. Even when he was very tired the native wisdom of the folk gave him satisfaction, clarity and indicated the right order of the eternal things.

By selecting what should be preserved in museums and archives, we distinguish the valuable from what we consider to be of little importance. With the dainas, Barons built a national and cultural Latvian identity. One of the functions of cultural heritage is to mark out specific features and difference—and the choice falls naturally on phenomena that we have but others lack. The collection and compilation of dainas is perhaps one of the clearest examples of this. In a time of confusion and disorientation—Latvia was under Russian rule as part of a long history with various supremacies—the search for a Latvian identity began. Barons dainas gave the Latvians a specific and independent cultural history that distinguished them from Swedes, Poles, Russians, and other influential neighbors. Barons's work gained renewed importance after Latvia's independence from the Soviet Union.

The Berlin Phonogramm-Archiv is a completely different type of archive—not only regarding the material, as the core of the collection is sound recordings, but also regarding the collection methods and ideology. It is fair to say that the birth of the Berlin Phonogramm-Archiv was a direct result of the technological achievements of the late 1800s—above all the phonograph, patented in 1877. It is often said that the invention of the phonograph was the very start of comparative musicology, which then led to the development of ethnomusicology as a university subject. And clearly, the collecting of ethnic music received a new breakthrough with the phonograph.

The ability to record sound marked the start of a more scientific approach to music collecting. Through the analysis of the recordings, more accurately based transcriptions could be carried out. The phonograph also enabled scientific criticism of the published material—you could check the result of the transcripts. Many music forms had earlier been very difficult to transcribe. But now complex polyphony and improvisation could be caught with the help of the phonograph. The American ethnologist Jesse Walter Fewkes made the first music ethnological phonograph recordings. During the years 1889–1890, he recorded music of Passamaquoddy and Zuni peoples of North America. In 1892 Hungarian collector Bela Vikar used phonograph for folk music collecting in Hungary. In the following years there were many recording projects of folk music in Europe (see Figure 4.2).

The Berlin Phonogramm-Archiv was established by Professor Carl Stumpf (1848–1936) at the Institute of Psychology at the University of Berlin. The starting point was the recording of a Thai theater performance at the Berlin Zoo in September 1900. Stumpf's main areas of interest were acoustics and music psychology, but together with other colleagues (and perhaps primarily Erich Moritz von Hornbostel and Otto Abraham, who by this time were Stumpf's assistants), he developed what came to be known as the "Berlin School" and its methods of comparative musicology. After Stumpf's recordings of the Thai musicians, other recordings with visiting musicians, including a Japanese theater company in November 1901, were made. The Berlin Phonogramm-Archiv was officially founded in 1905 with Hornbostel as the director. Hornbostel managed to ensure that German ethnological expeditions to other countries were provided with recording equipment, and the collections grew rapidly. The phonograph recording activities lasted until World War II. After Stumpf's retirement in 1922, the archive was taken over by the state and was attached to the *Hochschule für Musik*. Twelve years later the archive became attached to the *Museum für Völkerkunde*, with Marius Schneider as manager, and moved to Berlin-Dahlem.

FIGURE 4.2. Wax cylinders from Karl Tirén's yoik collection 1913–15. In Svenskt visarkiv.

Right from the start the archive had developed good contacts with scholars in different parts of the world, and the technical knowledge that existed in Berlin was a reason for them to send material to the archive. As early as 1905, the American anthropologist Franz Boas sent cylinders with Indian music to the Berlin archive for scientific processing, and in the coming years many researchers did the same. By 1954 the collections had grown to over 16,000 cylinders from different parts of the world. But until 1914 the greater part of the collection originated from the former German colonies in Africa and the Pacific.[17]

> The main concern of Stumpf, Hornbostel, and other members of the Archive was to collect as many examples of traditional music as possible in order to create and follow theories about the origin and evaluation of music in general. Thus, on the basis of the great number of recordings on wax cylinders from all over the world, a new university came in to being: Comparative musicology or "ethnomusicology," as it is called today.[18]

The goal of the archive thus was primarily to investigate and compare music from different ethnic groups and cultures, often with an evolutionary perspective. A central idea was that the study of various aspects of music, like rhythm or tonality, could reveal principles of the functioning of the human mind. The research could teach us about our own music's development in history. The Berlin School's researchers also stressed the importance of field recordings and the need for thorough knowledge in order to understand the music culture.

> It is always the best if the scientist learns the songs or instrumental pieces so well that he can perform them for the natives to get their approval. One should choose a critic with musical talent (who is considered knowledgeable also by his countrymen) and insure that the approval is not given by courtesy or disinterest.[19]

The Berlin School, with its scientific approach, in many ways turned the study of music into a laboratory science, where the sounding object's physical characteristics and psychological effects were in focus; at the same time, there was a great respect for the musicians and an interest in music practice and its social functions. Comparative musicology's quest for human universals is basically a reflection of Johann Gottfried von Herder's ideas about how the cultural diversity of species forms a kind of whole. The evolutionists' basic idea is a vision that we all are branches of the same tree of humanity. But the new cultural sciences developed in the epoch of imperialism, and one can also see a different tendency, that is, the notion of a hierarchy of cultures in a Darwinian sense.[20] In such a system (often ethnocentric) the cultures represent different stages of development, from the primitive to the highly civilized, and the "primitive" may then serve as an example of lower stages of human "progress."

Rationales for Archiving Today

In the article "'For My Own Research Purposes?' Examining Ethnomusicology Field Methods for a Sustainable Music," Janet Topp Fargion discusses backgrounds and rationales for ethnomusicological collection of music through audio recordings. Fargion assumes that the strongest motive is preservation, but that collection is also linked to an aim of the continuation of traditions.

> The idea of archives is inextricably linked with the concept of preservation, a word, if not a concept shied away from in today's ethnomusicology: we no longer do ethnomusicology to "preserve" music, to keep it from extinction. Aware of the range of activities actually engaged in by today's ethnomusicology archives, I suggest a much broader definition of preservation, namely, do describe it as the *facilitation of the continuation of tradition*.[21]

Topp Fargion is right that for the ethnomusicological archives, preservation also includes facilitation of the use of the music—but my question here is of a different kind. Which traditions' continuation is facilitated, and which traditions never get the chance because they are not being collected at all? Archiving always involves choices—when some objects are chosen to represent or to continue certain traditions. This is, of course, at the expense of others. Those that are not collected therefore will fall by the wayside and eventually disappear.

The collection and documentation of folk music and music-making has most often not been governed by democratic principles of equal rights, but by utopian visions of individuals and organizations, and sometimes by state and national interests and needs. The lack of minority or immigrant cultural expressions and traditions, for instance, within archives and museums is normally not the result of malice or racism—but that might be a consequence. Instead, it is more often the effect of the museums' and archives' role in the creation of official versions of our common history, and the value placed on what is determined to be worthy of being collected and archived, and what can be discarded.

From an ideological perspective, there are many good arguments for music archiving.

Music is history. All music, new or old, carries with it traces of earlier times. This is an important reason to work with music in archives, museums, and libraries.

Music is identity. It can be argued that archives and museums are both democratic institutions and a human right. By depriving people of the access to archives, you deprive them of the possibility of a continuous cultural/ national identity.

Music is human interaction and communication. Music making is an activity that can be charged with many, and widely differing, types of messages, opinions, and meanings. With music as a cultural icon, people not only can enhance the self-esteem of their group, but also can demonstrate to others who they are or what they sympathize with.

Many of today's more important music archives have long histories with aims and ambitions that have varied over time. The goals have had to be reformulated to adapt to new issues and needs in society. An important question to ask is what position the national archives should take in today's multicultural contexts. Which music should be collected? Whose history should be written?

The Concept of Folk Music

That a scientific discipline devotes considerable effort toward precise definitions of key concepts and activities in its own fields of expertise is, of course, neither surprising nor uncommon. One finds endless discussions in other aesthetic disciplines about what can really be regarded as dance, theater, or art. This approach is, in itself, interesting and shows thoroughness within traditional music research and a willingness to problematize its own field. But it also reveals that the concept is loosely defined and difficult to use. Part of the problem, of course, is found on the semantic level; the term's meaning can vary, and continues to vary over time. Major changes have occurred within the folk music scene and in the use of folk music during the last 100 years. Musical forms that earlier had clear roots in the rituals of peasant cultures have, over the years, undergone shifts in both class and geography. We can use various terms in describing this process: aestheticization, institutionalization, professionalization, or symbolization. In other words, the complex meaning of the concept of folk music is characterized by its delocalization from older meeting spaces (such as community halls and the open spaces at crossroads) to concert stages, recording studios, music education institutions, and various media. Folk music has always had a strong connection to place—it is nestled in the very name, in the romantic sense of the word "folk." But today we see how music styles are disconnected from their original context and gain new uses, functions, and meanings in new contexts. And music is perhaps the aesthetic expression that can most easily travel across cultural and political boundaries. This has perhaps always been the case, but it seems clearer now than ever in an increasingly globalized media world.[22] Nevertheless, different understandings of the concept of folk music, from different time periods, persist, continuing to compete over its meaning.

It is clear that the discussion about meaning, in part, has to do with these major changes. But it is also clear that the discussion has its origins in the complex ideological points of departure that characterize the concepts' emergence. Folk music, as a contrasting designation—the other music—that which is not church or court music, which belonged to "high culture" or the culture of the emerging bourgeoisie of the late eighteenth century. In this positioning lies a clear judgment as well: that folk music does not belong to the dominant cultural stratum.[23] From having involved a majority of the people, folk music was turned into a subculture.

The Cultural Heritage Process and the Archives

In the article "Theorizing Heritage," the American folklorist Barbara Kirshenblatt-Gimblett discussed cultural heritage as a value-adding process:

> Heritage adds value to existing assets that have either ceased to be viable (subsistence lifestyles, obsolete technologies, abandoned mines, the evidence of past disasters) or that never were economically productive because an area is too hot, too cold, too wet or too remote. Heritage organizations ensure that places and practices in danger of disappearing because they are no longer occupied or functioning or valued will survive. It does this by adding value of pastness, exhibition, difference, and where possible indigeneity.[24]

In several publications, the Swedish ethnologist Stefan Bohman has developed ideas around cultural heritage in what he calls "the cultural heritage process," a mechanism in which phenomena are selected and given special status as symbols of a culture. Bohman's model is concerned with museums and the conscious or unconscious selections that result in museum collections; perhaps more important, his model addresses the consequences that these choices have for our understanding of the collections and for their cultural value. But Bohman's argument is also applicable to archives and other memory institutions. In the cultural heritage process, not only does the status of the collected objects change, but also the way we understand them. In *Historia, museer och nationalism* (History, museums and nationalism), Bohman presents a model that also has been explained and further developed by the Finnish folklorist Johanna Björkholm in her dissertation thesis *Immateriellt kulturarv som begrepp och process* (Intangible cultural heritage as concept and process).[25] Bohman's model assumes that cultural heritage is dependent on active staging and maintenance, which means that objects and phenomena are identified and re-created in accordance with the prevailing ideals of society. Therefore, they will also be reinterpreted in line with changes in the surrounding culture.

Based on Stefan Bohman's ideas, I will discuss the cultural heritage process in relation to the collecting and archiving of folk music. Bohman's model departs, as I stated earlier, from the museum's activities and has a clear focus on the construction of new symbolic values for the items collected and exhibited. This kind of value shift does, of course, also take place in the archive context, but a very important difference is that many music archives, especially folk music archives, have as one of their primary goals to be a resource for the music scene. For today's creative folk musicians, archives play a very important role as a source or stock of musical material. The musicians use the archives to find tunes as well as inspiration. In this way the archive turns out to be an important, and sometimes the only, link to previous music traditions. The archive becomes a keyhole for tradition, and archivists' and researchers' work can thus be seen as a kind of gatekeeping.

To describe archives from a theoretical cultural heritage perspective I have identified four steps of the process: *identification–classification–standardization–symbolization*.[26] In the description below, I speak mainly about instrumental music, but examples might as well have been vocal genres.

Identification

The first step includes identification of the music form. This may sound simple, but music forms are constantly changing, and in many cases are more "blurred at the edges" than they might appear at first glance. Questions about origin, instrumentation, and playing technique are relevant in the identification of a music form. This leads to discrimination and reduction. Loosely related or "impure" forms are often removed.

Key issues:

- What is the music form? And what is not?
- In what ways does it differ from other genres/musics?

Classification

The next step is to organize various musical expressions within the identified music practice. This may involve the identifying of sub-styles and hierarchies. Here authenticity, even though this is a very much debated concept, is often used as a criterion. The history and origin of a musical form may be the basis for this step in the process.

Key issues:

- Are there different forms?
- Is there a hierarchy (values)?

Standardization

A consequence of the identification and classification in the establishing of an archive or a collection is that the identified music form often becomes more homogenized. Publications and other resources, such as books, phonograms, theoretical tools, and standardized repertoire, together with the designation of "rights and wrongs" in the performing style, can also promote a standardized musical behavior. The selected repertoire and perhaps also playing techniques and styles will dominate, at the expense of others. Diverse and ambiguous sub-styles of the music form can be altered in order to fit the model.

Key issue:

- Purification; to remove the "wrong" repertoire, interpretations, and expressions.

Symbolization

An unavoidable result of any institutionalization in archives, as well as in museums, is symbolization. The symbolic value of a chosen music form can represent a culture, nation, or style. Symbolization often leads to new forms and uses of the music. This can also be followed by a re-diversification "on the other side," that is, when material from the archive is used in new contexts.

Key issues:

- Development of a musical canon
- Creation of a musical "grammar,"

Swedish Folk Music as Cultural Heritage

To exemplify the cultural heritage process and how the archives' and the collectors' work affects the music community, I have chosen to describe the Swedish Folk Music Commission's work during the first half of the twentieth century.

When Professor Jan Ling wrote the textbook *Svensk folkmusik. Bondens musik i helg och söcken* (Swedish folk music. The peasants' music in festivities and daily life) in 1964, he saw Swedish folk music from a fairly strict historical perspective. Folk music was still a living tradition, but the number of practitioners was steadily declining. And it was reasonable to expect that the genre in the near future was in danger of complete disappearance. What he did not know was that his book would be highly significant for the strong revival of Swedish folk music that emerged in the 1970s. In the "folk music vogue"[27] that washed over the country, scholars and collectors such as Ling became important inspirations and guides for young musicians who grew up in new environments, often with very little connection to rural society. Archival materials were then—which is still the case—often the only sources of older folk music forms.

Since the 1970s, folk music has developed into a genre that can be said to stand side by side with other recognized art forms. Folk music has been established in education, courses and programs in folk music are given at most Swedish universities, and folk musician education is offered at Swedish music conservatories. Today, the number of professional folk musicians is greater than ever. The importance of archives for this development can hardly be overstated—archives are essential for repertoire, but also a filter. The collections of the nineteenth and twentieth centuries are keyholes to the music history and usually the only way to find repertoire.

In the article "Sweden" in the *Garland Encyclopedia of World Music*, the ideological and filtering effect of the archives is emphasized:

> Swedish folk music is a composite of many heterogeneous styles and genres, accumulated for centuries. These traditions, genres, forms, and styles seem homogeneous in comparison to today's musical diversity. Their homogeneity is, however, a result of powerful processes of ideological filtering-processes that have seriously reduced the heterogeneity of rural musical traditions.[28]

The Swedish term *folkmusik* (folk music) usually denotes music of the rural classes in old peasant society, while *populärmusik* (popular music) normally refers to modern music.

> As a result of the interchange between these two concepts, there emerged an urban folklore, which, around 1920, was embodied in *gammaldans* old-time dance-music. Since about the 1970s, the term *folklig musik* (vernacular music) has served as an umbrella term for folk music, *gammaldans,* and some other forms of popular music. In the 1990s, the terms *ethnic music* and *world music* were introduced, most often for modernized forms of non-Swedish folk and popular music.[29]

Since the 1980s, new forms of ensemble music have been developed with inspiration from other European folk ensembles, primarily Irish and Hungarian.

The Folk Music Commission

In the early 1900s, the ideas that encouraged the pioneers of folk music collection at the end of the 1700s was revitalized in Sweden. One might speak of a second or maybe even third wave of the interest in recording and collecting folk culture. Also at this time, interest in the older folk music was primarily rooted in intellectual and academic circles. An appeal in the Nordic Museum's publication *Fataburen*, in the summer of 1908, was signed by the Swedish prince Eugene, as well as some of the most significant intellectual leaders of that time: Karl Silverstope, member of the ministry of justice and President of the Swedish Royal Academy of Music; Anders Zorn, internationally well-known painter; Nils Andersson judge; Lars Johan Zetterqvist, concert master; Richard Steffen, rector; Bernhard Salin, director of the Nordic Museum; and Nils Keyland, assistant at the Nordic Museum. The aim was to generate interest in the newly formed FMK, a body that would promote the collecting of important elements of a rapidly disappearing cultural heritage and preserve it for future generations. The Commission had been formed the previous year and in a call-to-action that was sent out it was written:

> It is a known fact that the Swedish folk music for decades been undergoing decline, that our genuine old songs and ballads, which by connoisseurs are said to be among the most beautiful in the world, are about to disappear, and are supplanted by songs that lack almost all musical value. Degeneration is quick. In the younger generations these beautiful melodies are already forgotten. Without our intervention they would now no longer be able to survive in tradition.[30]

It is stated that the interest is in "genuine old songs and ballads," and later in the text the commission declares that there is a particular need for contributions as "transcriptions of folk songs and old hymns, herding tunes, walking tunes, wedding songs, long dances, polskas, old waltzes etc."[31] Apparently, the interest is largely focused on instrumental music. This is partly new. In the childhood of the collection of folk culture, the interest was more focused on vocal music and lyrics. The change of focus can be explained ideologically but also by the simple fact that the driving enthusiasts had a special interest in instrumental folk music.

When the Commission was founded at the Nordic Museum at the "First Meeting for Swedish Folk Knowledge," Nils Andersson, who was the Commission's strong man and the driving force behind the petition, gave a speech that resulted in the following statement from the assembled:

> The first meeting of the Swedish folk knowledge states that the assembly considers that it is, from a scientific, ethnographic and nationally musical interest, highly desirable that in the near future, records of folk-like melodies may with utmost passion be conducted. The meeting finds it equally desirable, that in the near future a large

central collection of Swedish folk melodies may be established. The meeting agrees to the principles for music collecting that were presented by the speaker.[32]

Nils Andersson succeeded in his ambitions, and FMK was formed with the aim to be "a central collection of Swedish folk songs." Its mission was to collect and store selected repertoires of Swedish folk music. The main task was to implement the survey of Swedish folk music, region by region, which resulted in the 24 volumes of *Svenska låtar* (Swedish tunes) (see Figure 4.3).[33] The work was led initially by Nils Andersson and was then taken over by Nils's companion, Olof Andersson. The latter had been engaged to assist with fair copies and field transcriptions, but after Nils's death in 1921 the collecting was conducted entirely by Olof Andersson. In 1940 the last of the 24 volumes of *Svenska låtar* was published, and the Folk Music Commission's work was completed.[34]

But what ideas about folk music were discussed in the circles around FMK? What was good music and what was bad—and what music was worth collecting? There are no clear indications within FMK's own materials, but when Nils Andersson suggested at the meeting at the Nordic Museum that the collecting of folk melodies should intensified, he had a particular repertoire in mind. Nils Andersson draws a clear line between what

FIGURE 4.3. Polska from Ore, Dalarna in the FMK collection. Transcribed by Nils Andersson 1906. In Svenskt visarkiv.

should be collected and preserved, and what should, in fact, preferably be forgotten. But the line does not run between folk music and some other genre. He seems to rather consider which music is good, and which music is bad, within the folk music genre itself. He calls for the collecting of walking tunes (*gånglåtar*), polskas, herding music, and so on. But he also makes it clear that polkas, polkettas, mazurkas, and Viennese waltzes should not be collected, despite the fact that he undoubtedly sees that these were a large part of that time's contemporary folk culture. My understanding is that FMK's work had an enormous influence on what has come to be the core of the genre, and therefore also its meaning—and without the committee explicitly stating the meaning of the concept folk music. Today, we can also conclude that the collecting work had practical repercussions. The work within FMK had as a goal to collect, but also to keep the music alive—publications were intended to follow. And the publication of *Svenska låtar* (Swedish tunes) meant a fundamental canonization of Swedish folk music—perhaps to a greater degree than the collectors themselves imagined. By means of what was selected, one decided what would be preserved and, therefore, what would be played by coming generations of musicians. In this way, one can say that FMK defined Swedish folk music through its selections and its work.

The Discussions

The meaning of the concept of folk music has, as mentioned earlier, been discussed by many Swedish ethnomusicologists. As a starting point, I would like to talk about some of the more influential proposals of definitions made over the last 30 years by Swedish scholars. But I would also like to refer to discussions found within the framework of academic theses about Swedish folk music in more recent years.[35]

To begin the discussion on the effects of today's use of the concept, I will highlight four proposed definitions that have been often used and discussed: Ling (1979), Ronström (1989), Ramsten (1992), and Lundberg and Ternhag (1996).[36] But first I will reveal that I will be using quotations from these authors, perhaps a little unfairly, in order to deliberately polarize the concept of folk music.[37]

I begin with two definitions, which address the concept's ideological meaning: Jan Ling and then Owe Ronström, who uses and deepens Ling's ideas, 10 years later.

In his classic article, "Folkmusik—en brygd" (Folk Music—a Brew) (1979), Ling grounds his definition on the aspect of power. The concept of folk music was recognized and established by an acknowledged cultural elite at the end of the 1700s, and this has had an almost distancing effect. Ling writes that folk music is an "ideological concept, coined by the bourgeoisie of the eighteen and nineteen hundreds as a designation for 'the others', the people's music, which they observe, study, and attempt to incorporate within their culture." Ling states that the prerequisite for the development of folk music as a concept concerns the social changes that took place during the eighteenth century.

In my view, there are two main aspects of Ling's observation: (1) that folk music is the culture of "the other," and (2) that the designation of *folk music* was a way to gain control by making the music part of the designator's own cultural identity. In both cases, it is about positions of power. It is the new bourgeois class that defines and chooses. "The people" in this sense, are passive practitioners of the cultural expressions that are attributed to them. From the viewpoint of those in power, the *folk* do not choose their culture, while the bourgeoisie, to some extent, choose their means of expression.

Owe Ronström, in *Nationell musik? Bondemusik? Om folkmusikbegreppet* (1989) (National Music? Peasant Music? On the Concept of Folk Music), builds on Ling's ideas and further develops what the concept of folk music can be thought to stand for—in theory and in practice. In the end, he comes up with a sort of sociolinguistic definition of the term. According to Ronström, folk music is ". . . that which we call folk music. The people who use the word often decide what it will mean. Musicians, researchers, politicians, and audiences are all involved in an ongoing tug of war about which direction, and how far the meaning can be stretched."[38] Ronström observes, unlike Ling, the participants within the music community, from different social classes and with various roles. They actively take part in the power struggle over the meaning of the concept of folk music. It is basically Ling's line of thinking, but shifted to a more modern platform. In the research project *Music, Media, Multiculture*, Ronström's thoughts were developed around the model "doers—knowers—makers," three roles in a kind of discursive and performative power struggle.[39]

Ling and Ronström view folk music from its importance as an ideological marker. Folk music is defined, or rather singled out, as "the other." But the designation of subculture also means that folk music ends up in a defined relationship to the majority's culture and becomes, indirectly, a part of it. "Outsider-ness" becomes "insider-ness" as well—folk music "is incorporated" into the culture of the majority, as Ling expresses it.

A different way to approach the concept of folk music is to consider the music itself. Folk music has, since the 1700s, been defined through its function. But in its modern context it hardly differs from other aesthetic music forms—folk music stands side by side with jazz and art music on the concert stage.

Two definitions that deal with folk music as a genre, or musical style, include Märta Ramsten's in her dissertation, *Återklang. Svensk folkmusik i förändring 1950–1980* (Echoes: Swedish folk music in transition, 1950–1980) (1992), and four years later, my own and Gunnar Ternhag's definition in the textbook *Folkmusik i Sverige* (Folk music in Sweden).

Ramsten views folk music as ". . . a music genre, in other words, an established repertoire and a conventional way of performing this repertoire. This performance, of course, varies during different time periods, but which, even today, is highly dependent on nineteenth-century folk music collectors' approach to the material."[40] Ramsten connects it to an established repertoire that is performed in a generally accepted way—folk music as musical material played in a specific style. In addition, Ramsten links this to the work of collecting and the collectors' ideological frameworks. Lundberg and Ternhag (1996) take the discussion a step further. Folk music is "a family of styles. And as a style, folk music has certain characteristic traits that one can find in the use of tonal language, rhythmic patterns, or sound—or in a combination of these."[41] In this definition, the authors let go of the connection between collecting and an established repertoire—the music's attributes are determined solely by its style/sound or musical codes. The folk music genre, in this version, could be dominated by totally newly composed music that sounds like folk music.

Schematically described, one could say that the four definitions of folk music are overlapping, yet still represent a line of development; from the view of folk music as an ideologically constructed category, to the approach that folk music is an established form for creating music where the practitioners themselves influence the style's musical codes through their musical practice. It is tempting to see these as extremes within a spectrum of possible definitions, but the paths of thinking definitely complement one another. There is no obstacle to experiencing folk music as a musical code, while at the same time recognizing its strong links to national ideologies. It is clear that folk music can represent both ideology and style—and perhaps this is already captured in Ramsten's definition. The definitions themselves, in actuality, represent various levels of meaning within the folk music concept. Through their differences, they also describe folk music's relocations. The historically oriented definitions are, on the one hand, closely tied to folk music's social contexts; folk music is folk music because it is connected to a social class and to a diffuse and loosely defined past. The definitions that pertain to today's use of folk music instead refer to musical codes; folk music is characterized by a type of instrumentation, playing technique, type of repertoire, and so on.

Everyday Meaning and the Practitioner's Perspective

One can, of course, ask oneself whether or not the above definitions are included in some sort of "everyday meaning" of the concept of folk music. If one should ask "the man on the street," that person would hardly be answering that folk music is an ideologically constructed category, or that it is defined based on a sustained drone effect or modal melodic structures. In our daily use of the concept, we are more likely influenced by the ideas of folk music's social connections to rituals, as well as the daily work within a rural community—"the peasants' music in festivities and daily life."[42]

While teaching "Swedish folk music" in various situations, I have often discussed the everyday meaning of "folk music" with the students in order to see which criteria one can agree upon, without analyzing the concept more deeply. It is interesting that it is actually pretty easy to come to an overall agreement on some sort of meaning of the concept. The following key criteria almost always come up:

Oral tradition
Passed on across generational borders
Tied to rituals
Rural music
From the past.

All of these criteria point to music's social context and connection to older rural society. It is quite seldom that the criteria of musical styles come up during such a discussion.

During the fall of 2008, I taught the first-year students of the folk music department at The Royal College of Music in Stockholm. On this occasion I also asked if any of the students considered themselves to be a *spelman* (Swedish folk musician or folk fiddler, considered to be embedded in a specific playing tradition). Of the group's 11 students, there was only one who thought of himself as a *spelman*. One can ask oneself why? Except for the three students who studied singing, all of the others were, more or less, established practitioners and instrumentalists within folk music. These are knowledgeable musicians who should have identified themselves as *spelmän/spelkvinnor* (male/female folk musicians)—otherwise, who else would identify themselves as such? Historically, it would have been a bigger problem for them to call themselves "musicians," a title that, at least in earlier times, would have brought to mind an educated, professional, and experienced music practitioner in art music. But, according to this student group at the music academy, which I believe is relatively representative, it is less pretentious to call oneself a (folk) musician than a *spelman*.

> "I will never be a spelman." said one.
> "I would never be able to play so faithfully in one style. To be a spelman involves adherence to a bunch of impossible requirements."

This is a complete turn-around of the meaning and value given to the terms "musician" and *spelman*. I believe that this is, in part, an important effect stemming from FMK's efforts to connect the music to place and local culture, and not least, to raise the status of the individual, instrumental musician within folk culture—the *spelman*. In order to put some light on this change, we can compare it to the reaction of the folk music collector Karl Sporr, who became very upset when he was called a *spelman*. In an article in the newspaper *Falukuriren* in 1940, he pointed out that he wanted to be called "a violinist and music researcher, and not a *spelman*." The background was that when Sporr received the Hazelius Medal for his contributions to folk music, he refused to accept it, as the Nordic Museum had presented him with the title *spelman*.

The Folk Music Commission's Folk Music

In order to discuss FMK's ideas about what folk music is, or rather what good folk music is, I have chosen to start with Nils Andersson's lecture, "About Swedish Folk Music," which he held in various locations in the region of Skåne during the late winter of 1909.[43] Nils Andersson's lectures were often presented in the press in a summarized or abstract form, and these were later commented upon by the Finnish musicologist and collector Professor Otto Andersson, in an article in 1958.[44] Among other things, Otto Andersson remarks on the fact that the summaries are very much alike and have, for the most part, the same form. Otto Andersson draws the conclusion that Nils wrote these abstracts himself and sent them to the newspapers, or gave them to some newspaper reporter. It is certainly possible that this is true, as Nils Andersson was very eager to get his message out, and a clever way to do it, of course, was to "do the job" for the journalists. It was easy to just take the completed summary to the newspaper. But, one can also consider that the newspapers got their news from one another. Otto Andersson comments on four lectures from around the same time: in Trelleborg on February 8, in Lund on March 2, in Ängelholm on March 11, and in Kristianstad on April 1. In my example, I will be using the abstract that was published in the daily newspaper *Sydsvenska Dagbladet Snällposten* on March 5, 1909.

Nils Andersson's lecture presents a clear statement about several aspects of the nature of folk music, its function, and value. In many ways, Nils Andersson's evaluation goes back to Johann Gottfried von Herder's ideas about folk culture as a sort of expression of the collective folk soul (*Volksgeist*)—even though he does not use that term.

Folk Music's Essence and Origin

Nils Andersson begins by claiming that there are two types of folk music, instrumental and vocal—a fundamental and, understandably, elemental observation that is interesting only in light of the fact that he never returns to the topic of vocal music in the lecture. He comments further:

- *Embedded in the term "folk music" is that it belongs to the peasantry.*
  - It has not merely been preserved within tradition, but has originated there as well.
- *[Folk music] is... among the finest and best expressions of a people's temperament and character.*

- ... *as well as a reflection of the people's way of perceiving the environment in which they live.*
  - *Each country has, thus, its own particular folk music.*
  - *And in Sweden, it can be said that each province has its own folk music.*
- *Of the folk music of all countries, Sweden's is of the highest rank.*

Nils Andersson's thoughts about the essence and origin of folk music fall in line with the Romantic era's ideas of folk music's connection to the soul of the people. The basis for this is the late eighteenth-century ideas of nation, race ideology, and the idealization of the simple, wild, or the uncultured. A consistent view was that everything, or rather every culture, had its own character—a soul. Humans had, of course, their souls, but people as a whole, as well as nature, had a soul. These ideas can be seen as a reaction against the Enlightenment's espousal of reason and rationalism. The new Romantic currents instead emphasized the importance of the soul of the arts and the emotions. Music was given a double role as both an expression for, and the bearer of, the soul of the people.

Philosopher and historian Johann Gottfried von Herder is often cited as the author of the concept of "folk." Through Herder, the term "folk" began to be used in a way that can be likened to today's use of "culture." People are, at the same time, individuals, and representatives of a collective. In the latter role, a person expresses a kind of folk character. Herder's view of the folk as a collective unit was relative. He meant that all cultures are different, that human nature is not uniform, but that we all have different capabilities within our respective basic characters that express the soul of the folk. At the same time, the various different folk souls are expressions for one and the same God.[45] It is interesting that Nils Andersson maintains that Swedish folk music is foremost among all countries. We Swedes are hardly known for emphasizing that our own culture, celebrating ourselves, is better than the culture of others.[46] Nils Andersson's choice of accenting Swedish folk music's superiority can understandably be his belief that it really is outstanding, but also may be an expression of a kind of alienation—a sort of distancing himself from folk culture. It is easier to highlight Swedish folk music if one is not actually a part of the folk culture, but only its promoter.

The Bearers of Tradition

"The bearers of folk music were the old fiddlers who, as a rule, were highly regarded." One of the most distinctive features of Nils Andersson's approach and presentation of folk music material is that he places the fiddler (*spelman*) in the center (see Figure 4.4). In the publication *Svenska låtar* (Swedish tunes), the presentation of the *spelman* receives a central place. The folk musician functions also as a principal category for the tunes, something that Nils Andersson was criticized for by contemporary colleagues from various quarters. In earlier collections, anonymity of authors functioned just the opposite way—as a sort of lofty ideal. The collective, creative process of folk culture stood in the

FIGURE 4.4. The music collector Nils Andersson in the home of the fiddler Ante Sundin. Photo from Svenskt visarkiv.

center. The Serbian collector Vuk Karadžić, who gathered epics and ballads in parts of the Balkans in the beginning of the 1800s, wrote: "Everyone denies their involvement, even the actual poet, and they say that they heard it from someone else."[47] It is a sort of faith in the process, that people—audience, storytellers, and singers—act as a kind of filter or selection mechanism. The individual can write poetry and compose music, but it is the folk who actively choose what will be preserved. One can, in fact, see this as a kind of process of canonization on an everyday level. FMK's approach of accenting the importance of the musician can instead be seen as a new and modern way of presenting the folk music and its practitioners. Then, of course, one can wonder if Nils Andersson was correct when he claims that musicians "as a rule, were highly regarded."

THREATS

One reason for the formation of FMK was that folk music was considered to be dying out fast. Through the work of collecting, at least parts of the quickly disappearing cultural heritage could be saved for coming generations.

This is reflected in newspaper summaries of Nils Andersson's lectures, where he notes that

> [t]he real folk music in Sweden is almost extinct.
> What now goes by the name is extremely trite and burlesque, and infinitely inferior to the genuine, old folk music.

Popular music is a particular threat in this scenario. It is interesting in that it seems that poplar music gradually evolved into folk music's leading opponent during the 1800s. It becomes increasingly clear that art music, in many ways, is allied with collectors—folk music was used by many classical composers as source material for the composition of national music during the Romantic period. Popular music, instead, stood directly in the firing line, and the most pronounced object of hate was the accordion. Nils Andersson asserts in the lecture that the threats include:
Accordion
One attributes this [folk music's death] commonly to the accordion.
... the old folk music cannot be played on the regular accordion, since it does not have the notes found in these [folk music's] scales.
It would be fortuitous if one could eradicate the accordion.
Musical sense and, perhaps even, emotional life [has] become superficial and diluted.
Contributing factors are:
Popularity of quartet songs,
And even more so, brass music.
One reason for the extinction of folk music has also been pietism.
The German instrument maker, Friedrich Buschmann, constructed the first accordion in 1822. He named his invention Handäoline. The instrument had a diatonic tonal range and each button, connected to two lamellae, produced different tones depending on if it was pressed on the intake or the output of air. In 1829, Austrian Cyrill Demian took out a patent on his Akkordion, a development variation of Buschmann's instrument. Through industrial production that enabled relatively low prices, the accordion spread rapidly over Europe and North America. The accordion fit well to the new repertoire of dance music that was spreading throughout these regions at the time, around the turn of the century. The accordion belongs to the family of instruments called free-reed and includes, for example, harmonica (mouth harp) and pump organ, and is related to Asian instruments such as the mouth organ (for example, the Chinese *sheng*), which has existed in southeastern regions of Asia for at least two thousand years. It is believed that the idea for the accordion was modeled on these Asian mouth organs. But the accordion also has much in common with European bagpipes, mostly in the construction that includes a bellows, and base and melody functions.

By the middle of the 1800s, there were different kinds of accordions with various names. The accordion was also called by many local, vernacular names such as *hand klaver, knäorgel, piglock,* and *drängkammarorgel* (hand keyboard, knee organ, maid charmer, workman's organ)—that witness to the fact of the importance of the accordion among Sweden's lower classes. The accordion's rapid spread also put its mark on folk music. In many ways, one can say that the accordion represents an important shift in musical thinking. In the older stratum, the music was built with only the melody in mind. The most important components in the music were melody and rhythm—one used to say that music was "linear." But, in that one can begin to harmonize and put chords to the melody, there arises a new way of thinking about music. Music gains a vertical dimension. The accordion's huge popularity meant that much of the older music was adapted to a harmonic way of thinking. And it was exactly that which upset Nils Andersson and other folk music enthusiasts. They felt that the accordion simplified the older music and made the intricate melodies coarser. But the accordion also stood for the new era—industrialization and urbanization. In this way and in many people's eyes, it became a symbol of the culture's superficiality—something that must be fought against if folk music was to be preserved.

The accordion, along with the harmonica, was manufactured industrially during the latter part of the 1800s and spread quickly across Europe. Together with modern brass orchestras and string ensembles, accordion players began to gradually take over more and more of the dance music function, previously held by violin and clarinet musicians.[48] Local instrument traditions were also regarded as threatened—as for instance the Swedish *nyckelharpa* and older types of wind instruments belonging to the herding traditions.

But it was not only the changing trends that threatened folk music. It had more enemies. During the latter years of the nineteenth century, a religious revivalist movement campaigned against alcohol, dancing, and other worldly pleasures of indulgence—a crusade that also affected music making, which was closely associated with contexts in which immorality and sin could be expected to occur.[49]

The Identification of the "Authentic" Folk Music

In FMK's archive there are many examples of clarifications on what is valuable or what is reprehensible from a collecting perspective. In a letter to Professor Tobias Norlind in 1912, Nils Andersson explains that his collections consist "of truly ancient fiddle tunes and therefore, do not bother with the likes of polkett, mazurka, Viennese waltz, galop, etc."

In the commentary in *Sydsvenskan*, Nils Andersson describes the oldest and the "most peculiar" material as the most important.

- Among the oldest and most peculiar were
    - Those so-called herding tunes, which the herders played on animal horns or birch-bark trumpets (*näverlurar*).
    - Walking tunes were those played while walking [and] wedding processions.

- Dance music comprised, however, a considerable part of folk music.
  - The foremost here being polskas.
  - While the names of these indicate foreign origin, it is not the music that matters, but only a certain kind of dance.
  - Of old, some of these melodies have been played for a long dance.

Folk music's value was dependent on its ability to symbolize a national character, and to be authentic, distinctive, and not least, very old. In addition, it must differ from the folk culture of other countries. Swedish music must have something different from that of the Danish or Finnish. Thus we see the worthiness that Nils Andersson puts on the most peculiar songs. Nils Andersson saw a very special value in the herding music, thanks to its archaic sound, but also because it is distinctly Swedish.

THE END GOAL

FMK's aim was to preserve folk music. But, above all, the Commission wanted to make the music available through the publication of *Svenska låtar* (Swedish tunes). In his lecture, Nils Andersson points out two goals for FMK's activity:

- ... that the rich treasure, that our folk music contains and which, at the last moment was captured, could again become alive and be assimilated by our people and used for cultivating and enriching spiritual life.
- And even our composers would have a very rewarding goldmine from which they could take motifs and ideas.

The work of collecting carried out in the 1800s had, in many cases, the aim to publish songs and tunes so that they could be sung and played. But the intended audience was not the musicians and singers of the rural society. An example is Richard Dybeck's efforts to implement folk culture in a theatrical setting. One form of this was the so-called evening entertainments, which he arranged in Stockholm. He combined different folk traditions in scenes that he named, for example, "festive pieces," "dance rhapsodies," "lyrical folksongs," and "scenes from the herding woods" (where cattle grazed). The pieces were arranged with a wide variety of instrumental groups, choirs, orchestras, and soloists. An important detail is that, as stated before, the performances never made use of peasant musicians or singers. Dybeck let professional musicians, singers, and college music students take the roles. Dybeck's efforts show how important it was for him to find a balance between what was aesthetically acceptable to the bourgeois audiences of Stockholm, and the "authentic" folk music as it was performed in the farming communities—in church, for dancing, or in the summer pastures. FMK had a very different target group in mind—those musicians who were interested in finding good repertoire from their own regions. And this came to be. The publication *Svenska låtar* functioned as a priceless source for the organized fiddle groups. But FMK also wanted to make the collections available to composers and researchers.

New Perspectives on Folk Music

It is clear that, according to FMK, the threats to folk music do not come from art music, but from popular culture and new music trends coming from continental Europe, spread across Europe through new media. In his lectures, Nils Andersson points out that young people are misled into forgetting the old melodies by new, foreign, trendy melodies and instruments. For him, classical music and its composers were rather allies in the fight for the preservation of folk music. This was, of course, not unique for FMK but, in fact, was a common feature of the Romantic era. The fear that the youth would be misled by foreign influences was ongoing in many later events during the twentieth century.[50]

On the basis of Nils Andersson's lectures and FMK's other writings, one can construct a of hierarchy of values that coincides well with the Romantic era's ideals about national culture.[51] The scale stretches between poles that can be designated in different ways:

Good–Bad
Old–New
Authentic–Modern
Natural–Artificial
Rural–Urban
Minor key–Major key
Polska dance–Polka
March–Foxtrot

With the help of Nils Andersson's lectures, we can construct FMK's value scale (see Figure 4.5).

FMK's Impact and the Cultural Heritage Process

Nils Andersson's lecture is a sermon—a proclamation of the folk music gospel. He took his arguments about the folk culture that springs from the collective soul and which mirrors nature from ideologies of the Romantic era. And he had a burning passion for this work.

Nils Andersson did not work with some explicit definition of folk music, but in his arguments, one can catch a glimpse of the same conceptual content as in the "everyday

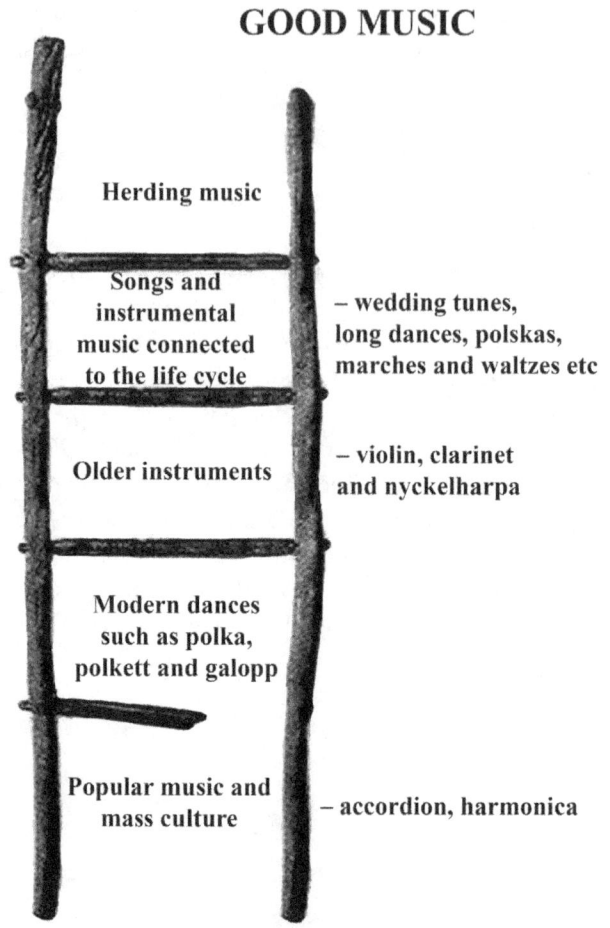

FIGURE 4.5. The ladder is an illustration the value scale of FMK. At the bottom we find the music that represents modernity and international influences. At the top we find pastoral music that stands for the good old peasant society

meaning" that I described earlier. Nils Andersson's folk music is rural music, from older times that have a clear connection to function—rituals, work in the woods and at the summer pasture. Folk music's lifeblood is the old farming community, which was passed down from generation to generation. Consequently, folk music was threatened by modernity, internationalization, and fast-paced changes.

For Nils Andersson, it seems that it was not necessary for him to define folk music—it was self-evident. Even so, one can say that he and FMK, through their work more than any other, shaped the concept. Through the clear focus on instrumental music, from certain geographical regions, a focus on certain types of tunes, and sanctioning of certain instruments, FMK has, in tangible ways, narrowed down the concept.

Through their extensive and diligent work, FMK created a clear and distinct repertoire for future generations—a canon for Swedish folk music that is still in use.

FMK's work can be described by the four steps of the cultural heritage process.

Identification

The Folk Music Commission concluded that certain styles and dance types would be preserved, so identification is perhaps the most obvious part, and it was the Commission's very starting point. Here is an outspoken appreciation of the older layers of folk music and this, combined with a clear desire to preserve the most distinctive musical forms in Swedish folk music, with the aim that Swedish music should be conceived as different from other countries' folk music. One consequence of this was that melodies collected close to the Norwegian border sometimes sounded too Norwegian. A collected material of this type was in some cases sent to Norwegian collectors.[52] The hunt for elderly and distinctive forms of music directed the collecting work toward shepherd music and dance music with roots in the eighteenth-century folk culture.

Classification

This step is especially evident in the presentation of the material in the publication *Svenska låtar*, where the folk musicians' repertoires were consistently presented by melody type. Another result of FMK's work is that the polska melodies were grouped into three main types, based on the notated rhythm. The publication in *Svenska låtar* also creates a clear geographical division of the Swedish folk music by region, with regions profiled against each other. We can also observe that the classification of a tune as "polska" led to a rise of its status and thus increased the tradition bearer's prestige. It is clear that many musicians adapted their repertoire after collectors' preferences—explicit or implicit—and this meant a shift of the folk music genre toward older repertoires.

Standardization

The Swedish folk music of today is based very much on the collections created by FMK. The polska has become the overall dominating melody and dance type in Swedish folk music. As a result of FMK's focus on a few musical instruments, folk music today is largely dominated by violin music. The orientation toward older folk music practice has also counteracted the ensemble types developed in the 1900s with the accordion as a central instrument. Until the last few decades, this kind of ensemble has not been regarded as folk—unlike in many other European countries, where the ensembles have been seen as a natural development within the tradition. FMK's ideal folk musician was the nineteenth-century *spelman*, a romanticized and mythical maverick, a strong-willed natural artist who maintained traditions without allowing himself to be influenced by contemporary trends and musical fashions. The musician was a man, an instrumentalist who usually played to dance, alone without accompaniment. The effect of this was, of course, that the Swedish folk music by FMK became a more male-dominated instrumental genre throughout most of the twentieth century.[53]

Symbolization

A fundamental effect of FMK's collecting work has been the creation of a distinct "Swedish" folk music idiom. The nationalistic ideas during the Romantic era had their roots in Johann Gottfried von Herder's ideas of national folk characters. These ideas were the basis for FMK's collections and the publication of *Svenska låtar*. The collectors' focus on typical or distinctive features, in terms of melody types and modal structures, have turned these into stylistic cannons. From this perspective, it is possible to say that FMK made Swedish folk music more Swedish, or at least more distinct. In the early twentieth century, instruments such as the Swedish *nyckelharpa* were threatened by new factory-made musical instruments, especially the accordion and harmonica. In the work of FMK, the *nyckelharpa* was identified as particularly important to preserve. The result that we can see today is that the *nyckelharpa* has developed into a national symbol. Without FMK, this would hardly have been possible.

Conclusions

FMK's ideological importance to the folk music concept in practice may be summarized as the following:

- The *spelman* as the focus
  - The individual musician becomes visible in the tradition
  - Sorting of good and poor musicians
  - The older the better as a basic idea
  - Focus on "passing on to the next" (tune learned from . . . which was learned from, etc.)
  - Collecting becomes focused on instrumental music
  - A shift from a female to a male focus
- Local distinctiveness
  - From national to regional
- Certain types of tunes become established standards
  - Polska dances, waltzes, marches, herding music, and long dances
- A clearer picture of the threat from popular music
  - Art music composers considered to be allies
  - Accordion music and popular dances end up on the outside

- Strong demands on helpers and other collectors to avoid collecting polkas, polkettas, and galops
- The instruments are standardized.
  - Focusing on fiddle, clarinet, and *nyckelharpa*—as well as the cow and sheep horn and bark trumpet (*lur*).
  - Less focus on bagpipe, fipple flute, diddling—singing of dance tunes (*trall*), bowed lyre (*stråkharpa*)
  - Absolutely no accordion, harmonica, other bowed instruments, or transverse flutes.

Music collecting and archive work were important parts of the homogenization and establishing of Swedish folk music—a Swedish folk music that was different from other countries' musics. From this perspective, the work of FMK is definitely a form of applied ethnomusicology, where the aim was to interact with and influence the music community and, in a way, on a higher level, take an active part in the creation of a Swedish identity. The quote "history is written by the victors" is sometimes said to originate from Winston Churchill. That is possible, but more important is the meaning of the sentence—that history writing is a matter of the exercise of power. This is also true for memory institutions. The records of bygone times are, of course, important for our understanding of history. By taking the initiative in the collecting work, FMK could decide what should be preserved concerning genres and tunes. And this was not unproblematic—in several cases there were tensions and power struggles between competing collectors and institutions. FMK emerged victorious from this power struggle, and the material that became published in *Svenska låtar* is dominant among Swedish practitioners of folk music today.

FMK employees had very little contact with other European collectors. Apart from the Nordic network, where scholars exchanged ideas and materials, there were, as far as one can see in the documentation, almost no contacts with collectors in Central Europe, the Berlin School, or with British or Hungarian collectors. This might explain why they so stubbornly clung to the use of pen and paper without using the modern technical aids of that time. But in the work of FMK, which of course was conducted much later, the phonograph was used only on a few occasions. Perhaps this had to do with the fact that FMK had as its primary goal to publish the material in printed form and that the collectors were very skilled at transcribing and felt that it was unnecessary to lug heavy equipment for fieldwork. But it is also possible that this was a way to control the situation—to have the exclusive right to the interpretation. Because there have not been recordings available, FMK's transcriptions are the only sources. There is thus little opportunity to question the versions published in *Svenska låtar*.

Anthony Seeger is probably right when he says that ethnomusicologists in the first place will be remembered for their collections, not for their theories or methods.[54] But possibly, one can draw his reasoning a step further and argue that it is primarily the collections themselves that will live on, and in most cases, both the collectors and the motives for the works will be forgotten. However, from a research perspective, this is extremely important—if we do not understand how and why the collections were generated, we cannot fully interpret or comprehend them.

> No one can predict the ways their collections will be used. Some will become one of the building blocks of cultural and political movements; some will bring alive the voice of a legendary ancestor for an individual; some will stimulate budding musicians, some will soothe the pain of exile, and some will be used for restudies of primary data that may revolutionize approaches to world music.[55]

A very important and difficult task of responsibility for applied ethnomusicology is to try to ensure that the fruits of ethnomusicological work cannot be misused. In Sweden, nationalistic and xenophobic forces in recent years often used folk culture archives as arguments, as examples of the "real" Swedish culture that must be defended against other cultures that threaten to take over. FMK's efforts to describe Swedish folk music as something distinctly different from the music of other countries by identifying and collecting older distinctive music forms of course appealing to such forces. Applied ethnomusicology then then has a particular responsibility to explain the origin of our archives and provide a perspective on their background and role in history. And folk music is still a question of definition.

NOTES

1. Cf. Fargion (2009).
2. Lundberg, Malm, and Ronström (2003).
3. Reinhard (1962).
4. Slobin (2010: 1). The concept is also recently discussed in connection to "world music" by Philip Bohlman (2002).
5. The work of the Folk Music Commission has been discussed and described by the Swedish ethnomusicologist Mathias Boström (2006, 2010). Different aspects of the Commission's activities are investigated in the anthology *Det stora uppdraget* (2010).
6. Pattinato (1991).
7. Cf. Lidman (2012: 5–6).
8. Ibid.
9. Cf. Hammarlund (2015).
10. Lönnrot (1835).
11. Cf. Hugh Trevor-Roper's article "The Invention of Tradition: The Highland Tradition of Scotland" (1983).
12. Ronström (2010). My translation from Swedish.
13. http://www.unesco.org/new/en/communication-and-information/flagship-project-activities/memory-of-the-world/homepage/.
14. Hammarlund (2015).
15. Quote from Barons reprinted in Nordiska museet (1985). "Folkdiktning från Lettland. About the Latvian folk poem collector Krišjānis Barons." My translation.
16. Hammarlund (2015).

17. Koch et al. (2004: 228).
18. Ibid.
19. Abraham and Hornbostel (1909: 15). *Am besten ist es, wenn der Forscher selbst die Gesänge oder Instrumentalstücke so erlernt, dass er sie zur Zufriedenheit der Eingeboren en wiedergeben kann. Als Kritiker muss man sich musikalisch besonders Begabte—(wieder nach dem Urteil ihrer Landsleute)—wählen und auch die Sicherheit haben, dass die Zustimmung nicht nur aus Höflichkeit oder aus Interesselosigkeit erfolgt.*
20. Cf. Hammarlund (2015).
21. Fargion (2009: 76).
22. Cf. Lundberg et al. (2003: 400–412) in the chapter "The Play of Opposites," and Anthony Giddens's concept "disembedding mechanisms" (1990).
23. Mark Slobin uses the term "superculture" to mean the dominant culture (*Subcultural Sounds: Micromusics of the West*, 1993). Slobin, in his turn, builds on the Italian Marxist philosopher Antonio Gramsci. Peter Burke 2009, makes the same distinction between what Robert Redfield called "the great" and "the little tradition" in *Popular Culture in Early Modern Europe*.
24. Kirshenblatt-Gimblett (1995: 370).
25. Bohman (1997) and Björkholm (2011).
26. Cf. Bohman (2010) who uses: defining—coding—change of context—objectification. See also Lundberg, "It Goes Without Saying" (2011).
27. Kjellström (1985).
28. Kjellberg, Ling, and Ronström (2000: 437).
29. Kjellberg, Ling, and Ronström (2000: 436–437).
30. "Upprop" (Call). Archive of the Folk Music Commission.
31. "Polska" is a very common dance in the Swedish folk culture. The word means "Polish." At the end of the sixteenth century couple dances came to Sweden. The most significant types had their origin in different parts of Northern Europe. The term probably has its roots in the Polish dances danced in the Swedish noblemen's halls from the late 1500s. The popularity of the polska is manifested through the great variety of the dance types called polska. Many older dances (also different chain dances) had locally been called polskas. The pol-ska of the Renaissance had a two-part form, in full accordance with the demands of balance and proportion in art (cf. other two-part dances, such as pavan-gaillard). The original Polish dances were composed of a slow first part in duple meter and a more lively second part in triple meter. Eventually, the second part, the livelier spring dance, became more and more important. And it is that part that survived and became the polska that is still danced in Sweden.
32. *Fataburen* (1908: s. 186).
33. *Svenska låtar* published by Nils Andersson and Olof Andersson (1921–1940).
34. The entire collection from FMK was published on the Internet by Svenskt visarkiv (the Centre for Folk Music and Jazz Research) *Folkmusikkommissionens notsamling och Musikmuseets spelmansböcker* (2007). The collection consists of around 45,000 handwritten pages with folk melodies. http://www.smus.se/earkiv/fmk/index.php?lang=en. The original collection is kept in Svenskt visarkiv (FMK's archive III.1 N.A.s arkiv vol. 1K).
35. In her dissertation, *Bland polskor, gånglåtar och valser. Hallands spelmansförbund och den halländska folkmusiken* (2004) (Among Polskas, Walking tunes, and Waltzes: Halland's Fiddler's Association and the Music of Halland), Karin Eriksson discusses Swedish folk music as an "open concept" in which the meaning is always recharged with new meanings.

She highlights how Halland's (region in southwest Sweden) Fiddler's Association, through its activities, presents, in various ways, what can be considered to be a regional folk music of Halland, and what the consequences are for the repertoire that is emphasized as folk music from Halland. In *Med rösten som instrument. Perspektiv på nutida svensk vokal folkmusik* (2007) (With the Voice as Instrument: Perspectives on Contemporary Swedish Vocal Folk Music), Ingrid Åkesson, from the Svenskt visarkiv (Centre for Swedish Folk Music and Jazz Research) discusses, among other things, how the process of transmission within the genre of folk music involves more than a direct taking over of the older singers' (and fiddlers') practices. In his book *Från bondson till folkmusikikon. Otto Andersson och formandet av "finlandssvensk folkmusik"* (2007) (From Farmer's Son to Folk Music Icon: Otto Andersson and the Forming of "Finnish-Swedish Folk Music"), Niklas Nyqvist takes up a discussion of Otto Andersson's large collecting project of music of the Finland Swedes. Andersson's work went, in many ways, parallel to that of the FMK and also had significant implications for the meaning of the folk music concept within the context of the Finland Swedes. Finally, I will also name American ethnomusicologist David Kaminsky's *Hidden Traditions. Conceptualizing Swedish Folk Music in the Twenty-First Century* (2005), in which he discusses, in detail, the folk music concept within the Swedish academic tradition and sets it against the practical use of the term by musicians and those interested in music.

36. David Kaminsky has done a thorough examination of these definitions in his thesis from 2005.
37. It can thus seem like the authors completely disagree on the question of what folk music means. It is not that way, of course—all the authors recognize a much more nuanced picture of what the concept of folk music stands for. I have simply chosen to use the quotes that draw the apart the meanings and create apparent contradictions between the authors. I hope that they forgive me for this.
38. Ronström (1989: 7).
39. The model in *Musik, Medier, Mångkultur*—"doers-knowers-makers"—is based on the roles of three different actors within a music culture. See also Lundberg and Ternhag, *Folkmusik i Sverige* (2005), and Lundberg's "*Bjårskpip in blossom: on the revitalization process of a folk music instrument*" (2007).
40. Ramsten (1992: 7–8).
41. We wrote the book together and, during the process, put the definition of folk music through the ringer, but the basic wording is Gunnar Ternhag's (Lundberg and Ternhag, 2005: 14).
42. The subtitle to Jan Ling's textbook from 1964, *Svensk folkmusik. Bondens musik i helg och söcken.*
43. The Swedish title of the lecture was "Om svensk folkmusik."
44. The article "Melodisamlaren Nils Andersson. Minnen och anteckningar" is part of *Budkavlen* XIX, 1940. Nils Andersson's lecture was also commented upon by Otto Andersson in *Spel opp, I spelemänner: Nils Andersson och den svenska spelmansrörelsen* (1958).
45. Johann Gottfried von Herder, *Stimmen der Völker in Liedern* (1978).
46. Cf. Kaminsky (2007).
47. Peter Burke (2009: 134); cf. Owe Ronström (1989).
48. Cf. Dan Lundberg and Gunnar Ternhag, *Folkmusik i Sverige*, och Owe Ronström "Inledning" in Arwidsson, 1989.

49. Cf. Lundberg and Ternhag (2005: 82).
50. Cf. The Swedish ethnologist Jonas Frykman (1988) in his book "Dansbaneeländet"—*The Dance Pavilion Misery*.
51. Cf. Richard Carlins interesting article about folk music aesthetics, "The Good, the Bad, and the Folk" (2004).
52. Roempke (1994).
53. In much of the earlier collection works the interest was on the texts and, to some extent song melodies. This meant that more women were recorded. Folk Commission's focus on the instrumental folk tradition was a clear new trend. The male dominance among folk practitioners has been broken in recent years and today many music educators report a preponderance of women among the students.
54. Seeger (1986: 267); cf. Fargion (2009: 76).
55. Seeger (1986: 264).

References

Abraham, Otto, and Erich Moritz von Hornbostel. (1909). Vorschläge für die Transkription exotischer Melodien. *Sammelbände der Internationalen Musikgesellschaft*. Berlin: Franz Steiner Verlag.

Åkesson, Ingrid. (2007). *Med rösten som instrument. Perspektiv på nutida svensk vokal folkmusik* [With the Voice as Instrument: Perspectives on Contemporary Swedish Vocal Folk Music]. Stockholm: Svenskt visarkiv. Svenskt visarkivs handlingar.

Andersson, Otto. (1940). "Melodisamlaren Nils Andersson. Minnen och anteckningar" [The melody collector Nils Andersson. Memories and notes]. *Budkavlen* XIX.

Andersson, Otto. (1958). *Spel opp, I spelemänner. Nils Andersson och den svenska spelmansrörelsen* [Play, fiddlers, play! Nils Andersson and the Swedish folk music movement]. Stockholm: Nordiska museet.

Björkholm, Johanna. (2011). *Immateriellt kulturarv som begrepp och process* [Intangible cultural heritage as concept and as process]. Turku: Åbo Akademis förlag.

Bohlman, Philip V. (2002). *World Music. A Very Short Introduction*. Oxford: Oxford University Press.

Bohman, Stefan. (1997). *Historia, museer och nationalism* [History, museums and nationalism]. Stockholm: Carlsson.

Bohman, Stefan. (2010). Kanon som samhällsföreteelse. Beethoven—västerlandets kulturelle hjälte [Canon as feature of society. Beethoven—the cultural hero of the West]. In *Att sätta ansikte på samhällen: om kanon och personmuseer*. Stockholm: Carlsson.

Boström, Mathias. (2006). "Folkmusikkommissionens verksamhet och arkiv. En översikt och vägledning" [The work and archive of the Folk Music Commission. An overview] I *Dokumenterat. Bulletin från Statens musikbibliotek*. No. 37. Stockholm: Statens musikbibliotek.

Boström, Mathias. (2010). "100 år med Folkmusikkommissionen" [100 years with the Folk Music Commission]. In *Det stora uppdraget. Perspektiv på Folkmusikkommissionen i Sverige 1908-2008*, edited by Mathias Boström, Dan Lundberg, and Märta Ramsten, pp. 13-38. Stockholm: Nordiska museets förlag.

Boström, Mathias, Dan Lundberg, and Märta Ramsten. (2010). *Det stora uppdraget. Perspektiv på Folkmusikkommissionen i Sverige 1908–2008* [The great mission. Perspectives on the Folk Music Commission 1908–2008]. Stockholm: Nordiska museets förlag.

Burke, Peter. (2009). *Popular Culture in Early Modern Europe*. Farnham, UK: Ashgate.

Carlin, Richard. (2004). "The Good, the Bad and the Folk." In *Bad Music: The Music We Love to Hate*, edited by Christopher Washburne and Maiken Derno, pp. 173–189. New York: Routledge.

Eriksson, Karin. (2004). *Bland polskor, gånglåtar och valser. Hallands spelmansförbund och den halländska folkmusiken* [Among Polskas, Walking tunes, and Waltzes: Halland's Fiddler's Association and the Music of Halland]. Göteborg: Institutionen för musik- och filmvetenskap, Göteborgs universitet.

Fargion, Janet Topp. (2009). "'For My Own Research Purposes'? Examining Ethnomusicology Field Methods for a Sustainable Music." *the world of music* 51(1): 75–93.

FMK. (1909). The protocol from FMK's first meeting. In FMK's archive I.A1; "Upprop," *Fataburen* 1909.

FMK's archive *III.1 N.A.s arkiv vol 1*. Svenskt visarkiv.

Folkmusikkommissionens notsamling och Musikmuseets spelmansböcker. (2007). Internet resource published by Svenskt visarkiv. http://www.smus.se/earkiv/fmk/index.php?lang=en.

Frykman, Jonas (1988). *Dansbaneeländet. Ungdomen, populärkulturen och opinionen*. Stockholm: Natur och kultur.

Giddens, Anthony. (1990). *The Consequences of Modernity*. Stanford, CA: Stanford University Press.

Grimm, Wilhelm, and Grimm, Jacob. (1812). *Kinder und Hausmärchen*. Göttingen: Gesammelt durch die Brüder Grimm.

Hammarlund, Anders. (2015). *Documentum*. Stockholm: Svenskt visarkiv (manuscript).

Herder, Johann Gottfried von. (1978). *Stimmen der Völker in Liedern*. Leipzig: Reclam.

Kaminsky, David. (2005). *Hidden Traditions. Conceptualizing Swedish Folk Music in the Twenty-First Century*. Dissertation. Harvard University.

Kaminsky, David. (2007). "The Zorn Trials and the Jante Law: On Shining Musically in the Land of Moderation." *Yearbook for Traditional Music* 39: 27–49.

Kirshenblatt-Gimblett, Barbara. (1995). "Theorizing Heritage." *Ethnomusicology* 39(3): 367–380.

Kjellberg, Erik, Jan Ling, and Owe Ronström. (2000). "Sweden." In *The Garland Encyclopedia of World Music*, edited by Ruth M. Stone, James Porter, James, Timothy Rice, and Chris Goertzen, Chris. Vol. 8, *Europe*. New York: Garland.

Kjellström, Birgit, ed. (1985). *Folkmusikvågen* [The Folk Music Vouge]. Stockholm: Rikskonserter.

Koch, Lars-Christian, Albercht Wiedmann, and Susanne Ziegler. (2004). "The Berlin Phonogramm-Archiv: A Treasury of Sound Recordings." *Acoustical Science and Technology* 25(4): 227–231.

Lidman, Tomas. (2012). *Libraries and Archives: A Comparative Study*. Cambridge: Woodhead Publishing.

Ling, Jan. (1964). *Svensk folkmusik. Bondens musik i helg och söcken* [Swedish folk music. The peasants' music in festivities and daily life]. Stockholm: Prisma.

Ling, Jan. (1994 [1979]). "Folkmusik—en brygd" [Folk music—a brew]. In Texter om svensk folkmusik, edited by Owe Ronström and Gunnar Ternhag, pp. 24–278. Stockholm: Kungl. Musikaliska akademien.

Lundberg, Dan, and Ternhag, Gunnar. (2005 [1996]). *Folkmusik i Sverige* [Folk Music in Sweden]. Hedemora: Gidlunds.

Lundberg, Dan. (2007). *Bjårskpip in Blossom: On the Revitalization Process of a Folk Music Instrument*. STM-online. http://musikforskning.se/stmonline/vol_10/lundberg/index.php?menu=3.
Lundberg, Dan. (2011). "It Goes Without Saying." *Musiikkikasvatus* 14(1): 80–82.
Lundberg, Dan, Krister Malm, and Owe Ronström. (2003). *Music, Media, Multiculture: Changing Musicscapes*. Stockholm: Svenskt visarkiv.
Lönnrot, Elias. (1835). *Kalevala*. Helsingfors: Alternativt namn.
Nyqvist, Niklas. (2007). *Från bondson till folkmusikikon. Otto Andersson och formandet av "finlandssvensk folkmusik"* [From Farmer's Son to Folk Music Icon: Otto Andersson and the Forming of "Finnish-Swedish Folk Music]. Åbo: Åbo Akademis förlag.
Pettinato, Giovanni. (1991). *Ebla: A New Look at History*. Baltimore, MD: Johns Hopkins University.
Ramsten. Märta. (1992). *Återklang. Svensk folkmusik i förändring 1950–1980* [Echoes: Swedish Folk Music in Transition, 1950–1980]. Göteborg: Musikvetenskapliga institutionen, Göteborg Univ.
Reinhard, Kurt. (1962). "The Berlin Phonogramm-Archive." *Folklore and Folk Music Archivist* 5(2): 1–4.
Roempke, Ville. (1994). *På spelmansfärd med Lapp-Nils* [On a folk music journey with Lapp-Nils]. Östersund: Jämtlands läns museum. Se även: Jamtli.
Ronström, Owe. (1989). "Nationell musik? Bondemusik? Om folkmusikbegreppet" [National Music? Peasant Music? On the Concept of Folk Music]. In *Folkmusikens historia på Gotland*, edited by Bengt Arwidsson. Visby: Länsmuseet Gotlands fornsal.
Ronström, Owe. (2010). "Folkmusikens manus—en läsanvisning" [The manuscript of folk music—a reading instruction]. In *Det stora uppdraget*, edited by Mathias Boström, Dan Lundberg, and Märta Ramsten, pp. 207–224. Stockholm: Nordiska museets förlag.
Seeger, Anthony. (1986). "The Role of Sound Archives in Ethnomusicology Today." *Ethnomusicology* 30(2): 261–276.
Slobin, Mark. (1993). *Subcultural Sounds: Micromusics of the West*. Hanover, NH: Wesleyan University Press.
Slobin, Mark. (2010). *Folk Music: A Very Short Introduction*. Oxford: Oxford University Press.
Trevor-Roper, Hugh. (1983). "The Invention of Tradition: The Highland Tradition of Scotland." In *The Invention of Tradition*, edited by Eric Hobsbawm and Terence Ranger, pp. 15–42. Cambridge: Cambridge University Press.

CHAPTER 5

THE APPLIED ETHNOMUSICOLOGIST AS PUBLIC FOLKLORIST

Ethnomusicological Practice in the Context of a Government Agency in the United States

CLIFFORD R. MURPHY

In the United States, the work of applied ethnomusicologists often intersects with the sister discipline of public folklore. While it is understood that the term "folklore" is problematic and that the discipline has been the subject of a thorough international critique, its history in the United States is considered less problematic (Kirshenblatt-Gimblett, 1998). While folklore in the United States includes the study of myths and tales of "the folk" (*das volk*), its primary focus has been—for nearly 50 years now—the ethnographic inquiry into what our international colleagues call "intangible cultural heritage" (ICH), and what will be referred to throughout this article under the American term of practice, "folklife." This disciplinary shift is due in no small part to the progressive work of folklorists trained in universities, but not necessarily employed by them (Kirshenblatt-Gimblett, 1998). The majority of public folklorists working in the United States are affiliated or funded in some way by state and federal initiatives to document, celebrate, and sustain living traditions (folklife) in their region, and in collaboration with the cultural communities documented therein. As such, references to "public folklore," "folklorists," and "folklife" are to be understood in the context of practice in the United States, where the institutional structures and nomenclature of public folklore grow out of a practice distinct to the United States, but with likely equivalencies worldwide.

In 2008, I began working in the state of Maryland as a public folklorist—the same year that I graduated with a Ph.D. in Ethnomusicology from Brown University. Prior to graduate school, my working life had consisted mainly of touring and recording as a member of two professional rock and country bands. After nearly a decade spent at the intersection of music and corporate commerce, I felt increasingly drawn toward field recordings of American vernacular music made by the likes of Alan Lomax for the Library of Congress in the mid-twentieth century. It was these recordings—made by public folklorists and applied ethnomusicologists in the service of government agencies in the United States—that drew me to pursue a degree in ethnomusicology. And, as director of Maryland Traditions—the folklife program for the state of Maryland—it is the making and archiving of such recordings that constitute an important component of my career as a public folklorist.

This essay chronicles the work of the ethnomusicologist-as-public-folklorist in the United States, explores disciplinary connections between applied ethnomusicology and public folklore, and asks the question "How can an applied ethnomusicologist work meaningfully within the institutional and intellectual framework of public folklore?" While public folklore has an established history and theoretical framework (Baron and Spitzer, 2007), the terms "public folklore" and "public folklorist" are being used here more narrowly to mean those trained ethnographers who work in local, county, state, and federal government folklife programs, as well as nongovernmental organizations (NGO), such as the National Council for the Traditional Arts (NCTA), that work in close concert with governmental folklife initiatives. Such work entails connecting folklife practitioners (individuals and communities) to resources such as grant monies, public programs (festivals, documentaries, exhibitions, media projects), and infrastructures (archives, long-term community partnerships), primarily through documenting, promoting, and presenting the expressive traditions of cultural communities. Grant making—that is, the deskwork required to extend monetary governmental grants to folklife practitioners—is the tool by which public folklorists justify their employment, while the fieldwork carried out in advance of such grant making and the interpretive work of curating public programs from such fieldwork are their occupational lifeblood. Public folklorists working in service of governmental agencies are tasked with engaging broadly with folklife (cultural knowledge learned through oral transmission or by example). This finds the ethnographer documenting everything from the traditional nonverbal communication of steelworkers to the decorative tack of horse-drawn carriages. Fieldwork documentation is archived and serves as the foundation for public programs, grant making, and scholarly research. The frequent focus on the non-musical challenges the ethnomusicologist-as-public-folklorist to apply disciplinary training in new ways. And while the output of public folklorists over the course of the twentieth and twenty-first centuries has shown a substantial focus on music and dance traditions, fieldwork inquiry must have—by nature of the job description—a narrow focus on *traditional* music and dance, however defined by the agency's folklife program. So while the focus on folklife (occupational, devotional, architectural, musical, material, etc.) may appear wide open at first glance, it can at times feel constraining for the ethnomusicologist on account of its focus on the "traditional."

Origins of Public Folklore and Applied Ethnomusicology in Federal and State Government

Federal government folklife programs emerged slowly from the late nineteenth century until the 1930s. We are writing in an age when ethnomusicologists are typically persons with academic degrees in ethnomusicology. This has not always been the case, of course, as many of the first few generations of ethnomusicologists held (and hold) degrees in related fields, from anthropology to folklore to musicology and American studies. So in addressing the history of ethnomusicologists in federal government, there is a rather murky period from the late 1800s, when ethnographers like Fewkes and Densmore were recording Native Americans, through the rise of early to mid-twentieth-century comparative musicologists like Herzog and Seeger, when the discipline of ethnomusicology was in its primordial stages of development.

Contemporary government folklife programs can look to ethnomusicologist Charles Seeger as their logical starting point (Dirksen, 2012). When the Society for Ethnomusicology (SEM) was founded in 1955, Charles Seeger had spent most of the previous two decades working for the federal government. Trained in comparative musicology, Seeger had a series of teaching positions from 1912 to 1935. With the nation mired in the Depression, the Roosevelt administration created a series of initiatives through the New Deal that were intended as employment opportunities and became places where artists and folklorists flourished. Benjamin Botkin, one of the foremost folklorists of his time, oversaw the Federal Writers Project (1938–1941), and directed the Archive of Folk Culture at the Library of Congress (1942–1945). Seeger worked for several different New Deal programs, including the music division of the Resettlement Agency, and the Federal Music Project (a program of the Works Project Administration, or WPA). Seeger's work involved many different forms of musical inquiry, style, and engagement, and—unlike the work of many contemporary applied ethnomusicologists in government—was not restricted to vernacular musics. Behind the work of scholars like Botkin and Seeger (and on account of their dynamic work together), significant inroads and administrative infrastructure were built for the support of working folklorists and ethnomusicologists in federal government.

It was through his work with New Deal programs that Charles Seeger became a close ally and collaborator with folk song collectors John and Alan Lomax at the Library of Congress's Archive of Folk Song. The relationship between the Seegers (Charles and his wife, composer Ruth Crawford Seeger) and the Lomaxes spawned a wide-ranging variety of public folklore and applied ethnomusicological projects. The Library of Congress had established the Archive of Folk Song in 1928 under the guidance of Robert Winslow Gordon, who conducted extensive field recordings and accessioned the early field recordings of John A. Lomax. Carl Engle, head of the Library of Congress's

Music Division, had hoped to create a Department of Musicology at the Library, and saw the Archive of Folk Song as part of its foundation. However, the Department never materialized. Gordon was an ineffective administrator and was unable to secure the requisite grant funding to keep his position afloat. He left the Library of Congress in 1932 (Kodish, 1978). Direction of the Archive soon fell to John A. Lomax in 1933 (under the title of Honorary Consultant and Curator, which came with no salary) and his son, Alan, held the title of Assistant in Charge from 1937 (when the library secured funding for the position) until 1942. In time, the collection expanded to contain far more than music, and it was renamed the Archive of Folk Culture. When the American Folklife Center (AFC) was founded at the Library of Congress in 1976, the Archive of Folk Culture became a component of the AFC.

John and Alan Lomax were folklorists who carried out their most noteworthy fieldwork under the auspices of the Archive of Folk Song at the Library of Congress. Their extraordinary experiences documenting musical traditions in rural and incarcerated communities is the stuff of legend. By 1934, the Lomaxes had published their first collection of American folk songs, *American Ballads and Folk Songs* (Lomax, Lomax, and Kittredge 1934), followed by *Our Singing Country* (Lomax et al., 1941) and *Folk Song, U.S.A.* (Lomax et al., 1947). Charles Seeger provided some guidance for these latter two projects (*Our Singing Country* and *Folk Song U.S.A.*), but it was Ruth Crawford Seeger who carried out the exhaustive work required to create accurate (and highly innovative for the time) musical transcriptions of field recordings for the publications. Alan and his sister, Bess, were deeply involved in selecting songs for these projects, inspiring Bess to make a career as a folk singer, music instructor, and public folklorist. Alan published one final collection of American folk songs, the ambitious *Folk Songs of North America, in the English Language*, with musical transcriptions made by Charles and Ruth Seeger's daughter, Peggy (Lomax, 1960). While Alan Lomax was not shy in his critique of the fields of folklore and ethnomusicology—and at times distanced himself from both—it was his yeoman work for the Library of Congress that provided the serious study and documentation of American vernacular music within the federal government, and his collections became a cornerstone of the American Folklife Center in 1976 (Szwed, 2010).

Overview of Federal Folklife Programs

There are three programs of the federal government that have a lengthy history of employment for ethnomusicologists: the American Folklife Center at the Library of Congress (which today contains the Archive of Folk Culture), the National Endowment for the Arts, and the Smithsonian Center for Folklife and Cultural Heritage. All of these came about in the wake of the folk revival, of which Charles Seeger's children—folksingers Pete, Mike, and Peggy—played significant roles in fostering.

In 1967, the Smithsonian Museum—which originated as the nation's central educational museum in the mid-nineteenth century—launched the Festival of American Folklife (since renamed the Smithsonian Folklife Festival), a two-week festival on the National Mall in Washington, DC. Folklorists Jim Morris, Ralph Rinzler, and Henry Glassie planned the first festival, and it featured a strong focus on American vernacular music. The festival became a major annual event, drawing millions over the 4th of July holiday, and began employing ethnomusicologists as ethnographers and curators as early as 1974. Tom Vennum, an expert on Native American music and folklife, was the first ethnomusicologist to work for the Festival. By 1975, Bess Lomax Hawes was hired by the Smithsonian as Deputy Director for Presentation to curate the 1975 festival and the 1976 Bicentennial Festival of American Folklife on the National Mall, focusing on the expressive culture of every state and territory in the United States over three summer months. Hawes was familiar with ethnomusicologist Dan Sheehy, who was then completing his Ph.D. at UCLA, and contracted him to conduct fieldwork with Mexican and Mexican-American mariachi musicians in Los Angeles in advance of the 1975 and 1976 festivals. Sheehy recalls his first serious conversations with Hawes as being "mind opening. She began to put new tools into my intellectual toolkit" (Sheehy, 2013).

Following the 1976 festival, Hawes moved to the National Endowment for the Arts (known as the NEA, this is an independent agency of the federal government that funds artists, arts activities, and arts organizations nationwide), where she spearheaded the creation of the NEA's Folk Arts division. Prior to Hawes's arrival, folklorist Alan Jabbour, with the assistance of anthropologist Claire Farrar, had handled all folk arts projects that came to the NEA for consideration (he left the NEA in 1976 prior to Hawes's arrival); under Jabbour's watch, folk arts projects would eventually find their way into larger disciplines (music, theater, dance) for consideration alongside fine art projects. Hawes observed that folk arts projects were at a consistent and significant disadvantage within such an arrangement, and so the Folk Arts program began in 1977 (Hawes, 2008: 118–139). Hawes had a small staff, consisting of a secretary, a folklorist (Sally Yerkovich), and an ethnomusicologist. She hired Dan Sheehy for this latter role, believing that Yerkovich's knowledge of the folklore field and material culture would complement Sheehy's strengths in music and fieldwork (Sheehy, 2013). Hawes directed the Folk and Traditional Arts Division from its inception in 1977 until 1992, and her tenure at the NEA yielded remarkable results. She proposed the creation of the National Heritage Fellowships—the nation's highest federal honor given to traditional artists—which was inspired by the Japanese government's Living National Treasures of Japan program, whose mission since 1950 has been to identify "Important Intangible Cultural Properties." Hawes's proposed program was shaped over the course of years through dialogue and debate with folklorists and ethnomusicologists, and was approved by the National Council on the Arts (the NEA's governing council) and launched by the NEA in 1982 (Hawes, 2008: 161–168). Hawes also helped seed state folklife programs at state arts agencies in nearly every state and territory in the United States. Upon her retirement in 1992, Sheehy succeeded Hawes as Director of the Folk and Traditional Arts Division and remained there until moving to the Smithsonian Center for Folklife and Cultural Heritage in 2000.

Through their work at the NEA, Hawes and Sheehy shaped the future of Public Folklore and Applied Ethnomusicology. Not only did they cultivate a more nuanced and sophisticated understanding and appreciation for vernacular culture within an organization possessed of a strong orientation toward conservatory arts, they engaged a great many folklorists and ethnomusicologists (Bill Ivey, Barbara Hampton, Jeff Todd Titon, and Robert Garfias, to name but a few) in the process of evaluating applications for grant funding and in deliberating over nominees for the National Heritage Fellowships. Their most significant achievements were seeding state and regional folklife programs throughout the country, creating a program of folk arts apprenticeships (whereby a master traditional artist was funded to pass his or her knowledge on to a dedicated apprentice—a wildly successful program that was subsequently turned over by the NEA to state folklife programs), and successfully proposing the creation of the National Heritage Fellowships. In turn, each of these accomplishments created a significant resource for—and about—folklife practitioners in the United States and generated permanent and part-time employment for hundreds of folklorists, ethnomusicologists, and anthropologists over the ensuing decades. It is a testament to Hawes's dedication to elevating the appreciation of the profession of public folklore that President Bill Clinton appointed ethnomusicologist and folklorist Bill Ivey (MA Ethnomusicology and Folklore, Indiana University) to be the Chair of the NEA, where he served in that role from 1998 to 2001.

Hawes was not the first folklorist at the NEA, however, having been preceded by Alan Jabbour. Jabbour, who received a Ph.D. in English from Duke University in 1968 (with a focus on folk ballads), taught Ethnomusicology at UCLA in 1968–1969, after which he directed the Archive of Folk Culture at the Library of Congress (1969–1974), and then worked at the NEA (1974–1976). While Jabbour's tenure at the NEA was brief, he made a significant contribution to the field by creating the first federally funded state folklife programs in the United States in 1974 at the Maryland State Arts Council and the Tennessee Arts Commission. He left the NEA to become the Director of the American Folklife Center from its inception in 1976 until his retirement in 1999.

When the American Folklife Center was established at the Library of Congress in 1976, with a significant lobbying assist from folklorist Archie Green, the topics Green held most dear (American vernacular music, working-class culture) helped form the focus of the Center and have influenced the work of public folklorists through today. The topics covered by the American Folklife Center's collections mirror the strengths of a staff that consists of both folklorists and ethnomusicologists and demonstrates an evolving sense of what constitutes an "American." Disciplinary lines between staff folklorists and ethnomusicologists are somewhat hazy, yet affiliations come to the fore when staff chooses which academic conference they will attend. Staff members tend to self-select with regard to attendance at American

Folklore Society (AFS) or SEM annual meetings. This dynamic has existed since Jabbour's days at the AFC:

> At the American Folklife Center we had something of a division of labor, with some of us concentrating on AFS and some on SEM, so I chose the AFS assignment. By now it's been so long since I attended an SEM meeting that I feel like a fellow traveler, whereas I identify myself as a folklorist without any qualification.
>
> (Jabbour, 2013)

"Fellow travelers" is an apt description of ethnomusicologists and folklorists on staff of the American Folklife Center, as well as at the Smithsonian Center for Folklife and Cultural Heritage and beyond. Funds typically do not allow for staff to travel to both SEM and AFS, and divisions of labor such as Jabbour describes appear to exist today, with notable exceptions.

Over the years, the AFC has employed a number of ethnomusicologists, as well as other scholar/ researchers with training in ethnomusicology, including Nora Yeh, Ron Wolcott, Joe Hickerson, and Ed Schupman (today, Schupman is the Education Product Developer at the Smithsonian's National Museum of the American Indian). AFC has also directed special projects involving ethnomusicologists, such as the Native American component of the Federal Cylinder Project, on which David McAllester, Maria La Vigna, Tom Vennum, Dorothy Sara Lee, and Judith Gray played an important role (Myers 1992: 410–411). Today, the AFC employs three ethnomusicologists on staff: Jennifer Cutting, Judith Gray, and Nancy Groce. SEM's President serves as an ex-officio member of the AFC's Board of Trustees, and Kay Kauffman Shelemay was a long-standing Congressional appointee on the AFC's Board.

The mid-1970s through the early 1980s marked the most significant time of growth for the field of public folklore (and, by extension, applied ethnomusicology), with the creation of the AFC, the Folk Arts division of the NEA, the proliferation of state folklife positions seeded by the NEA, the high-profile bicentennial Festival of American Folklife, and the formal creation of the Smithsonian Center for Folklife and Cultural Heritage (CFCH). The CFCH's chief initiative was—and remains—the annual Smithsonian Folklife Festival. However, the Center was augmented substantially with the acquisition of Moe Asch's Folkways record label, which became Smithsonian Folkways in 1987, and the Ralph Rinzler Folklife Archives and Collections. More than any other governmental organization, the Smithsonian—and Smithsonian Folkways in particular—has been an employer of—and a tool for—applied ethnomusicologists. Ethnomusicologists—or persons with significant training in ethnomusicology—work in a variety of Smithsonian museums: Rayna Green and John Edward Hasse at the National Museum of American History, Adrienne Kaeppler at the National Museum of Natural History, and Michael Wilpers at the Freer Gallery of Art and Arthur M. Sackler Gallery. Nevertheless, the most significant concentration is at the CFCH, and at Smithsonian Folkways in particular: Jeff Place (Curator and Senior Archivist), Stephanie Smith (Archives Director), and Greg C. Adams (Assistant Archivist), and

Merideth Holmgren (Program Manager). Most visibly, anthropologist and ethnomusicologist Anthony Seeger, grandson of Charles Seeger, served as the Director of Smithsonian Folkways from 1988 until 2000, at which point Dan Sheehy (Director and Curator, Emeritus) assumed direction of the label until his retirement in 2015. Ethnomusicologist D. A. Sonneborn was Associate Director at the label from 1998 until his retirement in 2018 (Heritage, 2013).

Anthony Seeger made ethics of cultural ownership and copyright a hallmark of Folkways' engagement with global musics (Seeger, 1996) and was a significant shaping force behind the creation of Smithsonian Global Sound (launched in 2005 with the involvement of ethnomusicologist Jon Kertzer). For Sheehy, the work of the CFCH and Smithsonian Folkways helps to "right a wrong" that he was personally awakened to while playing music in the late 1960s in R&B bands in the Compton neighborhood of Los Angeles, in mariachi groups, and with West African drummers while a student at UCLA. "I had been done an injustice," Sheehy recalls feeling. "I felt the artists [and] the cultures had been done an injustice. And I thought the public at large had been done an injustice." The injustice was what Sheehy saw as the privileging of Western art music in childhood education (and cultural education) in the United States. Sheehy felt he—and the public at large—had been misled to believe that the Western art aesthetic was a culturally superior form (Sheehy, 2013). Sheehy's interest in cultural equity is well matched to the mission of Smithsonian Folkways:

> We are dedicated to supporting cultural diversity and increased understanding among peoples through the documentation, preservation, and dissemination of sound. We believe that musical and cultural diversity contributes to the vitality and quality of life throughout the world. Through the dissemination of audio recordings and educational materials we seek to strengthen people's engagement with their own cultural heritage and to enhance their awareness and appreciation of the cultural heritage of others.
>
> (Folkways, 2013)

Folkways' founder Moses Asch worked closely with artists associated with Alan Lomax (Lead Belly, Woody Guthrie, Pete Seeger). Asch also produced fieldwork projects by folklorists and ethnomusicologists, such as Ruth and Verlon Stone's "Music of the Kpelle of Liberia" (1971). Under Seeger, Sonneborn, and Sheehy, however, Smithsonian Folkways has become more deeply engaged with ethnomusicologists on field recording projects as diverse as Stephen Feld's *Voices of the Rainforest* (1991), Jeff Todd Titon's *Old Regular Baptists: Lined-Out Hymnody from Southeastern Kentucky* (1997), and most recently, Jeff Summit's *Delicious Peace: Coffee, Music and Interfaith Harmony in Uganda* (2013), based on Summit's field recordings from an interfaith coffee cooperative in Uganda. On the whole, the content of the Smithsonian Folkways catalog—much like the staff of the CFCH and the American Folklife Center—is profoundly shaped by the work of "fellow travelers": ethnomusicologists and folklorists working side by side.

By 2003, federal government folklife programs engaged with enough "fellow travelers" as to make up a substantial percentage of applied ethnomusicological careers, as witnessed by the fact that over half of the speakers at the first-ever conference on applied ethnomusicology, convened at Brown University in 2003 (not to be confused with a second conference on applied ethnomusicology that was convened later that year in Venice [Pettan, 2008]), consisted of people who had been involved in some way (many significantly) with the NEA (through state folklife programs or grant review panels), the AFC (through the Federal Cylinder Project or through collaborative research and archival repatriation initiatives), or the CFCH (through Smithsonian Folkways or the Smithsonian Folklife Festival) (Titon, 2003).

Overview of State Folklife Programs and State Folklorists

While Alan Jabbour and Bess Lomax Hawes created the blueprint for folklife programs at state arts agencies across the United States in the 1970s, the nation's first state folklorist position was created by the state of Pennsylvania in 1948 and was filled by Henry W. Shoemaker at the Pennsylvania Historical Commission until 1956. A journalist and former Ambassador to Bulgaria, Shoemaker was much derided by his folklore colleagues in academia, such as Samuel Bayard, for being a "fakelorist"—a play on the derogatory term "fakelore," coined by folklorist Richard Dorson to describe "deliberately contrived" folklore such as the tales of legendary North American woodcutter Paul Bunyan (Dorson, 1949). Nevertheless, Shoemaker was a significant popularizer of folklore, and the position stuck for several decades (Bronner, 1996). From 1967 to 1969 folklorist Henry Glassie served as Pennsylvania state folklorist (under the title of "Director of the Ethnic Culture Survey"), and was succeeded in that role by David Hufford. Though the program was dissolved when Hufford departed to teach at Newfoundland University in 1970, it had established enough institutional credibility to positively influence the neighboring state of Maryland to seek out the creation of a comparable program. While in the role of Pennsylvania State Folklorist, Glassie consulted with University of Maryland folklorist George Carey on the Maryland Gubernatorial Commission to Study the Need for the Establishment of an Archive of Maryland Folklife. The ensuing public report, commissioned by Governor Spiro Agnew in 1968 and issued in 1970, reflected the nation's growing introspection with regard to heritage as it approached the bicentennial, and an anxiety that all that was once beautiful was being lost to mass culture and interstate highways. The report concluded (in all caps) that

THE UNRECORDED HISTORY OF MARYLAND AND ITEMS OF MATERIAL FOLK CULTURE AND FOLKLORE ARE DAILY BEING LOST PERHAPS FOREVER TO THE PEOPLE OF THE STATE AND THEIR CHILDREN. THERE

IS INTEREST AMONG THE PEOPLE OF THE STATE IN THIS HISTORY, MATERIAL CULTURE, AND FOLKLORE, AND IN THEIR PRESERVATION. THERE ARE PROFESSIONAL FOLKLORISTS IN THE STATE WHO WOULD AID IN THIS PRESERVATION. COOPERATION OF OTHERS IS ASSURED. BUT GUIDANCE IS NEEDED.

TODAY, MARYLAND HAS THE OPPORTUNITY TO BE IN THE VANGUARD OF STATE GOVERNMENTS AS THEY COME TO REALIZE THAT THE PRESERVATION OF ONE'S FOLKLIFE IS NOT ONLY IMPORTANT BUT VITAL.

(Carey, 1970: 25)

Anxieties aside, Carey's report presented a convincing argument for the creation of a state folklorist position and a state folklore archive and laid the groundwork for the creation of the Maryland Folklife Program. In 1972, Carey was involved in producing the Smithsonian's 1972 Festival of American Folklife Maryland Program. In 1973, Alan Jabbour—then at the NEA—initiated discussions with Maryland State Arts Council (MSAC) Director James Backas about the possibility of creating a pilot program that could be used as a national model for state folklife programs that—unlike the Pennsylvania program, which was hosted at the Pennsylvania State Historical Museum—would be based at state arts agencies. These programs were to be directed by a state folklorist. The MSAC and the NEA developed a formal agreement and hired George Carey as its first state folklorist in 1974. The agreement set in motion a federal-state funding dynamic that remains mostly intact today, whereby the NEA provides some seed monies for a folklorist position; the host agency is responsible for making the position financially sustainable within a fixed number of years. Jabbour also created a pilot program that same year in Tennessee, but the Tennessee program closed shop within two years. Today, the Maryland Folklife Program (renamed Maryland Traditions in 2001) is the longest-running state folklife program in the nation.

The Maryland program was fruitful within its first three years, producing an annual Maryland Folklife Festival beginning in 1975 (based entirely on fieldwork), producing films, books, and symposia, and generating a groundswell of support from Maryland residents, administrators, and government officials. As such, it became an effective example of success for the NEA to promote to other state arts agencies throughout the country. When Bess Lomax Hawes started the Folk Arts division at the NEA in 1977, she made it a goal to have a state folklife program at every state arts agency in the nation, famously using a map with multicolored pins to show where folklife programs had been funded (Hawes, 2008). During Hawes's 15 years at the NEA, she grew the division's budget from $100,000 annually to $4 million, created folklife programs in 50 of the 56 states and territories, and expanded the folk arts staff from one to six (Heritage, 2013). Dan Sheehy worked alongside Hawes for much of this time, though he was not immediately employed in the Folk Arts Division; rather, he first served as an in-house expert on non-Western art musics before moving into the Folk Arts Division. Through both Hawes and Sheehy, ethnomusicologists became a known entity within state and federal folklife agencies and a disciplinary orientation that was considered an acceptable fit for state folklife programs.

The roots of Hawes's considerable success at the NEA is to be found in her work at the Smithsonian, where she had directed the 1976 Bicentennial Festival of American Folklife on the National Mall. The Bicentennial festival had enabled Hawes to consolidate a number of experts and folklife practitioners state by state, which ultimately became a rich resource when it came to fostering new state folklife programs. Indeed, many of the participants in the Smithsonian's 1972 Maryland Program were engaged with the Maryland Folklife Program at MSAC as soon as it began. This was a pattern that repeated itself elsewhere, both with regards to artists and ethnographers. As Hawes remembered it,

> Almost every person I know who is active today in the area of public folklore participated at least in some small fashion in the 1976 Festival. Historians will eventually look in wonder at the far-reaching effects of the 1976 Festival of American Folklife.
>
> (Heritage, 2013)

A rising generation of new professionals coming of age in the arts world in the 1970s expected to see festivals involving music and dance. The Smithsonian Folklife Festival, the National Folk Festival (NCTA), and the Newport Folk and Jazz Festivals (not to mention Woodstock and the Monterey Pop Festival) had inspired an entire generation of Americans to engage in fieldwork; many of these individuals filled the professional ranks of folklorists and ethnomusicologists by the late 1970s. The Smithsonian Folklife Festival had, in particular, become an innovator in folklife studies and a generator of work for folklorists and ethnomusicologists as fieldworkers, curators, writers, and presenters. As burgeoning state folklife programs looked for ways to showcase traditional folklife on the local level, they turned frequently to the festival format. Likewise, the post–Alex Haley/ Roots world had been awakened to the rich expressive traditions of multicultural urban centers. As such, folklorists who had cut their teeth solely on the rural English-language American vernacular musical styles found in the Lomaxes' songbooks were not always prepared to curate programs on Lithuanian, Chinese, Senegalese, or South Indian cultural traditions. Ethnomusicologist Jill Linzee recalls that the growing demand for such expertise was readily met by ethnomusicologists who not only had sophisticated musical training, but had also learned "well developed cultural sensitivities toward working with different cultural and/ or ethnic groups (especially those very different from one's own ethnic origin)." Bess Lomax Hawes recognized that—in the 1970s—ethnomusicologists tended to be internationally focused, whereas their folklore contemporaries tended to be domestically focused; this was a strength that ethnomusicologists could, and did, contribute in collaborative settings with folklorists (Sheehy, 2013). Ethnomusicology's focus on cultural context was (and is), in Linzee's view, a transferrable skill to non-musical activities (Linzee, 2013).

The first ethnomusicologist to hold the position of State Folklorist in the United States was Roberta Singer, who held the position in Massachusetts from 1983 to 1984. The position was created after ethnomusicologist Jeff Todd Titon and folklorist Jane Beck (founder of the Vermont Folklife Center), both of whom served on the NEA Folk Arts Panel under Bess Lomax Hawes, approached Massachusetts Arts Council Director Anne Hawley with the idea of launching a state folklife program using the NEA's typical "ramp-up-ramp-down" funding model (three years of funding to get the position started, after which the host agency would fund the position). Singer left the position to return home to New York City, where she helped develop the New York State Council on the Arts' (NYSCA) Apprenticeship Program within NYSCA's Folk Arts Program directed by Robert Baron. A group of folklorists formed the New York City Chapter of the New York Folklore Society, which, in 1986, incorporated as City Lore— The New York Center for Urban Folk Culture, a part of NYSCA's state-funded network of folklife partnerships. Singer has worked for City Lore since its inception, where her ethnomusicology training and experience laid a foundation for the research, documentation, and presentation of Puerto Rican and Cuban music. At City Lore, Singer has produced several CDs of New York Puerto Rican music, a national tour of Afro-Cuban and Puerto Rican music and dance, a documentary film on the Afro-Puerto Rican bomba tradition, and an exchange between Puerto Rican musicians from New York and Puerto Rico (Singer, 2014).

Singer was succeeded in Massachusetts by Dillon Bustin to direct the state's Folklife and Ethnic Arts Program. Bustin held that position from 1985 until the Massachusetts Arts Council was shuttered in 1991 in the wake of controversial public funding of art exhibitions deemed "obscene" by some members of the state legislature. The agency re-emerged soon after as the Massachusetts Cultural Council, who re-launched their folklife program in 1999 as the Folk Arts and Heritage program under the direction of state folklorist Maggie Holtzberg. Holtzberg majored in ethnomusicology as an undergraduate at Wesleyan (1979) and went on to receive a Ph.D. in Folklore from University of Pennsylvania in 1987. A fiddle player who identifies professionally as a folklorist, Holtzberg has done significant documentation and interpretation of living traditions in Massachusetts, which she has summarized thusly:

> With camera and sound recorder in hand, we have interviewed scrimshanders on Nantucket, feast-day organizers in Boston's North End, contra-dance fiddlers in Greenfield, and Native American regalia makers on Cape Cod. Vital folk art traditions are being carried on all across the state within both long-settled ethnic and new immigrant communities.
>
> (Holtzberg et al., 2008: xi)

Holtzberg has observed that ethnomusicologists bring special skills to musical fieldwork that many folklorists lack. In part because the festival format was such an important point of origin for the field of public folklore, traditional music has been a major component of folklife programs and an important entry point for cross-cultural understanding. Holtzberg feels that ethnomusicology plays an important role in documenting and interpreting living musical traditions. Though she is perhaps best known for her examination of the occupational folklife and craft of the printing trade (Holtzberg, 1992), as well as her work with traditional Irish musicians like accordionist Joe Derrane, Holtzberg has documented a broad range of musical traditions, from Trinidadian carnival music to African-American tap dance (Holtzberg et al., 2008). In her previous roles with the Alabama State Council on the Arts (1988–1989) and as state folklorist in Georgia (1992–1997), she worked with African-American sacred and occupational singers and produced the documentary film *Gandy Dancers* (1994) with Barry Dornfeld. Adding an additional layer to the state/federal/NGO folklife relationship, Holtzberg has been on "loan" from the state of Massachusetts to the National Park Service in the post-industrial mill city of Lowell, Massachusetts, where she coordinates programming for the state folklife program, the Lowell National Historical Park, and for the annual Lowell Folk Festival, produced by the NCTA.

Other states have hired ethnomusicologists in central positions (the so-called "state folklorist" position) or as folklorists who directed regional partnerships. Ethnomusicologist Steve Grauberger has been a Folklife Specialist at the Alabama State Council on the Arts' Alabama Center for Traditional Culture since 1998. Ethnomusicologist Jill Linzee was the Traditional Arts Coordinator (state folklorist) for the New Hampshire State Council on the Arts from 1993 to 1996. By this time, the presence of an ethnomusicologist in the role of a folklorist had become common enough. Indeed, today the Tennessee Arts Commission employs two Ethnomusicologists—Bradley A. Hanson (Director of Folklife) and Langston Collin Wilkins (Traditional Arts Specialist) as state folklorists. For some folklore professionals, this was—and remains—a source of mild frustration, as can be seen in this anecdote from Linzee:

> One of my public folklore colleagues who had been formally trained in the field of folklore once confronted me with this question: As an ethnomusicologist, you are competing with folklorists for public folklore jobs—but what kind of jobs has the field of ethnomusicology helped to establish that folklorists can apply for?
>
> (Linzee, 2013)

For most, however, like folklorist Robert Baron—the New York State folklorist and a significant figure in the development of public folklore theory—the increase in numbers of ethnomusicologists in state folklife programs is both welcoming and non-threatening. In Baron's opinion, the joint meeting of MACSEM (the Mid-Atlantic Chapter of SEM) and MAFA (the Mid-Atlantic Folklife Association) in 2007 was particularly fruitful (Baron, 2013). Baron's sentiment—that joint meetings of regional chapters of SEM and AFS, as well as of the parent organizations, are mutually beneficial and should be more frequent—is common in conversations among public folklorists and applied ethnomusicologists. As Holtzberg has observed, "good fieldwork is good fieldwork, whether it was done by someone trained in Folklore, Ethnomusicology, or American Studies" (Holtzberg, 2013).

From State Folklorists to State Folklife Partnerships

The work of the state folklorist has changed over the course of four decades of state folklife programs. At the Maryland State Arts Council (MSAC), where I worked as the state folklorist since from 2008–2017, that change can be characterized as a shift from a mostly singular pursuit to that of a partnership approach. Founded in 1974 as the Maryland Folklife Program, the program changed its name to Maryland Traditions in 2001 as part of an evolution in state folklife programs nationwide. For its first 26 years, the Maryland Folklife Program—like most in the nation—was an office of one (the state folklorist), operating out of the city of Baltimore, with occasional discretionary projects that employed ethnographers of varying disciplines on short-term contracts. In 2001, MSAC and the Maryland Historical Trust (the state's historical preservation office) collaborated on the creation of a state folklife infrastructure program. The state folklife infrastructure program (an NEA term) was modeled after innovative programs in the states of Louisiana, Pennsylvania, New York, and New Jersey, where the state folklife program seeded networks of regional long-term partnerships throughout the state. Each partnership would employ a folklorist to conduct regional fieldwork. Fieldwork would be archived both locally and in a central statewide folklife archive. Regional partners would connect local folklife practitioners to statewide grants (apprenticeships) and local nonprofits to statewide project grants. In its most basic sense, the state folklife infrastructure concept grew out of the idea that it is hard to develop trust and long-term resources for local communities when working remotely out of a centralized government office. Likewise, regional partners could engage in a kind of local, grassroots work that is impossible and not always appropriate for a state agency to become involved in.

Partnerships add significant flexibility for state folklife programs, enabling local partners to engage in grassroots initiatives, to act as mediators of community conflict, and to develop long-term support for communities involved in maintaining living traditions. Each partnership has a focus distinct to its parent organization's mission and the needs and demands of the communities in the region. As such, one partner might require a folklorist to have significant expertise in material culture, or occupational folklife, while another requires an ability to work with a broad range of musical traditions. As such, state folklife infrastructure programs such as Maryland Traditions provide additional opportunities for which ethnomusicologists are well suited.

In Maryland, musical inquiry has been an effective ambassador for the program's continued support by the state. In 1974, the aim of the Maryland folklife program was to "amplify" the voice of Maryland tradition bearers, in vernacular performing, verbal, occupational, architectural, and material arts through public programs and publications based on fieldwork (Carey, 1976). Today the aims of the program mix pragmatism with the ideals of cultural equity that inspired the program's founding: to document, celebrate, and sustain living traditions in Maryland. These living traditions can be indigenous, or they can be new to Maryland. Maryland Traditions works to achieve its mission primarily through the aforementioned seed grants for the development of regional folklife programs statewide, and the development of more sophisticated means of extending the resources of the state to celebrate and sustain living traditions through apprenticeship grants and project grants. As such, the program is built to work statewide and regionally, with organizations (through Project Grants and Partnerships) and with individuals (through Apprenticeship grants and other awards and programs for individual artists).

Public Folklore as Strategic Governmental Outreach

In government folklife work, there are political and philosophical motivations behind the focus on traditional arts and culture. A governmental agency is at its core a public service entity with an obligation to serve all of its residents in a wide variety of capacities from roadways to revenues to research. So, politically, any agency that is not serving the entirety of its residents is vulnerable to critique, censure, and defunding. Given that government work is public service, there are those residents who are readily "served" and those who are not. In the language of government, this latter category is defined as "underserved." In the realm of state arts agencies, where the vast majority of state folklife programs are housed, there are both underserved *communities* and *expressive forms*. These tend to be communities and expressive forms of working-class, rural, agricultural, maritime, occupational, or non-Western orientation, as well as the disabled. Very often, these same underserved communities consist of persons of color, non-native English speakers, and/ or persons who do not tend to fill out grant applications. Folklife programs focus on those communities and their expressive cultural traditions that are passed on through word of mouth or by example. This is what is implied in "traditional" and can be a source of consternation for those who astutely point out that some musical traditions that rely on oral tradition (such as heavy metal music) are excluded, just as many conservatory arts are also endowed with "tradition." These latter traditions, however, are not associated with either underserved expressive forms or communities in the realm of arts funding. The political value of government folklife programs is to be found in their effectiveness at reaching underserved communities.

The philosophical value of folklife programs comes from ideas of social and cultural equity—this is a philosophy espoused by a great many culture workers engaged in folklife programs, rather than an explicit part of the mission of the programs themselves. There are folklife programs with overt social justice missions, but they are NGO programs, such as the Philadelphia Folklore Project (PFP), which utilizes folklorists, ethnomusicologists, and other ethnographers to carry out grassroots social justice work

(Kodish, 2011) (Debora Kodish, the founder and then Executive Director of PFP, was brought by the Applied Ethnomusicology Section of the Society for Ethnomusicology to speak at the 2011 annual conference about the intersection of applied ethnomusicology and social justice work). Finally, a history of government folklife programs shows a recurring and problematic interest in developing, galvanizing, and promoting nationalistic and regional identities. This latter philosophical mission was most prominently on display during the World War II era. Each of these political and philosophical strands is at work at some level in government folklife programs, and the federal government is responsible for creating the blueprint that has been replicated by state, county, and municipal governments.

Strategic outreach in a state such as Maryland comes with its own distinct challenges, ones well met by partnerships that can respond to specific regional/ community needs. Maryland is the ninth smallest state in the United States and is bordered to the south by Washington, DC, and Virginia, to the east by Delaware and the Atlantic Ocean, to the north by Pennsylvania and Delaware, and to the west by Virginia and West Virginia. Its northern border constitutes the Mason-Dixon. Maryland is the 19th most populous state (5.8 million) and the fifth most densely populated state in the nation (2011 US Census). It is both highly urbanized—with urban centers in Baltimore and Metro DC—and has long-standing agricultural, maritime, and mining occupational groups. Maryland's defining geographical attributes are the Chesapeake Bay and the Atlantic Ocean to the east and the Appalachian Mountains to the West. The city of Baltimore is home to the second-largest deepwater port on the Eastern Seaboard—this distinction has, historically, meant that the city has been a major port of entry for immigrants. In the late twentieth century, however, Baltimore's port and its close proximity to the Eastern seaboard cities of New York, Philadelphia, Washington, DC, and Richmond made it a major port of entry for illegal drugs, a fact that—combined with mass deindustrialization and the devastating effects of race riots in the 1970s—has created a swath of crippling poverty and urban blight. This urban blight—the backdrop to Baltimore's drug culture, as portrayed on David Simon's popular HBO television series *The Wire*—stands in stark contrast to the state's enormous wealth. Maryland is the wealthiest state in the nation, and its proximity to Washington, DC, has transformed it into one of the most multicultural regions in the nation. Such diversity in geography and demographics makes for a region of significant variation in areas of cultural inquiry.

With such a diverse cultural geography, Maryland Traditions has worked to build strategic regional partnerships in distinct sub-regions of the state. Partnerships over the first 12 years of the program have consisted of a mixture of museums, universities, county arts councils, local municipalities, and nonprofits. Maryland Traditions' partnerships currently include organizations as different as the National Council for the Traditional Arts in Silver Spring, Maryland (the nation's oldest folk arts nonprofit, producers of the annual National Folk Festival since 1934), and the Ward Museum of Wildfowl Art in Salisbury (a museum dedicated to Maryland's indigenous, functional duck decoy carving/ painting traditions and the international fine art wildfowl sculpture tradition). Over the past decade, Maryland Traditions' partners have employed ethnomusicologists in a variety of roles—from targeted short-term contracts (e.g., Dr. Harold Anderson, who documented the musical traditions of Old West Baltimore in 2004, and African-American sacred expressive traditions in Prince George's County in 2010) to longer-term, full-time positions (ethnomusicologist Mark Puryear was a staff folklorist at the Arts and Humanities Council of Montgomery County from 2005 to 2010). Ethnomusicologists are also active in other partner institutions, such as the NCTA, whether as employees (such as Anne Kogan) or as fieldworkers and stage presenters. Additionally, ethnomusicologists are active in the archives: Maryland Traditions has employed ethnomusicologists Greg C. Adams and Hannah Rogers to process and organize 40 years of ethnographic materials.

For the average ethnomusicologist, the working list of living traditions in Maryland folklife is dizzying—ranging from boatbuilding to hog-butchering, Native American regalia-making to quilting, South Indian Kuchipudi dance to Piedmont blues, and silversmithing to muskrat-skinning. Clearly, such a list encompasses far more than the study of people making music. However intimidating such a range might appear at first glance, in practice it is invigorating and a constant reminder that, no matter our academic credentials or the size of our archives, we really know very little about anything. In my five plus years as state folklorist, I have found the broader context of folklife to be a healthy reminder that music is not always the primary point of cultural expression for everybody. In fact, while Titon defines ethnomusicology as the study of people making music (Titon, 2009), for the ethnomusicologist-as-state-folklorist, it is also the study of music in context (Merriam and Herbert M. Halpert Collection, 1964). And sometimes that context is highly non-musical, pushing the ethnomusicologist into "the study of people making _____."

On the Job

The work of the ethnomusicologist-as-folklorist requires administrative and production skills not imparted during graduate school: management of budgets and personnel, evaluation of grant applications, convening of grant review panels, advocating for budget increases from senior administrators and government officials, producing festivals, advocating for artists, producing media projects, curating museum exhibitions, negotiating salaries with university provosts, advocating for cultural policies that acknowledge and respect the existence of folklife, writing grants, working with university and community scholars, or advising on all of the above. In short, the job requires a fair amount of diplomacy and fieldwork and a steady diet of desk work.

When Curt Sachs critiqued comparative musicology's practice of "desk work" (Sachs and Kunst, 1962: 16–32), he was addressing the privileged place that transcription and analysis of sound artifacts (field recordings and fieldwork conducted by others) had within the discipline over ethnographic inquiry. David McAllester's *Enemy Way Music* signified a departure from "desk work" (or "armchair" ethnomusicology) in favor of ethnography augmented by transcription and analysis of one's own fieldwork (McAllester, 1954). For the contemporary director of a statewide folklife program—or, for that matter, for equivalents in federal programs—the job requires both fieldwork and deskwork: conducting one's own fieldwork and frequently coordinating, transcribing, analyzing, and interpreting the fieldwork efforts of colleagues and contract fieldworkers conducted in service of the state program. And while armchair ethnomusicology is carried out to some degree by the public folklorist in the manner that Sachs, Hood, and others would have defined it (Hood, 1971: 30), there is an altogether different form of armchair ethnomusicology distinct to this work that is far more engaging and meaningful. A team of collaborating folklorists and ethnomusicologists, each with a distinct set of strengths, expertise, and objectives, can be of far greater service to the people of the state than a singular ethnographer who is averse to armchair ethnomusicology. Collaborative presentations and symposia about Maryland folklife are invigorating and informative, particularly when they involve community members ("tradition bearers" in the language of public folklore; "informants" in the language of anthropologists), but such presentations have their limitations as well, with regard to both logistics and clear narrative, and are not always the right choice in cases of cultural policy and institutional advocacy.

Another positive piece of armchair ethnomusicology comes in curating events and exhibitions that draw from the entirety of the ethnographic inquiry of the full Maryland Traditions partnership, including now-historical fieldwork (that is, archived fieldwork conducted in decades past by ethnographers who no longer work for the folklife program). In 2009, I was invited, as state folklorist, to participate in the programming committee for the Asian-Pacific-American (APA) Program of the 2010 Smithsonian Folklife Festival. The Program, which sought to celebrate the APA community of Metropolitan DC as a microcosm of the APA experience broadly, included five other ethnomusicologists: Dan Sheehy, Dr. Joanna Pecore (Education Specialist, Smithsonian Freer and Sackler Galleries), Michael Wilpers (Performing Arts Programmer, Smithsonian Freer and Sackler Galleries), Dr. Terry Liu (Educational Specialist at the NEA), and Mark Puryear. At the time, Puryear was directing the Maryland Traditions partnership at the Arts and Humanities Council of Montgomery County. Pecore was—and remains—an active musician in the DC region's Cambodian music and dance community (her dissertation focused on this music/ refugee/sacred community). The overall committee was quite large, and each of us was called upon to introduce artists for consideration in the Program. In Pecore's case, this was deep ethnographic inquiry into local Khmer classical court music and dance traditions. For Puryear and myself, we introduced artists that had been vetted by Maryland Traditions fieldwork, though not always fieldwork that had been carried out ourselves. Rather, we were introducing participants for consideration who had been documented by ourselves and our colleagues, past and present. As such, the APA artists documented in our archives constituted a kind of roster that could be considered for inclusion in the program. Ultimately, Maryland-based artists and cultural communities were represented in significant numbers over the course of the two-week program, ranging from Cambodian pin peat musicians to Nepalese sarangi players to Kuchipudi dancers.

Such collaboration between federal, state, and local governmental folklife programs is common and also fosters a professional environment that is conducive for lateral and horizontal movement. Many professional colleagues in public folklore have moved within federal, state, and local programs, including ethnomusicologists such as Jill Linzee (American Folklife Center, Smithsonian, NEA, NH State Council on the Arts). Other ethnomusicologists have moved from governmental work to NGO/nonprofit work, such as Lisa Richardson (folklorist for the L.A. County Arts Commission and the City of L.A. Dept. of Cultural Affairs), who is currently the Director of the nonprofit California Traditional Music Society (Richardson, 2011).

Terry Liu has been another long-standing applied ethnomusicologist who has moved in and out of federal, state, and local folklife programs, though he is most closely associated with his longtime service for the NEA. Liu has served the NEA as Folk and Traditional Arts Specialist (1990–1996) and as Arts Education Specialist (2000–2017). In 1989 he taught ethnomusicology at Kent State. He has also served as an administrator, grants panelist, and consultant in arts funding at the federal, state, regional, and local government levels, as well as for private foundations across the country. Originally a conservatory violinist, Liu studied ethnomusicology at University of Hawai'i at Manoa (M.A. in 1982) and at Kent State University (Ph.D. in 1988). From 1996 to 1999 Liu was a program specialist at the Arts Council for Long Beach, California, where he conducted fieldwork and offered technical assistance to traditional artists. He also served as regional coordinator to develop folk arts infrastructure in Southern California in coordination with the California Arts Council. He was a cofounder of the Alliance for California Traditional Arts (ACTA) and served on grant review panels across the country. Terry is also an active musician, playing violin with Mariachi Los Amigos (Dan Sheehy also plays trumpet with this group) in the Metro DC region.

Liu's work at the NEA requires a great deal of grants management and consultation to hundreds of applicants from nonprofit organizations throughout the country. At the time of this writing, Liu was managing 170 applications for arts education projects, with a total request of over $9 million. Each grant application is reviewed by a panel of 20 evaluators, and four separate panels will be convened (Liu, 2013). Each division of the NEA recruits experts in a variety of disciplines for its review panels, and ethnomusicologists are often called upon to serve as reviewers for music, folklife, education, and National Heritage Award panels. The same is true for state arts agencies, which draw upon folklorists and ethnomusicologists to review their folklife grant applications. My first interaction with this aspect of public folklore occurred in graduate school, first as an observer of the Massachusetts Cultural Council's Folk Arts Apprenticeships panel, and soon after as member of a folklife panel for the Rhode Island State Council on the Arts. Panels serve as a driver of professional community, providing opportunities for young ethnographers to interact (and debate) with senior colleagues and fellow travelers from across the country (and from both public sector and university places of employment) in a collegial environment.

Such panels are also a tremendous opportunity to gain insight on issues affecting the field and the communities with which applied ethnomusicologists engage. From funding crises to political or community strife, grant panels—like a miniature SEM or AFS meeting—help provide a broad view of the field and its various challenges. For example, Maryland is experiencing a period of robust support for state folklife initiatives, but the same cannot be said for many other states in the country. Personal and professional bonds developed at conferences and panel meetings help to forge a strong network of advocacy and political capital that can be drawn from in key moments (a recent example being the mobilization of public folklorists and applied ethnomusicologists to save the National Heritage Fellowships from being eliminated in 2011). Advocacy and cultural policy are part and parcel of the work of public folklorists.

In the realm of cultural policy—engaging with elected officials, governmental agencies, and community organizations—it is not only highly effective to have an armchair ethnomusicologist (or folklorist) involved, it is often critical to any hope of sensitive cultural intervention on the part of the government. For the state folklorist, they must utilize their perspective and their insight to advocate for greater attention and equity for traditional artists and underserved communities. This sort of work must be done with great diplomacy; otherwise, equitable allocation of funding and other resources is jeopardized. Outside the state arts agency, such a role is most often demanded in the realm of cultural/ heritage tourism.

Cultural policy work constitutes an important, if small, part of the job, however. The bread-and-butter of most state arts agencies is grants administration. For the state folklorist—as for the regional partner—reviewing grant applications and convening grant panels to evaluate grant applications is a major part of the job. Being able to evaluate narratives as well as budgets is critical to long-term success. It may sound ridiculously obvious, but being able to show up to staff meetings is also important, despite the fact that the day-to-day work of the agency as a whole is conducted in a different administrative dialect than that of the folklife program. Likewise, the job requires fieldwork, making the job description significantly different from that of one's arts agency peers. For too many state folklorists, this has been a fatal flaw, magnified by the very earnest and intense sense of purpose the ethnographer often brings with him to work. This means that the incoming state folklorist has often been stereotyped before arriving on the job, and it is a stereotype that is best addressed head-on by showing up on time, following dress codes, attending meetings and other mandatory events—all while connecting the relevancy of folklife to the work of arts agency colleagues approaching culture work from a decidedly different angle.

The state folklorist must be able to effectively justify her existence and her ongoing fieldwork activities in order to build credibility and institutional support. Connecting fieldwork engagement to grant work is crucial to achieving this transformation. For example, for several years I was engaged in ongoing fieldwork with a community in northeastern Maryland that came about as a result of a Depression-era migration of Appalachian people. This migration contained a number of musicians significant in the early history of country and bluegrass music: Ola Belle Reed, Fields Ward, and Hazel Dickens foremost among them. While I have an intellectual interest in this migration and in regional forms of country music that persist primarily as "people's music" (Keil,

1985), I also wished—as an applied ethnomusicologist, and as a public folklorist who was hired to conduct outreach work to underserved communities—to connect this community to the resources of the Maryland State Arts Council. This was accomplished by engaging the community with Maryland Traditions Project Grants and Apprenticeship Grants. Project grants help to fund not-for-profit organizations such as the Cecil County Public Library conduct a community gathering focused on the oral testimony of first- and second-generation Appalachian migrants. Apprenticeships have focused on a number of first- and second-generation musicians from the migration who seek to pass on living traditions from one generation to the next. Apprenticeships pair a master artist (e.g., banjo player David Reed, son of the late Ola Belle Reed) with an apprentice for one year to fortify the transmission of living traditions. Apprenticeships consist of a monetary award as well as publicity that can sometimes be significant. Apprenticeship teams are documented through photographs and field recordings, and audiovisual vignettes are produced and published on YouTube. Field documentation is placed in the Maryland Traditions Archives.

For the host agency, fieldwork is, then, practical work. Folklife apprenticeships focus primarily on traditions rooted in working-class, agricultural, rural, and immigrant communities—communities that do not always prioritize grant-writing. Applicants often do not to have a college education, or when they do, many speak English as a second (or third) language. Without fieldwork—or, in the language of the state arts agency, "outreach" or "technical assistance"—these artists would never find their way into the grant programs of the agency. And for a state agency whose mission is to serve all of the residents of the state, it is a liability when one's grant programs fall short of this mission. So fieldwork/ outreach is crucial, as the state folklorist—and the regional folklife partners throughout the state—offers considerable technical assistance with regard to grant work. The apprenticeship demographic also has a very high percentage of applicants who do not use computers at all. As such, the Maryland Traditions Apprenticeship grants are the last grants of MSAC that are able to filled out by hand—all others (including Maryland Traditions Project Grants) must be completed via electronic/online grant applications. And so the technical assistance work provided by the state folklorist is decidedly out of step with the high-tech grant world of the twenty-first century, but would be entirely at home in Charles Seeger's WPA era of government work that spawned the field of public folklore.

In addition to grant work, the state folklorist produces public programs such as festivals, radio programs, and symposia. The quality of such public programs can do wonders for building credibility and institutional buy-in. Since 2011, the Maryland Traditions Folklife Festival has greatly elevated the profile of not only the Maryland Traditions program, but of MSAC and folklife in Maryland in general. As mentioned before, the bread-and-butter of state arts agency work is grant making. And while this means the thoughtful and careful infusion of millions of dollars of state funds into nonprofit arts activities ranging from symphony orchestras to arts in education to theater programs for persons with special needs, grant making does not always appear to be "active" engagement with the public. So the state folklorist is also an unusual colleague at a state arts agency in this respect: she is involved in a good deal of public programming. These programs generate considerable good will toward the agency through publicity and through the events themselves. Nowhere is this more apparent than at the Maryland Traditions Folklife Festival, where programs make it plain that the festival participants have also been recognized by Maryland Traditions/MSAC folklife grants and awards. So in this arena, the festival induces a form of performative grant making (and fieldwork).

Radio programs are by far the most gratifying work for the Maryland state folklorist. Ongoing collaborations with the Baltimore NPR affiliate (88.1-FM, WYPR) have resulted in a considerable body of feature-length (one-hour) radio programs focused on Maryland's musical folklife. These features use key individuals as the lens through which a given cultural community is understood, and each is based entirely on interviews and field recordings. Features have ranged from Piedmont blues musicians in Metro DC to Persian classical musicians in Baltimore; African-American sacred music to bluegrass; West African griots to Lumbee Indian pow-wow musicians and dancers. Each of these programs has been the result of considerable fieldwork, and each provides a stage not only for the airing of field recordings and interviews, but for thoughtful reflection and interpretation of culture by the applied ethnomusicologist. These programs not only help to serve the public through education and awareness—the fact that each radio program is also available for download and podcast has made it an effective tool for featured artists to promote themselves within their home communities, to repurpose on social media, or to provide the validating stamp of community outsiders that has been one of the hallmarks of public folklorists for a century.

Disciplinary Challenges to the Ethnomusicologist as Government Folklorist

For the aspiring applied ethnomusicologist considering a career in public folklore, the most obvious disciplinary challenge is likely to be the prodigious amount of non-musical areas of inquiry. This is as true for the state folklorist as it is for an ethnomusicologist such as Jennifer Cutting on the reference desk at the American Folklife Center:

> Truth is, though, that all of us who work on the Reference Desk ... end up answering questions about everything from Norwegian sod houses to "How the Leopard Got His Spots." So we have to have a passing knowledge of folklore genres from vernacular architecture to folk tales and everything in between.
>
> (Cutting, 2011)

A secondary challenge is the narrower "folklife" or "traditional" paradigm that is not necessarily applied by ethnomusicologists in other professional realms. Disciplinary challenges to the ethnomusicologist-as-folklorist are not restricted to the focus on traditional music, however: the nature of public service and state-funded public programs complicate the application—in public settings—of bi-musicality and participant observation. Public displays of bi-musicality by a state employee give the appearance of contradicting the mission of state-driven public service. However, effective fieldwork requires the ethnomusicologist-as-folklorist to practice bi-musicality behind the scenes. Traditional music communities tend to be somewhat skeptical of government employees until bi-musicality comes into play. Likewise, fieldwork communities expect the government folklorist to be useful to them in some way. Sometimes, however, the most useful action calls for overt advocacy. A veteran of state and federal folklife programs, ethnomusicologist Jill Linzee has found greater freedom as the Executive Director of Northwest Heritage (an NGO based in Lake Forest Park, Washington) to become involved in the intersection between applied ethnomusicology and social justice work. For the state folklorist constrained from overt acts of social justice, then, the challenge is to connect fieldwork communities to organizations that can effectively collaborate with (or advocate for) them in a dynamic and open way not available to (or appropriate for) a state agency.

Other challenges may seem small on the surface: primarily, Jabbour's "fellow traveler" syndrome. For the ethnomusicologist as public folklorist, it can be difficult to justify (to one's host agency) attendance at the annual meetings for the Society for Ethnomusicology (let alone ICTM or others). State arts agencies have hard-earned battle scars from the culture wars of the 1980s, when political forces tried to eradicate the National Endowment for the Arts. During this time, federal (and, often, state) funding for the arts was cut deeply, and equally deep skepticism of arts funding was stoked by such politicians as US Senator Jesse Helms over cases such as the 1989 NEA-funded "The Perfect Moment" exhibit of Robert Mapplethorpe fine art photographs. As such, state arts agencies have been conservative in their expenditures. In other words, a state arts agency does not cover the cost of conference travel as much as a university might. Typically, I am financially (and philosophically) supported to attend the annual meeting of the American Folklore Society. And while I am an Americanist and a working folklorist and find AFS utterly relevant and enriching, I am a trained ethnomusicologist who has much to gain (professionally, personally, and intellectually) from attending SEM. Indeed, SEM is my disciplinary "home." However, in seven years of working at MSAC, I received conference travel support for only two of seven SEM conferences. This has an effect, over time, of distancing the state folklorist from professional colleagues and innovative new thinking within the field of ethnomusicology. My host agency does not think of me as an ethnomusicologist—to them I am a folklorist—and so I have to choose my SEM conferences with great care.

In a similar way, scholarly publication is not a priority for the state arts agency. For the state agency, there is little obvious benefit to publication of scholarly articles. Popular publications are another matter, so long as they serve the core mission of the agency and the state folklorist can convince the administration that time spent on publishing will not interfere with the day-to-day work of the folklorist. This encompasses CD releases, liner notes, digital publications, book projects and the like. The benefits of scholarly publications are more elusive to the agency. However, I would argue that it is crucial to the field of applied ethnomusicology and public folklore that we prioritize publication—whether this be on our own personal time, or that we advocate to do so on work hours. Without publication, we will miss countless opportunities to educate and train those who will someday replace us at our work. We also risk that the field will not advance to a stronger position within the world of government work. Not publishing will continue a dynamic lamented by many applied ethnomusicologists in the folklife field—that we are not presented as professional or intellectual role models to graduate students (Dirksen, 2012; Holtzberg, 2013; Sheehy, 2013). And, finally, we risk continuing a "road of no return" dynamic in which an applied/public career path is perceived as incompatible with entering the academic workforce. In my opinion, the academy would be greatly served by using public folklore as a training ground for its graduate students and for its junior professors. Seeing a broad diversity of music in culture/context via fieldwork is a far cry from learning about it in a classroom. Connecting ethnomusicologists' international work with the diasporic communities with whom local folklife programs have built trust (and archival documentation) is good common sense. Doing cultural interpretation in close proximity of those communities we are interpreting is also healthy—if utterly inconvenient—for culture is dynamic and ever-changing. Often, our cultural interpretations as both applied and university-based ethnomusicologists are instantly outdated. In the realm of applied work, cultural communities will point this fact out onstage at public events and in museum galleries. This is good for all ethnographers to be mindful of when teaching ethnography or when presenting our work. Finally, it would be hard for any ethnomusicologist to emerge from working as a public folklorist without the profound sense that any and all fieldwork inquiry should benefit the community as well as the ambitious scholar. State arts agencies can and should be both ethnographic training grounds for graduate students, just as state folklife archives can and should be a deep research resource for scholars and folklife communities.

For the ethnomusicologist-as-public-folklorist, there is a reversal of the pressures facing our tenure-track university colleagues. For instance, aspiring university professionals are reminded that applied work will not count toward tenure, so any applied work done during the first seven years on the job is to be conducted on one's own personal time. The priority, then, is research/publication and teaching. For the applied ethnomusicologist, research (fieldwork) is also a priority. But so is applied work. Publication, however—at least peer-reviewed scholarly publications such as books published by university presses and academic journals—is something to be done on one's own time, unless it is perceived as being central to the public folklife program's core mission. For academic publications, the core audience is typically not the local community—rather, it is fellow colleagues and researchers. Public folklorists publish a great deal of material in a broad range of mediums (film, radio, television, print, digital, etc.), but the primary audience is the local/regional constituency. How, then, do we move both of these worlds forward? How do we convince agencies—universities and state arts agencies alike—of the value of publications and programs of community engagement, both applied and theoretical? It is in the best interest of our society to do so, and it is in the best interest of our discipline to do so. Some of this requires that we apply our ethnographic skills to our own host institutions: What are the value systems of these institutions? How do we communicate in the language of this culture? How do we learn to communicate cross culturally/institutionally? In learning the answers to these questions, we can better argue the merits of those changes we seek to effect.

REFERENCES

Baron, Robert. (2013). Author's notes on conversation with Robert Baron. Baltimore, MD, July 31.

Baron, Robert, and Nicholas R. Spitzer. (2007). *Public Folklore*. Jackson: University Press of Mississippi.

Bronner, Simon J. (1996). *Popularizing Pennsylvania: Henry W. Shoemaker and the Progressive Uses of Folklore and History*. University Park: Pennsylvania State University Press.

Carey, George. (1976). State Folklorists and State Arts Councils: The Maryland Pilot. https://scholarworks.iu.edu/dspace/bitstream/handle/2022/1440/9%281%291-8.pdf?sequence=1.

Carey, George G. (1970). Final Report of the Study Commission on Maryland Folklore, edited by O. o. t. Governor: State of Maryland.

Cutting, Jennifer. (2011). Re: Query about Ethnomusicologists Working as Folklorists. Baltimore, MD, October 12.

Dirksen, Rebecca. (2012). "Reconsidering Theory and Practice in Ethnomusicology: Applying, Advocating, and Engaging Beyond Academia." Review of Reviewed Item. *Ethnomusicology Review*, http://ethnomusicologyreview.ucla.edu/journal/volume/17/piece/602.

Dorson, Richard M. (1949). "*Wisconsin Is My Doorstep* by Robert E. Gard (Review).: The Journal of American Folklore 62(244): 201.

Folkways, Smithsonian. (2013). About Us—Mission. http://www.folkways.si.edu/about_us/mission_history.aspx (accessed September 20, 2013).

Hawes, Bess Lomax. (2008). *Sing It Pretty: A Memoir*. Urbana: University of Illinois Press.

Heritage, Smithsonian Center for Folklife and Cultural. (2013). Bess Lomax Hawes. http://www.folklife.si.edu/center/legacy/hawes.aspx (accessed September 30, 2013).

Heritage, Smithsonian Center for Folklife and Cultural. (2013). *Staff*. http://www.folklife.si.edu/center/staff.aspx (accessed October 3, 2013).

Holtzberg, Maggie. (1992). *The Lost World of the Craft Printer, Folklore and Society*. Urbana: University of Illinois Press.

Holtzberg, Maggie. (2013). Notes from a conversation with Maggie Holtzberg. Baltimore, MD, October 1.

Holtzberg, Maggie, Jason Dowdle, Massachusetts Cultural Council, and National Heritage Museum (Lexington, MA). (2008). *Keepers of Tradition: Art and Folk Heritage in Massachusetts*. [Boston, MA] Lexington, MA [Amherst, MA]: Massachusetts Cultural Council; National Heritage Museum; Distributed by the University of Massachusetts Press.

Hood, Mantle. (1971). *The Ethnomusicologist*. New York: McGraw-Hill.

Jabbour, Alan. (2013). Re: Applied ethno question. Baltimore, MD, September 20.

Keil, Charles. (1985). "People's Music Comparatively: Style And Stereotype, Class And Hegemony." *Dialectical Anthropology* 10(1–2): 119–130.

Kirshenblatt-Gimblett, Barbara. (1998). "Folklore's Crisis." *The Journal of American Folklore* 111(441): 281–327.

Kodish, Debora. (2011). "Envisioning Folklore Activism." *The Journal of American Folklore* 124(491): 31–60.

Kodish, Debora G. (1978). "'A National Project with Many Workers': Robert Winslow Gordon and the Archive of American Folk Song." *The Quarterly Journal of the Library of Congress* 35(4): 218–233.

Linzee, Jill. (2013). Re: Folklorists who were trained in Ethnomusicology. Baltimore, MD, September 30.

Liu, Terry. (2013). Re: Question about applied ethnomusicology. Baltimore, MD, September 24.

Lomax, Alan. (1960). *The Folk Songs of North America, in the English Language*. London: Cassell.

Lomax, John A., Alan Lomax, and George Lyman Kittredge. (1934). *American Ballads and Folk Songs*. New York: Macmillan.

Lomax, John A., Alan Lomax, Charles Seeger, and Ruth Crawford Seeger. (1947). *Folk Song: U. S. A.* (1st ed.). New York: Duell.

Lomax, John A., Alan Lomax, Ruth Crawford Seeger, and Harold William Thompson. (1941). *Our Singing Country: A Second Volume of American Ballads and Folk Songs*. New York: Macmillan.

McAllester, David P. (1954). *Enemy Way Music*. Cambridge: The Peabody Museum, Harvard University.

Merriam, Alan P., and Herbert M. Halpert Collection. (1964). *The Anthropology of Music*. Evanston, IL: Northwestern University Press.

Myers, Helen. (1992). *Ethnomusicology* (1st American ed.), 2 vols. The Norton/ Grove Handbooks in Music. New York: W. W. Norton.

Pettan, Svanibor. (2008). "Applied Ethnomusicology and Empowerment Strategies: Views from across the Atlantic." *Muzikoloski zbornik/Musicological Annual* 44(1): 88–99.

Richardson, Lisa. (2011). Re: [PUBLORE] Query about folklorists who were trained in ethnomusicology. Baltimore, MD, October 6.

Sachs, Curt, and Jaap Kunst. (1962). *The Wellsprings of Music*. The Hague: M. Nijhoff.

Seeger, Anthony. (1996). "Ethnomusicologists, Archives, Professional Organizations, and the Shifting Ethics of Intellectual Property." *Yearbook for Traditional Music* 28: 87–105.

Sheehy, Daniel. (2013). *Interview with Dan Sheehy by Clifford R. Murphy*. Washington, DC: Rinzler Archives, Smithsonian Center for Folklife and Cultural Heritage.

Singer, Roberta. (2014). Re: Interview request—applied ethnomusicology question. Baltimore, MD, January 20.

Szwed, John F. (2010). *Alan Lomax: The Man Who Recorded the World*. New York: Viking Penguin.

Titon, Jeff Todd. (2003). "Ethnomusicology & Musical Advocacy." Paper read at Invested in Community: Ethnomusicology & Musical Advocacy, March 8–9, 2003, at Brown University, Providence, RI. https://library.brown.edu/cds/invested_in_community/Titon_Closing.html

Titon, Jeff Todd. (2009). *Worlds of Music: An Introduction to the Music of the World's Peoples* (5th ed.). Belmont, CA: Schirmer Cengage Learning.

CHAPTER 6

APPLIED ETHNOMUSICOLOGY IN CHINA

An Analytical Review of Practice

ZHANG BOYU

General Introduction

Scope

When I first heard the term "applied ethnomusicology" 10 years ago, I did not understand its exact meaning, but I was nevertheless intrigued.[1] Years of study have rewarded me with a more thorough understanding of applied ethnomusicology, which I now see as a music-related activity that engages in or manages, from the perspective of ethnomusicology, traditional music in different nations throughout the world. It is a practice that utilizes music within society.

At the present time, there are few academics in China who would refer to themselves as applied ethnomusicologists, but we can nevertheless trace the nature and meaning of applied ethnomusicology in China, as well as its contributions to Chinese society, through events and activities such as various types of traditional music festivals, the publication of traditional music CDs, the organization of academic conferences and seminars on traditional music, the selection of "intangible cultural heritages," which are organized in China by various levels of government as well as the United Nations, collections of musical instruments as museums, the production of programs on traditional music by radio and television stations, and so on. These combined elements create a clear picture of applied ethnomusicology in China.

Meanwhile, the significance of "music" to social development, as well as to the lives of the Chinese people, can be perceived from the community musical events organized by the government at all levels. It is important to note that the term "music" here is not restricted to the traditional or folk music that usually concerns ethnomusicologists; it also refers to Western music, as well as to popular music. These practices therefore fall under the umbrella of "applied musicology." However, this chapter also examines the subject at the individual level, addressing my own exploration and practice of applied ethnomusicology while I was director of the Musicology Department in the Central Conservatory of Music.

Although the word "applied" as used in this chapter refers to the ways in which music is used in social and personal activities, the section headings may lead readers to think that this chapter is proposing a catalogue for all music activities in China, including those that may not be seen as applied. For example, a music database seems far more research-oriented than concerned with anything "applied." It is worth discussing this issue here for the following reasons. Chinese music scholarship is currently divided into theoretical discussion and material collection. The difference between these two domains is that the former offers increased knowledge and better understanding of the music from across the world, whereas the latter offers practical access to a variety of materials, some of which may be accessible via other resources. Generally speaking, databases are based on research; however, they may be considered part of the archiving work of applied ethnomusicology where the catalogues may at some point be made accessible to the general public, including the people whose music is contained within. In fact, it is the data collected in these databases that lead to the development of research theories; a database is also a way to organize data, making access more convenient for its users. Potential financial benefit coming from databases is also an important factor differentiating research and applied ethnomusicology.

If we can understand why this chapter has devoted so much time to databases, we can also understand why the organization of conferences and the establishment of music museums are discussed as personal applied ethnomusicology practices. A research activity and an activity for research may not be the same thing.

Another important factor to be considered is that many types of traditional music in China are functional music, in that they perform various social functions, including religious, funerary, marital, medicinal, and educational, as well playing a role in communal work. These functions do not reflect "applied ethnomusicology," since they are the main focus of ethnomusicological research. Rather, the domain of applied ethnomusicology is those functions that have been created in order to negotiate contemporary social situations. These divisions may or may not be totally appropriate in Western applied ethnomusicology.

It is worth emphasizing again that applied ethnomusicology is still a relatively new field in China; Chinese ethnomusicologists have not yet developed an applied ethnomusicology to suit China's specific circumstances. This chapter is the first true dialogue between Chinese ethnomusicologists and their colleagues in the West.

Research Findings

"Applied ethnomusicology" is a relatively new term in China, and so far there has been little in-depth research on this topic. Only one translated book specializing in this subject has been published, and articles discussing applied ethnomusicology are few and far between. A search for "applied ethnomusicology" on http://www.cnki.net,[2] a database of Chinese academic journals and dissertations, returned just five results.

In "Chinese Minorities' Music in View of the Protection of Intangible Cultural Heritage: The View and Methodology of Applied Ethnomusicology," published in 2008, Yang Xifan discusses the protection and utilization of ethnic minority music in China from the perspective of applied ethnomusicology. This article borrows Japanese ethnomusicologist Yamaguti Osamu's definition of applied ethnomusicology, which argues that "as a study of humanities, musicology derives from society and should be applied to society. Applied musicology is the result of a mutually beneficial interaction between the study of music and society" (2008: 123). In view of this interaction, Yang explores the various problems that ethnic minority music in China has encountered, addressing the difficulties such music has confronted against the backdrop of social changes caused by "demographic structure," "transformation of society," and "external culture," as well as emphasizing the role of government and the importance of educational continuity. However, with regard to the theory of applied ethnomusicology, this article primarily tackles the continuity of ethnic minority music in China from the perspective of the relationship between music and society (Yang Xifan, 2008).

Lü Lulu was the first to discuss the difference between ethnomusicology and applied ethnomusicology. In her 2012 article, "Applied Ethnomusicology and Local Music Education," Lü argues that the First Annual Conference of the Chinese Traditional Music Association, which was held at the Nanjing University of Arts in 1980, set the tone and direction of the professional development of China's ethnomusicology scholarship for 30 years, and that all future study of Chinese ethnomusicology should be directed toward applied ethnomusicology. This article takes local music education as its starting point, exploring the practice and application of Chinese ethnomusicology in the education and continuity of local music (Lü, 2012).

In the article "On Ethnomusicology's Role in Chinese Music Education: Applied Ethnomusicology, Current Music Education and the Course Syllabus in China" (2012), Cao Jun argues that it is necessary to integrate the theory of ethnomusicology into the present Chinese music education system, so as to help reverse or eradicate—both in methodology and ideology—engrained, unhelpful practices negatively affected by Eurocentrism. He goes on to argue that applied ethnomusicology can provide scientific and discussable solutions in terms of methodology for other musical subjects such as music history, music morphology, music analysis, music recording, and music communication. Lü also suggests that courses such as "Chinese Cultural Studies," "Guqin (seven-stringed zither) Music," "Beijing Opera," "*Kunqu* Opera," and "World Music" be added to the current music educational system.

Zhou Xianbao's "Western Ethnomusicology and Chinese Traditional Music Research: Reviews of the Theory and Methodology of Applied Ethnomusicology" (2012) is chiefly a discussion of the spread and application of Western ethnomusicological theory in China, which spurred a transition within the study of Chinese traditional music from focusing on the music itself to emphasizing musical culture. The author poses this question: Since we already have applied mathematics, applied economics, and applied anthropology, isn't it fair to have applied ethnomusicology as a part of musicology? Above all, "the ultimate goal of the establishment of any subject is not the study of this subject itself, but to apply the theory and methodology of this subject so as to explore the unknown, and to see whether studies of this subject could be applied to benefit society and the nation as well as the survival and development of mankind" (2012: 16). Zhou does not provide a specific theory or methodology of applied ethnomusicology; rather, he offers a hypothesis, which intends to integrate the study of ethnomusicology into the realities of society, so as to give full play to the social value of ethnomusicological studies. Zhou also offers his opinion on the relationship between ethnomusicology and musicology, stating unequivocally that ethnomusicology is part of musicology.

Zhang Xiaoyan and Su Qianzhong's "Approach to Applied Musicology: A Review of Japanese Ethnomusicologist Yamaguti Osamu's Academic Summit Series," which was published in 2007, serves as an introduction to a series of lectures made by the famous Japanese ethnomusicologist Yamaguti, speeches given at the invitation of Shanghai Conservatory of Music. Yamagutii defined the study of music as being divided into three categories: historical musicology, comparative musicology, and applied musicology, and illustrated the historical contributions made by applied ethnomusicology to the renaissance of Vietnamese court music (Zhang Xiaoyan and Su Qianzhong, 2007).

The above articles reveal that the theoretical exploration of applied ethnomusicology is still very limited in China, lacking precise subject orientation and in-depth studies of the definition, scope, and methodology of this subject. It is fair to say that the study of applied ethnomusicology is a field that still requires cultivation. The lack of theoretical studies, however, does not mean the absence of practical explorations. The practice of applied ethnomusicology manifests itself in various ways. The following sections will introduce two aspects of this practice in China: the social, and the personal.

From the Social Perspective

Applied Ethnomusicology in Political Construction: Music Activities within Communities

There are multiple levels within each Chinese administrative district. The highest level consists of the Communist Party of China Central Committee, the State Council, and the People's Congress. Ministries that report to the State Council, including the Ministry of Culture, are viewed by the Chinese people as national institutions. Second to this is the provincial level, which includes those four municipalities directly under the central government (Beijing, Shanghai, Tianjin, and Chongqing), as well as the 23 provinces and five autonomous regions.[3] Each province and autonomous region has its own Culture Department or Culture Bureau. Below the provinces and autonomous regions is the prefecture level, each city or district with its own Culture Bureau. Fourth is the county level; each region is composed of several counties, and each county has its own Culture Institute. The final level includes towns and villages, which have their own Culture Stations. These levels, as well as their respective cultural establishments, can be illustrated by this simple list:

The State Council
The Ministry of Culture
The Culture Department (Provincial level)
The Culture Bureau (Prefectural level)
The Culture Institute (County level)
The Culture Station (Town level)

It is clear from this that there is a huge network in place for the management of culture in China, from the national Culture Ministry down to the provincial Culture Departments, the prefecture-level Culture Bureaus, the county-level Culture Institutes, and finally, the town-level Culture Stations. At each level, there are professionals in charge of the management of music-related events and activities. Music activities are used at all levels of government to enrich people's cultural and spiritual lives; cultural management is an essential part of government. There are also numerous music organizations and groups affiliated to the Ministry of Culture, such as the Central National Music Orchestra, the Central Symphony Orchestra, the Central Opera House, the Beijing Opera Theatre of China, the Central Ballet Theatre, the National Theatre Company of China, and so on. These groups represent the best of Chinese professional music and performance. In addition, each province and autonomous region has its own professional musical groups, including symphony orchestras and local opera theaters. According to the annual report issued by the Chinese Musicians Association (China Federation of Literary and Art Circles, 2013: 113–139), there are 57 symphony orchestras in China (including Hong Kong and Macao). In 2006, the Ministry of Education, Ministry of Culture, and Ministry of Finance jointly initiated the "Advanced Arts Going into Campuses" program[4] to enrich college students' humanistic understandings and expand their cultural horizons (China Federation of Literary and Art Circles, 2013: 116). In the wake of the cultural institutional reforms of recent years, many professional music groups are now taking the economic road to independent management. However, according to national requirements, each province and city still maintains at least one group or institution sponsored by the government, in order to protect the local arts.

On the national and provincial levels, it is professional musical groups that play the most prominent role. On the prefecture and county level, however, the Culture Institutes and Stations take charge of organizing and managing the people's cultural activities. A balanced relationship between material affluence and spiritual development has in fact been emphasized by the Chinese government, and managing the people's cultural activities is seen as an important part of government business, aiming to enrich people's lives with a variety of musical and cultural activities. This is also a path to the construction of a harmonious society, which is not an empty political slogan but a government requirement at all levels. Such activities include the performance of music by local folk musicians, who are managed by the cultural institutes and stations, with various types of musical ensembles, such as the Western brass band and the Chinese traditional orchestra; ethnomusicological researches, such as recording, transcription, ethnographical introduction, done by the local officials; folk activities, such as the performance of folk music as well as exhibitions at temple fairs and during festivals; and local music competitions. It is important to note that performances organized by the government have played an essential role in the development of Chinese musical culture. Currently there are more than 300 types of local opera, one-third of which emerged and developed after the founding of the People's Republic of China. This was a direct result of governmentally organized art performances, which encouraged the production of arts that represented local cultures and customs, rather than historical legacies (Zhang Zhentao, 2008). In June 2013, I took part in a music fair organized by the Beijing Financial Street Administration.[5] Beijing Financial Street is famous for being home to the headquarters of many Chinese national banks and foreign financial corporations. The street administrative office recruited college graduates from Wuhan Conservatory of Music to work in the area, making music the bridge linking government departments, companies, and the people. They also invited famous musicians from overseas to perform on a regular basis. Figure 6.1 shows Finnish jazz musicians playing on Financial Street in June 2013. The music featured in activities organized by the government is generally local. This protects and preserves local music on the one hand, while serving the people and society on the other.

Discussion

Although Socialist China has undergone hardships, it is now enjoying a golden age; under the leadership of the Chinese Communist Party, the economy is developing swiftly and strongly. In fact, the Chinese government has attached great importance to the building and development of mass culture, not only during boom times but also during periods when economic development is flagging. In most Chinese cities, it is not uncommon to spot elderly people in matching costumes dancing popular rural folk dances together. In remote towns and villages, people get together to play cards and Mahjong. When the people are enjoying themselves, the government's efforts to enrich their cultural lives are well rewarded.

At the same time, however, we should also be aware that top-down administrative cultural management has the potential to produce conformity within cultural activities throughout China. Events and developments at one particular place or time can also be seen at other places or times, which is not conducive to displays of individuality within a

FIGURE 6.1. Finnish Jazz musicians playing at the Financial Street in Beijing. Photographed by Zhang Boyu in June 2013.

diversified culture. Under this management system, many activities also risk acquiring a political flavor.

Applied Ethnomusicology in Social Construction: The Local Application of Musical Intangible Cultural Heritages

In China, the management of intangible cultural heritage is currently divided into five levels: the United Nations level, the national level, the provincial level, the prefecture level, and the county level.

In 2004, the Chinese government signed the "Convention for the Production of Intangible Cultural Heritage" issued by the United Nations Educational, Scientific and Cultural Organization (UNESCO). Since then, the concept of "intangible cultural heritage" has been widely recognized in China. Government at all levels, from the central to the local, sees the task of protecting intangible cultural heritage as a significant one, and systematic protective measures have been carried out with positive results. By 2012, the Chinese State Council had announced three lists of national intangible cultural heritages, containing 1,219 items in total, as well as four lists of national intangible cultural heritage representatives, with a total of 1,986 people. By 2013, 37 Chinese intangible cultural heritages had been added to the "Representative List of the Intangible Cultural Heritage of Humanity" and six to the "List of Intangible Cultural Heritage in Need of Urgent Protection," making China the country with the most intangible cultural heritages on these lists. Meanwhile, the provinces and autonomous regions also began to identify and name intangible cultural heritage items and representatives at various levels. In the first three rounds, a total of 6,332 people were named as representatives of the provincial-level intangible cultural heritages, while 870,000 intangible cultural heritages were named on the recommendation of various regions.[6] In 2008, the government began to sponsor national intangible cultural heritages, providing 200,000–300,000 yuan for each project. In 2017, sponsorship for national intangible cultural heritage representatives was increased to 20,000 yuan from the previous 8,000–10,000 per year. The provinces and autonomous regions also began to sponsor their local intangible cultural heritages and representatives according to their own circumstances.[7]

Government officials at various levels have organized a series of events and activities to promote intangible cultural heritages. These activities reflect the nature of applied ethnomusicology. First celebrated in 2006, the second Saturday in June is China's "Cultural Heritage Day," when regions and institutions throughout China hold cultural events and activities. Below are some examples of such activities:

1. In February, 2006, the first "Chinese Intangible Cultural Heritage Exhibition" was held at the National Museum in Beijing. The exhibition period was extended from 10 days to a month.[8]
2. The biennial "China International Intangible Cultural Heritage Festival" was held in Chengdu from 2007 to 2017.[9]
3. During the Lantern Festival in 2009, 14 members of the Interministerial Conference for the Protection of Intangible Cultural Heritage, including the Ministry of Finance, the Ministry of Culture, and the National Reform and Development Commission, jointly held the "China's Intangible Cultural Heritage Traditional Craft Exhibition"[10] in Beijing's Agriculture Exhibition Centre.
4. In February 2012, the "Productive Protection of China's Intangible Cultural Heritage Exhibition" was held in the Agriculture Exhibition Centre in Beijing.[11]
5. From 2011 onward, the Zhihua Temple in Beijing held annual activities to commemorate "Cultural Heritage Day," inviting folk music groups from different regions to give performances in Beijing.[12]
6. In November 2012, the first "Chinese Intangible Cultural Heritage Traditional Craft Exhibition" was held in Huangshan, Anhui province.[13]

Improvement of facilities represents an important aspect of intangible cultural heritage protection. According to Kuaner (2011), the provinces (including autonomous regions and municipalities) have established a total of 424 intangible cultural heritage museums, 179 folk museums, and 96 galleries, as well as 1,216 training institutes. These facilities and sites assume the responsibility of collecting, protecting, studying, and ensuring the continuation of intangible cultural heritages.

When it comes to local applications for musical intangible cultural heritages, the question of local traditional music and tourism is unavoidable. The tourist industry has developed very rapidly in China. 10 years ago, Chinese tourists were an unusual sight in most countries; now they come in droves. This is especially true for domestic tourism: since the vast majority of people are still unable to go abroad, domestic travel has become a way for them to see more of the world. International tourism is only available to the middle classes; domestic tourism suffers from no such limitations. As a result, the domestic tourism industry is booming. Besides natural and historical sites, people are increasingly focusing on local cultural life. Although modernization helped the Chinese people escape poverty, it also resulted in the loss of many of their traditions. Postmodernism allowed the Chinese to value their traditions once more, with the result that they now appreciate these traditions from a modernized perspective.

Since tourism is an important path to economic development, naturally, regions with tourism resources will make use of these resources. In fact, even those who possess few such resources have been exploring the potential for tourism, and local traditional music has become an essential tourism resource. The Naxi traditional music of Lijiang, Yunnan, is a well-known example of a successfully explored tourism resource. The *Dongjing* music of Yunnan is a subgenre of Han Chinese Taoist music, which usually takes the form of scripture recitation to accompany worship ceremonies. According to historical records, *Dongjing* performances were once held in Lijiang, the home of the Naxi people; however, performance ceased a long time ago, and many elements have now been lost, particularly the scriptures and worship ceremonies. Only a few instrumental pieces, played on Naxi instruments such as the *pipa* (a four-stringed lute bigger than the Han *pipa*) and the *suogudu* (three-stringed lute), remain. As these instruments possess significant Naxi characteristics, pieces played with them are generally considered to be Naxi traditional music. *Dayan Guyue She*, a group that performs these pieces, gives daily concerts at the center of Lijiang, and has become a must-see for any tourist who comes to Lijiang.

At the same time, some scholars are unhappy with the concept of "Naxi traditional music," arguing that such music was never exclusively played or owned by the Naxi ethnicity. One scholar went so far as to write an article asking "What Kind of a Thing Is Naxi Traditional Music?" (Wu Xueyuan, 2003). The *Dayan Guyue She* were so offended by this that they sued the scholar in question, who was later requested by the court to pay 20,000 yuan in compensation, while the journal that published the article paid 100,000 yuan. In this case, there was a significant discrepancy between academic truth and the commercial interests of society. Many scholars sympathized with Mr. Wu; however, according to the court, the decision was made based not on academic truth but rather the words used in the title, "What Kind of a Thing Is Naxi Traditional Music?" (*Naxi Guyue Shi Shenme Dongxi*) which were perceived as implying disrespect for the music. If nothing else, this served as a reminder to Chinese scholars that all critical opinions expressed should be based on rational analysis rather than emotion, even though most scholars today agree that Naxi traditional music is little more than a fabrication. Ironically, a theater for the performance of Naxi traditional music was constructed just opposite *Dayan Guyue She*, but was not popular with tourists, and the *Dongba Palace*, as it was known, eventually was turned into a bar.

Discussion

The significance of protecting intangible cultural heritages in China is multifaceted, with different elements having different significance at different levels. At the national level, the protection of intangible cultural heritage also protects China's traditional culture, establishing China's own cultural system and striving to make Chinese culture prominent in the vast mosaic of world cultures. At the 2009 "Bo'ao Youth Forum" in Hong Kong, Vice-Minister of Culture Zhou Heping delivered the keynote speech "Protect Intangible Cultural Heritage: Build a Spiritual Paradise for the Chinese Nation." He argued that "the renaissance of the Chinese nation should start from the renaissance of the Chinese culture" (Zhou Heping, 2009).[14]

Guided by the idea that cultural renaissance plays an important role in national revitalization, the government has invested heavily in the protection of intangible cultural heritage; each national project receives 200,000–300,000 yuan to be used in the maintenance of heritage continuity. Contradictions are not uncommon in the protection process. Intangible cultural heritage represents the extension and legacy of history; in many projects, elements left over from the agricultural era come into conflict with modern developments. Meanwhile, the folk beliefs reflected in some of these projects contradict the atheism officially advocated by the Chinese Communist Party. *Dongjing* performances in Yunnan are effectively the recitation of scriptures, and are mostly held in local temples that were not approved by local government. There is therefore a conflict between protecting something that has been recognized as an intangible cultural heritage and allowing chanting in unauthorized temples (Zhang Boyu, 2012). It is worth mentioning that the government has not removed those temples or restricted *Dongjing* performance activities, which shows that since the beginning of the Reform and Opening Up policy, the scope of "opening up" has expanded from the economic to the social. It also suggests that the Chinese government, faced with the might of Western culture, has found a way to counterbalance its impact with China's own unique traditional culture.

On the local level (provincial, prefecture, and county level), the protection of intangible cultural heritage has a different meaning. Although China's Reform and Opening Up policy began in the economic realm, it has now extended to almost all aspects of society. Reform and Opening Up has provided us with the opportunity to realize the "Chinese Dream," which is not solely materially defined but also has spiritual connotations. It has already become a consensus among the Chinese people that culture plays an essential role in realizing the "Chinese Dream," and the significance of culture has therefore been repeatedly emphasized as the economy has developed. People from different regions and districts are eager to display the unique nature of their own local cultures so as to strengthen their sense of identity. At the same time, however, economic benefits are always a motivating factor, even in the protection of intangible cultural heritage, as most people would prefer to accumulate rather than spend money in the process of protecting these heritages. Unlike the central government, local governments are exploring the economic potential of intangible cultural heritages, on the one hand, and protecting them

FIGURE 6.2. Folk instrumental ensembles competition held in Jincheng city Shanxi province in 2013. This is one of the village folk bands joined the competition. Such activities can be found everywhere across the country. Photographed by Zhang Boyu in January 2013.

for the sake of their local identity, on the other (see Figures 6.2 and 6.3). The phrase "Protection for Development; Development for Better Protection" exemplifies the idea that only through proper utilization can protection be effective. Tourism has become a major and viable method to utilize traditional music resources, whether or not a region has tourism resources. For those regions that do have tourism resources, traditional music will often form part of local tourism projects. In regions with few or no tourism resources, local governments will often encourage private investment in recreation sites such as vacation villages, which is an important path to economic development for many towns and villages. As a result of this process, local folk music resources have attracted attention from government officials at a number of different levels.

The owners of these intangible cultural heritages are the common people, most of whom are underprivileged, rooted in their local cultures, and unable to adapt to external cultural influences. Such people can benefit in a small way from their own customs and cultures by giving traditional cultural performances. In the past, this was looked down upon, and musicians who performed for money were often seen as inferior. However, the establishment of the intangible cultural heritage system transformed the current crop of village musicians overnight into representatives of China's local traditional cultures, recognized nationwide. They are frequently invited to give performances by cultural institutions in Beijing, Shanghai, and other large cities, and they make frequent appearances on television. Some of them even enjoy national subsidies simply for being cultural representatives, a state of affairs that they could never have dreamed of before. This new social identity has not only promoted them in terms of social hierarchy, but has

FIGURE 6.3. Villages in Wuan county Hebei province are joining a local opera performance during a Taoist temple affair. This is still an important way of spiritual life for current Chinese in rural areas. Photographed by Zhang Boyu in January 2013.

also brought them huge economic benefits. Unfortunately, this has led to fake "intangible cultural heritages" popping up in regions across the country. Take percussion music, for example: there are more than 10 types of percussion ensembles in Shan'xi province, and while all of them have been identified as "intangible cultural heritages," some of them are in fact newly created, with few or none of the historical values they supposedly possess.

From the multiple manifestations of the protection of intangible cultural heritage discussed above, we can understand the following with regard to applied ethnomusicology. Intangible cultural heritages, when applied to the development of society, can be tainted with strong political flavors but are nevertheless powerful cultural weapons, as traditions inherited from thousands of years ago, against the impact or intrusion of Westernization and globalization.

Intangible cultural heritages, both when used to satisfy a need for recreation and amusement in people's lives and as tourist resources, are targets for research in the study of applied ethnomusicology.

Intangible cultural heritages, when used for academic purposes, are spiritual food for ethnomusicologists and sources of deductive thinking for scholars. (For more information, see the following discussion.)

Applied Ethnomusicology in Academia: The Establishment of a Musical Database

In the study of Chinese applied ethnomusicology, research for the purpose of research—that is, the establishment of a database for a certain type of music—has recently been given a lot of attention. Such databases generally concern Chinese traditional music, and are intended for practical use. In this they share certain characteristics with applied ethnomusicology. The target beneficiaries of these databases, however, are ethnomusicologists, and they are mainly used for the sole purpose of research. In this sense, such databases are also representative of research-oriented ethnomusicology. The following two databases can be seen as typical of the various traditional music databases.

Uyghur Muqam Database in the Xinjiang Autonomous Region

Muqam is a famous example of Uyghur musical art, a form of large-scale musical performance that includes vocals, instrumental music, and dancing. Since the Uyghur people live in different districts throughout the Xinjiang autonomous region, there are different types of Muqam, which can be further divided into various branches, such as Daolang Muqam, Hami Muqam, Turfan Muqam, and Twelve Muqam, the most representative branch. The art of Muqam was listed by UNESCO as a "Masterpiece of Oral and Intangible Heritage of Humanity" in 2005 (Li Jilian, Zhou Ji, and Li Kairong, 2005).

Muqam has been a focus of Chinese music academic research, with a large number of related research findings. In order to organize the music, images, graphics, scores, and lyrics of Uyghur Muqam, and record them through modern digitization for long-term storage and ease of retrieval, the Central Conservatory of Music, Xinjiang Arts Research Institute, and the Cultural Department of Xinjiang Autonomous Region jointly initiated the Uyghur Muqam Database in 2007. The database includes research papers, performances (audio and video), instruments, bands, costumes and stage sets, important figures, associations, musical events, historical records, scores and lyrics, and relevant materials, as well as information on Muqam in foreign countries.

The Central Conservatory of Music, Xinjiang Arts Research Institute, and the Cultural Department of Xinjiang Autonomous Region have invested 600,000 yuan for the construction of this database. Meanwhile, the Central Conservatory of Music and Xinjiang Arts Research Institute have held several joint seminars and have organized scholars as well as students to do field research in Moyu, Pishan, Hetian, Akesu, Kuche, and Tashikurgan. Unfortunately, the death of Zhou Ji, the director of the database project and a preeminent scholar of Muqam, has made it difficult for the project to proceed. The database was completed in 2011, but not as expected. It still lacks any practical applications.

Chinese Guqin Musical Culture Database

The 2006 "Key Project" planned by the Musicology Research Institute affiliated with the Central Conservatory of Music (a key research base for the humanities, recognized by the Education Ministry of China) and the 2008 "Third-Phase Building of Key Disciplines" of the "211 Project" both listed the Chinese Guqin Musical Culture Database as an important research project. This database was established in 2006, led by Professor Yuan Jingfang from the Central Conservatory of Music.[15]

The Chinese Guqin Musical Culture Database contains 68 theoretical books on Guqin from the pre-Qin dynasty to the Qing dynasty, as well as 77 on modern Guqin. It collects a total of 5,679 articles on Guqin music in the Ming and Qing dynasties (1,612 of which were written after 1911), 9 collections of theses, 126 issues of periodicals published since the year 1911, 51 reports, and 165 collections of musical scores from different dynasties (both written by hand and printed), containing a total of 4,799 pieces and covering all the Guqin scores handed down since the Tang Dynasty. There are also 9,481 minutes of recorded Guqin music, with 1,411 tracks on 129 CDs. The database also includes information on 841 Guqin performers from the pre-Qin period to the Qing dynasty, as well as hundreds of performers since the founding of the Republic. There are more than 30 groups established after the late Qing dynasty, as well as a total of 82 commemorative activities, gatherings of literati, academic seminars, and concerts. The database also includes more than 749 articles on performance techniques, indexed in each dynasty's collection of musical scores. In addition, there are 1,080 poems, 25 iambic verses, 31 articles, 25 poetic essays, 8 frescos, 55 sculptures, 51 paintings, and other literature and images. Construction of this database was completed in 2011 (Yuan, 2009).

Discussion

Database-building is of great practical value and significance to the study of ethnomusicology. China has a great many types of music; however, database capacity was inevitably limited in the era of paper media, and data retrieval relatively difficult to conduct. Advances in technology have resolved many issues that could not be addressed before, and the future is bright for the development of database building. However, none of these musical databases has been put to use, with the exception of CNKI. The reason for this is that there was no clear purpose for building these databases. Should a database be used for data collecting and compilation, or for research purposes? The intention of the former is to collect and store traditional music before it disappears, while the latter aims to provide literature for the study of a certain type of music, as well as creating commercial value through the operation of the database. Since most musical databases are run by music scholars, many databases are more like paper archives that happen to exist in electronic forms. A great deal of effort goes into the construction of the databases, and their creators often hesitate to let others use their work for free. Unfortunately, if fees were charged for the use of these databases, few people would be willing to pay them. For this reason, most music databases are currently left unused.

Applied Ethnomusicology in Mass Entertainment: China Central Television (CCTV) Programs on Chinese Traditional Music

There are any number of options for entertainment available to the masses: go to a concert, see a movie, sing at a karaoke television, dance in a public park, and so on. All of these are common pastimes for the Chinese people. What cannot be denied, however, is that television, in China as well as other parts of the world, is a major form of entertainment and an indispensable part of modern life. In China, the connection between applied ethnomusicology and television manifests itself in several TV programs on Chinese folk music. CCTV, for example, broadcasts the Television Grand Prix, Folk Music Performance Competition, Elegant Chinese Music, and the Opera Channel (Channel 11).

Television Grand Prix for Young Singers

The Television Grand Prix for Young Singers is a program launched by CCTV, which integrates music and entertainment with an element of competition. Every two years, local TV stations send their chosen candidates to participate in a competition held in Beijing. The Grand Prix has been successfully held 15 times since the first competition in 1984. The judging panel is usually made up of famous singers. There used to be three categories within the contest: bel canto, Chinese style singing, and popular singing. However, in 2006, original-style singing[16] was added as a fourth category. Mongolian *"Changdiao (Wurdindu)"* and *"Humai* (Throat singing)," as well as the Dong people's *"Dage (Kalau)"* and the Yi people's *"Haicai Qiang,"* have all won prizes in this competition. This original-style singing has been the subject of much discussion among China's ethnomusicologists. How do we define "original-style singing?" Does to refer to original voices, or is it that the style itself should present an original context? It is fair to say that the discussion on original-style singing reflects what applied ethnomusicology has done for ethnomusicology. The Television Grand Prix has received wide recognition in China, and the program itself is a major topic of discussion among the masses. Because of this, entering the competition is also an effective way for new singers to make themselves known.

Traditional Instrumental Music Performance Competition

CCTV has held two Traditional Instrumental Music Performance Competitions, one in 2009 and one in 2012. The candidates are selected or recommended by television stations in the provinces, autonomous regions, and cities, as well as by the following groups in Beijing: artistic and cultural organizations, art schools, university art departments, and art groups affiliated with the People's Liberation Army. The judging panel is composed of famous Chinese traditional instrument performers and composers, and the candidates are divided into juvenile and adult categories. The competition itself is divided into two categories: soloists and ensembles. Instruments for solo performance include *erhu* (fiddle), *banhu* (fiddle), *pipa* (lute), *yangqin* (dulcimer), *guzheng* (zither), *guqin* (zither), *dizi* (flute), *suona* (cornet), *sheng* (mouth organ), and percussion, with gold, silver, and copper prizes going to outstanding players. Ensembles may include local instrumental genres, ensembles composed of traditional instruments, and ensembles composed of both traditional and non-traditional instruments. There should be 2–15 performers in each group, and gold, silver, and copper prizes are awarded in each of the three categories. This competition has become a bridge to success for many professional Chinese folk instrument performers.

Fenghua Guoyue (Elegant Chinese Music)

Fenghua Guoyue (Elegant Chinese Music) is an entertainment program broadcast on CCTV. *Fenghua Guoyue* focuses on the appreciation of Chinese traditional music and instrumental performances, serving as an introduction to China's traditional music culture and providing a platform for traditional music performers to showcase themselves and their music. The program has three sections: *Jiaqu Youyue* (Fine Music), *Lingting Tianlai* (Elegant Voices), and *Women Yongyou* (What We have), each of which has a weekday edition and a weekend edition. The show airs at 6.20 p.m. Monday to Sunday, and is replayed at 6.30 a.m. Tuesday to Monday. Apart from instrumental performances, the program also includes vivid pictures and explanations, and is popular among fans of folk music instruments.

The Opera Channel (Channel 11)

Many people complain that traditional music is not paid enough attention when compared to the popularity and publicity enjoyed by popular music. Although that may be true in most other countries, it is not the case in China. As a matter of fact, Chinese traditional music receives special attention both from the government and from the public, and is strongly represented in the media as well as in concert halls. CCTV's Chinese Opera Channel is a typical example of this. The channel started broadcasting on July 9, 2001, and mainly presents performances of various types of Chinese music—not only Beijing Opera, but also music from other regions.

Apart from promoting Chinese opera culture, this channel also emphasizes the importance of mass participation and entertainment. Opera amateurs, for example, are often invited to give performances on this channel. Since all programs on this channel are opera-related and are broadcast non-stop during the day, they are grouped into several subdivisions: *Mingduan Xinshang* (Appreciation of Famous Stories), *Liyuan Leitai* (Opera Competitions), *Dianbo Shijian* (Request Time), *Xiqu Fengcai* (Opera Beauties), *Nanqiang Beidiao* (Northern and Southern Operas), *Xiyuan Baijia* (Various Types of Operas), *Difangxi Zhichuang* (Local Operas), CCTV *Kongzhong Juyuan* (CCTV Sky Theatre), *Genwo Xue* (Learn With Me), *Guoba Yin* (Enjoying Opera), and *Jiuzhou Daxitai* (Opera Stages from All Regions), among others.

Chinese opera possesses an intense musicality. There are 300 local operas in China, mainly distinguished by their different music. Promoting Chinese opera via mass media, and promoting traditional music through modern methods of communication, so as to integrate traditional music into modern musical life, represent another typical case for us to consider in our study of applied ethnomusicology.

Discussion

Having considered the promotion of Chinese traditional music via mass media, we can come to the following conclusions. First, culture is a group behavior. When people share and abide by common behaviors, a series of customs and conventions form, which evolve over time into a culture. Urbanization has separated people into different units, buildings, and residential compounds. Through such segregation, the space for group behavior has been shrinking, and so the common behaviors of the people are reflected instead via television. People in different units, buildings, and even cities all watch the same television program at the same time. As a result, television has created a new type of group behavior, one in which interactions between people are rendered redundant. The songs that should have been heard in traditional theaters and out in the fields are now broadcast via television channels. The songs remain, but the interactions between audience members do not.

Second, the introduction of original-style singing in the Television Grand Prix for Young Singers is an initiative that reflects both the organizers' love for Chinese traditional music and their sense of responsibility toward it. However, original-style singing can only present original sounds, for the original way of life for its performers cannot be re-created on a stage in Beijing. In this sense, the connection between the sound of traditional music and the way of life it represents has disappeared, replaced by a connection between sound and stage for the sake of professional performance. The beauty to be found only in a wild cry in the fields, therefore, has no value on CCTV's professional stage (Xu Shuyun, 2003; Wu Xiulin and Zhang Xia, 2010; Li Sue, 2006; Yu Renhao, 2006).

Third, the professional development of Chinese ethnic music has contributed to the development of Chinese ethnic musical instrument–playing techniques, as well as helping to nurture a large group of ethnic musical instrument performers, many of which are now prominent in the field. Professional Chinese instrumental music is the pursuit of superb performance skills; the ability to read music is essential. Sight-reading has been added to some musical instrument competitions. Chinese traditional music, however, employs traditional Chinese music notation, and the capacity to produce impromptu variations is not considered part of professional development. The original features of Chinese traditional instrumental music and the processes necessary to create it have been completely lost (Zhang Boyu, 2010a).

Applied Ethnomusicology in Social Life: The Musical Lives of Beijing Seniors

The capabilities of music are endless. In ancient China, Confucius's observations of society were not based on sociopolitical or economic factors; rather, he judged the merit of a society on the music that its people liked and disliked. He also believed that the best way to change social customs was through music.[17] In ancient China, people used music to deliver commands during war. The saying "Drive the soldiers forward when playing the drum, withdraw the army when beating the gong"[18] reflects the idea that music could encourage soldiers during a war. Chairman Mao Zedong used music to educate the people; as a result, music became a political tool. Today, music has a wide variety of functions in China. Several Chinese conservatories offer majors in music therapy; although many schools around the world now offer similar programs, fighting illness with music is particularly common in China. Traditional Chinese medicine emphasizes the balance between *Yin* and *Yang* in the human body, so emotional adjustment is an important method employed by Chinese medicine to treat the sick. In the Temple of Heaven, a famous park in Beijing and one of the most popular tourism sites, people gather every Saturday to sing together (see Figure 6.4). One of the groups is called *Shanting Teshu Hechangdui* (Fan Pavilion Unique Chorus). Most of the members are cancer patients, and they use their songs to fight against cancer. The female conductor teaches each new song to the group, in addition to conducting it. Every day the choir becomes more famous, and more and more people flock to join it. When singing, people forget their illnesses, reflecting a new, optimistic spirit; they find a new, beautiful world in music and integrate themselves into it. Through their singing, they taste the width and depth of life, and seek out another pillar of the soul. Beijing Television has reported on the

FIGURE 6.4. A Choir has its regular rehearsal at Temple of Heaven Park in Beijing on Saturday morning. Photographed by Zhang Hong on 3th August 2013.

chorus, noting that cure rates and life expectancies among its members are higher than the average.

Discussion

Currently, musical activities and events organized by the public are ubiquitous in Chinese cities. In parks and on the streets, groups of elderly people get together to sing, dance, and perform local operas. Such activities represent not only a valuable form of recreation but also an effective method of exercise, as well as reflecting the reality of life for Chinese seniors and their attitude toward that life (see Figure 6.5). Chinese people are generally reserved, and are seldom willing to sing, even in front of their families. In public gatherings such as these, however, singing is considered natural, and most people in the neighborhood are happy for them to take place. These activities are a beautiful illustration of the urban lives of many Chinese seniors.

Music is inextricably caught up with life, and ethnomusicology has a profound understanding of this relationship. Due to its artistic values, Western classical music is usually performed in concert halls, which makes going to a concert a spiritual benefit as well as a high art that is out of reach for the ordinary masses. The musical activities in Chinese parks and streets, however, are part of people's daily lives. It is fair to say that it is generally the socially privileged who go to concerts, with the ordinary masses more likely to

FIGURE 6.5. A Choir has its regular rehearsal at Zizhuyuan Park in Beijing on Sunday morning. Photographed by Zhang Hong on 4th August 2013.

participate in musical activities. However, in the fight against illness, everyone becomes equal, turning as one to music to combat their diseases. This is one of the reasons we see so many music activities in non-musical settings.

From the Individual Perspective

Background

Graduates of the Central Conservatory of Music's Musicology Department generally find jobs at music schools, concert halls, and television or radio stations. Due to the lack of a systematic approach in the courses offered, they often find it difficult to apply what they have learned to their jobs. That said, those who go on to teach in colleges find the program extremely useful, as they can simply review the material they studied and then start to teach. Could our graduates be better adapted to different jobs through the restructuring of the current academic program?

In 1999, the Central Conservatory of Music's Musicology Department initiated reforms to improve the courses and majors offered. At first, they intended to add a major in applied ethnomusicology to the course list, but later renamed it the "Major in Music Communication, Experimental Class." In later course restructures, "Music Communication" became "Music Management," a brand new major to parallel the Musicology major. Nevertheless, the Musicology Department still encourages involvement in applied musicology/ethnomusicology through the following activities: the holding of "World Music Days," encouraging students to participate in the organization of academic conferences; creating opportunities for students to take part in proofreading for the Central Conservatory of Music Press; English translations (English–Chinese/ Chinese–English); publishing CDs to showcase the folk music recorded in fieldwork; and establishing a musical instrument exhibition center.

Through activities such as these, the Musicology Department faculty and students have not only contributed to the construction and development of the Musicology Department and its courses, but also gained precious opportunities to learn, to further explore the significance of applied ethnomusicology, and to better understand what applied ethnomusicology is. Applied ethnomusicology not only includes specific practices and procedures, but also theoretical questions worthy of consideration, including reflections on the organization of the aforementioned academic activities. In the following passages, I will provide three examples, which illustrate the above: (1) the globalization of folk festivals manifested in the organization of "World Music Days"; (2) cultural continuity within translations of Chinese musical terminology in English-language editions; and (3) the migration and display of culture during the establishment of the Musical Instrument Exhibition Centre.

World Music Days: The Created Stage Reality and the Social Position of Traditional Music

In 2004, Professor Akin Euba from the University of Pittsburgh was invited to give a series of lectures at the Central Conservatory of Music. During our conversation, he expressed the desire to hold a small-scale seminar on African music, an idea that appealed to us and was supported by the head of the school. Later, the Central Conservatory of Music decided to make the seminar a conference that integrated academic discussions, musical performances, lectures, and musical workshops. We also invited scholars from China, the United States, and Africa to attend. During the conference, folk musicians from Hebei province, Yunnan province, and the United States gave special concerts, and a number of African-American musicians presented workshops on African drum music and African dancing for the students. Outside these activities, the dialogue and exchange between musicians from home and abroad were inspiring. The entire event was a success. In November 2006, while I was attending the Society for Ethnomusicology (SEM) Conference in Atlanta, I had the opportunity to have lunch with Professor Akin Euba, Dr. Kimasi Brown, and Dr. Kimberlin Cynthia. They had all attended the Sino-African conference held by the Central Conservatory of Music, and spoke highly of the experience. We all found the idea of holding a second Sino-Africa conference on music extremely exciting.

After two years of preparation, and with a great deal of support and guidance from school leaders, the second Sino-African Music Dialogue was held as planned. It was during this conference, composed of seminars, musical performances, lectures, and musical workshops, that the concept of "World Music Days" was first proposed. The workshops were held a week prior to the conference proper, with scholars from abroad arriving in Beijing in advance to give workshops on African music and dancing to Musicology Department students—who, for the first time since the founding of the department, held their own special concerts and performances (see Figure 6.6). With the second session of the Sino-African Music Dialogue complete, we realized that such activities would not only promote academic exchange and communication, but also provide valuable opportunities to learn from music in other parts of the world. Up until this point, there had been a lack of world music content in activities held by the conservatory, and the Sino-African Music Dialogue represented an effective supplement to the conservatory's current teaching and academic systems. We decided to continue with these activities, going on to hold World Music Days 2008: China-Finland Festival and Symposium Dialogue in Music, World Music Days 2009: China–New Zealand and Pacific Festival and Symposium Dialogue in Music, World Music Days 2010: China-India Festival and Symposium Dialogue in Music, World Music Days 2011: China-Japan Festival and Symposium Dialogue in Music, and World Music Days 2012: China–Indonesia Festival and Symposium Dialogue in Music. The name "Festival and Symposium Dialogue in Music" indicates that the conferences featured musical festivals as well as academic discussion and research.

FIGURE 6.6. Musicology Department students at the Central Conservatory of Music giving their first public performance ever at the Recital Hall of the Conservatory during the World Music Days 2010. Photographed by Zhao Liang in November 2010.

Discussion

Cultural diversity is not a new phenomenon; exchanges between different regions and cultures have been taking place since the early stages of human history. No culture can exist in isolation, and it is only by selecting, absorbing, and integrating elements from external sources that a culture can gain momentum for sustained development. As the Western world began to lead the process of industrialization and modernization, Western culture also ascended to a position of supreme global power. In this era of "superculture," exchanges between Western and non-Western cultures more closely resemble a one-way transfer of Western culture to non-Western areas. Many regional cultures confront a common dilemma: whether to cling to the traditional and reject modernization, or to embrace modernization and abandon tradition. During the same period, exchanges between regional cultures have diminished, swallowed up by the vast shadow of globalization. Today's world, however, is working hard to move out of this shadow. It is a world in which different cultures can and do coexist, and in which comprehensive exchanges between different regions are increasingly frequent. Today, the capacity to manage cross-cultural communication is an extremely significant asset (see Figure 6.7).

World Music Days, an initiative that promotes equal dialogue between cultures of different regions, is an active contribution to the world's multicultural development. Studying world music is one of the best ways to understand and appreciate the cultures of other countries and regions, and the current system for teaching world music represents an effective integration of academic research and practice. Through

FIGURE 6.7. Foreign professors and musicians visited Quantou village at the *Baiyangdian* lake region Hebei province and played the folk music with the folk musicians during the World Music Days in 2007. This was the first time for the villages to see foreigners in their village. Photographed by Rong Yingtao in October 2007.

a combination of seminars, lectures, workshops, and performances, the "World Music Days" project advances the development of course syllabuses, theoretical musicology, and ethnomusicology, as well as the attendees' personal experience and understanding of world music.

In practice, however, there are still some questions worthy of further consideration: notably, the relationship between "reality on the stage" and "reality in real life." The American ethnomusicologist Jeff Titon has noted that if intangible cultural heritages are placed on stage, this new context can have unintended negative consequences, one of which is that staged authenticity for tourists is self-defeating, for such a scripted performance can never be authentic (Titon, 2010). In the workshops organized for World Music Days, professors and students from the Musicology Department danced African dances, participated in the Samoa chorus, and enjoyed Cook Islands percussion music. The music and dances featured in these workshops were all altered to make the task of teaching them to foreigners easier, and although all the pieces chosen were authentic, they were also very carefully selected. Nettl once criticized the American method of instrumental teaching, pointing out that expecting students to understand the musical connotations of other cultures within a semester or two may cause them to come to incorrect conclusions (Nettl, 1983: 264). Some universities in the United States offer courses on Chinese instrumental ensembles, generally teaching simplified pieces such as *Xiyangyang* (Happiness) and *Bubugao* (Stepping High). The students lack basic training on the instruments, and could easily develop misunderstandings about Chinese instrumental ensembles during group performance. During World Music Days, students from the Musicology Department experience the beauty of multiculturalism and a sense of fulfillment by participating in the creation of cultural diversity. However, it is important to note that while this has helped us to nurture positive attitudes toward cultural diversity in our students, it does not necessarily enhance the students' capacity to understand a diversified culture, since these activities are out of our regular syllabus and the music itself is out of their social contexts.

The World Music Days project also invited several performance groups from other regions in China, and those folk musicians brought their local music to the Central Conservatory of Music, China's "musical shrine." Although they were excited to perform at the conservatory, they also found it difficult to adapt—partly for psychological reasons, and partly due to the change in performance space. Not only did this change influence the acoustics, it also gave rise to cultural contradictions. A local opera group from Shanxi province was once invited to give a concert during the festival. The performers employed a special kind of male singing, one that is very loud and husky. The sound was so ear-splitting that one-third of the audience left the concert hall; as it turned out, the sound system had not been properly adjusted. Musicians performing in different regions may also encounter cultural barriers. Performing folk music in its original setting is obviously different from performing it in a conservatory. Should the music be adjusted to fit to the space? Folk music festivals tend to showcase music from different cultures on the same stage without any attempt to reflect their different backgrounds. This is a new, self-inflicted kind of globalization, one in which it is impossible to ensure the authenticity of either music or context.

Music festivals are one of the ways in which applied ethnomusicology has contributed to the promotion of musical exchange and communication among different nations. At the same time, juxtaposing voices from different cultural systems can have unexpected results. The definition of "world music" (at least, in the Chinese sense) is the display of music from different cultures within a global context. But is it still world music? The World Music Days held at the Central Conservatory of Music were a showcase for different music cultures throughout the world, which is itself a kind of globalization, albeit in the name of "cultural diversity." Meanwhile, according to Li Xuanying's observations of the Nanning Folk Music Festival, "the success of folk music festivals contributes to a strengthening of national spirit and a sense of national identity, as well as playing an active role in enhancing national cohesion" (Li Xuanying, 2009: 294–295). She also notes that "traditional folk music, especially original-style singing, has not had a regular presence in recent festivals, reflecting the fact that there is a lack of confidence in traditional music; folk music is a combination of a number of different arts, and folk music festivals could lose their original spiritual aims and aesthetic purposes if they overemphasize modern and popular music just to satisfy the tastes of the masses" (2009: 296).

English Translations of Chinese Music Records: Transmissions of Knowledge, Culture, and Thought

Chinese scholars have spent decades in the study of music, accumulating rich experiences in the field. However, we still lack confidence when presenting our research findings at international academic conferences, due to our lack of foreign language abilities. Currently it is Sinologists, rather than Chinese scholars and professionals, who are the spokespeople for research in Chinese music. Many Chinese scholars do not agree with all of their research findings, but they are not able to present their own arguments due to language difficulties. Beginning in 2010, and supported by a "211" sponsorship, I initiated the translation and publication of several collected works on musicology, including *Discourse in Music: Collected Essays of the Central Conservatory of Music Musicology Department* (Zhang Boyu, 2010a), *Contemplations of Music: A Collection of Articles by Yu Runyang* (Yu Runyang, 2012), *Africa Meets Asia: Proceedings of the 2005 and 2007 International Symposia on African and Chinese Music* (Zhang Boyu, 2011), *Traditional Chinese Music in a Changing Contemporary Society: A Field Report and Music Collection of the Quantou Village Music Association, Baiyangdian Lake Region, Hebei Province* (Zhang Boyu, 2013), and an *English Translation of 900 Chinese Music Terms* (Zhang Boyu, 2010b).

The Central Conservatory of Music, China Conservatory of Music, and Shanghai Conservatory of Music, among others, are currently undertaking translation work for the publication of English versions of various Chinese books and periodicals on music. It is believed that such undertakings will only increase in the future.

Discussion

It is a common misconception that translation is all about language. In one sense, this is correct, but translation practices have proved that the most difficult part of translation is not language, but culture (Xu Yuanyong, 2006; Zhang Boyu, 2003).

First, there is the translation of specialized vocabularies. According to Merriam, the creation of music begins with concepts—that is, with the external expression of human thought. These concepts reflect the different ways in which different people think. The same holds true for music: Chinese music, for example, reflects the way Chinese people think about the creation of music. Some concepts are similar in Chinese and English, which reflects a common ground between the two peoples and makes translation much easier. This includes concepts such as *Yueqi* (musical instrument) and *Yinjie* (scale). Most of the time, however, there is no equivalent for a given Chinese musical term, whether it be a theoretical term such as *Qupai*, *Gongdiao*, or *Banyan*; an instrument name such as *pipa* or *erhu*, an operatic genre such as *Jingju*, *Chuanju*, or *Ganju*, a form of instrumental ensemble such as *Jiangnan Sizhu* or *Guangdong Yinyue*, or a type of folksong such as *Xintianyou*, *Shanqu*, and so on.[19] Each of these words has rich connotations, which translation cannot adequately reflect. But if we attempt to express those connotations, then we are not translating but merely explaining.

The second thing to consider is the historical and cultural backgrounds of such words. The study of music has been taking place in China for thousands of years, and there is a historical background to many of these musical terms. The term *zhudi*, for example, can be translated as "bamboo flute." However, the same translation also perfectly describes *xiao*, another traditional Chinese musical instrument quite different from a *zhudi*. A *xiao* requires the player to blow vertically, while a *zhudi* is blown horizontally. Because of this, *zhudi* was eventually translated as "transverse bamboo flute," while *xiao* was translated as "vertical bamboo flute." Not only do these translations indicate how the instruments are played, they also respect the long academic history of Chinese music: historically, the *zhudi* was also known as a *hengchui*—"transverse blowing"—while the *xiao* was called *Shuchui*, or "vertically blowing." The *pipa* is another example. A frequently used translation for *pipa* is "a pear-shaped lute with four-stringed and a bent neck." Here, several different elements are combined to describe the instrument in English: "pear-shaped," "lute," "four strings," and "bent neck." But how do we decide which of these to include when creating a shorter translation? In ancient times, two different types of *pipa* were popular in China: the *quxiang* (bent neck) and the *wuxian* (five strings). The terms "bent neck" and "five strings" are therefore essential in differentiating the two instruments. It is important to note that the phrase "pear-shaped" was never historically used, and that the commonly used translation "pear-shaped lute" is incompatible with historical practices. From this, it is clear that the process of translation is a process of comprehension and understanding. A good translation cannot exist without a profound understanding of the relevant culture and history.

Aesthetics are a particular difficulty in translation. For example, the titles of certain famous music compositions and books are inseparable from ancient Chinese aesthetic awareness. *Chun Jiang Hua Yue Ye*, a popular instrumental piece, can be translated literally as "Spring, River, Flower, Moon and Night." However, this title conveys not only a beautiful image but also the cadences of the tones; the Chinese characters are combined as *Chunjiang Huayueye*. The translation "Spring River and Flowery Moon Night," therefore, better respects the rhythm and 2 + 3 structure of the original Chinese title. Generally speaking, it is possible to translate basic connotations from one language to another, but it is impossible to maintain the original rhymes and rhythms.

Musical Instrument Exhibition Centre: A Decorative Art?

In 2009, the Central Conservatory launched the third phase of the "211" project, establishing the Musical Instrument Exhibition Centre. This project was expected to be completed in 2010.

At present, the Musical Instrument Exhibition Centre is located on the first floor of the conservatory's new teaching building, with an area of 150 square meters (see Figures 6.8 and 6.9). Three groups of instruments have been collected thus far for display. The first group consists replicas of ancient musical instruments, such as the *Ling* bell from Xiangfen, Shanxi province, and the *Ling* bell from Yanshi, Henan province, the originals of which are the oldest metal musical instruments to be found from the Shang period; a *Nao* set composed of three pieces, the originals of which were unearthed from No. 699 tomb at Yinxu, Anyang, in Henan province; *Bozhong*, a replica of one of the 65 bells from the "Chime-Bells of the Tomb of Marquis of Zeng"; *Duo*, a replica of one of the oldest bells made during the Spring and Autumn period; *Goudiao*, a replica of one of eight bells made during the Han dynasty for the King of Yue State; *Zheng*, a replica of the original gong unearthed from Zigui county, Hubei province in 1985; *Tonghuan Shouzheng*, a *Zheng* with a ring on the top, the original of which was unearthed from Hongshan Qiuchengdun in Wuxi, Jiangxu province, in 2004; *Zenghouyi Bianzhong*, replicas of 24 of the 65 bells from the "Chime-Bells of the Tomb of Marquis of Zeng"; *Zenghouyi Bianqing*, a replica of the "Stone-Chime of the Tomb of Marquis of Zeng"; *Xuangu*, a suspended drum, the original of which was unearthed from Hongshan Qiuchengdun in Wuxi, Jiangxu province, in 2004; *Luozhuang Bianzhong*, a replica of a set of 19 chime-bells unearthed from Luozhuang in Shandong province; *Erxing Zhong*, replicas of four bells made during the Western Zhou dynasty and unearthed from pit No. 1 at Fufeng

FIGURE 6.8. The Chinese music instruments exhibition room at the Central Conservatory of Music. Photographed by Wang Xianyan in May 2010.

FIGURE 6.9. A set of copied bells exhibited at the Chinese music instruments exhibition room the Central Conservatory of Music. Photographed by Wang Xianyan in May 2010.

in Shaanxi province; a large *Nao* with elephant ornamentations, the original of which was unearthed from Shiguzhai village, Ningxiang county, Hunan province in 1959; *Chunyu*, a replica of a metal jar used as a military instrument, the original of which was unearthed from Qianyuping village, Changyang county, Hubei province in 1964; *Tonggu*, a metal drum, the original of which was unearthed from Wanjiaba, Chuxiong city, Yunnan province, in 1975; and *Yangjiao Zhong*, a goat horn bell, the original of which was unearthed from Chuxiong, Yunnan province, in 1975.

The second group includes instruments collected from different areas in China, including Tibetan musical instruments, folk music instruments from the Xinjiang Autonomous Region, instruments from the Wa and Naxi ethnic groups in Yunnan province and of the Dong ethnic group in Guangxi province, and so on. There are also some Han musical instruments—some old, some newly made or polished—which were collected from Fujian, Chaozhou, Hebei, Shandong, Henan, Jiangsu, Tianjin, Beijing, and Heilongjiang. The last group consists of frequently used musical instruments of the Han majority such as the *erhu, pipa, guzheng* and *guqin*, and so on. The collection contains more than 250 items in total.

Discussion: Purpose of Construction

Establishing a musical instrument museum has been a dream for generations of Chinese music scholars. Professors from the Music Research Institute of the China Arts Academy worked for years to establish a new era of Chinese musical instrument collection (Zhang Zhentao, 2009). Research funds for Chinese universities are increasing year by year, which has provided scholars with the financial support required to realize the dream of building such museums. After the project was launched, more and more universities began to participate, investing varying levels of funds. China is a vast country, and it should not be considered unusual for such a country to have several musical instrument museums. After all, there are museums in each of the provinces as well as on the national level. The question is, should musical instruments be viewed as cultural relics? Of course, ancient instruments that have been excavated are cultural relics; however, these are already preserved in provincial museums. The Musical Instrument Exhibition Centre is closer to an exhibition of music cultures, or perhaps a small-scale display of cultural ornaments. In this sense, the items we choose to display can be viewed as cultural relics (as in other museums), cultural representatives (as in large-scale displays of musical instruments), and ornaments (as in small-scale displays). However, the significance of each of these three aspects is different. As cultural relics, the items on display represent the remains of history, glimpses into the workings of time; as cultural representatives, these items are tokens of another culture, offering insights into the lives of the people who played them; as decorations, we can observe the connection and interaction between the items and their environments. Each instrument is displayed in a precise order, according to how it is viewed. For example, cultural relics cannot be touched, whereas cultural representatives should be experienced by the visitors in person, and decorations should not upstage the other elements. It is only with thorough and in-depth consideration of these factors that the exhibition space can be rendered meaningful and rewarding.

Cultural Migration

Ethnomusicologists believe that it is their responsibility to protect the musical heritages of human beings. Under the flag of cultural relativism, they uphold the value of music in the past, the present, and the future. They emphasize the relationship between music and its environment, arguing that music cannot be studied alone but must be considered together with its home environment. A musical instrument museum, however, extracts its subject—the instrument—from its musical system, and places it in a new, relatively isolated environment, so as to determine targets and channels for cultural appreciation and comprehension, both by people inside and outside the original musical system. The building of such museums is a purely material affair, one that is separated from other factors such as sound, performance, and culture, and that leads to the removal of musical instruments from the cultural regions they originally belonged to. A pertinent example is the transportation of musical instruments from all around the country to the Exhibition Centre at the Central Conservatory of Music. There is a wooden drum from the Wa ethnic group in the conservatory's collection, which was purchased in Ximeng County, Yunnan province. With the assistance of the County's Culture Bureau and Culture Institute, we had selected a drum that was perfectly made, with almost no flaws. During the ceremony for moving the drum from Ximeng to Beijing, I said to it, "You are about to leave home, and you might feel lonely." The director of the Culture Institute added, "You are going to live a better life in Beijing." Unfortunately, due to the long journey and the change of climate, there are now some cracks on the drum. Not only does this represent the physical sacrifice of cultural migration, but it is also a shock to the original culture and spirits—for the Wa people do believe that these wooden drums have spirits.

Beneficiaries of Construction

Museums are an essential part of cultural development, with social responsibilities and the obligation to open to the public after construction is completed. The exhibition of musical instruments at the Metropolitan Museum of Art in New York functions as a collection as well as a public display. The Musical Instruments Museum in Stockholm focuses on exhibition and public education, allowing visitors to enjoy the subtle beauty of music while experiencing the wonders of technology. The Sibelius Museum in Turku, Finland, is part of the Abo Academi University's Musicology Department and, though small, reflects the academic structure of the department. All of the above museums are open to the public, and all have become destinations for local visitors. The Exhibition Centre at the Central Conservatory of Music is located inside the teaching building. The question must be asked: Who can visit this room? If the visitors are the Conservatory's own students, how can we update the collection to provide them with new information? The musical instrument display room in the China Arts Research Institute originates from the 1950s, and has relocated from a fourth-floor space in Xinyuanli to a new building in Xiaoying. The display room holds hundreds of instruments, including dozens of priceless *guqin*, and has been home to several Chinese and foreign traveling exhibitions (Zhang Zhentao, 2009). However, it must be acknowledged that there is still no musical instrument museum in any real sense at the present time in China.

Theoretical Bases

Museums are places of specialization, not only in the field of musicology, but also in any and all fields related to the items they have on display. Exhibitions of musical instruments, therefore, have much to do with the study of musical instruments, organology, and musicology. The classification, manufacture, use, and proscription of such musical instruments are all connected fields, as are fields related to the music, people, customs, and aesthetics behind the instruments on display. So what is the theoretical basis for the construction of these exhibitions? Zhang Zhentao believes that "we should not view the collection of musical instruments as a historical activity, but rather one that reflects both the national consciousness and the spirit of an era; the musical and historical significance of constructing musical instrument exhibitions gives rise to even more academic topics for further discussion" (Zhang Zhentao, 2009). Unfortunately, the collection of instruments that began with Li Yuanqing and Yang Yinliu, both former directors of the Music Research Institute, has not yet given rise to any such topics.

Conclusion

Applied ethnomusicology is steadily attracting more and more attention, as it combines academic research with real life practices and thus directly serves society. A conference convened by the International Community of Traditional Music (ICTM) in Hanoi, 2010, was themed "applied ethnomusicology"; a conference convened by SEM in Los Angeles, 2010, also took applied ethnomusicology as one of its themes. Topics covered at this conference included music migrations and disasters; music, copyright, and human rights; music and social activism; and film soundtracks (see http://www.ethnomusicol-ogy.org/?Groups_SectionsAE). As ethnomusicologists, we hope that our work can be of practical use to society, as well as providing perspectives for understanding music as a social phenomenon. Applied ethnomusicology is an ideal way for us to add practical value to the academic value of ethnomusicological study.

Social practice and theoretical reflection are two sides of the same coin, and any new practice must be tested through theoretical analysis. This is how social practice and social criticism can exist as opposing dimensions in a balanced relationship. There are two aspects of applied ethnomusicology in China: social activities of an academic nature performed by ethnomusicologists, and social practices that are supported and sponsored by the government. In this case, applied ethnomusicology is not only a social construction but the reflection of a social mechanism that balances the increase of economic benefits with the building of a harmonious society. The difference between the nature of applied ethnomusicology and that of theoretic ethnomusicology is clearly manifest in both of these aspects. Applied ethnomusicology concerns itself not only with individual choices but with group choices, and it has a positive impact on culture and on society. Applied ethnomusicology also explores how traditional music can be of value in today's society, both as a "living heritage" and as evidence for its own protection, demonstrating that such traditions are still of great value to the modern world. It is worth mentioning that reflections on current practices tend to focus on their problems, as well as providing a theoretical basis for their improvement. Applied ethnomusicology, therefore, should not be separated from theoretical ethnomusicology, for the latter has the potential to provide value judgments for applied ethnomusicology both from critical and practical perspectives.

Glossary

Akesu	阿克苏
Baiyangdian	白洋淀
banhu	板胡
Banyan	板眼

Bejing Jinrongjie Banshichu	北京金融街办事处
Bozhong	镈钟
Bubugao	步步高
Cao Jun	曹军
Changdiao	长调
Chuanju	川剧
Chun Jiang Hua Yue Ye	春江花月夜
Chunyu	大錞于
Chuxiong, Yunnan province	云南楚雄
Dage	大歌
Daolang Muqam	刀朗木卡姆
Dayan Guyue She	大研古乐社
Dianbo Shijian	点播时间
Difangxi Zhichuang	地方戏之窗
dizi	笛子
Dong ethnic group	侗族
Dongba Palace	东巴宫
Dongjing	洞经
Dongzu Dage	侗族大歌
Duo	铎
erhu	二胡
Erxing Zhong	二兴钟
Fenghua Guoyue	风华国乐
Fufeng in Shaanxi province	陕西扶风
Ganju	赣剧
Gaoya Yishu Jin Xiaoyuan	高雅艺术进校园
Genwo Xue	跟我学
Gongdiao	宫调
Goudiao	勾鑃
Guangdong Yinyue	广东音乐
Guoba Yin	过把瘾
Guqin (*guqin*)	古琴
guzheng	古筝
Haicai Qiang	海菜腔
Hami Muqam	哈密木卡姆
Han *pipa*	汉族琵琶
Hengchui	横吹
Hetian	和田
Hongshan Qiuchengdun in Wuxi	无锡鸿山丘承墩
Humai	呼麦
Jiangnan Sizhu	江南丝竹
Jiaqu Youyue	佳曲有约
Jingju	京剧
Jiuzhou Daxitai	九洲大戏台
Kongzhong Juyuan	空中剧院
Kuche	库车
Kunqu	昆曲

Li Jilian	李季莲
Li Kairong	李开荣
Li Sue	李素娥
Li Xuanying	李宣颖
Lijiang	丽江
Ling	铃
Lingting Tianlai	聆听天籁
Liyuan Leitai	梨园擂台
Luozhuang Bianzhong	洛庄编钟
Luozhuang in Shandong province	山东洛庄
Lü Lulu	吕路路
Mingduan Xinshang	名段欣赏
Moyu	墨玉
Nanqiang Beidiao	南腔北调
Nao	大铙
Nao set	编铙
Naxi	纳西
pipa	琵琶
Pishan	皮山
Qianyuping village, Changyang county, Hubei province	湖北长阳千渔坪
Quantou Village Music Association	圈头村"音乐会"
Qupai	曲牌
quxiang	曲项
Shanqu	山曲
sheng	笙
Shiguzhai village, Ningxiang county, Hunan province	湖南宁乡师古寨
Shuchui	竖吹
Su Qianzhong	苏前忠
suogudu	索古都
suona	唢呐
Tashikurgan	塔什库尔干
Tiantan Shanting Teshu Hechangdui	天坛扇亭特殊合唱队
Tonggu	铜鼓
Tonghuan Shouzheng	铜环首钲
Turfan Muqam	吐鲁番木卡姆
Twelve Muqam	十二木卡姆
Wa ethnic group	佤族
Wanjiaba, Chuxiong city, Yunnan province	云南楚雄万家坝
Women Youyue	我们有约
Wu Xiulin	吴修林
Wu Xueyuan	吴学源
wuxian	五弦
Xiangfen, Shanxi province	山西襄汾
xiao	箫
Xiaoying	小营
Ximeng County	西蒙县
Xintianyou	信天游

Xinyuanli	新源里
Xiqu Fengcai	戏曲风采
Xiyangyang	喜洋洋
Xiyuan Baijia	戏苑百家
Xu Shuyun	徐淑云
Xuangu	悬鼓
Yang Xifan	杨曦帆
yangqin	扬琴
Yangjiao Zhong	羊角钟
Yanshi, Henan province	河南偃师
Yigu Zuoqi, Mingjin Shoubing	一鼓作气, 鸣金收兵
Yinjie	音阶
Yinxu, Anyang in Henan province	河南安阳殷虚
Yizu Haicaiqiang	彝族海菜腔
Yu Renhao	俞人豪
Yu Runyang	于润洋
Yuan Jingfang	袁静芳
Yuansheng Tai	原生态
Yueqi	乐器
Zhang Boyu	张伯瑜
Zhang Xia	张霞
Zhang Xiaoyan	张晓艳
Zhang Zhentao	张振涛
Zheng	钲筝
Zhou Heping	周和平
Zhou Ji	周吉
Zhou Xianbao	周显宝
zhudi	竹笛
Zenghouyi Bianqing	曾侯乙墓编磬
Zenghouyi Bianzhong	曾侯乙墓编钟
Zigui county, Hubei province	湖北秭归

Notes

1. I am grateful to Sarah Stanton for her extensive editorial work on this chapter.
2. CNKI, China National Knowledge Infrastructure net.
3. According to the map of PRC, Taiwan is included as one of the 23 provinces.
4. *Gaoya Yishu Jin Xiaoyuan.*
5. *Bejing Jinrongjie Banshichu.*
6. As of 2013, there have been three evaluations of intangible cultural heritage on the national level in China. The first evaluation was published on May 20, 2006, with a total of 518 items being approved. The second evaluation was published on June 14, 2008, with a total of 510 items being approved. The third evaluation was published on June 10, 2011; 191 items were approved on this occasion, with 164 other items being placed on an expanded list of items from the second evaluation. According to Chinese selection criteria, a national-level

288   AGENCIES

   own evaluation before submitting a project for national-level protection.
7. The above data are available on the Ministry of Culture's Intangible Cultural Heritage Department website (http://www.ccnt.gov.cn/sjzznew2011/fwzwhycs/), as well as the Chinese Intangible Cultural Heritage website (http://www.ihchina.cn/). See also Wang Wenzhang's book *On the Research of Intangible Cultural Heritage Protection* (in Chinese) (Beijing: Culture and Arts Publishing House, 2013: 427, 437).
8. For a related report, see Zhu Yi's "Impressions of China's First Intangible Cultural Heritage Exhibition," *Newspaper of People's Political Consultative Committee (Renmin Zhengxie Bao)*. February 15, 2006. Also available at http://news.sina.com.cn/c/2006-02-15/09269105836.shtml.
9. Related reports, including videos, can be found on a large number of different Chinese websites.
10. See "Series of Activities from the 'Chinese Intangible Cultural Heritage Tradition Skills Exhibition,'" http://wenku.baidu.com/view/2e9edfaad1f34693daef3e75.html (accessed 29 July 29, 2013). This article can also be found in *Chaozhou Daily*, February 19, 2009, under the title "To make Traditional Skills Embrace Modern Life."
11. See "'Achievements in the Production and Protection of Chinese Intangible Cultural Heritage' Exhibition Opens in Beijing," http://www.gov.cn/jrzg/2012-02/05/con-tent_2058920.htm (accessed July 29, 2013).
12. Two of these activities were personally attended by the author.
13. See "The Inaugural China (Huangshan) Intangible Cultural Heritage Traditional Skills Exhibition Opened on the 7th," http://native.cnr.cn/city/201211/t20121106_511314960.html (accessed July 29, 2013).
14. See http://www.ccnt.gov.cn/sjzznew2011/fwzwhycs/ (accessed July 29, 2013).
15. There are two essential terms that need to be explained here. The Key Research Base for Humanities and Social Sciences was a plan executed by the education administration in 1999. It aimed to set up 151 key research bases for the humanities and social sciences in 66 universities. The Musicology Research Institute at the Central Conservatory of Music is currently the only research base for the arts. The "211 Project," on the other hand, was a strategic project proposed in the early 1990s. Looking toward the twenty-first century, it aimed to build around 100 high-level education universities, which was the largest key construction project in the field of high-level education since the founding of New China. The Central Conservatory of Music is the only art school listed in the "211 project." Chinese government defines a term as three years, and provided three terms' worth of capital for the Central Conservatory of Music's education facilities, teacher training, and research.
16. *Yuansheng Tai*.
17. See *Xiaojing (The Classic of Filial Piety)*, chapter 12, "Broad and Crucial Doctrine": *Yifeng Yisu, Moshan Yuyue*, English translation as "for changing the customs and traditions there is nothing better than music." For English version of *Xiaojing*, see website: http://www.tsoidug.org/Xiao/Xiao_Jing_Comment.pdf. For Confucius's music thought, see also *Lunyu (Confucian Analects)*, Book III. *Payi*, chapters 1, 20, and 25; Book VII. *Shuer*, chapter 13, translated by James Legge (Oxford: Clarendon Press, 1893, reprinted by Cosimo in 2006).
18. *Yigu Zuoqi, Mingjin Shoubing*.
19. *Qupai* (labeled tunes); *Gongdiao* (pitch and mode); *Banyan* (beat and eyes, or "metre"); *pipa* (four-stringed lute); *erhu* (two-stringed fiddle); *Jingju* (Beijing opera); *Chuanju* (Sichuan opera); *Ganju* (Gan opera, a local opera Jiangxi province); *Jiangnan Sizhu*

(silk-and-bamboo, a local ensemble popular in Southern Jiangsu province); *Guangdong Yinyue* (an instrumental ensemble in Guangdong); *Xintiannyou* (floating on sky, a type of folksong popular in West Shaanxi province); *Shanqu* (mountain songs, a type of folksong popular in Shanxi province).

REFERENCES

Cao, Jun. (2012). "On Ethnomusicology's Role in Chinese Music Education: Applied Ethnomusicology, Current Music Education and the Course Syllabus in China." (In Chinese.) *Chinese Music* 4: 185–194.

China Federation of Literary and Art Circles. (2013). *Chinese Arts Development Report 2012*. (In Chinese.) Beijing: Chinese Literature and Arts Association Press.

Kuaner (2011). "Continuous Promotion of Protection for Chinese Intangible Cultural Heritage." (In Chinese.) Accessed via the Ministry of Culture of PRC's website. http://www.ccnt.gov.cn/sjzznew2011/fwzwhycs/.

Li, Jilian, Zhou Ji, and Li Kairong. (2005). "An Interview on the Working Process of the Application for the Uygur Muqam to Be Selected as a Masterpiece of World Intangible Cultural Heritage." (In Chinese.) *The Journal of the Arts College of Xinjiang Autonomous Region* 2: 1–6.

Li, Sue. (2006). "Moving and Settling: A Discussion on the Modern National-Style Singing and Original-Style Singing." (In Chinese.) *Chinese Music* 2: 100–105.

Li, Xuanying. (2009). "Cultural Identity Crisis Exhibited in Nanning International Folk Songs Festival." (In Chinese.) *Marxism Aesthetics Research* 1: 292–307.

Lü Lulu. (2012). "Applied Ethnomusicology and Local Music Education." (In Chinese.) *Northern Music* 12: 142–143.

Nettl, Bruno. (1983). *The Study of Ethnomusicology: Twenty-nine Issues and Concepts*. Urbana and Chicago: University of Illinois Press, pp. 259–269.

Titon, Jeff. (2010). "Music and Its Sustainability." (In Chinese), translated by Zhang Boyu and Wang Xianyan. *The Journal of the Central Conservatory of Music* 3: 107–114.

Wang, Wenzhang. (2013). *Intangible Cultural Heritage Protection Research*. (In Chinese.) Beijing: Culture and Arts Publishing House.

Wu, Xiulin, and Zhang Xia. (2010). "Inheriting or Developing? Thinking on Original-Style Singing in the Television Grand Prix for Young Singers." (In Chinese.) *Arts Contentions* 8: 60–61.

Wu, Xueyuan. (2003). "What Kind of a Thing Is Naxi Traditional Music?" (In Chinese.) *Arts Criticism* 1,: 21–26.

Xu, Shuyun. (2003). "Gathering Wheat in the Field: Reflecting on the Television Grand Prix for Young Singers." *People's Music* 1: 46–47.

Xu, Yuanyong. (2006). "Discussion on the Translation of Chinese Music Terms into a Foreign Language." *Music Research* 4: 39–43.

Yang, Xifan. (2008). "Chinese Minorities' Music in View of the Protection of Intangible Cultural Heritage: The View and Methodology of Applied Ethnomusicology." In *Proceedings of the International Symposium on Musical Intangible Cultural Heritage Protections*, pp. 123–130.

Yao, Hui. (2012). "Construction of the Protection System at Local Levels for the Intangible Cultural Heritage: Taking Inner Mongolia as an Example." Conference paper presented at the International Symposium on the Anthropology of Chinese Arts.

Yu, Renhao. (2006). "Original Ecological Music and the Original Ecology of Music." (In Chinese.) *People's Music* 9: 20–21.

Yu, Runyang. (2012). *Contemplations of Music: A Collection of Articles by Yu Runyang.* Beijing: Central Conservatory of Music Press.

Yuan, Jingfang. (2009). "Integrating Chinese Ancient Music Culture and Modern Technology: The Meaning and Value of Establishing the Database of Chinese Guqin Music Culture." (In Chinese.) *Journal of the Conservatory of Music* 4: 31–36.

Zhang, Boyu. (2003). "Translation: Problems and Solutions When Translating Chinese Musical Terms into English." (In Chinese.) *Chinese Musicology* 3: 19–22.

Zhang, Boyu. (2010a). "On the Loss of Traditional Musical Thinking in the Current Development of Chinese Instrumental Music." (In English.) In *Discourse in Music.* Beijing: Central Conservatory of Music Press, pp. 146–152.

Zhang, Boyu. (2010b). *English Translation of 900 Chinese Musical Terms.* Beijing: People's Music Publishing House.

Zhang, Boyu, ed. (2011). *Africa Meets Asia: Proceedings of the 2005 and 2007 International Symposia on African and Chinese Music.* California: MRI Press.

Zhang, Boyu. (2012). "Who Is Audience? Local Religious Music Popular in Yunnan." (In English.) *Asian Musicology*, Vol. 19, edited by Chun In Pyong, pp. 97–115.

Zhang, Boyu. (2013). *Traditional Chinese Music in a Changing Contemporary Society: A Field Report and Music Collection of the Quantou Village Music Association, Baiyangdian Lake Region, Hebei Province.* English translation by John Winzenburg. Beijing: Central Conservatory of Music Press.

Zhang, Xiaoyan, and Su Qianzhong. (2007). "Approach to Applied Musicology: A Review of Japanese Ethnomusicologist Yamaguti Osamu's Academic Summit Series." (In Chinese.) *People's Music* 7: 54–56.

Zhang, Zhentao. (2008). "A Historical Reflection of Folk Arts Festivals: One Method of Folk Music Protection." (In Chinese.) *Journal of the Central Conservatory of Music* 3: 32–37.

Zhang, Zhentao. (2009). "Full of Ambition: Chinese Musical Instrument Collection and the Academic Consciousness of Li Yuanqing." (In Chinese.) *Chinese Musicology* 4: 9–22.

Zhou, Heping. (2009). "Intangible Culture Heritage Protection and Constructing a Spiritual Home for the Chinese People." (In Chinese.) Speech at the Bo'ao Youth Forum (Hong Kong), December 7, 2009. Accessed via the Chinese Ministry of Culture's Intangible Cultural Heritage Bureau website. http://www.ccnt.gov.cn/sjzznew2011/fwzwhycs/.

Zhou, Xianbao. (2012). "Western Ethnomusicology and Chinese Traditional Music Research: Reviews of the Theory and Methodology of Applied Ethnomusicology." (In Chinese.) *Music Research* 6: 12–18.

Websites: (accessed 29 July 29, 2013)

http://www.ethnomusicology.org
http://www.ccnt.gov.cn/sjzznew2011/fwzwhycs/
http://www.ihchina.cn
http://wenku.baidu.com/view/
http://www.gov.cn/jrzg/
http://native.cnr.cn/city/
http://www.gov.cn/jrzg/

CHAPTER 7

THE PROBLEM AND POTENTIAL OF COMMERCE

ALAN WILLIAMS

ETHNOMUSICOLOGY and its related disciplines, anthropology and folklore studies, have a long and often difficult history of commercial encounters. Examples of conflicting agendas and accusations of exploitation abound, and nowhere are they more present than in instances where concerned parties attempted to *do* something with the results of scholastic inquiry. John and Alan Lomax's representation of Lead Belly and Steven Feld's attempts to disseminate his recordings in the marketplace[1] are but two case studies of uneasy alliances between academy and industry (Feld, 1991a; Filene, 2000; Szwed, 2010).

Yet, the dictum of applied ethnography—serve those who contribute to the research—sometimes leads to partnerships in commercial endeavors, and examples of such partnerships have increased exponentially in the post-Internet age. This chapter investigates some of these historical case studies, and documents more recent projects that attempt to disseminate information while simultaneously generating capital, often with the ostensible goal of benefiting those whose musical activities provide the primary and most commercially valuable content.

I focus on the intersection of technology, media, and marketing—a cultural space where all three factors contribute to the creation, capture, and dissemination of musical practices transformed into musical products. Recorded music in any form can both inform and entertain, and there are numerous examples of research-generated artifacts becoming commoditized product, just as commercial releases form the body of material of thousands of research studies. Perhaps more important, communication technology provides a platform for distribution of these audiovisual artifacts far beyond the limited points of access provided by libraries and record stores.

The discipline of ethnomusicology emerged in part as a challenge to previously held conceptions of what constituted music scholarship. In the commercial realm, figures within the culture industry present alternative definitions of "scholar" and "institution." In recent decades, a number of popular Western musicians—Paul Simon, Peter Gabriel, David Byrne, Ry Cooder, Damon Albarn, and others—have served as cultural brokers, simultaneously exploiting and promoting music and musicians from outside the Western mainstream. Undoubtedly as complicated as the cases of Lomax and Feld, it is apparent that their efforts have benefited a number of musicians directly, while establishing a market that indirectly serves many hundreds more.[2]

Can such commercial ventures be viewed as applied ethnomusicology? Beyond the question of whether a pop star can be considered a scholar, or whether a multinational media conglomerate an academic institution, I argue that projects like Real World Records, or the Buena Vista Social Club, disseminate cultural knowledge far beyond the walls of the academy. While degree-validated scholars can certainly question the legitimacy of such "knowledge," the impact of these projects highlights the disconnect between traditional scholarly research and those outside the academy. To paraphrase the famous marketing slogan/album title, "50 million Ladysmith Black Mambazo fans can't be wrong."

But just as activist/curious pop stars used the power of the industry that produced them, seismic shifts in Internet-based communication have undermined the hegemonic power of the twentieth-century culture industries. Amateur music enthusiasts with little to no support from any institution, academic or commercial, have harnessed the power of the Web to initiate a discourse and system of knowledge exchange with a socially activist agenda. In turn, both the academy and the commercial industry have begun to mirror strategies and methodologies developed by wi-fi-enabled armchair activists. In recent years, largely as a result of the collapse of the record industry in the wake of peer-to-peer file sharing, a common truism has emerged in music business discourse—"we are no longer a product industry; we are a service industry." The emphasis (perhaps more accurately stated as a dependence) on *service* aligns neatly, if somewhat uncomfortably, with the aims of applied scholarship. And academic institutions, where the Open Source movement began (Friedman, 2007), have increasingly opened their storehouses of secrets to the general public, engaging in dialog concerned with access to knowledge, providing resource to community, and facilitating exchange.

From my own experience as an instructor in music business degree programs, I can attest to a shift in the interest, goals, and methodologies of the newer generation of culture industry managers. Rather than a focus on commercial exploitation and career advancement, many of these students approach the music business as a platform for connecting musicians and audiences, and see their role as facilitator rather than profiteer. This generation, raised on the connectivity of the Internet, sees grassroots activism as a given, a normative model for any exchange of music, commoditized or not. While prior generations of corporate-based moguls may tout "service" as the new mode of operations, the immediate future of the industry lies in the hands of people whose biggest challenge is sustainability, rather than distribution or promotion.

I argue that these are all positive developments, not inherently in conflict, and potentially transformative in ways that we have only begun to envision. As I see it, the role of an academically based applied ethnomusicologist will be to contribute to the discourse by providing guidance based on decades of lessons learned about the potential dangers of exploitation, unrealistic expectations, and missed opportunities. If the challenge is whether to get involved, or get out of the way, perhaps we can provide the wisdom to know the difference.

Cultural Merchants and Brokers

The primary goal of any academic research is to produce "knowledge" of some form or another. Data is knowledge; history is knowledge; ideas are knowledge. But what to do with all this acquired knowledge? For some, knowledge was produced for the benefit of the elitist cult of the academy, where encounters with knowledge produces still more knowledge. But for many, a good idea needs to be shared, and shared beyond the ivy-coated walls of the university. For almost any trained academician, publishing text is the natural outcome of knowledge production. But for ethnomusicologists and other field-centered, humanities-based researchers, it is often the people encountered in the course of research that should be "shared" with the world. Musicians present some of the most obvious non-text-related opportunities for public presentation, either in the form of sound (and video) recordings, or in concert performances. According to Daniel Sheehy, "the fundamental importance of the role of the folklorist is "transcontextualizing," if you will, or transferring the folk musician from a traditional context to a public, non-traditional setting" (Sheehy, 1999: 220).

The impulse to "share" is not unique to folklorists; indeed it is a common response for many who encounter culture that resonates on a personal level. But academics with institutional support are in a privileged position that amplifies their voices and disseminates their tastes and agendas beyond the means available to most music fans. In this way, when ethnomusicologists champion an artist, they are in essence promoting their personal ideologies. The power of the gatekeeper lies in their ability to have other voices substitute for their own, and for a multiplicity of those voices to more effectively communicate the ideas of the solitary "voice" of authority. When radio hosts select a collection of music for broadcast, they are certainly promoting the individual musicians given airtime, but the collection itself is a statement, authored by the equally identified on-air personality. Promoting the music of others is a form of self-promotion as well.

The role of ego in such promotion does not undercut the benefits that the promoted musicians receive. Income-producing, artistically validating careers often result from temporary partnerships with public folklorists and ethnomusicologists. Some performers have then gone on to eclipse their gatekeeping patrons in terms of impact and influence. My main argument here is that conditions of self-promotion *and* cultural promotion exist in any effort to share the outcomes of a collaborative endeavor, and that neither inherently negates the value of the other.

Consider the case of Alan Lomax, the first widely recognized folklorist, nearly as well-known as his most famous discoveries. The term "discoveries" is itself highly charged, implying that individuals, cultures, and indeed entire civilizations don't truly exist until encountered and subsequently represented by (historically Western male) cultural capitalists. But while folklorists like Lomax merely recorded musical practices that had been in play in some form since the dawn of time, the moment of their recording signals a decisive turn, one that in many cases permanently alters the course of both the culture captured by the recording device, and all of those who subsequently encounter the recorded sounds. In this regard, Lomax was a pyromaniac *non pareil*, with musical culture as tinderwood, recording technology as accelerant, and the folklorist striking the match.

Alan Lomax began his career assisting his father John on a number of song-collecting fieldtrips. But whereas Lomax senior was primarily concerned with collating texts, Alan became obsessed with the possibilities that sound recording had for both capturing and transmitting musical cultures as they existed, free from the mediation of scholars who often "corrected" the texts they compiled, or rearranged and composed in the form of notated "transcriptions." Of course, as many have observed, the act of recording is far from un-mediated, but this does not change the fact that Lomax viewed his efforts from that perspective. And while the results may be flawed, the sheer amount of recorded material he produced in his lifetime now serves as a repository of global musical practices that, while failing to represent the history of music over time and across borders, stands as a towering achievement in documenting sounds of human inhabitants of planet earth in the mid-twentieth century.

But documenting alone was never the end goal for Lomax. To be truly useful, the music had to be made available to the public. While many of his field trips were funded by government agencies such as the Library of Congress, ostensibly to be cataloged and archived, Lomax went to great efforts to share the results with the public by arranging for the commercial release of recordings, by broadcasting the music on radio programs that he conceived, scripted, and hosted, by promoting and staging concert events large and small, and in the case of Leadbelly, by acting as a professional agent and manager.[3] The significance of Lomax and his accomplishments lies in his dual role as archivist and popularizer. For Lomax, the music industry was a vital tool for establishing the value of folk cultures, and facilitating cross-cultural understanding in ways that had both artistic and political consequences, even as he would later lament the impact of the same industry in permanently altering the cultures he sought to praise and promote.

As biographer John Szwed points out, Lomax the folklorist was never far removed from Lomax the music business professional. For every instance of professional efforts following folklore-inspired enterprise (as was the case with Leadbelly), many contributions to folkloric scholarship resulted from field trips sponsored by commercial interests. For many observers, much of his work was conducted under suspicious circumstances, and accusations of conflicts of interest dogged him even from the earliest days of his career. Lomax was not insensitive to the potential for exploitation, even if inadvertent, and made considerable efforts to share in any financial rewards that his fieldwork produced. But as a man struggling to feed a family, he did not see himself as someone in the position to act out of purely altruistic motivation. According to Szwed,

> Alan (Lomax)'s view was that the folklorist who recorded a song in the field was obliged to ensure that the singer was paid for his work, but should also have a share

of the royalties in consideration for his or her role as a collector if the record was ever sold commercially. Alan's reasoning was that composers of folk songs were not likely ever to be recorded nor ever to earn any money from their songs without the help and guidance of someone devoted to the music and its preservation.

(Szwed, 2010: 294)

Profits resulted from combined forces of labor, and Lomax clearly understood the value of his efforts in the marketplace. The "help and guidance" that Szwed refers to encompass both his roles: as gatekeeper, assessing the musical worth of a song or performance, and as music industry liaison, establishing conditions that would transform artistic value into commodity value. The key word in Szwed's description is "devoted," a concept that ostensibly separates Lomax from artists and repertoire (A&R) scouts like Victor's Ralph Peer or ARC's Don Law. For me, the distinction is far from clear, with men like Peer and Law (as well as Columbia scout John Hammond, and later figures like Ahmet Ertegun and the Chess Brothers) acquiring and exercising enough understanding of the music they encountered to successfully document and present to appreciative audiences, while in many cases establishing long-term relationships with the musicians they "exploited" (Kennedy and McNutt, 1999).

For Lomax, his relationships with his informants resulted in partnerships where each collaborator brought a different set of skills and resources to the table. If Leadbelly contributed both a knowledge of a body of folksongs, and the ability to creatively mold those traditions to craft personal artistic statements, Lomax brought a critical ear that could filter those statements for maximum resonance with the audiences that Lomax knew how to reach through both public sector and commercial realms. If Leadbelly proved a quick study, learning to assess an audience, and provide what they were willing to pay for, Lomax also learned how to turn cultural traditions into vehicles for personal expression. On many occasions, Lomax was called upon to perform himself, singing ballads and worksongs learned in the course of fieldwork, and inextricably weaving his voice into the tapestry of American musical culture. If anything, Lomax's own performing career is evidence of an ego-driven exploiter-artist, content to receive the attention, accolades, and bounty otherwise due to those whose music and culture he endeavored to enact. Neither Peer, Law, Hammond, Ertegun, nor the Chess Brothers ever placed their picture on the cover of an album (though their names were often present in liner notes, or in the logos for the labels they worked for or owned).[4]

Issues of copyright ownership plague both the history of the music business and that of documented folklore. Publishing and licensing fees account for the largest source of music industry revenue, and many songwriters have seen others amass considerable wealth by controlling the copyright to their work. Lomax was not immune to these conditions, and while he often claimed copyright for music at the behest of book publishers and record companies hoping to avoid eventual litigation, his estate has received considerable income from more recent uses of some of the recordings and compositions under his control. In this regard, he is no different from any number of music industry giants, though in many instances he made considerable efforts to direct funds to those who contributed to his archive (a clear break from standard "industry practice").

Some of the most complicated aspects of folklore/commercial partnerships concern the visible presence of the folklorist in the end product, and Lomax is somewhat unique in this regard. As Lomax gradually amassed both more recordings and an enhanced public visibility, this name association took on a commodity value of its own. Though this conversion of cultural capital to commodity capital was greatly accelerated after his death, Lomax himself took advantage of his public reputation, and was well aware of the market value of his name. The notoriety of the public figure worked against Lomax in terms of his acceptance by the academy. Indeed, the value of an academic's scholarship is often inversely proportional to his or her existence as a public intellectual. The work of Henry Louis Gates or Neil Degrasse Tyson becomes less citation-worthy with every television appearance. For scholars whose work catches the public's attention, issues of exploitation become complicated further. While the impulse to share that often drives the collaboration between scholars and industry is borne from the kind of devotion Szwed attributes to Lomax, the results of a project that "hits" in the commercial realm are often more than anyone bargained for.

Steven Feld's participation in disseminating the music of the Kaluli peoples of the Bosavi region of Papua, New Guinea, is a case in point, made all the more vivid by Feld's grappling with the issues in scholarly forums (Feld, 1991a The *Voices of the Rainforest* CD, produced by Feld and Grateful Dead drummer Mickey Hart and issued by Rykodisc, illustrates many of the tensions that arise from conflicting agendas, even when those differences are matters of degree rather than diametric opposition. For Feld, a recording that highlighted the significant relationship between music and environment was an extension of scholastic enterprise, in a form that presented his ideas in ways that surpassed the capabilities of text-based publication. Even if the alliance required that the culturally sensitive scholar grapple with issues of representation posed by the realities of CD artwork packaging, and so on, the relationship with a globally distributed independent company held the promise that revenue would be generated and directed to the peoples with whom Feld had bonded after years of research. As cultural intermediary, Feld was well aware of the forces that threated the Kaluli and their way of life; a recording that made the case for environmental conservation and brought the precarious status of Bosavi to the attention of the world could potentially do even more to aid his informants than the profits generated by the enterprise.

But Feld was also keenly aware that the outside world was already encroaching on Bosavi, irrevocably impacting the Kaluli, and that his audio representation of a way of life was myopically idealistic in its exclusion of the sounds of the modern world, both industrial and musical. The fact that the roar of a jet airplane was already part of the environmental soundscape was not lost on Feld. Yet his desire to craft an idealized and heavily nostalgic Bosavi soundscape depended upon considerable technological mediation. Working methodically with his field recordings, he carefully layered fragments of environmental sounds interspersed with those of the Kaluli, to craft a sound collage meant to represent "twenty-four hours of a day in the life of Bosavi in one continuous hour" (Feld, 1991: 134). The presence of industrial engines in this soundscape would presumably have been as distressing for the consumer as it was for Feld. This (mis)representation is an example of how scholars frame their research outcomes according to their own agendas, as well as how the entertainment industry attempts to fulfill an audience's expectations, to "give the people what they want."

If the construct of *Voices of the Rainforest* gave Feld pause, his subsequent efforts at presenting the music of the region sought to acknowledge, and perhaps begrudgingly accept, the full range of sonic experience in New Guinea, including new forms of technologically mediated Kaluli culture. A three-disc set entitled *Bosavi*, compiled by Feld and issued by Smithsonian Folkways, included several examples of amplified guitar bands recasting older, now vanished, Kaluli musical practices in the timbres of the modern Western world.[5] The presence of these recordings alongside examples drawn from Feld's earlier field recordings gives the listener a more complete aural picture of the region, and illustrates how an increasingly hybridized global culture yields results counter to Lomax's oft-referenced "cultural grey-out."

Feld continued to explore the intersection of technology and musical creation in his subsequent work on jazz in Accra, Ghana. Encountering music in the field that is expressly the result of globalized networks of cultural distribution, Feld has imposed a similar impressionist framework to present his personal experience of the musical expressions of others. While continuing to publish books and articles in scholarly journals, he also produces recordings that simultaneously represent the music he researches while standing as expressions of his own artistic sensibilities. He is scholar, activist, and artist. He is also a willing participant in the commoditization of culture. In 2003, Feld founded VoxLox, a company that, according to its website, "publish(es) CD, DVD, and book projects at the crossroads of anthropology and sound and visual art" (http://voxlox.myshopify.com/pages/about-us, accessed August 27, 2013).[6] The VoxLox catalog is an intriguing mixture of field recordings, collaborations with musicians encountered in New Guinea and Ghana, and Feld's own artistic creative expressions. In this manner, he utilizes his understanding of music industry operations to extend opportunities for his research partners to reach audiences beyond their local region. At the same time, by placing his own creative output alongside his collaborators, he levels the hierarchical distance between resource-privileged Westerner and fieldwork informants.

In broad strokes, Feld serves as a model for how an applied ethnomusicologist can work with and within the music industry to both spread the knowledge gained through research beyond the walls of the academy, and serve the needs of his informants, in terms of publicizing their plight as well as generating income. For example, Feld established a foundation to direct funds toward initiatives intended to help battle the encroachment of disease, and the decimation of an environment that supplies food and shelter to the Kaluli (Feld, 1991a). Everyone wins, even if no one escapes without a few bumps and bruises. Examining the specifics of the case study reveals many of the potential pitfalls surrounding any enterprise that must balance the needs of commerce, the needs of the academy, and most important, the needs of the community. These collaborations generate another field of knowledge—the history of their own creation—that can aid in guiding the efforts of others endeavoring to promote, advocate, and provide for all those who contribute to research.

Creative Alliances: Mutually Beneficial Exploitation

In a film documenting the making of Paul Simon's *Graceland* album and subsequent promotional tours, South African guitarist Ray Phiri emphatically states, "It was two-way traffic; we used Paul as much as he used us. There was no abuse."[7] *Graceland* was both the product of and the leading example of the world music genre that emerged in the 1980s. In its wake, several musicians associated with the project experienced substantially increased exposure, resulting in commercial viability of their own in the global marketplace. Simon's record label Warner Brothers issued albums by Ladysmith Black Mambazo (produced by Simon's recording engineer, Roy Halee), and Miriam Makeba, whose career was resurrected as opening act and support vocalist for the *Graceland* world tour. Additionally, many of the musicians, such as Phiri, who served as backing musicians for Simon live and on record developed careers of their own as session musicians, in some cases leaving South Africa for the more lucrative session scene of New York. Clearly, their prominence in the marketing of the album established their names and faces in the public sphere, putting them in much better stead after their work with Simon than before he made his controversial trek to Johannesburg (Mientjes, 1990).

Here the benefits of exploitation worked in both directions. While Simon was a well-established star, with massive success for both his partnership with Art Garfunkel, and his early and mid-1970s solo work, his career trajectory took a downward turn following a lukewarm reunion event with Garfunkel in 1980. *Graceland* eventually not only brought Simon back to the top of the charts, but became his most successful solo recording to date. Whether intentional or not, the savvy marketing of late twentieth-century exoticism boosted Simon's commercial value to its highest point in decades, a peak he has not since come close to matching. Certainly many musical figures have benefited from generalized exoticized othering—Debussy, Stravinsky, Bartok, Colin McPhee, Lou Harrison, Bing Crosby, and Dizzy Gillespie come quickly to mind—but few have brought the sources of their inspiration to such prominence, preferring to keep their encounters as more generally "cultural" than to forge alliances with specific individuals.

While Simon did not abandon his own career to devote his energies solely to those of the South African musicians he championed, he clearly used his commercial and cultural capital to help his collaborators secure solid backing from the corporate-level music industry. This role as industry liaison put a new spin on earlier Western pop star/

world music performers alliances. When the Rolling Stones guitarist Brian Jones made a recording of Moroccan musicians (eventually released posthumously in 1971), the album was titled *Brian Jones Presents the Pan Pipes of Jajouka*. And while George Harrison maintained a long relationship with sitar virtuoso Ravi Shankar, frequently citing his mentor and providing exposure as an opening act in his 1970s live performances, he was less directly involved in Shankar's own industry connections (in large part because Shankar had already established himself to some degree on the world stage prior to his association with Harrison). Simon's efforts on behalf of the *Graceland* musicians are noteworthy in transforming his role from one of cheerleader to that of advocate.

It is one thing to celebrate the musical practices of others in the moment; it is another to make a long-term commitment to advancing the careers of under-supported musicians and the cultures they represent. David Byrne and Peter Gabriel are examples of Western pop artists drawn to non-Western music, who have in turn devoted energies toward promoting the music they admire and draw inspiration from. Both stars have leveraged their cultural capital to create enterprises that work within the structures of the music industry to further the cause of the music, and the careers of the musicians that make it. Byrne's Luaka Bop and Gabriel's Real World record labels present non-Western acts to Western audiences by issuing recordings that are created with the same care and attention to detail, and often in the same facilities, afforded their own recorded work, and benefit from the same distribution channels as their own commercial output. If Simon protégés Ladysmith Black Mambazo demonstrated the commercial viability of non-Western artists, the catalogs of both labels provided a bulk of content with which to populate the newly allocated bin space in the world music section of record stores across North American and Europe. Each label bore the unmistakable imprint of their founders, with Luaka Bop tending toward idiosyncratic pop music from around the globe, while Real World records presented more traditional regional styles, though recorded in state of the art facilities, and mirroring the sonic detail of Gabriel's own work.[8]

The packaging of these releases extends the mission of presenting alternative views of the value of non-Western music. Real World releases generally feature intriguing images that often have little to do directly with the cultures that produce the music, but firmly establish the recordings as "art" product. For Byrne, album artwork is a powerful tool for reframing the exoticized "other" as a contemporary cultural equal.

> Overall, we think of the music we work with as contemporary pop music, and we try to present it as such. While something like Zap Mama's first record could be, and sometimes was, perceived as an "ethnic" record, we did our damnedest to alter that perception. The CD covers go a long way, in my opinion, to creating this attitude. We don't do covers that look like folkloric records or like academic records of obscure material of interest only to musicologists and a few weird fringe types . . . we work with the designers to come up with a graphic statement that says "this music is as relevant to your life and is as contemporary as Prodigy, Fiona Apple, or Cornershop."
>
> (Byrne, 2013)[9]

Though one could argue that the sumptuous artwork and pristine sonics of Luaka Bop and Real World releases propagate an extension of a hegemonic contemporary Western aesthetic, packaging the recorded performances of non-Western musicians in the same manner as mainstream Western pop stars positions world music artists as equals in the record store bins and living rooms in which the product is intended to reside. Yes, the music is framed through Western ears and eyes, but these recordings are also evidence that a number of culture brokers have deemed the music worthy of the frame. Why shouldn't a musician from Sudan be afforded the opportunity to record in a state of the art facility, and be presented in a manner that differs markedly from commercially released "ethnic" recordings of the mid-twentieth century? Gabriel was particularly sensitive to accusations of exploitation as his 1980s musical statements began to borrow heavily from non-Western sources. In his view, he was collaborating with musicians in much the same way as he did with Western session musicians, exploring creative possibilities, in the search for something compellingly new.

> I know all the arguments concerning appropriation, but at the end of the day, providing you try and balance the exchange and allow for the promotion of the collaborating artist and their own music, rather than just taking, I feel very comfortable with this idea of dialogue. . . . So, given these parameters, more is gained than is lost . . . it is possible now for artists from different cultures and countries to reach a limited audience worldwide, making a living from it, and there is much more focus now than there was ten years ago.
>
> (quoted in Taylor, 1997: 50)

Gabriel's belief in the potential benefit to non-Western collaborators involved in his recorded work was not a naive dream, but rather the demonstrable results of his own substantial labors in creating a structure to facilitate these musicians' ability to reach a much broader audience. The outcome of extended promotional efforts from labels such as Real World and Luaka Bop did not simply stoke interest in global musical traditions for bored Western pop music consumers, but rather established ongoing careers for the stand-out performers of those traditions. According to Gabriel, "An artist can come from another country and get onto a circuit that they will find very hard to achieve anywhere else—and get visibility, get heard, and hopefully find an audience that will allow them the following year to come back and tour under their own steam" (quoted in Taylor, 1997: 51). Real World's focus on promoting identifiable "stars" such as Youssou N'Dour and Nusrat Fateh Ali Khan, rather than compilations of regional styles, parallels a trend in ethnomusicology during the 1980s and 1990s that emphasized the value of individual musicians over more generalized practices (for example, Rice, 1994), and record releases tied to individual names and faces accomplish the goal more effectively than the ever-changing line-up of the folk festival culture show.

Yet Gabriel pursued this path as well, launching the first WOMAD (World of Music and Dance) festival in 1982 near his home in southwest England. Though well attended, the festival ran considerably over budget in an effort to present the music most effectively, and to provide fair compensation to the performers. On the brink of bankruptcy, Gabriel was forced to approach his old band members in Genesis to stage a one-off reunion concert to pay the bills. Though WOMAD was on shaky ground in its early days, it has since flourished and is now in its third decade, with events staged around the world, reaching audiences in the millions. One benefit to understanding how industry practices such as concert promotion staging and marketing actually work is that once the machine is built and fired up, it can run without the constant attention of its founders.

Simon, Gabriel, and Byrne became the most visible cultural brokers in the popular music marketplace in part by underscoring the contemporary relevance of the non-Western musical practices they adopted and adapted. But a decade earlier, Van Dyke Parks and Ry Cooder, two Los Angeles–based musicians with pop music credentials[10] embarked on cross-cultural pathways with a decidedly nostalgic bent. Parks issued an album featuring re-recordings of 1930s calypso music entitled *Discover America* and later produced albums by the Esso Trinidad Steel Band and The Mighty Sparrow. Both *Discover America* and its Caribbean-flavored follow-up, *Clang of the Mighty Reaper*, were complete commercial failures, as much a result of Park's relative obscurity as it was of the contemporary irrelevancy of the music. But Cooder methodically established a mid-level career for himself by specializing in an amalgam of Depression-era American blues, jazz, and country music. Along the way, he began to collaborate with musicians who could lend a more directly associative authenticity to his music while simultaneously expanding his palette of stylistic borrowings—Earl "Fatha" Hines contributing a touch of stride piano, Flaco Jimenez on *norteno*-styled renditions of 1950s doo wop, and Gabby Pahanui bridging the gap between Hawaiian slack-key guitar and Cooder's renditions of Delta blues. Indeed, the selling point for Cooder's audience was the very out-of-sync nature of the music. Steadfastly avoiding any resemblance to current popular music trends, Cooder's 1970s catalog appealed to a similar nostalgic hipsterism found in the folk revivalists of the 1960s, or the British "trad" jazz scene intent on re-creating early twentieth-century New Orleans in the 1950s London suburbs. The longevity and sweep of Cooder's career bestowed upon him a measure of "authority," a public radio–validated gentleman scholar.[11]

Cooder's participation in the *Buena Vista Social Club*[12] project deserves closer inspection. His guitar work is present on many of the recordings, but is rarely featured. Instead, primary attention is given to the vocalists, and to some extent pianist Gonzalo Rubalcaba. If any non-Cuban is prominent, it is Cooder's son Joachim, whose percussion work is central to many of the performances. In essence, both Cooders are continuing a well-established history of musical collaboration in the search of knowledge and understanding. Since Mantle Hood first championed "bi-musicality" as a prerequisite for any aspiring ethnomusicologist, one-on-one musical exchanges have formed the basis for much of the discipline's canonical works of scholarship. Cooder's role as background support player, simply "one of the band," downplays his importance to the project. As shown in the similarly titled Wim Wenders film documenting subsequent recording sessions for an Ibraham Ferrer album and two concert performances in Amsterdam and New York,[13] Cooder hovers in the background, only occasionally commenting on the proceedings, choosing to shape the flow of the music with his guitar work. The cameras capture several moments where Cooder and the Cuban musicians exchange knowing smiles in response to one another's musical expressions. When the music begins, everyone is on equal footing. At least, potentially. In truth, Cooder adds far less musical input than in his supporting work with Western musicians from the Rolling Stones to John Hiatt, ceding the musical landscape to the local musicians, apparently acknowledging his neophyte status as a purveyor of Cuban *son*.

Though it would appear from scenes in the Wenders documentary that the Cuban musicians respect Cooder as a player, his key contribution is in lending the cultural capital of his name in the general marketing plan. The project was conceived and the musicians initially assembled by Nick Gold, the owner of British record label World Circuit. Cooder's presence in the studio helped quietly steer the musical performances in a direction that might prove more palatable to Western audiences looking for new sounds that fit their NPR-formed aesthetic. But he does not appear to have taken a direct role in producing the sessions, or directing the concert performances. He did oversee the mixing of the record, and to that extent employs his decades of professional studio experience in an area where he can claim a measure of expertise. But tellingly, the end product was not another time-traveling/globe-trotting Ry Cooder album meant to display his mastery of yet another musical genre. Nor is Cooder "presenting" a "discovery." Cooder on stage and in the studio fades into the background. Cooder as the figure with the most cultural capital to spend only becomes a featured star in the marketing of the project. To the extent that his own career benefits from the exposure, this prominence is, to a degree, self-serving. But clearly, the Cuban musicians stand to gain exponentially more from their collaboration. Ferrer and Rubalcaba were able to release new recordings using the same production team and label/ distribution deal following the commercial success of the initial release, and many of the musicians found agents and embarked on world tours that would never have happened without Cooder's participation in the project.

So, the activist/patron role is firmly established, but is the work they produce scholarship? The answer depends upon one's definition of "scholarship." Bertrand Russell famously established two categories of knowledge—that which is obtained by "description," and that which is derived from "acquaintance" (Russell, 2005 [1905]). Cultural brokers serve valuable roles in knowledge production both by helping to create a system for encounters with culture (acquaintance), and by providing a contextual framework for understanding those encounters (description). When an audience actively engages with the products of the culture industry as a result of their acquaintance with the creative expressions of others, even a modicum of description can lead to a deeper understanding of the human condition. Viewing a project like the *Buena Vista Social Club* through this lens, the recordings and films serve as evidence—"Hey folks, here's some music"—and the context provided by a culturally brokered marketing plan poses the questions: Where has this music been all this time? Who are these people? What are these songs about? What's Ry Cooder doing in the middle of all of this? When can we go to Cuba to hear some more?

Academically initiated recording projects have significantly contributed to the formation of hybridized world music culture and thus bear some responsibility for fostering the mediated encounter and encouraging creative individuals to do something with the knowledge they have gleaned. Writing in 1991, Kay Kaufmann Shelemay notes that

> [n]early a century of ethnic recordings, many prepared by or in collaboration with ethnomusicologists or "ethno-recordists," has contributed to a growing trend for cross-cultural synthesis in musical composition and performance.... Much of the inspiration and raw material for these new fusions stems directly from the ethnomusicological presence in the university, public-sector agencies, and the music industry itself.
>
> (Shelemay, 1991: 287)

Just as academics have played a significant role in establishing an emergent "world music" pop culture, Western pop stars have made meaningful contributions to music scholarship. If the results of cross-cultural encounters yield a body of knowledge, then perhaps those cultural intermediaries are doing ethnomusicological work. When Simon travels to Johannesburg, he is doing fieldwork—fieldwork that results in the production of a form of knowledge. When David Byrne pores through the vaults of EGREM, the record company of the Cuban government, searching for unreleased gems to issue on lavishly packaged compilations, he is doing fieldwork. When Peter Gabriel creates a platform for the presentation of various global traditions, he is advocating for the musicians who make the music. All of their endeavors have a broader impact than that measured by the record charts. It is not a stretch to say that Western awareness of South African politics was heightened by the attention paid to *Graceland*, and may have hastened the release of Nelson Mandela and the end of apartheid. The cross-cultural coalition of WOMAD performers and attendees does not merely reflect a growing multiculturalism; it facilitates it. In this way, pop star–driven projects utilizing the power of the music industry promotional machine benefit the communities they both work with and establish, and are therefore highly effective examples of applied ethnomusicology.

Shifting Industry: From Resource Exploitation to Service Enterprise

The discipline of ethnomusicology is built upon sound recording technology, which supplanted notated transcription as the primary data collected in the course of research. Moreover, field recordings were not solely in the domain of the academic. As Kay Kaufmann Shelemay points out,

> [i]f early ethnomusicologists and the record industry shared technologies through the first decade of the twentieth century, they also shared working methods and interests of a diverse repertory for an even longer period. In many instances, representatives of the early record companies preceded ethnomusicologists in the field, themselves functioning as fieldworkers in locating and then recording local talent.
>
> (Shelemay, 1991: 280)

The intersection of the academy and the music industry, though closely aligned in the early years of sound recording, became less common as record labels eschewed the limited commercial rewards yielded by "ethnic" records in favor of much more profitable popular musical forms. Though folklorists and record company scouts utilized many of the same technological processes and social practices in the course of capturing recorded performances, the purposes of their work "in the field" differed tremendously. Record companies sought to maximize profit from recordings by marketing each release as an excitingly new product, soon to be replaced by even more exciting new products in the near future, assuming a "shelf life" of weeks rather than years, decades, or centuries.[14]

Most ethnomusicologists made sound recordings as a means of documenting musical practices, intending that the recordings serve as the basis for research while simultaneously preserving examples of musical cultures on the verge of extinction. As Nicholas Spitzer writes, "To me, sowing the seeds of musical performances in the vinyl furrows of LPs or the digital fields of CDs is a way of documentary cultivation as a practicing folklorist" (Spitzer, 1992: 98). But what happens to the fruits of such cultivation? Are these the furrows of a garden plot? Is the harvest bound for the farmer's table, or is it destined to be converted into cash at the farmer's market? Once the seeds are planted, will the land and its crop become the property of the Archer Daniel Midlands Corporation? And what if those seeds are genetically altered, what sort of inorganic fruits does the harvest yield?

The nature of this form of documentation is that, once captured, the sounds can be as readily commoditized as they can be archived. In some cases, field recordings were made specifically to be packaged and sold in the marketplace. For example, Alan Lomax was commissioned by Columbia Records in the early 1950s to create a series of LPs entitled *World Library of Folk and Primitive Music* (Szwed, 2010). Lomax spent years traveling through Europe, amassing hundreds of hours of recordings, knowing that most of the documents would likely be kept in storage, while keeping an ear out for material that could be issued commercially through Columbia. In other cases, Lomax's efforts were initially intended as a means of preserving musical cultures that he worried would die off with their aging practitioners. But while considered archive material at the time of their capture, many of these recordings were later issued on commercially released LPs and CDs. Gray areas abound. Lomax is simultaneously a folklorist *and* an A&R talent scout. When Moses Asch released Lomax's recordings on his Folkways label, the recordings became commoditized, though the nearly nonexistent marketing of those LPs casts Asch's enterprise as closer to a one-man Library of Congress than a chart-topping, profit-generating machine. Even more curious is the desire of Columbia to create a series such as the *World Library of Folk and Primitive Music*. This project and others like it represent the first attempts at creating a world music market. A key difference between the 1950s and the 1980s versions of world music marketing lies in the assumed uses of the music for listening audiences. Whereas late twentieth-century world music was marketed as pop, intended to fill a never-quenched thirst for the "new," mid-twentieth-century commercial releases stressed the edifying quality of getting to know the world beyond the backyard. In many ways, this resembles other large media efforts to inform while entertaining, such as the CBS television broadcasts of Leonard Bernstein conducting programs for children (and their curious parents), a form of *noblesse oblige* exercised by corporations operating with the best interests of their customers in mind.

One further complication surrounding the act of the field recording concerns the assumptions and aspirations of the musicians being recorded. Far from fearing that their performances might become commercialized product, many contributors to field research desire just such an outcome and view the researcher as their conduit to the marketplace. Jeff Todd Titon has identified the many and varied expectations of fieldwork informants and the roles they may assign to the intruders in their midst, a condition he labels "stance" (Titon, 1985). Nicholas Spitzer describes experiencing a similar phenomenon while recording Cajun and Zydeco musicians in Louisiana.

> As I learned from musicians about their lives, ambitions, repertoires, and styles, I realized the value they placed on the tangible results of this project; their music and life stories on a recording. If the project was flawed, in their view, it was because I had no connections to Motown or any other national record company catering to black listeners that fulfilled some of their ideas about success as musicians.
>
> (Spitzer, 1992: 79)

If Spitzer were to truly serve his collaborators in the spirit of applied folklore, he would have to endeavor to make such connections to mainstream record labels, especially those that issued recordings that his informants were familiar with. It's all well and good to be in the Library of Congress, but having a record on the radio or local jukebox would be a far more validating result. In Spitzer's case, he subsequently oversaw the commercial release of some his recordings, albeit on the small Arhoolie label, a far cry from Motown. In later years as a widely syndicated radio host, he has helped to popularize all manner of American roots music, in essence adopting the stance that his fieldwork informants initially imposed upon him and, I would argue, effectively doing applied ethnomusicology in his capacity as cultural gatekeeper and broker.

It is important to clarify what is meant by "music industry." For many casual observers, the term signifies records in all their various format incarnations from 78s to down-loadable soundfiles. But record sales are but one component of a much larger system of revenue-generating uses of musical performance and related technologies. Concerts, broadcasts, print publications and associated merchandise, licensed uses for inclusion in film, television, and Web content all contribute to a musician's potential earnings. By focusing on records, it is easy to overlook other aspects of music industry practice that resemble some of the forms that applied folklore and ethnomusicology have already taken.

For several decades, the most publicly visible role for folklorists and ethnomusicologists has been in the presentation of traditional music in a festival setting. Academics often serve as cultural brokers, sometimes by promoting musicians they have worked with in the course of research activities to festival organizers, sometimes by providing scholarly validation of the merits of traditional music performers in the form of program notes, or as voices of authority in promotional campaigns. Accompanying these activities, many of these academics have published hand-wringing and soul-searching treatises attempting to resolve/absolve their role in shaping/diminishing/corrupting the music and musicians they champion.

Issues of representation abound in the realm of the culture show, as they do in any mediated presentation of culture. Some scholars have argued that the culture show inherently misrepresents the culture presented by performers framed by the stage proscenium, while others see the festival stage as an empowering space for claiming identity (Harker, 1985; Hobsbawm, 1983; Kishenblatt-Gimblett, 1992, 1998; Sarkissian, 2000).[15] For me, the more problematic aspect of the culture show is the illusory notion that these festivals operate outside the realm of the commercial concert promotion industry. Frequently, the intellectual discourse of the seminar room that has propelled the folklorist onto the festival grounds fades into the background when confronting the logistics of the concert stage. The challenge for the folklorist involved in the culture show enterprise is to navigate the myriad issues surrounding "culture" while simultaneously grappling with the practicalities of the "show."

For example, the National Council for the Traditional Arts (NCTA) organizes the annual Lowell Folk Festival, one of many large-scale arts festivals they oversee across the country. As a professor at the local university, I have frequently served as a "scholar/presenter," announcing the performing acts, supplying brief biographical information, and providing a small measure of cultural context about the music. In reality, I am an emcee, and the primary task at hand is to keep the show moving according to a highly regimented timetable. In the course of an afternoon, I will make numerous requests for donations and read extensive lists of sponsors for the event. This is perhaps the primary distinction between the folk fest and more pop music–oriented events such as Coachella, Bonaroo, Glastonbury, or Roskilde—it's free.

However, in all other respects, the folk fest operates like any of the above-mentioned commercial spectacles. All the acts receive payment; most of them are represented by booking agents who have mastered the fine art of calling for bids, negotiating fee for service, and stipulating conditions for travel, food, and lodging. Tents are set up for the specific purpose of selling CDs, T-shirts, and other merchandise. Robert Cantwell's probing consideration of the Smithsonian Folklife Festival, *Ethnomimesis*, took issue with the treatment of individual humans as little more than troublesome artifacts that failed to show up for a 6 a.m. bus, or seemed to need to eat at some point during the day

(Cantwell, 1993). Even more troubling for Cantwell were the forms of representation imposed upon the performers by the festival organizers, and the basic construct of the festival itself. His point is well taken, but in recent decades, the goals and outcomes of most folk festivals are right in line with those of the acts that are presented—a studied professionalism is demonstrated by both performers and organizers: from set lists that time out to the second, practiced stage banter that entertains and informs like a jocular World Book entry, to carefully mapped stage plots, piezo pick-ups mounted in all manner of "traditional" instruments, to checks made out in advance, with federal tax dutifully reported.

All of this is to say that a professional circuit exists to serve a growing legion of musical performers who have benefited directly and indirectly from the efforts of applied folklorists and ethnomusicologists to present specific musicians and musical practices to audiences much more sizable than the local communities from which they sprang. And for many academics working in the public sphere, these musicians are the most effective "transcontextualizers." As Daniel Sheehy writes,

> Many musicians, once known to but a few, became important communicators of their cultural group's values, worldview, life-style, and potential for creating expressions of beauty. I think it is fair to say that the public impact of these collaborators has been great, and they have done much to bring traditional arts, artists, and even communities the respect they deserve, but all too often do not receive.
>
> (Sheehy, 1992: 222)

What gives some observers pause is the degree to which many traditional performers master the art of transcontextualization, deftly sizing up their audiences, and targeting their messages and performances to fit. Some would argue that this professionalism signifies the incarnation of "fakelore," an empty sham of gestures meant to satisfy an audience's desire for the "real thing," a ruse made all the more convincing due to its performers' "authentic" cultural history. But I would argue that such a view severely underestimates the abilities of these professional transcontextualizers to craft performances of real depth and meaning, working with an audience's expectations, manipulating the surface gestures to communicate something about themselves as individuals, and about the cultures they represent. As George Lipsitz cautions in his conclusion to *Dangerous Crossroads*,

> It is important to document the harm done by uncomprehending appropriation of cultural creations, to face squarely the consequences of mistakes in reception, representation, and reproduction of cultural images, sounds, and ideas. But the biggest mistake of all would be to underestimate how creative people are and how much they find out about the world that the people in power never intended for them to know in the first place.
>
> (Lipsitz, 1994: 169)

Recent endeavors within the business world parallel the concept of applied work in the academic sector. Their successes and failures provide some useful insights as to how applied ethnomusicologists can more effectively partner with commercial enterprise. Nicholas Negroponte's One Laptop Per Child (OLPC) initiative and the One for One project developed by Toms Shoes founder Blake Mycoskie are two high-profile exercises in corporate-based activism. Both endeavors have received praise for their plans to use private sector manufacturing and distributions models to advance social causes, while simultaneously enduring criticism for the inconsistent effectiveness of their attempts to put theory into practice.

Negroponte, former director of the MIT Media Lab and author of *Being Digital* (Negroponte, 1995), identified a significant problem for non-industrialized nations in the post-Internet era—the inability of those populations to connect with the digital world, further increasing the marginalization of those societies. His solution was to make connectivity possible by getting computer technology into the hands of children, and utilizing satellite technology to link those computers to the Internet. Transforming dream into reality required significant innovation in technological design and manufacturing processes. Negroponte announced his plan to create "$100 Laptops" for sale to the governments of under-industrialized nations (Warschauer and Ames, 2010). These computers were built to withstand harsh environmental conditions, and to operate with hand-cranked battery chargers. The education-based software emphasized graphics to facilitate learning for non-literate children.

Immediately, the project stumbled on obstacles both technological and economic. When the OLPC computers were brought to market, their cost was nearly double that of the announced $100 price tag—though surely a $200 laptop was a minor miracle of its own. Distributing the units and providing sufficient instruction and support to the new owners proved more difficult than OLPC had anticipated. While the laptops were relatively intuitive to operate, communicating the concept of advancement through connectivity to governments, teachers, parents, and even students presented an even greater challenge. One persistent issue that dogged the project was the disparity between the "have-not-a-lot" and the "have-none-at-all." Nations that were able to pony up the funds necessary to obtain the laptops balked at the notion that they would be subsidizing those that could not afford the purchase price. Smaller orders in turn meant higher manufacturing costs for OLPC. Confusing the issue further, OLPC was the recipient of several grants, legitimizing the claims of unfair competitive practices made by other manufacturers.

In 2010, a solution was reached that addressed both of these concerns. The organization was split into two—the OLPC Foundation would provide fully subsidized laptops to politically and economically unstable regions such as Iraq, Afghanistan, and Gaza, while the OLPC Association operated as a for-profit enterprise, providing low-cost though unsubsidized laptops in developing markets such as Uruguay and Peru. Though the laptops themselves were never made available to Western consumers, a recent initiative by the OLPC Association to make low-cost tablets available through giant retailers like Walmart and Amazon directly challenges the hegemony of technological giants such as Apple and Hewitt Packard in the United States and elsewhere. The profits gleaned from the sales of these tablets will in turn lower the cost of the laptops for the association's customers, a condition in which Western consumers in effect subsidize the market for computer technology outside the industrialized world.

Blake Mycoskie, the founder of Toms Shoes, has established a model that makes such consumer subsidy its overt mission. The One for One project directly correlates the act of purchase with an act of charity—for every set of shoes bought by a customer, another pair is donated to an individual in need (Chu and Weiss, 2013). The most important aspect of the enterprise is that it uses altruism as a marketing strategy, a strategy geared to earn profit for the company. The global economy based upon the production of wearable goods has a far uglier history of exploitation than that of the culture show or music industry. To counter this, Toms Shoes uses workers from impoverished nations, but pays a fair wage and is vigilant in monitoring the conditions of its laborers. Outsourcing labor has a negative impact on domestic economies, but serves the greater good by elevating the global workforce. The effect is twofold—low-cost shoes introduce competition into Western markets, while providing higher standards of living for their factory workers induces other manufacturers to better the pay and working conditions of their own employees.

The endeavor hit some bumps in its earliest years. Ineffective manufacturing oversight led to defective products making their way to dissatisfied customers. The imperative to better the labor conditions proved more costly than originally anticipated, and the differential substantially cut into the profit margin. But the company has effectively addressed many of these issues, and has been able to deliver on the promise of its mission, while adding revenue to its coffers. Perhaps most strikingly, the charitable component of One for One operates increasingly in the background, a corporate altruism that is the pleasant side effect of having a hit in the marketplace. The product line is now popular with consumers who may have little awareness of the impact of their purchase—they just like the shoes.

Though neither Real World nor Luaka Bop operate as nonprofits, they do have a mission to connect audiences with music, while simultaneously providing previously marginalized musicians with the means to expand their audiences and benefit directly from the commoditization of their creative endeavors. This mission can only be met if the product itself is appealing to music consumers, and in this way, the success of these record companies mirrors that of the One for One product line. I underscore the importance of harnessing the power of commerce by creating product or presenting performances that have viability in the marketplace. Music is rarely completely free from notions of value exchange—instruments never materialize from nothing, and individuals and communities often endeavor to demonstrate an appreciation for musical expression by providing food, services, or other forms of compensation. While issues of representation and exploitation are always present in these exchanges, intersections between music and commerce are nearly unavoidable. Simon Frith maintains that

> [t]he industrialization of music cannot be understood as something which happens *to* music, since it describes a process in which music itself is made—a process, that is, which fuses (and confuses) capital, technical and musical arguments.
>
> (Frith, 2006: 231)

The music industry that emerged in the wake of sound recording technology bore a close resemblance to the primary economic engine of the nineteenth century—mining. Companies sought out raw materials that could be quickly and efficiently excavated, then sold as the basic elements of a developing world—steel for constructing the bridges and skyscrapers of the industrial world, coal to burn in the furnaces and engines of the machinery produced in the factory. Likewise, musicians were discovered, molded, shaped and refined, packaged and sold, the profits held by the companies behind the products. In industry parlance, "exploitation" is what the music business *does*. Just as the search for ore and gold brought European interests into the mountains, valleys, and plains of Africa, Asia, and the Americas, the corporate interests behind the music industry spread across the globe in search of both raw material and customers. As Jacques Attali contends, "Show business, the star system, and the hit parade signal a profound institutional and cultural colonization" (Attali, 1989: 4).

The global music industry was built by Western interests at first content to operate within their own geographic sphere. But even as manufactured culture for consumption generated substantial revenues, companies looked to further increase profits by expanding into foreign territories. Though the Gramophone Company sponsored recording field trips across the globe in the early 1900s with the purpose of creating product that would appeal to regional tastes, it became apparent that it was far easier and cheaper to create a demand for Western musical practices over indigenous ones. The hegemonic reign of the Western pop star, from Elvis to Madonna, continued well into the twenty-first century. As Keith Negus wrote in 1992, "The globalization of communications media and geographical expansion of transnational corporations has provided more opportunities for, and increased the significance of the marketing and promotion of recording artists across the planet" (Negus, 1992: 7). The structure Negus describes had the potential to develop and promote music careers for non-Western musicians as well as Western ones, though, as he points out,

> [i]f the dominance of Anglo-American repertoire around the world provides opportunities for successful British and North American artists to gain extra sales, at the same time it severely restricts the opportunities for local artists. Although the major corporations are—in theory—concerned with finding and developing local talent throughout the world, in practice this has taken second place to the marketing of acts from Britain and the United States.
>
> (Negus, 1992: 11)

Yet, curious developments were already taking place, operating just below surface of global superstars and multiplatinum albums. As Simon Frith points out, vibrant music scenes, supported by regional systems of creation, promotion, and distribution, are beginning to challenge the hegemony of Western pop, a process he labels "globalization from below" (Frith, 2000: 319). These subterranean rumblings of the late twentieth century gave way to earth-shaking seismic events at the dawn of the new millennium. Suddenly, non-Western acts like Shakira were taking their place on the Western charts, while performers like Khaled could sell multiple millions of copies without ever mounting an American promotional campaign. These changes occurred simultaneously with the rise of the Internet, and the emergence of information as the primary commodity of the global economy.

The popular music business of the twentieth century grew into a multibillion-dollar industry built upon the commodification of sound recording technology. In the rock era, record sales generated the largest profits, and the album served as the centerpiece for most associated promotional activity, from radio airplay to concert tours. But in the post-Napster Internet age, the sales of recorded music plummeted, and the collapse of the record-centric industry model dramatically altered the way the music business operated. While a few entrepreneurs found ways to monetize the exchange of information happening over fiber optic lines and cellular networks, the Internet largely enabled voices to be heard, but not to be sold. Audiences exercised a newfound agency, exerting far more control over the ways they accessed music, and demanding far more interaction with the artists they supported. Social media served as the conduit for artist/ fan exchanges, and recorded music became one of many elements that formed a fan's experience. Artists and companies began to cater to this hunger for experience, and soon the music business began to reconfigure itself from a system based on commodity exchange into one geared toward providing "service."

The term "service" is also central to the tenets of applied ethnomusicology, folklore, and anthropology, and while the relationship may appear merely semantic, I argue that the shared use of the term reveals some commonly desired outcomes, even if the methodologies and motivations differ considerably. When any life is enhanced by an encounter with knowledge, or more specifically the *expression* of knowledge, a service has been provided. Rather than view the goals of the academy and the corporate industry as antithetical, it may be useful to recognize one another as partners in service. And if it's true that the academy and the industry are giant behemoths casting large shadows over creative endeavors, there are figures within both institutions who have taken on the role of activists and advocates: Alan Lomax is to Dan Sheehy is to Peter Gabriel. It is equally useful to consider the power exerted by technologically empowered individuals operating without the support of a university or record company. Audiences and consumers, too, are potential partners in affecting social change. The following section examines a few examples of informed activism, using the tools of music distribution and the dissemination of information without the support of government grants, the validation of a Doctoral degree, or the notoriety of a magazine cover.

Pop(ulist) Activism

The oft-debated democratizing power of the Internet enables users to circumvent traditional centers of control and authority, including academic institutions and music industry corporations. Likewise, the role of gatekeeper once served by scholars and record company executives is now shared by an entire population, a condition that essentially nullifies the concept of the gate itself. Rather than protect the exclusivity of existing territory, a number of populist activists have engaged in endeavors designed to make connections and facilitate exchange, to transform fences and gates into bridges. Working outside the academy, many of these individuals have established new models of applied fieldwork that might be emulated by future folklorists and ethnomusicologists. Two such projects illustrate the common goals shared by both academic and non-academic service initiatives, harnessing the potential of the Internet for connecting individuals and disseminating ideas to an immense audience. Though differing somewhat in the methodologies they employ and the philosophies they espouse, the Voice Project and Playing For Change are both ongoing efforts to effect social change through collective music-making.

The Voice Project grew from an encounter between American NGO volunteer Hunter Heaney and a group of Ugandan women in 2008 (Macsai, 2011). In a move reminiscent of Anthony Seeger's experience with the Suyá people of the Amazon region wherein he was asked to share his music with his informants in the same spirit with which they shared theirs with him, Heaney taught the Ugandan women a song by American folk musician Joe Purdy entitled, "Suitcase." After leaving Uganda, Heaney was emailed a video in which the women performed a brief version of "Suitcase." Heaney was struck by the connection the music had made, and wondered if this connection could be extended. He contacted Purdy, sent him the video, and asked if he might wish to contribute a response. Unfamiliar with Ugandan music, Purdy elected to perform a song by American rock group R.E.M., mirroring the act of connecting via someone else's music. Heaney then came up with the idea of a song chain wherein one musician covers the song of another, and that musician in turn covers a song by an artist of their choice, and so forth.

Heaney realized that this kind of musical exchange could be the centerpiece of a grassroots political initiative to address the plight of the Ugandan women whose families had been wrenched apart by sectarian violence. Partnering with Chris Holmes and Anna Gabriel (daughter of Peter), Heaney founded The Voice Project in 2009. Through Gabriel's industry connections, the foundation was able to enlist a variety of Western pop stars to the cause. With recognizable faces—and voices—attached, the project gained validation, and the Voice Project enticed a number of mid-level indie-rock artists, with the occasional contribution by stars such as Peter Gabriel and members of R.E.M., to create a number of "song chains." Each performance is captured on video with minimal technology employed, often with the musicians performing in their living rooms or basement practice spaces. The constructed candid intimacy serves to humanize the stars as they run through often charmingly unpolished versions of the song they have selected. Each video includes brief moments of awkward conversation before the songs begin, and is presented in widescreen black and white imagery, establishing a highbrow low-fi aesthetic that provides a measure of consistency from video to video.

The videos are made available through streaming sites such as YouTube and Vimeo, and point the viewer to the organization's website, where one can find out about the most recent contribution, get information about the history of the project and any current initiatives, and support the cause with a donation or by purchasing merchandise. The website is designed to resemble, and in many ways functions in the same way as the online homes of pop stars and record labels. But the activist mission of the organization is always front and center. The video performances are the promotional devices meant to lure fans to the site where the real work of the organization is presented in well-crafted informational videos and images. Interestingly, the mission of the Voice Project maintains its focus on the use of music to affect social and political change. While the first influx of funds was utilized for job-training courses and micro-loan programs, the current initiative, conducted in partnership with the United Nations, involves constructing radio towers in Uganda and other regions of central Africa, and broadcasting messages and songs meant to reach the thousands of children kidnapped and conscripted by Joseph Kony's notorious Lord's Resistance Army (LRA). Songs sung by the mothers of these children, urging them to return home and forgiving them for their participation in horrific acts of violence, have proven remarkably effective. According to the organization's website, 50 such children recently appeared in refugee camps, having fled Kony's army after hearing the broadcasts.

An interesting contrast can be made with Playing For Change, a less overtly political project that has reached a considerably wider audience. The published mission statement reads like a typical beauty pageant parody—"to inspire, connect, and bring peace to the world through music."[16] Whereas the musical content of the Voice Project is primarily concerned with luring in contributors to an activist cause, the videos created by Playing For Change are an example of a McLuhan-esque medium as message. Though the Playing For Change Foundation has founded a number of music schools in Africa and Asia, the primary purpose of the project appears to be to demonstrate that peoples from around the world can find common ground in performing (decidedly Western) pop songs together.

"Together" is a decidedly more complex construct in the creation of the Playing For Change videos, though this complexity is also its most effective marketing ploy. Founders Mark Johnson and Enzo Buono hit upon the idea after persuading a Los Angeles–based street musician, Roger Ridley, to allow them to capture his performance on video, using simple but professional quality audio and video recording technology. They then traveled the world, enlisting the participation of other street performers who played along to recordings of Ridley and others. Johnson and Buono then carefully pieced together fairly elaborate arrangements, layering fragments of the various recorded performances to create a composite ensemble performance. In this manner, each musician "collaborated" in the creation of the video.

The results highlight several interesting aspects of music making in the early twenty-first century. The technology that makes these performances possible is incredibly powerful, allowing for an assembly of sonic and visual elements that would have been nearly impossible just a few decades prior. Even more noteworthy is the portability of the technology, a fact made quite obvious to the viewer as each musician is filmed in a variety of locations, often on street corners where they would normally perform, or on postcard-perfect vistas that present the beauty of the natural (and somewhat exoticized) world. The message seems to be that "it's a rather large world made smaller by music." To underscore the breadth of the undertaking, each musician is identified by name and by location; a generic street corner becomes "Rome," a grassy hilltop "South Africa."

The songs that the musicians work with demonstrate the extent to which Western pop music has traversed the globe. While some of the performers appear to have learned the songs especially for the video, others seem completely at ease, their familiarity with Ben E. King or Bob Marley evident in the confident command of the material. The role of the directors of the project in selecting and presenting the songs to the musicians deserves further inquiry. Clearly, some of the early contributors simply ran through their standard repertoire, and it is not surprising that two American musicians well into their golden years would find some overlap in their song bags. But it seems unlikely that every performer of "Stand By Me" already knew the song before Johnson and Buono arrived with their cameras and microphones. Disappointingly, there are no examples of music flowing in the other direction, with New Orleans street musicians grappling with a folk song from Nepal. One unspoken message of Playing For Change is that "*Western pop* music is a universal language."

Though both Playing For Change and the Voice Project have succeeded in furthering their causes, there is a significant difference in the size of their respective audiences, and this difference raises questions about the efficacy of their approaches to culturally situated social activism. As is the case with all US-based nonprofits, the organization must disclose its financial statements. Remarkably, the Voice Project does so with a link directly from the website. Such transparency is laudable, and the graphs illustrating the relatively low administrative costs, coupled with a detailed explanation of how the funds are allocated, serve to assuage any reluctant supporters that their contributions will be well spent. But the numbers themselves in the 2011 statement are less than impressive. Despite attention from media outlets such as *Rolling Stone*, and the glossy business-oriented *Fast Company*, the organization managed to raise little more than a quarter million dollars. Certainly the Voice Project is accomplishing demonstrable results, but in financial terms, perhaps not on a scale commensurate with the star power used to promote their endeavors. It is likely that the overtly political message of the Voice Project inherently limits its appeal. The cause may be noble, and the song threads "cool," but they aren't necessarily "fun." The Playing For Change videos are celebratory, communicating a message that is far more encouraging and comforting, and therefore succeed in the marketplace as a form of escapist entertainment—indeed, the 1999

Playing For Change tour included performances of Bobby McFerrin's oft-derided hit, "Don't Worry, Be Happy."

But the impact of the projects and the size of their receptive audiences may also reflect the degree to which the required presence of "pop stars" is no longer the dominant paradigm in popular music experience. Once the viewers get over the novelty of the technologically enabled collaboration, their eyes and ears are open to the power of music made by people they may have literally passed on the street. To be a fan of Playing For Change is to champion the artistic merit of the unheralded, everyday musician, unsupported by the culture industry machine. The videos initially posted to YouTube consisted exclusively of unknown faces, voices, and fingers. Once the project became more visible, other professional musicians began to appear, notably Israeli guitarist David Broza, American folk-blues musician Keb Mo, and, most disconcertingly in a Bob Marley medley of "War/No More Trouble," U2's Bono. Bono's appearance comes as a shock after watching a stream of unfamiliar figures producing remarkably captivating performances, and illustrates how out of place the music industry of the late twentieth century is in the Internet age. Greil Marcus insightfully critiqued the star-powered charity spectacles of the 1980s, such as "We Are The World" and the Live Aid concert event, contending that such projects functioned mainly as career-enhancing self-promotion for its stars more than as truly effective forms of social activism (Marcus, 1993). A holdover from that era, Bono may have the best of intentions, but his presence dulls the impact of the celebratory, everyman quality of most of the Playing For Change videos, though it would appear that the creators of the project are quite pleased with his participation. They shoot the rock star as a rock star, then apply many of the tropes of rock music videos to the rest of the "War/No More Trouble," with African children moving in slow motion, dreadlocks swaying in sun-drenched silhouette.

The contrasting aesthetics of the Voice Project and Playing For Change illustrate two different approaches to trading on the cultural capital of the "star." Whereas the pop star contributors to the Voice Project are presented as ordinary musicians, the minimal technology employed and lack of editing and other enhancements serving to humanize the performers, the Playing For Change videos take the opposite tack, letting the faces of the musicians fill the screen, or framing them in artfully positioned locales, shot in full color, and carefully filtered and mixed so that their performances take on the sheen of million-dollar-budget pop releases. The resulting disparity in audience reception is equally telling. Slumming pop stars are far less interesting than "untainted" and "authentic" unknowns, and this distinction is reflected in realm of YouTube, where the difference between the most successful viral amateur videos and those calculated to reach audiences as part of a marketing campaign is substantial. A case in point, the first Playing For Change video, "Stand By Me," has amassed well over 50 million views on YouTube; the Bono-included "War/No More Trouble" has reached less than 5% of that audience.

Like Simon's *Graceland* and Gabriel's Real World releases and WOMAD festival, Playing For Change greatly enhanced the professional status of many of its participants. Partnering with the Concord Music Group label (responsible for massive hit records from mainstays such as Ray Charles and Paul McCartney), a CD/ DVD package was released in 2009. Later that year, a full-length documentary, *Peace Through Music*, further promoted the phenomenon, and the following year, Playing For Change undertook a concert tour, presenting many of the musicians from the project performing on their own, and in the more traditional sense of "together" for sold out performances across North America. In doing so, the founders of the project harnessed both new forms of media communication via the Internet, and more traditional music industry structures with commercial recordings and concert tour packages. The crucial distinction for both Playing For Change and the Voice Project is that the impetus for establishing each endeavor came from outside either the industry or the academy, initially bypassing the channels of communication, creation, and distribution established in the previous century. These outsiders found ways to reclaim aspects of the existing music industry to serve as tools in creating new models of a more holistic intersection between entertainment, edification, and activism.

The university can also play a role in redefining how institutions, both academic and corporate, can provide resource and support for the public good. The 100 Songs Project, a joint undertaking between Queensland University of Technology and several recording industry professionals, is such an example. A call for submissions of songs and performers goes out to all of Australia. Thousands of demos are submitted, and a panel of producers, publishers, journalists, and academics narrows the list to 100. These performers are then given four hours of free studio time in QUT's commercial facilities, overseen by a group of seasoned record producers, assisted by students earning degrees in sound engineering and production. The resulting recordings are owned and controlled by the musicians, who are free to sell or use them in any way they wish to promote their music. A select group from the 100 is afforded more studio time to craft a more professional final mix, and the results are collected on a CD, promoted to radio, and sold in major retail outlets.[17]

While the university benefits from the visibility of the project, even more significantly, its students gain invaluable "real world" experience during the sessions. The industry is able to use the submissions as a way of scouting for new talent, and then can test the acts' commercial potential based upon the reaction at radio and retail. And the hundreds of musicians from across the country are given access to high-quality recording facilities and guidance from recording professionals, with the top results presented to the general public, supported by a promotional machine far beyond the means of most self-managed performers.

At this date, the existing music industry functions as less of a hegemonic monstrosity than a sometimes useful skeleton of its former self. Commercial releases and concert tours can aid in connecting musicians to fans, but they are not the sole, nor even the most effective, ways of reaching and creating audiences. Projects like Playing For Change and the Voice Project operate in a similar fashion to many professional pop musical acts, harnessing the power of the Internet initially to broadcast their messages, then subsequently to maintain a dialog with their fans, extending that discourse to include older industry mainstays such as recordings for sale and concert performances. The nineteenth century depended upon the arterial networks of transportation facilitated by railways, but by the twenty-first century, thousands of miles of track lay abandoned, their purpose usurped by superhighways and airliners. Those same tracks are now often reclaimed as bike paths and walking trails, and I propose that the music industry structure is undergoing a similar reclamation.

Conclusion: All for One

Playing For Change and the Voice Project are but two examples of applied ethnomusicology that fall outside the purview of the academy or the culture industry. Bypassing traditional gatekeepers—whether they be journal editors or record company A&R scouts—these projects connect musicians, promoters, and audiences at a speed and scope that dwarfs the "competition" of universities and corporations. Crowd-sourced, crowd-driven, crowd-funded enterprises challenge the hegemonic power of both industry and the academy. Perhaps the clearest counter to the irrelevancy of both institutions is to recognize commonalities, and to develop partnerships that create shared agendas and serve them effectively. Product-line managers and marketing geniuses have much to contribute to the success of activist endeavors; intellectually engaged advocates can help to shape the agendas behind the initiatives.

The role of the applied ethnomusicologist is not to be the sole voice of authority, but rather to be a useful contributor to a network of actors involved in the endeavor. The value of the contribution stems from the training that has heightened an awareness of the potential pitfalls of (re)presentation of culture from macro to micro levels. As culture brokers, applied ethnomusicologists should be less concerned with preventing misrepresentation, than with facilitating forms of representation that serve the needs of performers and promoters alike, to help guide these forces to arrive at mutually beneficial outcomes. In other words, the profit-driven motivations of the industry are not inherently antithetical to those of either the performing musician *or* the research academic. The forces of business are far less concerned with the forms of representation than they are with the efficacy of those forms in generating revenue. The practicalities of marketing require condensed, simple images and text that can communicate a rich spectrum of meaning. Ugly cultural stereotypes do this well, and thus have been effectively used for centuries. The challenge lies in constructing reductionist representations that respect traditions, performers, and audiences alike. Here is an area for the applied ethnomusicologist to make a useful contribution—not to avoid dirtying the hands by delving into marketing campaigns, but rather to make marketing campaigns less dirty.

The history of the music business is fraught with examples of crass exploitation, examples that highlight the forms of abuse that have often been standard industry practice. A knowledge of this history, even if only cursory and apocryphal, has led many folklorists to attempt to steer their informants away from the inevitably doomed outcomes of any encounters with culture merchants. But academics must also be receptive to the desires of their collaborators—including those that dream of a professional career within the music industry. In this case, applied ethnomusicologists can make significant contributions to the communities they work with by helping musicians to navigate unchartered waters of copyright ownership, contractual obligations, and marketing strategies. Indeed, an understanding of the basic operations of the music industry may be the most valuable information they can share with their partners in research.

In many ways, the knee-jerk casting of music industrialists as arbiters of evil is as condescending as those of the images the music industry has often used to sell its products. The history of the record business, for example, is filled with figures who approached the music they profited from with love and respect, even if their fortunes far exceeded those of the musicians they championed. And even as the record industry became ever more absorbed by larger corporate interests, the people at the helm of these companies did not set out to destroy the music they marketed, but inadvertently damaged the culture that gave rise to the music by opting for short-term gains over long-term profit. In all of these instances, a more insightful voice attuned to the needs of commerce as well as art would have helped prevent some of the worst abuses, and could have created a more viable and sustainable culture of music-related commerce, where artistic expression generates profits, and the system facilitates expression.

There are many examples of such systems, though historically they have often been relegated to the very few stars whose industrial clout ensured that the system worked for them. While the most successful musicians of all time, the Beatles, were the recipients of only a small fraction of the moneys they generated, they also clearly benefited from the technological resources provided by the corporate interests that owned their recorded output, utilizing the machines of the machine as vehicles of creative expression. The key now is to make the technology that enables creative expression and the means to present those creations to welcoming audiences available to a much larger number of musicians. In turn, these individuals will reclaim their agency over a system that was either completely closed to them, or only briefly open, in order to find new bodies—and bodies of work—to exploit. George Lipsitz notes, "the interconnectedness of capitalist culture might help create collective solutions to the systematic and unrelenting injustice and austerity which characterizes life for so many people on this planet" (Lipsitz, 1994: 17).

Many such endeavors are already underway. The world music market, so markedly shaped by successful pop artists establishing systems of musical exchange that value musicians and musical cultures, is a prime example of "long tail" viability (Anderson, 2008). Inarguably, many more figures currently earn comfortable livings from their music than even two or three decades ago. Perhaps there are fewer musician-owned yachts and jet planes, but there are significantly more two-bedroom home mortgage payments being made by professional musicians. Countering the outdated stereotypes of the rock star lifestyle is another area where applied ethnomusicologists can make a contribution, clarifying what is possible for aspiring musicians and helping to reshape fantasy into a more practical and sustainable reality.

"Sustainability" is the current buzzword, applied as often to the production of food or energy as to that of culture and its byproducts. A sustainable business model engenders a fundamental sense of respect for both the consumers of products and for those responsible for providing the products for consumption. The products themselves must be cultivated and renewed. Fields are harvested, but are also enriched in cycles of productivity and rest. Such an approach requires that a commercial institution develop *patience*, reducing the amount of immediate profit in exchange for longer-term continual rewards. I have seen this philosophy enacted by my own students earning degrees in music business. Far from embodying the stereotypical cigar-chomping exploiter of musicians and audiences, squeezing the last bit of profit out of a performer before discarding him on the slag heap of irrelevant pop stars and moving on to the next vein of unrefined ore/talent, this generation is primarily concerned with facilitating musical encounters, helping musicians and audiences find one another, while simultaneously enriching the experience for all involved. They are coming of age at a time when concepts like "service enterprise" and "open source" are no longer novel ideas, but practical realities. The next generation of music industrialists may have a social agenda equal to that of the growing numbers of applied ethnomusicologists. The future of both academia and the industry may indeed hinge upon a redefinition of the terms "service," "institutions," "scholarship," and "activism" as a nexus of music production and dissemination, placing the academy within the culture industry, acknowledging commercial interests as knowledge producers, and empowering music fans as social activists.

Notes

1. Feld published articles on the issues that arose in his efforts to create and release *Voices of the Rainforest* (Rykodisc 10173, 1991a), see Feld, Steven. "Voices of the Rainforest" *Public Culture* 4(1) (1991b): 131–140.
2. For context, the following sources have laid the groundwork for research in the areas of music industry (Chapple and Garofalo 1977; Negus 1999), applied anthropology and ethnomusicology (Foster 1969; Titon 1992; Harrison 2012), and the impact of a global industry on local music traditions (Wallis and Malm, 1984; Mitchell, 1996), among others.
3. John Lomax was most responsible for the initial presentation of Leadbelly to the general public, and many of the issues of representation subsequently identified by scholars also troubled Alan Lomax. Even more perplexing for the younger Lomax was Leadbelly's continued use of the prison overalls and hay bale stage sets originally conceived by the elder Lomax, even after Alan took over the role of agent and manager.
4. Jeff Todd Titon suggests that Lomax's marketing of self may have something to do with his familiarity with the academy and its notions of authored scholarship, in contrast to "company men" such as Peer et al., whose accomplishments were recognized with a paycheck, or ownership stake in the products. I thank him for this insight.
5. *Bosavi: Rainforest Music from Papua, New Guinea* (Smithsonian Folkways, 40487, 2001).
6. VoxLox website, http://voxlox.myshopify.com/pages/about-us, accessed August 27, 2013.
7. *Classic Albums—Paul Simon: Graceland*, Rhino Home Video 105845RHDVD, 1997.

8. Luaka Bop's stable included such artists as Brazilian experimentalist Tom Ze, Indian *filmi* music composer Vijaya Anand, Zap Mama, the female vocal group from Zimbabwe, and the British *bangrha* band, Cornershop. Real World Records initially focused on Gabriel collaborators such as Senegalese vocalist Youssou N'Dour and Pakistani *qawwalli* singer Nusrat Fateh Ali Khan before branching out to more traditional global folk musics, albeit wrapped in a cloud of digitally enhanced sonics (see Laing, 2010).
9. Byrne, David. "Luaka Bop History" (http://luakabop.com/history/, accessed August 26, 2013).
10. Parks wrote the lyrics for Brian Wilson's aborted *Smile* album, and Cooder played on several Rolling Stones sessions, famously showing Keith Richards the open G tuning that became central to the band's classic 1970s recordings.
11. Jeff Todd Titon points out that Taj Mahal, Cooder's former bandmate in The Rising Sons, pursued a similar musical career in the 1970s, moving from electrified Chicago-style blues, through a sepia-toned embrace of 1920s and 1930s American delta blues, to an extended survey of traditional and contemporary Haitian musical practices. I posit that race factored into the difference in visibility and viability in the careers of Ry Cooder and Taj Mahal, with racial "othering" positioning Cooder as the more "unique" of the two musicians.
12. *Buena Vista Social Club* (Nonesuch/World Circuit 79478, 1997).
13. *Buena Vista Social Club* (Artisan DVD 10176, 1999).
14. The value of back catalog became most apparent to the industry only in the late 1980s when compact disc reissues of product from the vaults, such as Columbia's Robert Johnson boxed set, *Robert Johnson: The Complete Recordings* (Columbia C2K 46222, 1990), generated millions of dollars in hitherto unexplored revenue streams.
15. Eric Hobsbawm demonstrated that once an authored work has been naturalized as "traditional," it replicates and evolves in the same manner as non-authored work, in time becoming as traditional as the form it was crafted to resemble (Hobsbawm, 1983). Dave Harker calls attention to the political agendas and commercial interests that such invented traditions often serve (Harker, 1985). Hobsbawm and Harker have a point, but such logic rests on the assumption that an "authentic" exists, a *real* lore to contrast the *fake* lore they identify. Barbara Kirschenblatt-Gimblett counters that, "the folkloristic enterprise is not and cannot be beyond ideology, national political interests, and economic concerns" (Kirshenblatt-Gimblett, 1992: 32), and that folkloric festival representations push these undercurrents to the visible surface (Kirshenblatt-Gimblett, 1998). Margaret Sarkissian makes a convincing argument that festival staging empowers marginalized populations to establish and reclaim their cultural and political identity (Sarkissian, 2000).
16. Playing For Change website, http://playingforchange.com/journey/introduction(accessed August 25, 2013).
17. Howlett, Mike, and Phil Graham. "Creating New Music Ecologies: QUT's 100 Songs Project," presented at the 2013 Art of Record Production Conference, Université Laval, Quebec City, Canada, unpublished paper.

REFERENCES

Anderson, Chris. (2008). *The Long Tail: Why the Future of Business is Selling Less of More.* New York: Hyperion.

Attali, Jacques. (1989). *Noise: The Political Economy of Music*, trans. Brian Massumi. Minneapolis: University of Minnesota Press.

Byrne, David. (2013). *Luaka Bop History*. http://luakabop.com/history/ (accessed August 26, 2013).

Cantwell, Robert. (1993). *Ethnomimesis: Folklife and the Representation of Culture*. Chapel Hill, NC: University of North Carolina Press.

Chapple, Steve, and Reebee Garofalo. (1977). *Rock 'N' Roll is Here to Pay: The History and Politics of the Music Industry*. Chicago: Nelson Hall.

Chu, Jeff, and Jessica Weiss. (2013). "The Cobbler's Conundrum." *Fast Company*, Issue 177 (July/August 2013): 98–112.

Feld, Steven. (1991a). *Voices of the Rainforest: A Day in the Life of the Kaluli People*. Salem, MA: Rykodisc 10173.

Feld, Steven. (1991b). "Voices of the Rainforest." *Public Culture* 4(1): 131–140.

Feld, Steven. (2000). "The Poetics and Politics of Pygmy Pop." In *Western Music and its Others: Difference, Representation, and Appropriation in Music*, edited by Georgina Born and David Hesmondhalgh. Berkeley: University of California Press.

Filene, Benjamin. (2000). *Romancing The Folk: Public Memory & American Roots Music*. Chapel Hill, NC: University of North Carolina Press.

Foster, George. (1969). *Applied Anthropology*. Boston: Little, Brown and Company.

Friedman, Thomas L. (2007). *The World Is Flat: A Brief History of the Twenty-First Century*. New York: Picador.

Frith, Simon. (2000). "The Discourse of World Music." In *Western Music and its Others: Difference, Representation, and Appropriation in Music*, edited by Georgina Born and David Hesmondhalgh. Berkeley: University of California Press.

Frith, Simon. (2006). "The Industrialization of Music." In *The Popular Music Studies Reader*, edited by Andy Bennett, Barry Shank, and Jason Toynbee. London: Routledge.

Harker, Dave. (1985). *Fakesong: The Manufacture of British 'Folksong' 1700 to the Present Day*. London: Open University Press.

Harrison, Klisala. (2012). "Epistemologies of Applied Ethnomusicology." *Ethnomusicology* 56(3): 505–529.

Hobsbawm, Eric. (1983). "Introduction: Inventing Traditions." In *The Invention of Tradition*, edited by Eric Hobsbawm and Terence Ranger. Cambridge: Cambridge University Press.

Kennedy, Rick, and Randy McNutt. 1999. *Little Labels-Big Sound: Small Record Companies and the Rise of American Music*. Bloomington, IN: Indiana University Press.

Kirshenblatt-Gimblett, Barbara. (1992). "Mistaken Dichotomies." In *Public Folklore*, edited by Robert Baron and Nicholas R. Spitzer. Washington, D.C.: Smithsonian Institution Press.

Kirshenblatt-Gimblett, Barbara. (1998). *Destination Culture: Tourism, Museums, and Heritage*. Berkeley: University of California Press.

Laing, David. (2010). "'Hand-made, Hi-tech, Worldwide': Peter Gabriel and World Music." In *Peter Gabriel, From Genesis to Growing Up*, edited by Michael Drewett, Sarah Hill and Kimi Kärki. London: Ashgate.

Lipsitz, George. (1994). *Dangerous Crossroads: Popular Music, Postmodernism and the Poetics of Place*. London: Verso.

Macsai, Dan. (2011). "Rock Stars Lend Their Sound to Ugandan Women of the Voice Project." *Fast Company*. http://www.fastcompany.com/1747592/rock-stars-lendtheir-sound-ugandan-women-voice-project (accessed July 11, 2013).

Marcus, Greil. (1993). "Number One with a Bullet." In *In The Fascist Bathroom: Punk in Pop Music, 1977–1992*. Cambridge, MA: Harvard University Press.

Meintjes, Louise. (1990). "Paul Simon's Graceland, South Africa, and the Mediation of Musical Meaning." *Ethnomusicology* 34(1): 37–73.

Mitchell, Tony. (1996). *Popular Music and Local Identity: Rock, Pop and Rap in Europe and Oceania*. London: Leicester University Press.

Negroponte, Nicholas. (1995). *Being Digital*. New York: Knopf.

Negus, Keith. (1992). *Producing Pop: Culture and Conflict in the Popular Music Industry*. London: Arnold.

Negus, Keith. (1999). *Music Genres and Corporate Cultures*. London: Routledge.

Rice, Timothy. (1994). *May It Fill Your Soul: Experiencing Bulgarian Music*. Chicago: University of Chicago Press.

Russell, Bertrand. (1905 [2005]). "On Denoting." *Mind* 114(456): 873–887.

Sarkissian, Margaret. (2000). *D'Albuquerque's Children: Performing Tradition in Malaysia's Portuguese Settlement*. Chicago: University of Chicago Press.

Sheehy, Daniel. (1992). "'Crossover Dreams': The Folklorist and the Folk Arrival." In *Public Folklore*, edited by Robert Baron and Nicholas R. Spitzer. Washington, D.C.: Smithsonian Institution Press.

Shelemay, Kay Kaufman. (1991). "Recording Technology, the Record Industry, and Ethnomusicological Scholarship." In *Comparative Musicology and Anthropology of Music*, edited by Bruno Nettl and Philip V. Bohlman. Chicago, IL: University of Chicago Press.

Spitzer, Nicholas R. (1992). "Cultural Conversation: Metaphors and Methods in Public Folklore." In *Public Folklore*, edited by Robert Baron and Nicholas R. Spitzer. Washington, D.C.: Smithsonian Institution Press.

Szwed, John. (2010). *Alan Lomax: The Man Who Recorded the World*. London: Penguin Books.

Taylor, Timothy D. (1997). *Global Pop: World Music, World Markets*. New York: Routledge.

Titon, Jeff Todd. (1985). "Stance, Role, and Identity in Fieldwork Among Folk Baptists and Pentacostals." *American Music* 3(1): 16–24.

Titon, Jeff Todd. (1992). "Music, the Public Interest, and the Practice of Ethnomusicology." *Ethnomusicology* 36(3): 315–322.

Wallis, Roger, and Krister Malm. (1984). *Big Sounds from Small Peoples: The Music Industry in Small Countries*. New York: Pendragon.

Warschauer, Mark, and Morgan Ames. (2010). "Can One Laptop Per Child Save the World's Poor?." *Journal of International Affairs* 64(1): 33–51.

Index

Note: Tables and figures are indicated by t and f following the page number

ʿAbbāsid Caliphate, 148
Abdurashidov, Abdulvali, 135, 136f
Abo Academi University, 283
Abraham, Otto, 190, 197
Academia
    applied ethnomusicology in, 266–268
    music business degree programs, 292
    scholarship, 250–251, 302–303, 319
Academy of Maqâm, 135, 139, 140, 140f
Access to education, 92–100
Access to musical traditions,
    instructional, 82–84
Accordions, 214–215
Activism, 312–317, 319
    environmental sound, 7
Adams, Greg C., 234, 244
"Advanced Arts Going into Campuses"
    program (China), 258
Advocacy, 6, 10, 21, 25, 27, 55, 59, 76, 79, 99, 119,
    146, 172, 245, 247, 253
    and cultural policy, 247
    early history of, 27
    and sustainability, 59
Aesthetics, cultural, 105, 279
AFC (American Folklife Center), 23, 231, 233–234
Africa, 37
African-American musicians, 83, 107
African American popular music, 159
AFS (American Folklore Society),
    233–234, 250
Aga Khan III, 134–135
Aga Khan IV, 134, 135
Aga Khan Humanities Project (AKHP), 58,
    135–138
    application, 138–141
    cinema group, 138

curriculum, 136–138
evolutionary phases, 138
Internet technology, 138
music, 119–151
pluralism, 144–146, 150–151
publications, 149
research, 141–144
sponsorship of, 135
status of, 149
truth in, 145–146
Aga Khan Music Initiative, 135, 137, 150–151
Aga Khan Trust for Culture, 150–151
Agnew, Spiro, 236
Agriculture Exhibition Centre
    (Beijing, China)
    China's Intangible Cultural Heritage
        Traditional Craft Exhibition, 261
    Productive Protection of China's Intangible
        Cultural Heritage Exhibition, 261
Akkordion, 214
Alabama Center for Traditional Culture, 240
Alabama State Council on the Arts, 240
Albarn, Damon, 291–292
Alexander, Delia, 89–91
Ali-Bouromand, Nour, 168
All-City Arts progams, 95
All-City Orchestra, 95
All for one, 317–319
Alviso, Ric, 26
Amazon, 309
American Ballads and Folk Songs (Lomax,
    Lomax, and Kittredge), 231
American Folklife Center (AFC), 23, 231
    collections, 233–234
    establishment of, 231, 233–234
    ethnomusicologists at, 233–234

American Folklore Society (AFS), 233–234, 250
American Musicological Society (AMS), 16
Analytical Studies in World Music (Tenzer), 166
Anand, Vijaya, 320
Ancient Greeks, 129–130
Anderson, Harold, 244
Anderson, William M., 166
Andersson, Nils, 205–207, 211–220, 213f, 224
Andersson, Olof, 206
Andersson, Otto, 224
Appalachian mountains, 5
Apple, 309
Applied: in other disciplines, 35–36
Applied anthropology, early, 19–20
Applied ethnomusicologists, 228–252
　role of, 317
Applied ethnomusicology, 80, 81–88, 119–120
　in academia, 266–267
　advocacy, 6, 27, 56
　Alexander on, 89–91
　archives and, 189–225
　being, knowing, and doing, 8–9
　Berger on, 33
　in China, 254–289
　as commerce, 291–292
　as conscious practice, 31
　contextualized definition of, 88–100
　contextualized strategies for partnerships for learning through music, 100–103
　cultural policy interventions, 5–6
　definitions of, 3–4, 7-8, 49–50, 88–100, 120, 255
　early work, 19–20
　education, 6
　in education, 69–108
　as emergent movement, 1
　in environmental sound activism and ecojustice, 7
　epistemological orientation, 8
　hermeneutic method, 121–127
　history of, 19–29, 41-49
　humane, 138–141
　humanist theory of, 127–132
　humanitarian, 133–138
　insularity, 9
　International Council for Traditional Music on, 46–49
　in journalism, 7
　in law and music industry, 7
　in libraries, museums, and sound archives, 7
　in mass entertainment, 268–270
　Maultsby on, 89–91
　in medicine, 7
　vs. non-academic work, 32
　in North America, 5–8
　opportunities for, 81–88
　origins of, 230–231
　in peace and conflict resolution, 7
　philosophical reflection on, 120–121
　power imbalance, 32–33
　professionalization, 17–19
　public, 8
　vs. public folklore, 7–8
　vs. public-sector ethnomusicology, 7–8
　scope, 3–4
　Sheehy on, 88–89
　in social life, 270–273
　strategies for, 88–100
　theory vs. practice, 120
　Titon on, 171
　as unified voice, 119–120
　in U.S., 9–29
Applied Ethnomusicology: Historical and Contemporary Approaches (Harrison, Mackinlay, and Pettan), 27, 31
Applied Ethnomusicology Section, SEM, 243
Applied musicology, 255
Apprenticeships, 247–248
al-'Arabī, 130–131, 133–134
Araújo, Samuel, 37, 56, 102–103, 108, 172
Archive of Folk Culture, Library of Congress, 23, 81, 230, 231
Archive of Folk Song, Library of Congress, 230–231
Archives, 189–225, 244. *See also* Databases
　cultural heritage process and, 201–203
　definitions of, 190–191, 192
　folk music, 189–225
　functions of, 191
　history of, 191–199
　objectives or purposes of, 189–190, 192–193
　public, 192

rationales for, 199–200
sound archives, 7
Archives of African American Music and Culture, 107
Archives of Traditional Music and Culture, Indiana University, 107
Arendt, Hannah, 121
Arhoolie label, 305
Armchair ethnomusicology, 244–245
Art: music as, 124
Arthur M. Sackler Gallery (Washington, D.C.), 234
Art Is Education project (YANEO), 76–77, 99–100
Artists
　in the schools, 58
　teaching, 69, 75–78, 83–84, 85–87, 98–99, 107
a/r/tographers, 78
Arts education
　high-quality, 106
　partnerships for, 57–58, 73–77, 106
Arts Education Partnership, 106
Arts integration, 72, 77–79
Arts opportunity gap, 86
Aryan philosophy, 142
Asch, Moses, 234, 235, 304–305
Asian-Pacific-American (APA) Program, 245
Association for Cultural Equity, 167
Atlanta Symphony Orchestra, 107
Attali, Jacques, 310
Australia, 36–37
Authenticity, 164, 175, 307, 315, 320
　of folk music, 215–216
　identification of, 215–216
Authority, 301
Avorgbedor, Daniel, 37
Azra project, 34–35

Backas, James, 237
Badakhshan, 126, 139, 142–143, 147, 148
Badakhshani lute *(rubab)*, 130, 142, 148, 150
Bailey, John, 168
Bakan, Michael, 26, 166, 168
Baldwin Wallace University Conservatory, 75, 94, 95

Balinese music education, 170
Baron, Robert, 239, 240
Barons, Krišjānis, 194–199
Bartok, Bela, 298
Barz, Gregory, 100
Bayard, Samuel, 236
Beck, Jane, 239
Beijing, China
　Financial Street, 259, 260f
　musical lives of seniors in, 270–273, 271f, 272f
Beijing Financial Street Administration, 259
Beijing Opera Theatre of China, 258
Beijing Television, 271–272
Being, knowing, and doing, 8–9
Being in the world *(dasein)*, 123
Belonging, sense of: deepening, 87–88
Berger, Harris M., 33
Berliner, Paul, 25, 169
Berlin Phonogramm-Archiv, 197–199
Berlin School, 190, 197, 198–199
Beste-s (classical songs), 135
Bezić, Jerko, 40
Bi-musicality, 17, 22, 250, 301–302
al-Bīrūnī, 128
Björkholm, Johanna, 202
Blackfoot, 167
Blacking, John, 121, 165, 168, 169, 178, 180
Bleibinger, Bernhard, 37
Bloco Vomit, 175
Blues, 159
Blues Archive, Chicago Public Library, 107
Blum, Stephen, 83
Boas, Franz, 10, 12
Bohman, Stefan, 201–202
Bono, 315
Borrowings, stylistic, 301
Bosavi, 297
Bosavi (Papua, New Guinea), 296–297
Bosnian refugees, 34–35
Boström, Mathias, 222
Botkin, Benjamin, 230
Brian Jones Presents the Pan Pipes of Jajouka, 299
Brown, Kimasi, 273
Broza, David, 315
Bubugao (Stepping High), 277

Buena Vista Social Club, 292, 301–302
Bukharan Judaism, 137
Bulgarian *gaida* (bagpipe), 168–169
Bunyan, Paul, 236
Buono, Enzo, 314–315
Burke, Peter, 223
Burnim, Mellonee V., 81, 100, 166
Burton, Bryan, 80
Buschmann, Friedrich, 214
Business. *See* Commerce
Business degree programs, 292
Bustin, Dillon, 239
Byrne, David, 291–292, 300–301, 303

CAEC (Cleveland Arts Education Consortium), 76–77
Ćaleta, Joško, 43
Campbell, Patricia Shehan, 21, 79–80, 166
Cantwell, Robert, 306–307
Cao Jun, 256
Carey, George, 236–237
Carlins, Richard, 225
Case Western Reserve University, 94
Castelo-Branco, Salwa El-Shawan, 29, 33, 54
Cavicchi, Daniel, 81
CBS, 305
CCP (Chinese Communist Party), 257–258, 263
CCTV. *See* Chinese Central Television
CD recordings. *See* Recordings
Center for Educational Partnerships in Music, Georgia State University, 107
Center for Folklife and Cultural Heritage (CFCH), 231, 234–235
Central Asia, 125, 143
Central Ballet Theatre (China), 258
Central Conservatory of Music (China), 266
 English translations of Chinese music records, 278–279
 Musical Instrument Exhibition Centre, 273, 280–283, 280f, 281f
 Musicology Department, 273, 274–277, 275f
 Musicology Research Institute, 267, 288
 Sino-African Music Dialogue, 274
 World Music Days, 273, 274–277, 275f
Central Conservatory of Music Press, 273

Central National Music Orchestra, 258
Central Opera House (China), 258
Central skylights *(chahar khaneh),* 142, 144f
Central Symphony Orchestra (China), 258
Ceribašić, Naila, 42
Cerna, John, 179
CFCH (Center for Folklife and Cultural Heritage), 231, 234–235
Chahar khaneh (skylights), 142, 144f
Channel 11 (Chinese Opera Channel), 269–270
Chant, 137, 193
Chavez, Carlos, 160
Chessin, Ethan, 179
Chicago, Illinois, 5
Chicago Public Library, 107
China, 254–289
 academia, 266–267
 "Advanced Arts Going into Campuses" program, 258
 applied ethnomusicology in, 254–289
 cultural diversity, 275
 Cultural Heritage Day, 261
 folk music, 263–264, 264f
 individual perspective on, 273–283
 intangible cultural heritages, 254, 260–265, 264f, 265f, 284, 287–288
 Interministerial Conference for the Protection of Intangible Cultural Heritage, 261
 mass entertainment, 268–270
 Ministry of Culture, 257–258, 288
 Ministry of Education, 258
 Ministry of Finance, 258
 music, 254–255, 263–264, 264f
 music activities in communities, 257–260
 musical databases, 266–267
 Musical Instrument Exhibition Centre, 280–283, 281f
 musical lives of Beijing seniors, 270–273, 271f, 272f
 People's Congress, 257–258
 political construction, 257–260
 Reform and Opening Up policy, 263–264
 research findings in, 256–257
 social construction, 260–265
 social life, 270–273

social perspective on, 257–273
spiritual life, 263–264, 265f
symphony orchestras, 258
tourism in, 261–262, 264
World Music Days, 274–277, 275f, 276f
Xinjiang Autonomous Region, 266
China Arts Academy, 281–282
China Arts Research Institute, 283
China Conservatory of Music, 278
China-Finland Festival and Symposium Dialogue in Music, 274
China-India Festival and Symposium Dialogue in Music, 274
China-Indonesia Festival and Symposium Dialogue in Music, 274
China International Intangible Cultural Heritage Festival, 261
China-Japan Festival and Symposium Dialogue in Music, 274
China–New Zealand and Pacific Festival and Symposium Dialogue in Music, 274
China's Intangible Cultural Heritage Traditional Craft Exhibition, 261
Chinese Central Television (CCTV)
    Chinese Opera Channel (Channel 11), 269–270
    Fenghua Guoyue (Elegant Chinese Music) program, 269
    Television Grand Prix for Young Singers, 268, 270
    Traditional Instrumental Music Performance Competition, 268–269
    traditional music programs, 268–270
Chinese Communist Party (CCP), 257–258, 263
Chinese Dream, 263–264
Chinese Guqin Musical Culture Database, 267
Chinese Intangible Cultural Heritage (website), 288
Chinese Intangible Cultural Heritage Exhibition, 261
Chinese Intangible Cultural Heritage Traditional Craft Exhibition, 261
Chinese Musicians Association, 258
Chinese music records: English translations of, 278–279
Chinese opera, 263–264, 265f

Chinese Opera Channel (Channel 11), 269–270
Chinese *sheng*, 214
Chinese traditional music, 279
    Chinese Central Television (CCTV) programs on, 268–270
Choirs, 167
Christensen, Dieter, 53
Christensen Fund, 151
Christians and Christianity, 128, 129–130, 137
Chun Jiang Hua Yue Ye (Spring River and Flowery Moon Night), 279
Cinema, 138
City Lore—The New York Center for Urban Folk Culture, 239
Clang of the Mighty Reaper, 301
Classical music (*shashmaqam*), 135, 140
Classical songs (*beste-s*), 135
Classification, 202–203, 219
Cleveland, Ohio
    All-City Arts programs, 95
    area arts scene, 82–83
    demographic characteristics, 96–97
    geographic characteristics, 96
    immigrant communities, 96
    minority populations, 96
    partnerships for arts education, 57–58
    poverty, 82, 93, 95, 96–97
    public education, 71–77, 81–88, 92–100
    racial segregation, 95, 96–97
    social barriers, 92–100
    University Circle district, 94
Cleveland Arts Education Consortium (CAEC), 76–77
Cleveland Foundation, 99, 108
Cleveland Institute of Music, 75, 94
Cleveland Metropolitan School District (CMSD), 74–75, 82, 95
    Academic Transformation Plan, 86
    All-City Orchestra, 95
    Department of Arts Education, 93
    East Technical High School, 86
    PASS (Premier Arts Specialty System), 93
    Transformation Plan, 93
Cleveland Music School Settlement, 75
Cleveland Music Therapy Consortium, 76
Cleveland Opera, 98–99

Cleveland Orchestra, 75, 82–83, 94
Cleveland School of the Arts (CSA), 93, 94
Clifford, James, 145–146
Climati, Antonio, 30
Clinton, Bill, 233
CMSD. *See* Cleveland Metropolitan School District
CNKI, 267
Code Napoléon, 127–128
Cognition of performance, 168
Collaborations
  with folklorists, 245, 297–298
  in video, 314–315
Collaborative process, 73
Collectivization, 126
The College Board, 79
Columbia Records, 304–305, 320
Commerce, 291–320
  all for one, 317–319
  as applied ethnomusicology, 291–292
  cultural merchants and brokers, 293–298, 302–303, 304–306
  cultural promotion, 293–296
  folklorists in, 296, 306
  music business degree programs, 292
  mutually beneficial exploitation in, 298–303
  pop(ulist) activism in, 312–317
  from resource exploitation to service enterprise, 303–311
  self-promotion, 293–296
  sustainability in, 318
  technology, media, and marketing, 291
Committee on Applied Ethnomusicology, SEM, 26
Commodification, 59
Communication: music as, 200
Communities. *See also specific communities*
  music activities in, 257–260
Community music, 58
  as field of practice, 156–157
  intersections with ethnomusicology and music education, 156–181
  popularity of, 170–173
  scope and applications of, 171–173
Comparative musicology, 12–13
  vs. ethnomusicology, 38–39, 38t, 163–164, 198
  vs. folk music research, 38–39, 38t
Concept-based arts integration, 78
Concord Music Group label, 315–316
Conflict resolution: music for, 7, 58
Confucius, 288
Connections, from music, 72
Conservation, cultural. *See* History of cultural conservation, U.S.
Conservatories, 126
Constructivist framework, 73
Contextualized applied ethnomusicology, 88–100
  strategies for partnerships for learning through music, 100–103
Convention for the Production of Intangible Cultural Heritage, 260–261
Cooder, Joachim, 301–302
Cooder, Ry, 291–292, 301–302, 320
Cooley, Timothy, 100
Coombs, Philip, 171–172
Copyright ownership, 295–296
Corn, Aaron, 36
Cornershop, 320
Croatia, 39–40, 42–43
Crosby, Bing, 298
CSA (Cleveland School of the Arts), 93, 94
Cuba, 303
Cultural aesthetics, 105
Cultural conservation. *See* History of cultural conservation, U.S.
Cultural democracy, 171
Cultural diversity, 275
Cultural equity, 28
Cultural grey-out, 297
Cultural heritage. *See* Intangible cultural heritage
Cultural Heritage Day, 261
Cultural heritage process, 201–203
  FMK's impact on, 217–222
Cultural institutions. *See specific institutions*
Culturally responsive education, 79–81, 82
Culturally Responsive Teaching: Theory, Research, and Practice (Gay), 106
Cultural merchants and brokers, 293–298, 302–303, 304–306
  Alan Lomax, 293–296, 304–305
  David Byrne, 300–301, 303

Peter Gabriel, 300–301, 303
Ry Cooder, 301–302
Steven Feld, 296–298
Cultural migration, 282–283
Cultural policy, 247
Cultural policy interventions, 5–6
Cultural resources. *See specific resources*
Cultural trauma, 5
Culture
  vs. folk music, 212
  high, 201
  management of, 258
  superculture, 223, 275
Culture Institutes and Stations, 258
Culture shows, 306
Curriculum. *See also* Education
  Aga Khan Humanities Project, 136–138
  applied domain in, 51–52
  ethnomusicology in, 165–166
Cutting, Jennifer, 234, 249
Cuyahoga Community College, 94, 107
  All-City Arts programs, 95
  Tri-C Jazz Fest, 75, 83
Cynthia, Kimberlin, 273

Dainas Collection, 194–199
Dance
  ecstatic, 131, 142
  folk dances, 160
  Mevlevî *sema*, 131–132, 132f
  mortuary dances, 132, 133f
  overlap with music, 121–122, 122f
  polskas, 223
Dance bands, 159
Dance music, 216
Darder, Antonio, 108
Dargie, David, 37
Dasein (being in the world), 123
Dastgāh, 135, 137
Databases, musical, 266–267
  Chinese Guqin Musical Culture Database, 267
  Uyghur Muqam Database, 266
Davis, Martha Ellen, 26
Dayan Guyue She, 262
Deasy, Richard, 72

Debussy, Claude, 298
Decision-making, among partners, 73–77
Decolonization, 25, 28
Deification, 127
Delicious Peace: Coffee, Music and Interfaith Harmony in Uganda, 235
Demian, Cyrill, 214
Democracy, cultural, 171
Derrane, Joe, 240
Derrida, Jacques, 145
Dervishes, Mevlevî, 131–132, 132f
Desk work, 244–245
Development programs. *See specific programs*
Devotional music, 149–150
Devotional songs
  ginan-s, 135, 137
  qawwali-s, 135
Diamond, Beverley, 29, 54, 101
Dickens, Hazel, 247
al-Dīn, Jalāl (Rumi), 131–132, 148, 149
al-Dīn, Shams (Shams-e Tabrīzī), 132
Direct mediation, 35
Dirksen, Rebecca, 27
Discover America, 301
Distantiation, 121, 124, 125
Diversity, cultural, 275
Documentaries, 316
Documentation. *See* Archives
Dongba Palace, 262
Dongjing music, 262
"Don't Worry, Be Happy," 315
Dornfeld, Barry, 240
Dorson, Richard, 17
Drama, Iranian *(ta'ziyeh)*, 135
Dudley, Shannon, 166
Dumnić, Marija, 55
Dunbar-Hall, Peter, 80
Duncan, Arne, 86
Dushanbiyev, Janbaz, 133f, 147
DVDs, 137. *See also* Recordings
Dybeck, Richard, 216
Dyen, Doris, 26

East Technical High School (Cleveland, OH), 86
Ebla, 191
Ecojustice, 7

Ecomusicology, 7
Ecstatic dance, 131, 142
Edda, 193
Education, 6–7. See also Music education
   access to, 92–100
   arts education, 57–58, 73–77, 106
   culturally responsive, 79–81, 82
   ethnomusicology in, 164–167
   expansion of access to musical traditions in, 82–84
   higher education, 162–164,
      music as core subject of, 106–107
   opportunities for applying ethnomusicology in, 81–88
   partnerships for, 89
   systemic school education, 158–162
Education sector, U.S., 69–108
   arts integration, 77–79
   background, 69–71
   cross-institutional applications, 81–88
   ethnomusicologist strategies in, 71
   examples from Cleveland, 73–77, 81–88
   foundations for pedagogy for music, 77–81
   frames for learning through music, 71–73
   multicultural music education in, 79–81
   outcomes, 71
   professional roles in, 77
   strategies for applied ethnomusicology in, 88–100
   summary and suggestions for, 103–105
EGREM, 303
Elegant Chinese Music *(Fenghua Guoyue)*, 269
Ellis, Alexander, 12
Empathy, 121
Empowerment
   commercial or festival, 306, 320
   cultural democracy for, 171
   of ethnomusicologists, 92
   of students, 99
Engle, Carl, 230–231
English translations of Chinese music records, 278–279
Environmental sound activism, 7
Epistemological orientation, 8
Equity, cultural, 28
Eriksson, Karin, 223–224
Esso Trinidad Steel Band, 301
Ethnic records, 304
Ethnomimesis (Cantwell), 306–307

The Ethnomusicologist, 8
Ethnomusicologists. *See also specific individuals*
   decisions, 100–103
   empowerment of, 92
   fellow travelers, 234, 235, 236, 250
   as folklorists, 244
   as government folklorists, 249–252
   personalities and attitudes, 8–9
   places of employment, 3–4
   as public folklorists, 23–24, 228–252
   as state folklorists, 239–240, 241, 244–249
   strategies, 71
Ethnomusicology, 81. *See also applied ethnomusicology and specific topics*
   applied, 80, 81–88, 119–120
   armchair, 244–245
   vs. comparative musicology, 10, 12-14, 16, 23, 38–39, 38t, 163–164
   definitions of, 3, 13–14, 244
   disciplinary challenges, 249–252
   in education, 81–88, 164–167
   vs. folk music research, 38–39, 38t
   hermeneutic method, 121–127
   in higher education, 162–164
   history of, 10-29
   humanized, 25
   as an interdisciplinary field, 14–18
   macro level, 57
   medical, 7, 81, 119
   micro level, 57
   in music education, 156–181
   music pedagogy and, 77–81
   opportunities for, 81–88
   personal practices, 57
   philosophical reflection on, 120–121
   public, 8
   public-sector, 7–8
   social practices, 57
   in U.S. government agency, 228–252
   work in, 5–6
Ethnomusicology (journal), 8, 14, 15
Ethno-Musicology (Kunst), 13
Ethnomusicology: A Very Short Introduction (Rice), 55
Ethnomusicology Review (journal), 27
Euba, Akin, 274
Europe
   applied ethnomusicologies in, 41–43

ethnomusicologies in, 38–41, 38t, 41–43
music education in, 158–159
Evaluation. *See specific programs and types*
Exchange, musical, 312–313
Excursions in World Music (Nettl), 166
Exoticized othering, 298
Experts, knowledge-based, 101
Exploitation
  in music industry, 310, 317–318
  mutually beneficial, 298–303
  of resources, 303–311
Explorer series (Nonesuch Records), 164–165
Eyes on the Prize II, 91

Fakelore, 236, 307, 320
Fan Pavilion Unique Chorus *(Shanting Teshu Hechangdui)*, 271
al-Fārābi, 128, 129
Farrar, Claire, 232
Fast Company, 314
Fataburen, 205
FDA (Frederick Douglass Academy), 173–176, 181
Federal Cylinder Project, 234
Federal Music Project, 230
Federal Writers Project, 230
Feld, Steven, 178, 235, 291, 296–298, 319
Fellow traveler syndrome, 234, 235, 236, 250
Fenghua Guoyue (Elegant Chinese Music), 269
Ferrer, Ibrahim, 301–302
Festival of American Folklife (Smithsonian Folklife Festival), 5, 232, 238
Fewkes, Jesse Walter, 197
Fieldwork, 240, 244–245, 303
  connecting with grant work, 247–248
  expectations of informants in, 305
  field recordings, 304–305
  Titon on, 151
Film, 138, 316
Finnish jazz musicians, 259, 260f
Firth, Simon, 311
Fletcher, Alice Cunningham, 11
Fletcher, Samantha, 172
FMK. See *Folkmusikkommissionen*
Folk and Traditional Arts Division, NEA, 23–24, 232–233, 234, 237–238
  budget, 237–238
  staff, 237–238
  state folklife programs, 237–238

Folk Arts Panel, NEA, 239
Folk Arts Program, NYSCA, 239
Folk dances, 160
Folklife, 228
  state partnerships, 241–242
  U.S. federal programs, 231–236
  U.S. state programs, 236–240
Folklife paradigm, 249–250
Folklife Specialists, 240
Folklore
  and activism, 24
  fakelore, 236, 307, 320
  history of ethnomusicology and, 10, 12, 17, 23, 40–41, 44
  as intangible cultural heritage, 228
  Lomax, Alan, and, 23–24
  public, 7-8, 23–25, 55, 228, 229, 242–244
  public sector, 80
  as strategic governmental outreach, 242–244
  in U.S., 7-8, 23–24
Folklore Forum, 27
Folklorists
  collaboration with, 245, 297–298
  in commerce, 296, 306
  as cultural merchants and brokers, 293–298, 304–305
  public, 228–252
  role of, 293
  state, 239–240, 241, 244
Folk music, 159, 160, 190–191. *See also specific regions and types*
  "authentic," 215–216
  bearers of tradition of, 212–213
  in China, 263–264, 264f
  concept of, 200–201
  as cultural heritage, 203–204, 212, 217–222
  definitions of, 207–209
  essence and origin of, 211–212
  everyday meaning and practitioner's perspective on, 209–210
  instrumental, 211
  key criteria for, 210
  new perspectives on, 217
  research on, 38–39, 38t
  revival of, 23
  Swedish, 203–204, 212, 217–222
  threats to, 213–215, 220
  value of, 215–216
  vocal, 211

Folk Music: A Very Short Introduction (Slobin), 190–191
Folk music archives, 189–225. *See also* Archives
   Berlin Phonogramm-Archiv, 197–199
   fundamental perspectives on, 194–199
   Karl Tirén's yoik collection, 198f
   key issues, 194
   "The Nation in a cabinet" (Krišjānis Barons's work), 194–199
   Swedish *Folkmusikkommissionen* (FMK, Folk Music Commission) collection, 191, 196f, 205–207, 206f, 211, 220, 223
Folk musicians *(spelmän/spelkvinnor)*, 210, 212–213, 213f
Folkmusikkommissionen (FMK, Swedish Folk Music Commission), 213, 225
   collection, 191, 196f, 205–207, 206f, 211, 220, 223
   founding and early history, 205–207, 213
   goals of, 216–217
   identification of "authentic" folk music, 215–216
   impact on cultural heritage process, 217–222
   value scale, 58, 217, 218f
Folk Songs of North America, in the English Language (Lomax), 231
Folk Song U.S.A. (Lomax et al.), 231
Folkways label, 234–235, 304–305
France, 127, 158–159
Frederick Douglass Academy (FDA), 173–176, 181
Freer Gallery of Art, 234
Freire, Paolo, 103
From Bangkok and Beyond (Phoasavadi and Campbell), 166
From Rice Paddies and Temple Yards (Nguyen and Campbell), 166
Frykman, Jonas, 225

Gabriel, Anna, 312–313
Gabriel, Peter, 291–292, 300–301, 303, 311, 312, 320
Galileo Galilei, 127
Gandy Dancers, 240
Gånglåtar (walking tunes), 206–207

Gardner, Howard, 121
Garfias, Robert, 25, 165, 167, 233
Garfunkel, Art, 298
Garland Encyclopedia of World Music, 204
Gaston, E. Thayer, 178
Gates, Henry Louis, 296
Gay, Geneva, 106
Gaye, Marvin, 86
Genesis (band), 301
Georgia: state folklorist in, 240
Georgia State University Center for Educational Partnerships in Music, 107
Gerberg, Miriam, 26
Germany, 127, 158–159
Gharanas, 168
al-Ghazzālī, 130
Gillespie, Dizzy, 298
Ginan-s (devotional songs), 135, 137
Giorgoudes, Panicos, 56
Giving back, 11
Glassie, Henry, 232, 236
Global arena, 30–54
   Africa, 37
   applied ethnomusicology definition and scope in, 31–33
   Australia, 36–37
   European views on applied ethnomusicologies, 41–43
   European views on ethnomusicologies, 38–41, 38t
   individual views, 49–52
   International Council for Traditional Music, 43–46
      on applied ethnomusicology, 46–49
      Society for Ethnomusicology and, 53–55
   intervention in, 30–31, 32
   North America, 37–38
   personal stance on, 33–35
   power imbalance in, 32–33
   South America, 37
   Southeast Asia, 37
   vignette on, 30–31
Global music, 161–162. *See also* World music
Global music industry, 310–311
The Global Music Series (Wade and Campbell, eds.), 166
Global Voices in Song, 167

Goetze, Mary, 167
Gold, Nick, 302
Good Neighbor Policy, 160
Gordon, Robert Winslow, 230
Gourlay, Kenneth, 25
Government folklorists, 230–231, 249–252. *See also specific government-sponsored programs*
Graceland, 298, 299, 303
Gramophone Company, 310
Gramsci, Antonio, 223
Grant, Catherine, 36
Grant panels, 246–247
Grants, 229, 246, 247–248
Grauberger, Steve, 240
Gray, Judith, 234
Greater Cleveland Head Start, 84–85
Green, Archie, 233
Green, Rayna, 234
Gregorian chant, 193
Grimm brothers (Jacob and Wilhelm), 193
Groce, Nancy, 234
GroundWorks Dance Theater, 75
Gujarati, 135
Guqin music, 267
Gurminj Museum, 140
Guthrie, Woody, 235

Halee, Roy, 298
Halpert, Herbert, 12
Hamann, Johann Georg, 195
Hammarlund, Anders, 195
Hampton, Barbara, 233
Han Chinese Taoist music, 262
Han Kuo-Huang, 166
Harker, Dave, 320
Harlem Samba, 173–176
Harmonica (mouth harp), 214
Harrison, George, 299
Harrison, Klisala, 27, 56, 101–102, 119–120
Harrison, Lou, 298
Hart, Mickey, 296
Haskell, Erica, 26, 27
Hasse, John Edward, 234
Hawes, Bess Lomax, 231, 232–233, 237–238, 239
Hawley, Anne, 239

Haydon, Glen, 12, 13
Hazelius Medal, 210
Head Start, 84–85, 97–98
Head Start Program, 107
Heaney, Hunter, 312–313
Heidegger, Martin, 127–128, 145
Helbig, Adriana, 55, 56
Helms, Jesse, 250
Hemetek, Ursula, 38–39, 42
Herder, Johann Gottfried von, 195, 199, 212, 220
Heritage. See *intangible cultural heritage*
Hermeneutic approach, 147
Hermeneutic method, 121–127
Herzog, George, 12–13, 14–15, 23
Heth, Charlotte, 25, 166
Hewitt Packard, 309
Hickerson, Joe, 234
High culture, 201
Higher education, 162–164
Hinduism, 137, 148
Hines, Earl "Fatha," 301
History
  music as, 200
  public, 80
History of cultural conservation, U.S.
  American Folklife Center (AFC), 231–236
  NEA Folk Arts Division, 23–24
  Office of Folklife Studies, 23
History of ethnomusicology, U.S., 9–29
  advocacy, 6, 27, 56
  Boas in, 10, 12
  comparative musicology, 12–13
  critiques, 27–28
  doctoral training, 22
  Dorson in, 17
  Dorson-List-Merriam era in, 17
  Dyen and Davis in, 26
  Ethnomusicology, 14, 15
  European roots of, 12–13
  Fletcher in, 11
  Folk Arts Division of NEA, 23–24
  folklore, 23
  folk music revival, 23
  founding generation's research, 21
  giving back, 11
  Herzog in, 12, 14–15, 23
  Hood in, 21

History of ethnomusicology, U.S. (*cont.*)
   humanistic turn, 25
   institutional demand for professors, 22
   institutional growth, 21–22
   International Folk Music Council and, 16–17
   Keil in, 25
   Kunst in, 10, 13
   Lomax in, 5, 11–12, 23
   Matthews in, 10
   McAllester in, 14–15
   McAllester, Merriam, Rhodes, and Seeger's new direction, 15–16
   Merriam in, 14, 16–19
   music as culture move, 24
   Nettl in, 13–15
   Newsletter, 15
   in 1950, 10, 13
   origins and early work, 17–21
   popular interest, 21–22
   postcolonial applied ethnomusicology, 25
   pre-1950, 10
   professionalization, 18
   Seeger in, Anthony, 12
   Seeger in, Charles, 12
   Sheehy in, 11, 25
   skepticism in, 19
   Smithsonian in, 23–24
   Society for Ethnomusicology, 14, 15
      Committee on Applied Ethnomusicology, 26
      current activity, 27
      Section on Applied Ethnomusicology, 26
   theorization in, 27
Hobsbawm, Eric, 320
Hochschule für Musik, 197
Hofman, Ana, 55
Holmes, Chris, 312–313
Holmgren, Merideth, 234–235
Holtzberg, Maggie, 239–240
Homer, 193
HONK! Festival, 172–173, 179
Hood, Mantle, 8, 14, 21, 37, 301
Hornbostel, Erich Moritz von, 197, 198
Howard, Keith, 170
Hufford, David, 236

Humane: music as, 58, 123
Humane humanism, 146
Humaneism, 129, 130
Human interaction and communication: music as, 200
Humanism, 25, 127–129, 148
   critics of, 128
   history of, 127–128
   humane, 146
   Islamic, 128–129
   standard account of, 127
Humanistic: music as, 58, 123
Humanist theory, 127–132. *See also* Humanism
Humanitarian projects: Aga Khan Humanities Project, 58, 135–138
Humanities
   Aga Khan Humanities Project, 58, 135–138
   philosophical reflection in, 120–121
Humanity: music and, 124–127, 144
Human sounds, 121–124
Hurston, Zora Neale, 12

Ibn al-ʿArabī, 130–131
Ibn Sīnā, 128
ICH. *See* Intangible cultural heritage
ICTM. *See* International Council for Traditional Music
Identification, 202, 219
Identity: music as, 200
IFMC (International Folk Music Council), 16–17, 43
IMC (International Music Council), 160
Immigrant communities, 96
Impey, Angela, 37, 172
Important Intangible Cultural Properties, 232
Indiana University Archives of Traditional Music and Culture, 107
Indian Hinduism, 137
Indirect mediation, 35
Institutional partnerships, 69–70
Instruction, music, 165–166. *See also* Music education
Instructional materials, 166–167
   access to musical traditions for, 82–84
Insularity, 9
Intangible cultural heritage (ICH), 202

in China, 254, 260–265, 264f, 265f, 284, 287–288
China International Intangible Cultural Heritage Festival, 261
China's Intangible Cultural Heritage Traditional Craft Exhibition, 261
Convention for the Production of Intangible Cultural Heritage, 260–261
fake, 264–265
folklore as, 228
folk music as, 203–204, 212, 217–222
Important Intangible Cultural Properties (Japan), 232
List of Intangible Cultural Heritage in Need of Urgent Protection (UNESCO), 260–261
musical, 260–265
Productive Protection of China's Intangible Cultural Heritage Exhibition, 261
Representative List of the Intangible Cultural Heritage of Humanity (UNESCO), 260–261
Swedish folk music as, 203–204
Titon on, 276
Intellectual property
copyright ownership, 295–296
World Intellectual Property Organization (WIPO), 7
International Council for Traditional Music (ICTM), 43–46, 283
on applied ethnomusicology, 46–49
current intention, 45
name, 56
objectives of, 44
origins of, 43–44
post-WW II intention, 44–45
and Society for Ethnomusicology, 53–55
International Folk Music Council (IFMC), 16–17, 43
International Journal of Community Music, 171
International Music Council (IMC), 160
International Society for Music Education (ISME), 160, 165, 166
Internet technology, 138
Intervention, 30–31, 32
Introduction to Musicology (Haydon), 13

Invested in Community: Ethnomusicology and Musical Advocacy, 56
Iranian *dastgāh*, 135
Iranian drama *(taʿziyeh)*, 135
Islam, 128–129, 130, 134–135
Islamic humanism, 128–129
Isma'ilis, 132, 133–135, 137, 149
ISME (International Society for Music Education), 160, 165, 166
Italian opera, 135
Itinerant proselytizers *(Pir-s)*, 135
Ivey, Bill, 233

Jabbour, Alan, 232, 233–234, 237
Japan, 167
Important Intangible Cultural Properties, 232
Living National Treasures program, 232
Jazz, 159
Jazz Age, 159
Jazz musicians, 259, 260f
Jimenez, Flaco, 301
Johnson, Mark, 314–315
Johnson, Robert, 320
Jones, Brian, 299
Jones, Fernando, 106
Journalism, 7
The Journal of Educational Thought, 78–79
Jovanović, Jelena, 55n11
Judaism, 137

Kaeppler, Adrienne, 165, 234
Kalevala, 193
Kaluli people, 296–297
Kaminsky, David, 224
Karadžić, Vuk, 213
Karamu House theater, 75
Karpeles, Maud, 43–44, 54
Keil, Charles, 25, 165, 171, 172, 178, 179
Kennedy Center for the Performing Arts, 86
Kertzer, Jon, 235
Keshavjee, Rafique, 125, 138, 139, 144–145, 145f, 150–151
Keyland, Nils, 205
Key Research Base for Humanities and Social Sciences, 288

Khan, Ali Akbar, 164–165
Khan, Nusrat Fateh Ali, 300
Khorog Time, 148
Khusraw, Nasir, 131–132, 149
Khusraw school, 150
al-Kindī, 128, 129
King, Ben E., 314
Kirshenblatt-Gimblett, Barbara, 201, 320
Knowledge-based experts, 101
Knowledge for its own sake, 4, 19
Kodish, Debora, 243
Kogan, Anne, 244
Kony, Joseph, 313
Kuhač, Franjo, 40
Kunst, Jaap, 10, 13, 43
Kvitka, Kliment, 56

Lach, Robert, 40
Ladysmith Black Mambazo, 292, 298, 299
Lane, Deforia, 73, 75–76, 84–85, 87–88, 97–98
Lantern Festival, 261
Latvian *dainas*, 194–199
Latvian National Museum, 195
La Vigna, Maria, 234
Law, 7
Le Van Toan, 56
Lead Belly (Huddie Ledbetter), 235, 291, 294, 295, 319
League of Nations, 128
Learning about music, 104–105
Learning in music, 105–106
Learning through music, 71, 84–85, 105–106. *See also* Education
  partnerships for, 100–103, 103–104
Ledbetter, Huddie (Lead Belly), 235, 291, 294, 295, 319
Lee, Dorothy Sara, 234
Lee, Earl, 179
Let Your Voice Be Heard (Adzenyah, Maraire, and Tucker), 166
Libraries, 7
Library of Congress
  American Folklife Center (AFC), 23, 231–236
  Archive of Folk Culture, 23, 81, 230, 231
  Archive of Folk Song, 230–231

Lin, Weiya, 37
Ling, Jan, 204, 207, 208, 224
Linzee, Jill, 238, 240, 246, 250
The Lion's Roar (Kuo-huang and Campbell,), 166
Lipsitz, George, 307, 318
List, George, 14
Liu, Terry, 245, 246
Live Aid, 315
Living heritage, 284
Living National Treasures program (Japan), 232
Li Xuanying, 277
Li Yuanqing, 283
Ljubljana University, 119
Locke, David, 166
Lomax, Alan, 291, 311
  "Appeal for Cultural Equity," 11–12
  artists associated with, 235
  collaboration with Lead Belly, 319
  as cultural merchant and broker, 293–296, 304–305, 319
  as early folklorist, 229, 230–231, 304–305
  encounter with Herzog, 23
  field recordings, 304–305
  folk music revival, 23–24
  on Lead Belly's representation, 319
  radio broadcasts, 5
Lomax, John A., 12, 230–231, 291, 294, 319
Lönnrot, Elias, 193
Lord's Resistance Army (LRA), 313
Loughran, Maureen, 26, 27, 37, 56, 100, 102, 173
Lowell Folk Festival, 240, 306
Lowell National Historical Park, 240
LP recordings. *See* Recordings
Luaka Bop, 300, 309, 320
Lü Lulu, 256

Mackinlay, Elisabeth, 27
MacPherson, James, 193
MACSEM (Mid-Atlantic Chapter of SEM), 240
Macumba, 175
Madah (poetry), 130–131, 135, 137, 142–144
  ecstatic dance that accompanies, 142
  mortuary dances associated with, 132, 133f
  research on, 139, 141–144

Madahkhans (praise singers or musicians), 130–132, 131f, 135, 137, 141–144
MAFA (Mid-Atlantic Folklife Association), 240
Mahjong, 259
Makeba, Miriam, 298
Malm, Krister, 42, 167
Malm, William, 14, 165
Mandela, Nelson, 303
Mao Zedong, 271
Mapplethorpe, Robert, 250
Maqāmāt, 129
Maqamboland, 143, 143f
Marcus, Greil, 315
Mariachi Los Amigos, 246
Mariachi Online website, 167
Marketing, 291
Marley, Bob, 314
Martinelli, Dario, 147
Maryland: population, 243
Maryland Folklife Festival, 237–238, 248–249
Maryland Folklife Program, 236–237, 238, 241–242
Maryland Historical Trust, 241
Maryland State Arts Council (MSAC), 233, 237–238, 241, 248, 250
Maryland Traditions, 237, 241–242, 243–244, 245
   Apprenticeship grants, 248
   Project Grants, 248
Mason, Lowell, 158–159
Massachusetts Arts Council, 239
Massachusetts Cultural Council, 239
Massachusetts Folk Arts and Heritage Program, 239
Massachusetts Folklife and Ethnic Arts Program, 239
Massachusetts State Folklorist, 239
Mass entertainment, 305
   in China, 268–270
Matthews, Washington, 10
Maultsby, Portia, 89–91, 166
Mayes, Nicola, 179
MAYV (Music Alive! in the Yakima Valley), 176–180
McAllester, David, 14–15, 15–16, 21, 165, 167, 234, 244–245

McFerrin, Bobby, 315
McPhee, Colin, 298
Media, and marketing, 291
Mediation, 35
Medical ethnomusicology, 7, 81, 119
MENC (Music Educators National Conference), 160, 165
Merchants and brokers, cultural, 293–298. *See also* Cultural merchants and brokers
Merriam, Alan P., 14, 16–19, 37, 53, 167–168
Metropolitan Museum of Art (New York), 283
Mevlevî dervishes, 131–132, 132f, 137
Meyer, Steven, 179
Mid-Atlantic Chapter, SEM (MACSEM), 240
Mid-Atlantic Folklife Association (MAFA), 240
The Mighty Sparrow, 301
Migration and migrant communities, 96. *See also specific communities*
   cultural migration, 282–283
Miller, Terry E., 166
Minakov, Mosavar, 147
Minority populations, 96. *See also specific minorities*
Mo, Keb, 315
Mondo films, 55
Monson, Ingrid, 81
Monteiro, Dana, 173–174, 175
Monterey Pop Festival, 238
Monts, Lester P., 79
Morra, Mario, 30
Morris, Jim, 232
Mortuary dances, 132, 133f
Mouth harp (harmonica), 214
Mouth organs, 214
MSAC (Maryland State Arts Council), 237–238, 241
Mukhammas (poetry), 142
Multicultural music education, 79–81, 161, 166
Multicultural Perspectives in Music Education (Anderson and Campbell), 166
Muqam, 266
Museum für Völkerkunde, 197
Museums, 7

Music
- as art form, 124
- as bridge between humanism and humaneism, 123–124, 129–132, 146
- of Central Asia, 125
- in China, 254–255
- classical *(shashmaqam)*, 135, 140
- community, 58, 156–181, 170–173
- for conflict resolution, 7, 58
- connections from, 72
- as core subject of education, 106–107
- cultural domain of, 4
- dance, 216
- as defining characteristic of humanity, 124, 144
- definition of, 122
- devotional, 149–150
- Dongjing, 262
- English translations of Chinese music records, 278–279
- FMK value scale, 58, 217, 218f
- folk music, 159, 160, 190–191, 207–209, 217
- Guqin, 267
- Han Chinese Taoist, 262
- as history, 200
- as humane, 58, 123, 144–147
- as humaneistic, 58
- as human interaction and communication, 200
- as humanistic, 58, 123
- and humanity, 124–127
- as identity, 200
- learning about, 104–105
- learning in, 105–106
- learning through, 71, 84–85, 100–103, 103–104, 105–106
- Muqam, 266
- Navajo, 167
- Naxi traditional music, 262
- new perspectives on, 217
- in non-arts disciplines, 72
- overlap with dance, 121–122, 122f
- Pamiri, 150
- pedagogy for, 77–81
- practice of, 122
- rock and roll, 83, 107
- role of, 121–124
- studying humanity via, 122–123
- in systemic school education, 158–162
- Taoist, 263–264, 265f
- traditional Chinese music, 268–270
- Western pop music, 314
- world, 22, 163, 303
- youth music, 165

Music, Media, and Multiculture, 189
Music activities: in communities, 257–260
Musical databases, 266–267
- Chinese Guqin Musical Culture Database, 267
- Uyghur Muqam Database, 266

Musical exchange, 312–313
Musical Instrument Exhibition Centre (China), 280–283, 280f, 281f
Musical Instruments Museum (Stockholm), 283
Musical intangible cultural heritages. *See also* Intangible cultural heritage (ICH)
- local application of, 260–265

Music Alive! in the Yakima Valley (MAYV), 176–180
Musical traditions: access to, 82–84
Music archives, 189–225. *See also* Archives
- purposes of, 192–193

Music business degree programs, 292
Music education, 6–7, 57–58. *See also* Education; Pedagogy; *specific programs*
- advisory work, 166–167
- Balinese, 170
- community music in, 156–181
- as core subject, 79
- culturally responsive approaches, 79–81
- curriculum and instruction, 165–166
- ethnomusicology in, 156–181
- in Europe, 158–159
- foundations for, 77–79
- Harlem Samba, 173–176
- higher education, 162–164
- instructional materials, 166–167
- multicultural, 79–81, 161, 166
- out-of-school enrichment, 95
- partnerships for, 57–58
- pedagogy, 167–170
- revolutionary potentials, 180
- in United Kingdom, 158–159

in United States, 158–159
world and global music in, 161–162
Music Educators National Conference (MENC), 160, 165
Music for Change, 173, 181
Musician and Teachers (Campbell), 80
Musicians. *See also specific musicians and communities*
    praise singers or musicians *(madahkhans)*, 130–132, 131f, 135, 137, 141–144
    spelmän/spelkvinnor (male/female folk musicians), 210, 212–213, 213f, 219–220
    Tajik, 125–126, 126f
    Uzbek, 126
Music in Childhood (Campbell), 79–80
Music industry, 7, 305–306
    exploitation in, 310, 317–318
    global, 310–311
    in pop(ulist) activism, 316–317
Music in Social Life (Turino), 178
Musicking, 81, 178
Musicking a public voice, 85–87
Music-making, 104
Music of the Whole Earth (Reck), 166
Musicologica: A Study of the Nature of Ethnomusicology, Its Problems, Methods, and Representative Personalities, 43
Musicology Research Institute, 267, 288
Music specialists, 69–70
Music therapy, 271
Muslims, 128–129
Mutually beneficial exploitation, 298–303. *See also* Exploitation
Mycoskie, Blake, 308, 309

Napoleon Bonaparte, 127–128
National Council for the Traditional Arts (NCTA), 229, 238, 243–244
    Lowell Folk Festival, 240, 306
National Council on the Arts, 232
National Endowment for the Arts (NEA), 231, 232–233, 237, 250
    Folk and Traditional Arts Division, 23–24, 232–233, 234, 237–238
    Folk Arts Panel, 239
    National Council on the Arts, 232

National Folk Festival (NCTA), 238, 243
National Foundation of Youth Music, 172
National Heritage Fellowships, 232–233, 247
Nationalism, 58
National Library (Riga), 195
National Museum (China), 261
National Museum of American History (U.S.), 234
National Museum of Natural History (U.S.), 234
National Museum of the American Indian (U.S.), 234
National Park Service (U.S.), 240
National Socialism, 128
National Task Force on the Arts in Education (U.S.), 79
National Theatre Company of China, 258
"The Nation in a cabinet" (Krišjānis Barons's work), 194–199
Navajo music, 167
Naxi traditional music, 262
Nazi Party, 128
NCTA. *See* National Council for the Traditional Arts
N'Dour, Youssou, 300, 320
Negotiation, 90–91
Negroponte, Nicholas, 308
Negus, Keith, 310
Nettl, Bruno, 37, 54, 166, 167, 276
    on consultants as teachers, 168
    early work, 13–16, 19–20
    Excursions in World Music, 166
    ICTM work, 54
Networks, partner, 73–77
Neuman, Daniel, 168–169
New Hampshire: folklife program in, 240
New Hampshire State Council on the Arts, 240
Newport Folk Festival, 238
Newport Jazz Festival, 238
Newsletter, 15
Newsome, Jennifer, 56
New York City, New York, 5
New York Folklore Society, 239
New York State Council on the Arts (NYSCA)
    Apprenticeship Program, 239
    Folk Arts Program, 239

Ney (end-blown reed flute), 130, 131–132
Ngoma tradition, 163
NGOs (nongovernmental organization), 229, 246, 250
Niles, Don, 53, 56
Nketia, J. H. Kwabena, 166
No Child Left Behind Act, 106
Non-arts disciplines, 72
Nonesuch Records, 164–165
Nongovernmental organization (NGOs), 229, 246, 250
Nonprofit organizations, 246
Nordic Museum, 205, 210
Norlind, Tobias, 215
North America, 5–8, 37–38
North India, 167, 168
Northwestern University, 164–165
Northwest Heritage, 250
Norway: Bosnian refugees in, 34–35
Numerology, 144, 150
Nyckelharpa, 220
Nyqvist, Niklas, 224
NYSCA (New York State Council on the Arts), 239

O'Connell, Edward, 165
O'Connell, John Morgan, 37
Office of Folklife Studies, 23
O'Jays, 82–83
Older adults: musical lives of, 270–273, 271f, 272f
OLPC (One Laptop Per Child), 308–309
OLPC Association, 308–309
Olsen, Dale, 166
Olsen, Paul Rovsing, 56
100 Songs Project, 316
One for One, 308, 309
One Laptop Per Child (OLPC), 308–309
Onishi, Pamela, 37
Onkey, Lauren, 73
Opera
    Chinese, 263–264, 265f
    Chinese Opera Channel (Channel 11), 269–270
    Italian, 135
Opetčeska-Tatarčevska, Ivona, 55

Opondo, Patricia, 37, 56
Orientation, epistemological, 8
Ossian's songs, 193
Ostashewski, Marcia, 56
Othering
    exoticized, 298
    racial, 320
Our Singing Country (Lomax et al.), 231
Out-of-school enrichment, 95
Ownership, copyright, 295–296

PAA. *See* Progressive Arts Alliance
PAA All-Stars, 86–87
Pahanui, Gabby, 301
Pamiri music, 150
Panels, 246
Panj River, 142
Papua, New Guinea, 296–297
Parks, Van Dyke, 301, 320
Participant observation, 250
Partnerships
    for arts education, 57–58, 73–77
    for education, 57–58, 73–77, 89
    institutional, 69–70
    for learning through music, 100–103, 103–104
    among music specialists, 69–70
    regional, 241–242
    state folklife, 241–242
PASS (Premier Arts Specialty System), 93
Peace Through Music, 316
Pecore, Joanna, 245
Pedagogy, 77–81, 165–166, 167–170. *See also* Education
Peer-to-peer file sharing, 292
Pennsylvania: folklife program in, 236
Pennsylvania Historical Commission, 236
Pennsylvania State Historical Museum, 237
People's Republic of China. *See* China
Performance. *See also specific artists, programs, and performances*
    cognition of, 168
    culture shows, 306
    video performances, 313, 314–315
Persian poetry, 134
Persian songs, 135

Personal-political-possible, "storying." *See*
    Decolonization
Personal practices, 57
Petrović, Ankica, 55
Pettan, Svanibor, 27, 120, 172
Pettinato, Giovanni, 192
Philadelphia Folklore Project (PFP), 242–243
Philanthropy, 134
Philosophical reflection, 120–121
Phiri, Ray, 298
Pilzer, Joshua, 37
Pinker, Steven, 121
Pipa (four-stringed lute), 262, 279
Pir-s (itinerant proselytizers), 135
Pitzer, Robert, 179
Place, Jeff, 234
Plato, 129
Playhouse Square theaters (Cleveland, OH), 82–83
Playing For Change, 313–316
Plotinus, 129
Pluralism, 144–146, 150–151
Poetry
    madah, 130–131, 135, 137, 139, 141–144
    mukhammas, 142
    Persian, 134
Polskas, 206–207, 206f, 216, 218f, 219, 220, 223
Pop(ulist) activism, 312–317
Popular music
    African American, 159
    Western, 314
Position, social, 108
"Position Statement against the Use of Music as Torture," 28
Postcolonial ethnomusicology, 9, 25. *See also* Decolonization
Poverty, 82
Power relations, 100–103
Praise singers or musicians *(madahkhans)*, 130–132, 131f, 135, 137, 141–144
Premier Arts Specialty System (PASS), 93
Preservation. *See specific cultures, types, and topics*
Productive Protection of China's Intangible Cultural Heritage Exhibition, 261
Professional roles, 77

Progressive Arts Alliance (PAA), 75, 83–84
    PAA All-Stars, 86–87
    RHAPSODY Hip-Hop Summer Arts Camp, 86
    teaching-artists, 85–87
Project grants, 247–248
Property, intellectual
    copyright ownership, 295–296
    World Intellectual Property Organization (WIPO), 7
Protopapa, Santina, 74, 75, 83–84, 85–87
Public archives, 192
Public education
    access to musical traditions in, 82–84
    in Europe, 158–159
    multicultural music education in, 161
    music education in, 158–162
    in U.S., 69–108, 158–159, 160–162, 181
    world and global music in, 161–162
Public ethnomusicology, 8
Public folklore, 23–25, 228, 229
    origins of, 230–231
    as strategic governmental outreach, 242–244
Public folklorists
    apprenticeships, 247–248
    collaboration with, 245
    in cultural policy, 247
    desk work, 244–245
    disciplinary challenges, 249–252
    federal, 230–231
    fieldwork, 244–245, 247–248
    focus and work of, 228–229
    grant making as tool for, 229
    grants administration, 246
    grant work, 247–248
    history of, 230–231
    job of, 244–249
    on panels, 246
    public program work, 248–249
    radio program work, 249
    state, 230–231, 239–240, 241, 244–249
    strategic governmental outreach, 242–244
    Terry Liu's work, 246
    U.S., 228–252
Public history, 80
Public programs, 248–249. *See also specific programs*

Public-sector ethnomusicology, 7–8
Public sector folklore, 80
Purdy, Joe, 312
Puryear, Mark, 26, 244, 245
Pythagorean principles, 129

Qawwali-s (devotional songs), 135
Queensland University of Technology (QUT), 316
Qurʾan, 128

Racial othering, 320
Racial segregation, 95, 96–97, 159
Racy, Ali Jihad, 124–125
Radio programs, 249
Raga music, 135
Ragtime, 159
Rakočević, Selena, 55
Ralph Rinzler Folklife Archives and Collections, 234
Ramnarine, Tina, 172
Ramsten, Märta, 207, 208–209
Rasmussen, Ljerka Vidić, 55
Reagan, Bernice Johnson, 166
Real World Records, 292, 300, 309, 320
Reck, David, 166
Recordings, 137, 250–251
    Buena Vista Social Club, 292, 301–302
    Clang of the Mighty Reaper, 301
    commercial, 305–306
    Discover America, 301
    English translations of Chinese music records, 278–279
    ethnic records, 304
    field recordings, 304–305
    Graceland, 298, 299, 303
    video performances, 314–315
    Voices of the Rainforest, 296
    World Library of Folk and Primitive Music, 304–305
Redfield, Robert, 223
Reed, David, 248
Reed, Ola Belle, 247
Reformation, 127
Refugees, Bosnian, 34–35

Regional partnerships, 241–242
R.E.M., 312–313
Renaissance, 127, 129–130
Representation, 306–307
Research, 141–144. *See also specific researchers and projects*
    for its own sake, 18
    pure *vs.* applied, 5
Resettlement Agency, 230
The Resonant Community, 34, 41
Resources: exploitation of, 303–311
RHAPSODY Hip-Hop Summer Arts Camp (PAA), 86
Rhodes, Willard, 15–16, 54
Rice, Timothy, 55, 147, 165, 168–169
Richards, Keith, 320
Richardson, Dianna, 74, 75, 82, 94, 95
Richardson, Lisa, 246
Ridley, Roger, 314–315
Rinzler, Ralph, 232, 234
Robert Johnson: The Complete Recordings, 320
Rock and roll
    African-American contributions to, 83, 107
    definition and scope of, 107
Rock and Roll Hall of Fame and Museum, 73–77, 94
    Department of Education, 107
    Library and Archives, 94, 107
    Toddler Rock program, 75–76, 84–85, 87–88, 97–98
    Voice Your Choice project, 107–108
Rock Your World Festival, 94
Rogers, Hannah, 244
Rolling Stone, 314
Ronström, Owe, 194, 207, 208
Rousseau, Jean Jacques, 193
Royal College of Music (Stockholm), 210
Roybal, Robert, 179
Rubab (Badakhshani lute), 130, 142, 148, 150
Rubalcaba, Gonzalo, 301–302
Rule of fives, 142
Rumi (Jalāl al-Dīn), 131–132, 148, 149
Russian Christianity, 137
Ryder, Judith, 74, 76, 88, 98–99
Rykodisc, 296

Sachs, Curt, 190, 244
Arthur M. Sackler Gallery (Washington, D.C.), 234
Safi al-Dīn, 129
Salin, Bernhard, 205
Samba New York, 173
Sambangra, 175
SamulNori, 170
Santaella, Mayco, 37
Sarkissian, Margaret, 320
Savage, Roger, 147
Savage Man Savage Beast, 30
Schippers, Huib, 36–37
Schneider, Marius, 197
Scholarship, 250–251, 302–303, 319
School education, systemic, 158–162
School of Music, University of Washington, 177, 178
School of Rock, 83
Schrag, Brian, 37
Schupman, Ed, 234
Schwadron, Abraham, 165
Seattle Fandango Project, 173
Seeger, Anthony, 37, 166, 221–222
 early ethnomusicology, 12
 Smithsonian Folkways work, 235
Seeger, Charles, 12, 165, 230, 231
Seeger, Mike, 231
Seeger, Peggy, 231
Seeger, Pete, 231, 235
Seeger, Ruth Crawford, 12, 230–231
Seeman, Sonia, 147
SEM. *See* Society for Ethnomusicology
Sema, Mevlevî or Turkish, 131–132, 132f, 137
Seniors: musical lives of, 270–273, 271f, 272f
Serbia, 40–41
Service, 319
Service enterprises, 292, 303–311
Settlement houses, 160
Shadows in the Field (Barz and Cooley), 100
Shahriari, Andrew, 166
Shakespear, Will, 168
Shanghai Conservatory of Music, 278
Shankar, Ravi, 164–165, 299
Shanting Teshu Hechangdui (Fan Pavilion Unique Chorus), 271
Sharpe, Robert, 123

Shashmaqam (classical music), 135, 137, 140
Sheehy, Daniel (Dan), 166, 311
 on applied ethnomusicology, 25, 32, 88–89
 on conscious practice, 34
 on folklorist role, 293
 on history of applied ethnomusicology, 11
 on making music happen in communities, 179
 as musician, 246
 NEA Folk and Traditional Arts Division work, 232–233, 237–238
 Smithsonian Folklife Festival work, 232, 245
 Smithsonian Folkways work, 235
 on traditional music circuit, 307
Shehan, Patricia, 165
Shelemay, Kay Kaufman, 166, 234, 303–304
Sherinian, Zoe, 37
Shīrāzī, Hāfez-e, 135
Shi'ism, 132, 133, 137, 143, 149
Shoemaker, Henry W., 236
Sias, Tony F., 74, 75, 93, 94, 95
Sibelius Museum (Turku, Finland), 283
Silk Raod Project, 135
Silverstope, Karl, 205
Simon, Paul, 291–292, 298–299, 301, 303
Singer, Roberta, 239
Singing societies, 158–159
Sino-African Music Dialogue, 274, 275f
Skylights (chahar khaneh), 142, 144f
Skyllstad, Kjell, 41
Slobin, Mark, 190–191, 223
Slovenia, 39–40, 42–43
Small, Christopher, 178
Smith, Stephanie, 234
Smithsonian Folklife Festival, 5, 232, 234–235, 238
 Asian-Pacific-American (APA) Program, 245
 Ethnomimesis (Cantwell) considerations, 306–307
Smithsonian Folkways Recordings, 81, 165–166, 234–235, 297, 304–305
 website, 167
 World Music Pedagogy certification, 162
Smithsonian Global Sound, 235
Smithsonian Institution

Center for Folklife and Cultural Heritage (CFCH), 231, 234–235
   employment of ethnomusicologists by, 23–24
   Office of Folklife Studies, 23
Social barriers, 92–100
Social justice, 28
Social position, 108
Social practices, 57
   learning through music, 84–85
Society for Applied Microbiology, 55
Society for Applied Philosophy, 55
Society for Applied Spectroscopy, 55
Society for Ethnomusicology (SEM), 5, 165, 233–234, 250
   current applied ethnomusicology activity, 27
   Education Committee, 165
   founding and early history, 14, 15–16
   and International Council for Traditional Music, 53–55
   MACSEM (Mid-Atlantic Chapter), 240
   Section on Applied Ethnomusicology, 26, 80, 243
   Section on Education, 80
Society for Ricoeur Studies, 147
Son de Madera, 179
Song chains, 312–313
Songs and singing
   devotional songs (*ginan*-s), 135, 137
   devotional songs (*qawwali*-s), 135
   praise singers or musicians (*madahkhans*), 130–132, 131f, 135, 137, 141–144
   Turkish classical songs (*beste-s*), 135
Sonneborn, D.A., 235
Soto, Amanda, 179
Sound
   Badakhshani concept of, 142
   human sounds, 121–124
Sound activism, environmental, 7
Sound archives, 7. *See also* Archives
Soundscapes (Shelemay), 166
South America, 37
Southeast Asia, 37
Spelmän/spelkvinnor (male/female folk musicians), 210, 212–213, 213f, 219–220
Spiritual life, 263–264, 265f

Spitzer, Nicholas, 305
Sporr, Karl, 210
Standardization, 203, 219–220
"Stand By Me," 315
State folklife partnerships, 241–242
State folklorists, 239–240, 241, 244, 250–251
   work of, 244–249
Steffen, Richard, 205
STEM subjects (science, technology, engineering, and math), 72
Stevenson, Lauren, 72
Stojkova Serafimovska, Velika, 55
Stone, Ruth, 235
Stone, Verlon, 235
"Storying," the personal-political-possible. *See* Decolonization
Stravinsky, Igor, 298
Student empowerment, 99
The Study of Ethnomusicology, 19
Stumpf, Carl, 12, 197–199
Stylistic borrowings, 301
Sufism, 149
"Suitcase" (Purdy), 312
Summit, Jeffrey (Jeff), 37, 235
Sundin, Ante, 213f
Sunnīs, 133, 137
Suogudu (three-stringed lute), 262
Superculture, 223, 275
Su Qianzhong, 257
Sustainability, 5, 59, 318, 319
Svenska låtar (Swedish tunes), 205–207, 206f, 216–217, 220, 221
Svensk folkmusik. Bondens musik i helg och söcken (Ling), 204
Svenskt visarkiv (Centre for Folk Music and Jazz Research), 223
Swedish folk music, 204, 212
   as cultural heritage, 203–204, 217–222
Swedish *Folkmusikkommissionen* (FMK, Folk Music Commission), 213, 225
   collection, 191, 196f, 205–207, 206f, 220, 223
   founding and early history, 205–207, 213
   impact on cultural heritage process, 217–222
   value scale, 58, 217, 218f
Sweers, Britta, 56
Swijghuisen Reigersberg, Muriel, 36
Symbolization, 203, 220

Širola, Božidar, 40
Štrekelj, Karel, 40

Tabrīzī, Shams-e (Shams al-Dīn), 132
Tajikistan, 126–127, 131–132, 149
Tajik musicians, 125–126, 126f
Taj Mahal, 320
Talam, Jasmina, 55n11
Tanglewood Symposium, 164–165
Tan Sooi Beng, 37, 56
Taoist music, 263–264, 265f
    Han Chinese, 262
Tavalayev, Mamadata, 147
Taʿziyeh (Iranian drama), 135
Teaching artists, 69, 75–78, 83–84, 85–87, 98–99, 107
Technology
    Internet, 138
    and marketing, 291
    One Laptop Per Child (OLPC), 308–309
    video performances, 314–315
Television: Chinese Central Television (CCTV) programs on Chinese traditional music, 268–270
Television Grand Prix for Young Singers (CCTV), 268, 270
Tennessee: folklife program in, 237
Tennessee Arts Commission, 233
Tenzer, Michael, 166
Ternhag, Gunnar, 224
Tetrachords, 129
Textbooks, 166
"Think Cleveland," 86
Thram, Diane, 37
Tirén, Karl: yoik collection, 198f
Titon, Jeff Todd, 26, 37, 233, 235, 239
    on applied ethnomusicology, 3–9, 171
    definition of ethnomusicology, 3, 244
    on expectations of fieldwork informants, 305
    on field research, 151
    on the history of applied ethnomusicology, 3–29
    on intangible cultural heritages, 276
    on Lomax's marketing, 319
    on power relations and decisions of ethnomusicologists, 100
    on practice, 120, 147
    on Taj Mahal, 320
    Worlds of Music, 166
Toddler Rock, 75–76, 84–85, 87–88, 97–98
"Together," 314–315
Tokayev, Haydar, 147
Toms Shoes, 308, 309
Topp Fargion, Janet, 199
Torture: use of music as, 28
Tourism, 58–59
    in China, 261–262, 264
Tracey, Andrew, 37
Tradition: bearers of, 212–213
Traditional Chinese medicine, 271
Traditional Instrumental Music Performance Competition (CCTV), 268–269
Traditional music
    Chinese, 268–270, 279
    Naxi, 262
Traditional paradigm, 249–250
Training. *See* Education; Music education
Transcontextualization, 307
Transfer, 72
Translation, English: of Chinese music records, 278–279
Trauma, cultural, 5
Treloyn, Sally, 36
Trevor-Roper, Hugh, 222
Tri-C Jazz Fest, 75, 83
Trimillos, Ricardo, 166
Trust for Culture Program, 135
Truth, 145–146
Tucker, Judith Cook, 166
Turino, Thomas, 178
Turkey
    Mevlevî *sema*, 131–132, 132f
    ney (end-blown reed flute), 130, 131–132
Turkish classical songs *(beste-s)*, 135
Tyson, Neil Degrasse, 296

Uganda, 313
Ultime grida dalla savana, 30
UNESCO, 6, 57
Unitarian Church, Vancouver, Canada, 172
United Kingdom: music education in, 158–159

United Nations Educational, Scientific, and Cultural Organization (UNESCO)
  Convention for the Production of Intangible Cultural Heritage, 260–261
  International Music Council (IMC), 160
  List of Intangible Cultural Heritage in Need of Urgent Protection, 260–261
  Representative List of the Intangible Cultural Heritage of Humanity, 260–261
United States
  applied ethnomusicology in, 9–29
  education sector, 69–108
  ethnomusicological practice in, 228–252
  federal folklife programs, 231–236
  folklore, 23–24
  Good Neighbor Policy, 160
  music education in, 158–159
  public education, 160–162, 181
  public folklorists in, 228–252
  Roosevelt administration, 160, 229
  state folklife programs, 236–240
  State Folklorists, 239
United States Department of Health and Human Services: Head Start Program, 107
University-based ethnomusicological activism. *See* Conflict resolution
University of Washington (UW), 176–180
Urdu devotional songs *(qawwali-s)*, 135
Usner, Eric Martin, 56
Uyghur Muqam Database, 266
Uzbek musicians, 126

Valdez, Ricardo, 179
Value scales, 58, 217, 218f
Van Buren, Kathleen Noss, 26, 37, 172
Van Buren, Tom, 26, 172
Van Willigen, John, 17–18
Vedas, 137
Vennum, Thomas (Tom), 232, 234
Venues. *See specific venues*
Vermont Folklife Center, 239
Video performances, 313
  collaborations, 314–315
Vikár, Béla, 197

Vimeo, 313
Voice Project, 312–313, 314–315, 316
Voices of the Rainforest, 296
Voice Your Choice project, 107–108
Von Hornbostel, Erich Moritz, 190, 197
VoxLox, 297

Wade, Bonnie C., 166, 167
Walking tunes *(gånglåtar)*, 206–207
Walmart, 309
Wa people, 282–283
Ward, Fields, 247
Ward Museum of Wildfowl Art, 243
Warner Brothers, 298
"War/No More Trouble," 315
"We Are The World," 315
Weil, Zoe, 123
Wenders, Wim, 301–302
Wesleyan Symposium on Becoming Human Through Music, 165
Western music, 126
Western pop music, 314
"What's Going On... NOW," 86–87
Wilpers, Michael, 234, 245
Wilson, Brian, 320
Wilson, Dave, 55
WIPO (World Intellectual Property Organization), 7
Wolcott, Ron, 234
WOMAD (World of Music and Dance) festival, 300–301, 303
Wong, Deborah, 32, 178
Woodstock, 238
Works Project Administration (WPA), 230
World AIDS Day, 172
World Circuit, 302
World Intellectual Property Organization (WIPO), 7
World Library of Folk and Primitive Music, 304–305
World music, 22, 163, 303. *See also* Global music; *specific artists, promoters, and types*
World Music (Bakan), 166
World Music: A Global Journey (Miller and Shahriari), 166

World Music Days (China), 273, 274–277, 275f, 276f
World music educators, 169
World music pedagogy, 167–170
World Music Pedagogy certification (Smithsonian Folkways), 162
World Music Press, 166
Worlds of Music (Titon), 166
WPA (Works Project Administration), 230
Wuhan Conservatory of Music, 259
WYPR (88.1 FM), 249

Xiao (vertical bamboo flute), 279
Xinjiang Arts Research Institute, 266
Xinjiang Autonomous Region Cultural Department, 266
Xiyangyang (Happiness), 277

Yakama Nation Tribal School, 179
Yakima Valley: Music Alive! in the Yakima Valley (MAYV) program, 176–180
Yale University, 164–165
Yamaguti Osamu, 256, 257
YANEO (Young Audiences of Northeast Cleveland), 76
Yang Xifan, 256
Yang Yinliu, 283

Yeh, Nora, 234
Yerkovich, Sally, 232
Yoik collection (from Karl Tirén), 198f
Yoshitaka, Terada, 37
Young Audiences of Northeast Cleveland (YANEO), 76, 99–100
    Art Is Education project, 76–77
Youth music, 165
YouTube, 313, 315
Yuan Jingfang, 267
Yugoslavia, 40
Yu Runyang, 278

Zap Mama, 320
Zaretti, Joan L., 73
Ze, Tom, 320
Zebec, Tvrtko, 43
Zetterqvist, Lars Johan, 205
Žganec, Vinko, 40
Zhang Boyu, 37, 278
Zhang Xiaoyan, 257
Zhang Zhentao, 283
Zhihua Temple (Beijing, China), 261
Zhou Heping, 263
Zhou Ji, 266
Zhou Xianbao, 257
Zhudi (transverse bamboo flute), 279
Zorn, Anders, 205
Zoroastrianism, 148